the
Picts

The Peoples of Europe

General Editors: James Campbell and Barry Cunliffe

This series is about the European tribes and peoples from their origins in prehistory to the present day. Drawing upon a wide range of archaeological and historical evidence, each volume presents a fresh and absorbing account of a group's culture, society, and usually turbulent history.

Already published

The Etruscans
Graeme Barker and Thomas Rasmussen

The Byzantines
Averil Cameron

The Normans
Marjorie Chibnall

The Norsemen in the Viking Age
Eric Christiansen

The Lombards
Neil Christie

The Serbs
Sima Ćirković

The English
Geoffrey Elton

The Gypsies
Second edition
Angus Fraser

The Bretons
Patrick Galliou and Michael Jones

The Goths
Peter Heather

The Romans in the Age of Augustus
Andrew Lintott

The Vandals
Andy Merrills and Richard Miles

The Russians
Robin Milner-Gulland

The Mongols
Second edition
David Morgan

The Armenians
A. E. Redgate

The Britons
Christopher A. Snyder

The Huns
E. A. Thompson

The Early Germans
Second edition
Malcolm Todd

The Illyrians
John Wilkes

The Picts
Benjamin Hudson

In preparation

The Angles and Saxons
Helena Hamerow

The Celts
John Koch

The Gauls
Colin Haselgrove

the
Picts

Benjamin Hudson

WILEY Blackwell

This edition first published 2014
© 2014 John Wiley & Sons, Ltd

Registered Office
John Wiley & Sons, Ltd, The Atrium, Southern Gate, Chichester, West Sussex, PO19 8SQ, UK

Editorial Offices
350 Main Street, Malden, MA 02148–5020, USA
9600 Garsington Road, Oxford, OX4 2DQ, UK
The Atrium, Southern Gate, Chichester, West Sussex, PO19 8SQ, UK

For details of our global editorial offices, for customer services, and for information about how to apply for permission to reuse the copyright material in this book please see our website at www.wiley.com/wiley-blackwell.

The right of Benjamin Hudson to be identified as the author of this work has been asserted in accordance with the UK Copyright, Designs and Patents Act 1988.

All rights reserved. No part of this publication may be reproduced, stored in a retrieval system, or transmitted, in any form or by any means, electronic, mechanical, photocopying, recording or otherwise, except as permitted by the UK Copyright, Designs and Patents Act 1988, without the prior permission of the publisher.

Wiley also publishes its books in a variety of electronic formats. Some content that appears in print may not be available in electronic books.

Designations used by companies to distinguish their products are often claimed as trademarks. All brand names and product names used in this book are trade names, service marks, trademarks or registered trademarks of their respective owners. The publisher is not associated with any product or vendor mentioned in this book.

Limit of Liability/Disclaimer of Warranty: While the publisher and author have used their best efforts in preparing this book, they make no representations or warranties with respect to the accuracy or completeness of the contents of this book and specifically disclaim any implied warranties of merchantability or fitness for a particular purpose. It is sold on the understanding that the publisher is not engaged in rendering professional services and neither the publisher nor the author shall be liable for damages arising herefrom. If professional advice or other expert assistance is required, the services of a competent professional should be sought.

Library of Congress Cataloging-in-Publication Data
Hudson, Benjamin T.
  The Picts / Benjamin Hudson.
    pages cm
  Includes bibliographical references.
  ISBN 978-1-4051-8678-0 (cloth) – ISBN 978-1-118-60202-7 (pbk.)   1. Picts–History. 2. Scotland–History–To 1057. I. Title.
  DA774.4.P53H83 2014
  936.1′1–dc23
                                                               2013049563
A catalogue record for this book is available from the British Library.

Cover image: Celtic Pictish symbol stone slab detail in Aberlemno churchyard, Tayside, Scotland Battle scene with horse cavalry and spearmen. © David Lyons / age fotostock / SuperStock.
Cover design by Nicki Averill Design and Illustration

Set in 10/12.5pt Sabon by SPi Publisher Services, Pondicherry, India
Printed in Malaysia by Ho Printing (M) Sdn Bhd

1 2014

Contents

List of Figures and Tables	vi
List of Lineages and Maps	vii
Preface and Acknowledgments	viii
Methodology	x
Abbreviations	xii
Introducing the Picts	1
1 Picts and Romans	15
2 Myth and Reality	40
3 The Early Middle Ages	57
4 People and Work	95
5 Spirituality	134
6 Art	162
7 Conquest and Obscurity	182
8 Literature and Remembrance	207
Conclusion	233
Select Bibliography	240
Index	255

Figures and Tables

Figures

3.1	Dunnottar Castle	72
3.2	The countryside round Dunnichen	77
3.3	Battle scene from Aberlemno Cross-slab no. 2	78
4.1	A harp from Brechin Stone	102
4.2	Detail of weapons on Aberlemno Cross-slab no. 2	108
4.3	Two men fighting, Glamis no. 2	109
4.4	Hunting scene, Aberlemno Stone no. 2	118
4.5	Boat on St. Orland's Stone, Cossans	127
4.6	Salmon on a stone at Kintore	132
5.1	Dunkeld from *Theatrum Scotiae* (1693)	157
6.1	Rudimentary cross at St. Fergus', Dyce	166
6.2	Symbols and ogams on Brandsbutt Stone	167
6.3	Angels adoring the cross, Aberlemno Stone no. 3	168
6.4	V-rod design at top of Aberlemno Stone no. 2	169
6.5	Samson wrestling a lion?, from Brechin	170
6.6	Geometric designs from a stone at St. Fergus', Dyce	172
6.7	Mirror and comb from Aberlemno Stone no. 1	172
6.8	Carrion bird from Aberlemno Cross-slab no. 3	174
6.9	Sueno's Stone from a nineteenth-century print	177

Tables

7.1	The last Pictish kings	194

Lineages and Maps

Lineages

3.1	Family of Deirili	81
3.2	Family of Drostan	83
3.3	Family of Angus Son of Fergus	88

Maps

1.1	Northern Britain	17
2.1	Kingdoms of Northern Britain	47
3.1	Churches and Fortresses	61

Preface and Acknowledgments

When James Campbell invited me to write this book, my first thought was a statement made almost a century ago by John Fraser, the Jesus Professor of Celtic at Oxford, who began his essay "The Question of the Picts" with the declaration "For a people who played no very great part in the history of Europe the Picts might very well be thought to have already received their due attention at the hands of historians and others." Since Fraser wrote those words the Picts have engaged the interests of even more generations of archaeologists, art historians, and linguists. Each year brings a new crop of studies on topics of Pictish life and work; so much so that no one book can hope to incorporate all the information and speculation. Was there anything left for an historian to say?

This book is an attempt to answer that question in a brief survey. What is currently known about the Picts is re-examined to answer the questions: who were the Picts? and what part did they play in the early Middle Ages? In keeping with the spirit of the series *Peoples of Europe*, this book uses different methodologies, from transnationalism to comparative history, to study the Picts within a European-wide context. These new ways of looking at the subject allows us to move beyond the historiography of an earlier era because ideas about nationhood or ethnicity need to be re-examined in the light of new understandings of organization, movement, and political dynamics. Complexity increases with the admission that we know very little about the Picts.

Of course, this begs the question "why bother with a book about the Picts?" Early in the twelfth century Henry of Huntingdon dubbed them the Vanishing People of Britain and the tag has remained. One answer is their very prominence. For almost five hundred years the Picts were the premier predators of Britain. In addition to confronting the mighty Roman Empire, they fought other incomers throughout the centuries. More intriguing are the remains of their vibrant culture. The Picts were the premier sculptors of Britain and among the finest in Europe using designs ranging from Christian religious imagery to still-mysterious geometric figures and fabulous creatures. References to the Picts in literature show that their royal courts were the destinations for Irish and Anglo-Saxon poets. After the end of the ninth century, when the Picts are usually consigned to the dustbin of history, we discover that the archdeacon of Huntingdon was wrong and that the Picts did not disappear. From the reworking of their history at the courts of the Scots kings Macbeth and Malcolm Canmore to their appearance in story and song such as John Buchan's story "No Man's Land" or the Pink Floyd's recording of "Several Species of Small Furry Animals gathered together in a cave and grooving with a Pict" they remain a part of our cultural horizon.

There remains only the happy task of acknowledging those individuals and institutions whose assistance has been invaluable in the writing of this book. I thank the editors of the *Peoples of Europe* series, Professor James Campbell and Sir Barry Cunliffe, for the opportunity to write this book, for their comments on it, and for their much appreciated encouragement. James Campbell read the entire manuscript in draft and asked those questions that authors find awkward, but essential. My son Robert kindly placed his interest in photography at my disposal and all the photographs used here were taken by him. He and my daughter Alison are veterans of visits to symbol stones and battle fields. As always, my wife Aileen has been a source of encouragement as well as a tireless proof-reader. A grant from the Institute for Arts and Humanities at Penn State provided some funding for research in Scotland. Thanks also to the librarians and staff of the Pattee/Paterno Library at Penn State, the Queen Mother Library at the University of Aberdeen, the Bibliothêque nationale de France, Trinity College, Dublin, and the Bodleian Library, Oxford. Tessa Harvey has been a superb editor. Any errors are, of course, my own.

Methodology

One of the difficulties facing anyone who works on the early period of European history is being consistent. The few surviving records are in manuscripts of different dates and have variations in spelling, explanation, and presentation. Often the particular meaning of a word is more a matter of conjecture than certainty. There is no one method that will satisfy everyone, often not even the person employing it.

Chronology is a particular problem, especially during the medieval period when the materials we consult are themselves trying to reconcile the chronology of the texts they are following. Unless otherwise noted the chronology of the *Annals of Ulster* is followed in this study. One reason is not only that these chronicles occasionally preserve the older form of their exemplar, but also because these annals cover the entire period, unlike the cognate *Annals of Tigernach*, which contain a gap that begins in the middle of the eight century. This leads to reconciliation among the various dates that are proposed for some events. Of course for affairs concerning the Anglo-Saxons, primacy is given to Bede's *Ecclesiastical History*.

Personal names are a greater problem. Names of persons active in northern Britain during the early Middle Ages have been spelled in various fashions, depending on the inclination of the author. Rather than confuse the reader with a name form that may or may not have been used, in this work modern English equivalents for names are given, or a familiar form. Thus the francophone-derived modern Kenneth rather than the Old/Middle Irish form Cináed, and similarly the name Fergus rather than the plethora of variations such as Urgus or Forcus. Since this was a society in which one was identified by one's father, Latin *filius* or Old/Middle Irish *mac* have been abandoned to be replaced by the more awkward, but neutral "son of." Similarly, place names are given in modern form even when, as in the case of Deer Abbey, the location of the later medieval foundation with that name might not be the same as that for the earlier church. If a modern name is not known, then the form found in the sources is employed.

The texts cited in the notes usually are chosen because they have the text in the original language together with an English translation. Occasionally a text without a translation is used either because there is no suitable translation or because that edition is particularly important for the casual reader to know. On all these points absolute consistency has not been achieved.

Abbreviations

CIIC   R.A.S. Macalister, *Corpus Inscriptionum Insularum Celticarum*, 2 vols. (Dublin 1945–49); vol. 1, reprinted with a preface by Damian McManus (Dublin 1996)

CPS   W.J. Watson, *The History of the Celtic Place-Names of Scotland* (Edinburgh 1926)

ECMS   J. Romilly Allen and Joseph Anderson, *The Early Christian Monuments of Scotland*, reprinted with introduction by Isabel Henderson, 2 vols. (Balgavies 1993)

EHR   *English Historical Review*

ESC   Sir Archibald Lawrie, *Early Scottish Charters prior to 1153* (Glasgow 1905)

ESSH   Alan Orr Anderson, *Early Sources of Scottish History* AD *500 to 1286*, 2 vols. (Edinburgh 1922), re-edited with corrections by Marjorie Anderson (Stamford 1990)

KCS   Benjamin Hudson, *Kings of Celtic Scotland* (Westport 1994)

KES   Marjorie O. Anderson, *Kings and Kingship in Early Scotland* (Edinburgh 1973)

MGH   *Monumenta Germaniae Historica*

PSAS   *Proceedings of the Society of the Antiquaries of Scotland*

RRS   *Regesta Regum Scotorum*, gen. ed. G.W.S. Barrow (Edinburgh 1961–)

SHR   *Scottish Historical Review*

Introducing the Picts

The best known pictures of the Picts come from a book about North America. Among the members of an expedition to Virginia in 1585 was Thomas Harriot who had been commissioned to gather data about the new land. His *A Briefe and True Report of the New Found Land of Virginia* was a report of his findings, which his patron, Sir Walter Raleigh, hoped would entice people to invest. Accompanying the expedition was the artist John White, who later became the governor of the lost Roanoke River colony.[1] His watercolors of the people and countryside of this new world became famous and were included in printed editions of Harriot's narrative. Among the images of colorful birds, a Potomack (sic) fishing expedition, and a Powhatan chieftain are pictures of a Pictish warrior, his wife, and daughter. All three are covered in designs and wearing metal bands around their necks and midriffs with no other clothing. The man holds a sword, small shield, and a severed head while the women have swords and spears. White had never seen a Pict, of course (he had never seen a Powhatan chief either), but based his pictures of the early inhabitants of Britain on "an old history" and his own imagination. The illustrations were included "to showe how that the inhabitants of Great Bretannie have bin in times past as sauvage as those of Virginia," in other words that the Native Americans differed little from the inhabitants of Britain at the beginning of the Middle Ages. As the cult of the "noble savage" began to develop, some European

---

[1] Thomas Hariot, *A Briefe and True Report of the New Found Land of Virginia. Thomas Hariot. The 1590 Theodor de Bry Latin Edition* (Charlottesville, 2007).

The Picts, First Edition. Benjamin Hudson.
© 2014 John Wiley & Sons, Ltd. Published 2014 by John Wiley & Sons, Ltd.

writers thought that "primitives" wherever and whenever found represented the unsullied spirit of true humanity.[2] While there are many representations made by the peoples themselves, they do not have the popular appeal of White's paintings, which are best known through a later reworking by Theodor de Bry, who published Harriot's account and redrew White's images for publication.

As White's watercolors reveal, the Picts have been the mystery savages of Britain for a long time. The name *Pict* was coined by the Romans for a people who lived in northern Britain beyond Hadrian's Wall. The name first appears at the end of the third century AD and for the next 600 years they fought the Romans, southern Britons, Irish, Anglo-Saxons, and Vikings. The Picts were more than just warriors; they had an artistic culture that was acknowledged by their name: "the painted people." Their art ranged from monumental stone carvings to designs on jewelry. They were also the last people in the British Isles to convert to Christianity. White's inclusion of the Picts with the native peoples of North America is testimony to their place in the minds of educated men by the sixteenth century. One did not have to travel far to find further examples. White's older contemporary the antiquarian John Leland referred to Hadrian's Wall as "the Picts' wall," a name based on his reading of the sixth-century author Gildas' *Ruin of Britain*, and knowledge of medieval maps; that of Matthew Paris has both the Hadrian and Antonine walls separating the Picts from the southern lands. He seems to be unaware that it had been built centuries before the name "Pict" was first used to describe anyone in the British Isles.[3] Leland was not alone – moving back a millennium to the sixth century, Gildas believed the Picts to be so wild and primitive that only a physical structure such as a wall was capable of keeping them at bay. The sheer extent of the construction was enough to increase respect for the people it was thought to have held back. Even a cursory reading of Bede's *Ecclesiastical History* (a work that every educated person in the British Isles after the eighth century was expected to know) leaves the impression of the Picts as formidable warriors with few rivals.

---

[2] Sam Smiles, "John White and British Antiquity: Savage Origins in the Context of Tudor Historiography," in Kim Sloan (ed.), *European Visions: American Voices*, British Museum Research Publication 172 (London, 2009): 106–112.
[3] John Leland, *The Itinerary of John Leland in or about the Years 1535–1543*, ed. Lucy Toulmin Smith, 5 vols. (London, 1964): v, 60; the name is incorrectly used for remains at Bowness (v, 51).

There are two assumptions behind the historical views and popular perceptions of White or Leland, which have continued to the present and which this book will examine. The first is that there was a single race of Picts, a homogeneous population which extended throughout the northern part of Britain with exactly the same beliefs, costumes, methods of waging war, and patterns of everyday life. Connected with that supposition is a second one, that the Picts lived unchanged in a state of chronological grace for 600 years from the first appearance of the name Pict to the last "king of the Picts" at the beginning of the tenth century. Like the characters encountered by St. Brendan in his famous voyages, the political geography never altered in the land of the ageless Pict while military evolution and cultural development were unknown even as the societies round them were undergoing momentous transformations. Simply observing the significant alterations in culture and political geography of the other peoples in the British Isles during the same period leads to the conclusion that something similar was happening in northern Britain. To give just a couple of examples from the last years of the Imperial Roman administration to the beginning of the High Middle Ages, there were important movements of people (such as the Anglo-Saxons) as well as advances in technology (stirrups) together with changes in religion (Christianity).

As the following chapters show, there were many aspects to the peoples known as "the Picts." One of these is also the best known: the Picts were the ruthless warriors of Britain for almost five centuries. Their raids south of Hadrian's Wall hastened the end of Roman control of Britain. The fourth-century soldier-turned-memoirist Ammianus Marcellinus claimed that much of the turmoil in Britain involved the Picts somewhere. Moving forward several centuries, the destruction of an invading Anglo-Saxon army at the battle of Dun Nechtan in 685 ended the northern expansion of the Northumbrians. This paved the way for successful Pictish princes such as the eighth-century empire-builder Angus son of Fergus to ally with the Anglo-Saxons on conditions of equality; together they forced terms on the neighboring kingdom of Strathclyde. The victory at Dun Nechtan was even more impressive because the Angles were at their military peak and had conducted a successful raid on Ireland.

The martial aspect to the Picts must be set beside their art. Unlike many warrior societies of the period, which are known only through written descriptions of victorious battles, these fighters had a culture that valued the creative. Whether sculpture stones or intricate metal work, the Picts produced some of the finest pieces of art in the early Middle Ages. Artistic remains reveal technical and cultural development, as well as suggesting centers of political or ecclesiastical patronage. The "Pict at home" is literally visible on massive boulders (the sheer size of which sparked comment from early travelers through Scotland who remarked on their magnificence) to small rocks that can be held in the hand where there are obscure symbols, animals both real and fantastic, and scenes of everyday life such as the hunt or craftsmen with the tools of their trade. Imaginative sophistication, often in the area of ecclesiastical sculpture, provides insight into the classes of people and society in general. Stone carving in the northeastern Atlantic was ancient and the Pictish symbol stones have aspects in common with other northern European sculpture, such as the Gotland Picture Stones. The important symbol stones remain intriguing, yet controversial, sources of information. The individual images on the stones have been collected, collated, and sorted, often in efforts to show that they support someone's particular theory in connection with social organization or political succession. Recent archaeological excavations have produced new interpretations of the symbol stones' importance for understanding settlement patterns as well as evidence of the relationship between land divisions and political organization.

Another aspect to the Picts is their North Sea or northern European context. While it is true that the world for many people was little more than the immediate neighborhood where they lived and died, few people were in complete isolation. Warriors accompanied by their retinues fought battles sometimes a hundred miles or more from their homes while artists could travel even greater distances to be trained or to pursue their craft. Especially after the conversion to Christianity the Picts were drawn into an international community and their clergy subscribed to ideas, symbols, and rituals found from the Mediterranean to the North Sea. Before that, however, the Picts were by far the most northerly of the Romans' neighbors and were a part of a world that was bounded on the north by the sub-Arctic seas. Pictish fleets are mentioned several times in the Irish annals and the people were acknowledged as a formidable presence along the eastern Atlantic. Naval power allowed them to indulge in diplomacy, initially to form confederations against the Romans and then to deal with two powerful groups of immigrants to Britain: the Irish colonists on the west coast in Dál Riata and the Angles on the east coast moving northwards from the Tyne. Because of their northern situation the Picts were also the first to face the raiders/settlers from Scandinavia now known as the Vikings, who hastened the demise of Pictish (as well as others') political independence.

We cannot hope to "know" the peoples called the Picts, but certainly we can progress in understanding and recognizing some features of their society. This approach means asking many questions, few of which can be answered definitively, and exploring new topics, which in turn leads to a willingness to consider new possibilities. A useful example is the Picts as a maritime power because their activity along the eastern Atlantic leads to a reconsideration of diplomatic sophistication on the part of people whom the Romans dismissed as savages. The alliance with the Irish and the Saxons in the Barbarian Conspiracy of AD 367 temporarily ended Roman control of Britain. Another aspect of new topics is the reading of familiar works for unusual information. Religious literature such as Adomnán's *Life of Columba*, for example, has been read for ecclesiastical and political information, but it is also a useful social and cultural record for slavery, attitudes to illness, and recreation. Even personal names make a contribution, providing echoes from Gaulish deities to Christian saints. To add to the material which has been available for centuries, new discoveries are appearing with an increasing number of excavations. To take one example, in the mid-twentieth century very little was known about housing and habitation during the early Middle Ages in northern Britain, but since then there has been a comparative avalanche of information due to excavations. A willingness to use new approaches to the investigation of a marginal society such as the Picts demonstrate how different types of material – chronicles, symbol stones, remains of fortifications or settlements, and artifacts – can be revealing when assembled together, leading to new and illuminating themes. In short, an appropriate subtitle for this volume would be "Questions about the Picts."

Despite their battle prowess, the independence of the Picts was gone by the mid-ninth century. Are they to be included among history's losers, making an appearance in the historical records of late Roman/early medieval Europe before vanishing from them? Certainly that was the verdict in the twelfth century, long after the last "king of Picts" had died, when an archdeacon of Huntingdon named Henry rewrote the Venerable Bede's *Ecclesiastical History* and added his famous aside on enumeration of the five languages spoken in Britain with the comment that the language of the Picts disappeared as completely as the people.[4] A harsh verdict on peoples who had fought the mighty Roman Empire and

---

[4] Henry of Huntingdon, *Historia Anglorum*, ed. T. Arnold, Rolls Series 74 (London, 1879): 12.

destroyed the armies of their neighbors while creating beautiful sculptures and brewing ales "red as wine." This was an obscure period, and a question is how to interpret the surviving chronicle entries, king lists, and legends. Were the Picts conquered in brutal battle defeats or was there a gradual merger of Scots and Picts? Did a distinct Pictish people continue, as suggested by the tenth-century Anglo-Saxon historian Aethelweard who claimed that Picts fought at the Battle of Brunnanburh in AD 937, or was he merely indulging in rhetorical embroidery? By the twelfth century, the Picts had entered into the literary world, and Henry of Huntingdon's contemporary Geoffrey of Monmouth has them as the foes of King Arthur in his *History of the Kings of Britain*. Throughout the Middle Ages the Picts reappear in literature in increasingly fantastic situations. Failure and success are relative terms.

Pictones, a Diversion

Even where the search for the Pict begins is a matter which needs to be revisited. Traditionally a hunt for answers starts with Roman rule in Britain, when the name *Pict* appears for the first time at the end of the third century. The name had a greater antiquity, however, and three centuries earlier as Rome began to expand north of the Alps, Julius Caesar allied with a people on the Atlantic coast known as the *Pictones* who were not in Britain, but in what is now France. When Caesar campaigned in Gaul during the period 60–50 BC, among the kingdoms along the Atlantic coast were the Pictones; one of their kings was named Duratios. They inhabited the region south of the river Loire on the borders of what, centuries later, became the medieval duchy of Aquitaine. The form of the name *Pictones* shows that the Romans had borrowed, not coined, it. The element *-on* indicates that the name came originally from the Greek, to which was added the Latin population termination *-es*. The Pictones were situated in the corridor that linked the Atlantic Ocean with the Mediterranean Sea or, to phrase it culturally, linking the Celtic Atlantic with the Hellenized/Romanized Mediterranean zones. They were economically sophisticated with a distinctive gold coinage (which they had been minting since the second century BC) used for trade throughout Atlantic Europe (including the British Isles) via their ports at Ratiatunni (modern Rezé) and Corbilo.

Caesar was most interested in the usefulness of the Pictones for his campaigns, which was considerable because they were a naval power and competed in the Atlantic seaways with other maritime peoples, such as the northern kingdom of the Veneti who lived in what is today Brittany. Since the Veneti controlled the sea lanes to Britain, their destruction became the next stop on Caesar's itinerary. The Pictones quickly allied with Rome and were ordered to provide ships for Roman legions in preparation for the forthcoming confrontation with their northern neighbor. They happily seized the opportunity to make a new friend while destroying an old rival. Caesar's trust went only so far, and however friendly the Pictones might seem, he had his own men sail the vessels. This almost led to disaster because the Veneti had stout ships and they were experienced in sailing them. Rome was a land, not sea, power and the Romans had almost no experience sailing in the Atlantic Ocean. They overcame their naval incompetence by directness. Instead of outmaneuvering the enemy, they used extended grappling hooks to cut the rigging. The destruction of the Veneti at the battle of Morbihan Bay in 56 BC allowed their rivals the Pictones to assert their supremacy on the waters of the Bay of Biscay and, more importantly, access to the salt pans of Bourgneuf Bay.

Roman control of the Pictones increased during the following three and a half centuries as they were incorporated into the province of Aquitainia. The geographer Strabo (*c.* 54 BC–*c.* AD 24) claims that in addition to their shipping, the Pictones exported timber.[5] The Pictones appear to have gradually abandoned their maritime-orientation following Caesar's campaigns in the last century BC. Their trading ports at Rezé and Corbilo eventually were eclipsed by the town of Poitiers in the fourth century AD. The town was originally called Lemonum, possibly because it was located within a forest of elm trees. The location of the town on a plateau above the rivers Boivre and Clain might explain why the Romans used it as an administrative center. Poitiers' increasing importance appears to have been the deliberate result of Roman investment, with the construction of an enormous amphitheater, aqueducts, and baths. Even though the Pictones had become absorbed in the province of Aquitanica Secunda by the fourth century, they retained their identity. They do not seem to have been "romanized" in depth and their name continued to be found in the records. By the third century AD, remembrance of the Celtic origin of the Pictones came from place names, such as the abandonment of Limonum as the name of their chief town in favor

---

[5] Strabo, *The Geography of Strabo*, ed. and trans. Horace Leonard Jones, 8 vols. (Cambridge, MA, 1917–32): ii, 215–217.

of Pictavi, which was occasionally called Civitas Pictavorum. By the fifth century they were referring to themselves as Picts once again, and had produced a famous Church Father, Hilary of Poitiers (c.300–c.368) who was instrumental in combating the Arian heresy.[6] In choosing the name Pict, the Romans might have been making a comparison between the people of northern Britain and those round the Bay of Biscay, but, if so, they fail to state this directly.

Historical Sources

Something needs to be said about what information is preserved about the history of the Picts in Britain. Two important collections of information, in English translation, were compiled by Alan Orr Anderson with the titles *Scottish Annals from English Chroniclers* and the two volumes of the *Early Sources of Scottish History*.[7] While the former is limited to writers in what is now England, the latter includes material from Irish, Welsh, Scandinavian, and continental sources. The materials range from genealogies to items from chronicles, often with explanatory notes.

Turning to individual works, the history of the Picts is written from materials composed by their neighbors and enemies. Only a few of the more important are mentioned here. The earliest information comes from Roman writers, many of whom give only the barest evidence. An important historian for this topic is the former soldier turned memoirist Amminanus Marcellinus (c.325–c.395). The surviving sections of his history, the *Res Gestae*, cover the important fourth century as the Roman authorities were faced by an increasingly sophisticated foe north of Hadrian's Wall. Amminanus had served in Gaul, certainly during the reign of the Emperor Constans II and possibly for the Emperor Julian. His work shows the intrigues and strategy from the viewpoint of some who was familiar with both. A second author who needs to be mentioned is the panegyrist Claudius Claudianus (c.370–c.404). His poems in praise of the Emperor Honorius and his leading general (and father-in-law)

---

[6] A. Riese (ed.), *Geographia latini minores* (Hildesheim, repr. 1964): 143.

[7] Alan Orr Anderson, *Scottish Annals from English Chroniclers AD 500 to 1286* (London, 1908); and *Early Sources of Scottish History AD. 500 to 1286*, 2 vols. (Edinburgh, 1922). The latter was issued in a limited run of 600 sets, but was reissued in 1990 by Paul Watkins, Stamford, with a preface and corrections by his wife M.O. Anderson (ESSH).

Stilicho give a useful impression of how Britain and its peoples were seen elsewhere in the Empire.

By the sixth century information about the peoples north of Hadrian's Wall was not coming through a Roman filter. This means that there was more interest in the peoples described as Picts rather than a mere list of clichés for savages. Nonetheless, information remains sparse and obscure, often little more than a name. This is clearly seen in a work that is always cited as a primary source of information about the Picts by the British writer Gildas (*c*.495–*c*.550) who is the link between the antique and medieval worlds. Of the tracts credited to him, his *Ruin of Britain* (*De Excidio Britonum*) gives a retrospective view of the end of Roman rule in Britain and even though the importance of the Picts is emphasized, they make only a couple of appearances. While this work is regularly quoted as though it were history, it is actually a sermon whose theme is the evils of his day. In order to make his point, he calls upon history and gives a brief summary of the end of Roman Britain and the role played by the Picts and Scots. Difficult to interpret and clearly confused in some places, the *Ruin of Britain* is an essential and obscure narrative of fifth-century British history. Gildas spares little sympathy for his villains (such as the Picts), but his account became even more significant for subsequent history because it was used as a source for the Anglo-Saxon writer Bede's *Ecclesiastical History* and, a little later, the British history attributed to Nennius with the modern title *History of the Britons* (*Historia Brittonum*).

Moving completely out of a Mediterranean or Christian context, vernacular materials appear by the sixth century. Although the eulogies on fallen warriors are formulaic (the name of the warrior with some comment on him) in the sixth-/seventh-century poem *Y Gododdin* they give an insight into the society that developed north of Hadrian's Wall. The text is obscure and there are debates about almost all passages, but the general outline is that a force from the kingdom of Gododdin, located round what is now Edinburgh, was destroyed in a major battle fought in what is now Yorkshire. The authorship of the poem has traditionally been ascribed to Aneirin who, together with Taliesin, was considered one of the foremost bards of Britain. The verses offer evidence of northern warrior society. Otherwise information about northern British history after the sixth century comes to us in bits and pieces such as the obits found mainly in the Irish chronicles.

Two of the most important works were not intended to be used as political histories: the *Life of Columba* by Adomnán and Bede's aforementioned *Ecclesiastical History*. The two men were contemporaries living at the end of the seventh and early eighth century (Adomnán died in 704 and Bede in 735) and both were clergy serving important churches, the former at Iona and the latter at Wearmouth/Jarrow. Adomnán was the head of the church of Iona whose interests ran to the law; his fame in the Middle Ages was as author of a treatise forbidding attacks on noncombatants in times of war, known as the Law of Innocents or *Cáin Adomnáin* (Law of Adomnán). Adomnán's *Life of Columba* is the *vita* (life) or saintly biography of Columba or Colum Cille, the founder of the church on Iona, composed at the end of the seventh century. This is an important work for social history, as the saint's power is demonstrated through meetings with a prince, healing the ill, and banishing monsters or other creatures of evil. Since the action is important, there is little chronological guidance and only occasionally an indication of location. The value of Adomnán's work is not only that he led a church involved with the Picts, but that his position as head of the church meant that he was involved with missions active throughout northern Britain. Other Irish missions were also active in the region and snippets of what might or might not be valid information are found in other saintly *vitae*.

Rather different is Bede's *Ecclesiastical History* with its study of the conversion to Christianity of the Anglo-Saxons and the progress of the church. Bede's importance for history is difficult to overstate, and we write history for the most part in imitation of his work. He used a linear chronological progress with *anno domini* (AD) dating and gave place names, often with alternatives in different languages, throughout the history. Bede wrote more than 60 works (of which only a few survive) on topics as diverse as history, science, and theology. Two important works for this study are his prose *Vita of St. Cuthbert* (completed about 720), on the career of the bishop of Lindisfarne, and his *Ecclesiastical History*, a history of Christianity among the Anglo-Saxons which was finished about 731. Bede's history was authoritative and popular, so much so that shortly after his death, a brief set of annals was written and attached to it. His influence was extended as the *Ecclesiastical History* was consulted for the *Anglo-Saxon Chronicles* and brief annals found in other texts such as those embedded in the *Historia Regum* of Symeon of Durham. Bede was interested in the peoples round the Firth of Forth because of the establishment of a bishopric at Abercorn late in the seventh century as well as the involvement of St. Cuthbert of Lindisfarne, about whom he had composed a *vita* about a decade before his history. This shows that because Bede was writing a history of the Christian church among the Anglo-Saxons he includes external information only when it is connected with events that touch on his theme. To take one example, Bede mentions three kings of Picts – Brude son of Maelcon, Brude son of Bile, and Nechtan – in his *Ecclesiastical History*. In each instance there is a connection with Bede's thesis, which is the conversion to Christianity of the Anglo-Saxons and the flourishing of the faith. Bridei son of Maelchon is the king credited by Bede with donating the island of Iona to Columba for the building of his church, and from Iona came several bishops for the peoples in Northumbria, beginning with Áedan. The second of the trio is Brude son of Bile who defeated the Northumbrian king Ecgfrith at the battle of Dun Nechtan and ended, so far as Bede could know, the political supremacy of the kingdom. Finally, the last individual, Nechtan, was the king who sent a request to the Northumbrians for aid in reorganizing the churches in his domain. In each instance there is a direct connection with one of Bede's preoccupations.

The main source of material for the Picts is the chronicles and annals of which the most informative are two Irish annals now known as the *Annals of Ulster* and the *Annals of Tigernach*. There is a growing consensus that they incorporate materials collected at some religious house(s) in Britain, and that the ultimate source for both records seems to be a now-lost compendium popularly known as the Irish World Chronicle.[8] Particularly visible in the *Annals of Ulster* is the incorporation of differing dates for events.[9] Both sets of annals now survive in late medieval (fifteenth-century) manuscripts and much of their information is common to both of them. There are items that are unique to each text and, for the *Annals of Ulster*, the language original to the earliest manuscript was not consistently modernized and it occasionally preserves forms consistent with an early medieval date of composition. One problem is that a section of the *Annals of Tigernach* is missing from the eighth to tenth centuries, so other works supplement the *Annals of Ulster* such as the seventeenth-century transcriptions of annals now known as the *Annals of Clonmacnoise*, *Chronicon Scotorum*, and the *Fragmentary Annals of Ireland*. The information preserved varies according to the time span.

---

[8] For a reconstruction of what such a text might have included see T.M.O. Charles-Edwards, *The Chronicle of Ireland*, 2 vols. (Liverpool, 2006).

[9] Specifically addressing the problems of chronology see Daniel M. McCarthy, "The Chronological Apparatus of the Annals of Ulster AS 431–1131," *Peritia* 8 (1994): 46–79, and "The Chronological Apparatus of the Annals of Ulster AD 82–1019," *Peritia* 16 (2002): 256–283.

For the period from the mid-sixth century to the year 685 the notices are mainly obits, occasionally with some detail about the cause of death, together with an occasional notice of a battle or siege. From the year 685 to 741 the entries become comparatively copious with more detail of battles, pursuits, and captures. Afterwards, until the year 862, the notices revert to their previously laconic state concerned primarily with deaths. In addition to the annals and chronicles are stray items of information given in literature, geographical texts such as the *dindsenchus* (history of places), and genealogies.

A stylistic feature found in both Irish and Anglo-Saxon materials that has confused commentators is the use of the phrase *rex Pictorum*. Reading it as a collective name has led to the error that there was a single kingdom of all the Picts. In fact the phrase probably means simply "a king of Picts" rather than "the king of the Picts" providing evidence for a single kingdom. A comparison with the titles awarded to Anglo-Saxon kings in the Irish annals is instructive. The *Annals of Tigernach* describe the early seventh-century Edwin son of Aella as "king of the English" (*rex Saxonum*), the same term is used for his rival Penda, Penda's contemporary Oswy, and Oswy's son Ecgfrith; the *Annals of Ulster* use the same term for Oswy's brother Oswald. None of the men was king of all the Anglo-Saxons, despite later efforts to claim as much with the use of the term *Bretwalda*, but Edwin, Oswald, Oswy, and Ecgfrith were kings of Northumbria and Penda was king of Mercia. This explains why Brude son of Maelcon is described as king of the Picts in the *Annals of Tigernach* when he routed the army of Dál Riata, but his contemporary Cindaeladh or Cennalath is also called king of the Picts in his obit *c.* 581, as is Brude when he dies the following year.

The final group of source materials comes from the kingdom of Scotland. Setting aside the later historical or pseudo-historical accounts attributed to John of Fordun and Andrew of Wyntoun (which are discussed in chapter 7), there are the lists of kings and verse histories of the Picts. These "Pictish king-lists," are often cited as primary source documents. The arguments against accepting this view are made elsewhere, but a few observations will be useful here.[10] The keeping of lists of kings is ancient, but the medieval European tradition grew out of the Roman

---

[10] They are identified by letters of the alphabet and were collected by W.F. Skene, *Chronicles of the Picts, Chronicles of the Scots and other* (Edinburgh, 1867) and KCS: 240–291 with a discussion at pp. 77–102. An English translation of the so-called list A is in ESSH: i, cxix–cxxviii, with variations from other lists.

lists of consuls combined with the Christian tradition of remembering the leaders of the religious community, particularly bishops. The surviving lists of kings of the Picts (none of which is found in manuscripts earlier than the late thirteenth or early fourteenth century) are based on exemplars from the late twelfth and early thirteenth century. The earlier catalog, designated Y, assumed its present form around 1166 while the later, designated X, is around 1214–1249. The registers are actually a compendium of names gleaned from other sources. Comparison of the names with entries in the Irish annals suggests that they were one possible source of information. This led to a problem that, as Fraser noted, the number of kings of the Picts found for a span of 270 years in this early period would suffice for the following 700 years of Scottish history.[11] This is revealed when Talorgan son of Drostan, the king of Atholl, is found in the king lists together with his contemporaries Angus son of Fergus, the king of Circenn, and Alpín son of Ferant, the king of Fortriu. One reason why this was not immediately obvious is the slight variations in the forms of names between the annals and the king lists. This is more apparent than real because several name forms seemingly different are actually the same name. An example to be discussed in another chapter is Drust, which is one form of the names Drost and Drostan. A similar statement can be made for the names Talorgg/Talurg/Talorgan.

Questions and More Questions

As the foregoing discussion shows, there are many questions about the Picts and different answers are found throughout the centuries. Who were the Picts? Did the name indicate a specific ethnic group or was it merely a term of convenience for peoples who lived in a particular area? If it was geographical, where were the Picts? If ethnic, were the Picts survivors of an earlier culture that had flourished across Europe? The couple of examples given above show a continuing scholarly argument as to whether the language of the Picts was cognate with Old Welsh or a non-Indo-European tongue. Even their name provokes question. Why is *Cruithne*, the Old Irish name for them, used to describe people in both northern Britain and northeastern Ireland, but the Latin term *Picti* is used in the Middle Ages only for peoples living north of the firths of

---

[11] John Fraser, "The Question of the Picts," *Scottish Gaelic Studies* 2 (1927): 180n1.

Clyde and Forth? What, if any, was their connection with the Pictones of Gaul who gave their name to Poitiers? How did this warlike and innovative society function? Did they practice matrilineal succession to the kingship? Did their name come from the practice of tattooing? Even when there is evidence, either written or physical, interpretation can be uncertain. To take an example, sculpture of the important symbol stones, for instance, is an intriguing, yet controversial, source of information. On the one hand it is usually assumed that images of warriors, animals, vehicles, and scenes of everyday life are an invaluable source of information on what life was like, how the social contract operated, and what kinds of materials they did or did not have. On the other hand, these easily identifiable images might have another entirely different meaning, especially when accompanied by other figures whose meaning remains obscure. Fabulous beasts, geometric symbols, and an arcane writing system known as ogam (which used lines rather than alphabetic letter forms) have invited speculation. Interpretations of the obscure symbols have ranged from boundary markers to statements of lineage to hieroglyphs. Part of the problem is physical as many of them have yet to be photographed in usable form, while the past two centuries have been particularly destructive of material remains. So recourse often has to be made to the surviving (and uncertain) records found in eighteenth-century diaries and modern topographical reports. Many of these necessary materials are either unpublished or in rare printed editions in archives, necessitating personal consultation.

While much can be suggested, little can be concluded. Many books and essays claim to have discovered definitive conclusions about the Picts. The following chapters make no such assertions and, in contrast, merely survey the written and physical remains while asking questions. Definitive answers are few, but new techniques and methodologies, such as the incorporation of transnational and comparative methodologies along with the abandonment of the outdated theories favored by an earlier generation of scholars and their current disciples open new vistas on an important and intriguing people.

1

Picts and Romans

If anyone had doubts about the origins of the Picts, the Romans were not among them. A document dating from the early fourth century called "The Barbarian Nations that sprang up under the [Roman] Emperors," claims that they created the Picts.[1] Setting aside the title, the text is essentially a roll call of the peoples living outside the empire with which the Romans had contacts and its thesis is clear even before the completion of the inventory of 53 "nations" located beyond the imperial frontiers. This is a jumble of anciently known peoples together with nations which had recently appeared in the written records. As well as such fresh names as the Picts and Alemani there are older names such as the Caledonians and Persians. The tract shows Roman bigotry (a barbarian was a barbarian regardless of antiquity or achievements) together with a keen awareness that they were not living in isolation and that some knowledge of the people outside their borders might be helpful.

Fifteen hundred years later there was less certainty about the Picts. In 1971 the BBC broadcast a television program, accompanied by a book, with the title *Who are the Scots?* Various authors contributed chapters describing the different peoples who had settled in Scotland,

---

[1] "Gentes barbarae quae pullulaverunt sub imperatoribus," in *Geographia latini minores*, ed. A. Riese (Hildesheim, repr. 1964): 128–129; the text is attached to an official list of Roman provinces. See also Ralph W. Mathisen, "Catalogues of Barbarians in Late Antiquity," in Ralph W. Mathisen and Danuta Shanzer (eds.), *Romans, Barbarians, and the Transformation of the Roman World* (Burlington, VT, 2011): 17–32 (at p. 22).

The Picts, First Edition. Benjamin Hudson.
© 2014 John Wiley & Sons, Ltd. Published 2014 by John Wiley & Sons, Ltd.

beginning with the earliest inhabitants and culminating with the francophone emigrants of the High Middle Ages.[2] With one exception, the chapter titles are simple, such as "Britons and Angles" or "Scots of Dalriada." The exception is a chapter with the title "The Problem of the Picts." The phrase was an acknowledgment of an influential book called *The Problem of the Picts*, edited by F.T. Wainwright and published in 1955, based on a collection of papers originally delivered at a conference in Dundee in 1952 held under the auspices of the Scottish Summer School of Archaeology. The individual essays fell into four categories that have largely defined the avenues of inquiry since then: history, archaeology, art history, and language. A dozen years later, Isabel Henderson published *The Picts* which drew together the separate topics into a continuous narrative. In those works, as in subsequent English-language studies, the Picts were limited to Britain and their history begun in the last centuries of the Western Roman Empire.

Before the Picts

The peoples of northern Britain were a military concern for the Romans even before the appearance of the name Pict.[3] Tacitus gives an account of the peoples of northern Britain in his *Agricola* where he uses the generic term Britons (which in its widest application referred to everyone in the island) while mentioning specific peoples such as the Caledonians and Borestras. When Claudius Ptolemeus (the second-century geographer better known as Ptolemy of Alexandria) described Britain north of the Antonine Wall in his *Geographia*, he identified 16 peoples living in what is now Scotland.[4] Suggestions on the locations of these groups place the Caereni, Cornavii, Lugi, and Smertae in the region of what is now Caithness and Sutherland, while the Decantae and Carnonacae were in Ross. Between the Moray Firth and the Firth of Forth were the Caledonii, the Vacomagi, the Taexali, and the Venicones in the east, with the Crenoes and Epidii in the west. The southern peoples, between the Antonine

---

[2] Gordon Menzies (ed.), *Who are the Scots?* (London, 1971).
[3] For an overview of this period a useful guide is Peter Salway, *Roman Britain* (Oxford, 1981).
[4] Following the translated extracts in I.A. Richmond, *Roman and Native in North Britain* (London, 1953): 150–153.

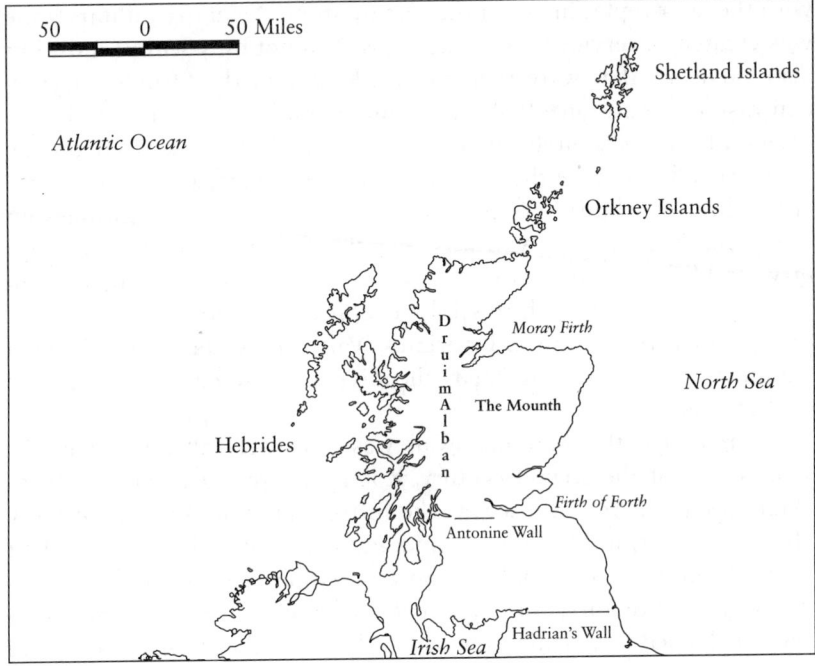

Map 1.1 Northern Britain.

and Hadrian walls, were the Novantae and Selgovae in Galloway and Dumfriesshire, the Damnonii to their east, and the Otadini in what is now Lothian.

The Romans constructed two walls – today called after the emperors Hadrian and Antonius – as part of their efforts to impose some control over their northern boundary in Britain (see Map 1.1). Building walls was not unique to Britain, of course, and they are found either on their own or in connection with other defenses, as at the Danube. They do show that the Romans felt that their opponents were too dangerous to be left unchecked. The earlier and more southerly barrier is now called Hadrian's Wall, built between AD 123 and 133 on roughly the same latitude as the southern boundary of Denmark. The more northerly construction, built a generation later, is known today as the Antonine Wall; situated between the inlets of the sea at the firths of Clyde and Forth, it lies farther north than Moscow. The two walls represent different levels of investment as well as longevity. Hadrian's Wall initially was constructed of stone in the east and turf in the west, with the later replacement of the turf by stone. An entire military zone was created to service it and Hadrian's Wall not only had portals, but also garrisons that were still stationed there in the fifth century. By contrast the Antonine Wall was built completely of turf and it is essentially a large ditch where the excavated soil was used on the southern side to make the defensive work. Compared with the southern wall, it was built hurriedly and cheaply. The debate continues on how long the Antonine Wall was an active feature of the Roman military establishment, but within the total time of Roman occupation in Britain it was brief, with possibly a total of 20 years of garrisoning. Except for a few decades, Hadrian's Wall was, so far as the Roman administration was concerned, the divider between barbarism and civilization.

Even though the Antonine Wall was effectively abandoned in the second half of the second century, Roman interest remained north of Hadrian's Wall. An outpost was the fortress built at Bremenium (now High Rochester) in Northumberland and it was occupied from the first to third centuries. The final Roman occupation of those lands came in the early third century, at the very end of the reign of Emperor Septimus Severus. He led a campaign for which the ostensible reason was to put down attacks from beyond the Wall. The emperor rebuffed efforts for a peaceful settlement in order (so the contemporary historian Herodian claimed) to give his indolent sons experience in warfare. Eager to avoid confrontation, the princes north of Hadrian's Wall sent envoys to treat with the emperor. Herodian noted that the ambassadors from the northern tribes were clothed only with iron bands round their necks and stomachs; otherwise they wore only tattoos that covered their entire bodies.[5] This sounds similar to the claim made three centuries earlier by Julius Caesar, who noted that the Britons wore few clothes and were covered in designs made with blue ink from the woad plant (*Isatis tinctoria*). Despite the determination of Severus, by the reign of his son Caracalla the imperial administration made Hadrian's Wall its northern extent.

Herodian's contemporary Dio gives an ethnic background to the expedition of Septimus Severus. He claims (book LXXVII) that the two principal peoples living north of Hadrian's Wall were the Caledonians and the Maeatae; the latter lived next to the wall while the former lived

---

[5] Herodian, *History of the Empire from the time of Marcus Aurelius*, ed. and trans. C.R. Whittaker, 2 vols. (Cambridge, MA, 1969): i, 358.

beyond them.⁶ The appearance of the Maeatae is a new grouping from the outline given by Ptolemy. Dio describes both of them as among the principal races of Britons. Both Herodian and Dio remark on the mountains and swamps inhabited by the northern peoples. Dio makes the added comment that the northerners did not touch fish, which seems supported by modern archaeology which has not found much evidence for mounds of fish bones (see chapter 4).

North and South

Anyone who traveled the length of Britain at the end of the third century, on the eve of the first appearance of the use of "Pict" for a people in Britain, would have been aware of a contrast between two general cultural areas marked by Hadrian's Wall. South of the wall were wide, paved roads that connected towns with markets, houses, government offices, and intersected with other roads leading to ports where ships sailed to continental Europe. North of the wall were a few paths (so inadequate for the Romans that Severus' troops had to build military roads for their use) leading to scattered fortified encampments usually on elevated ground and known by the Romans as *oppida* (sing. *oppidum*). Dio claimed that the inhabitants lived in tents. Security north of Hadrian's Wall was available to an individual within his own people, while to the south this security was mandated by imperial forces. The south had harbors, grain storage, and land reclamation projects (such as the Roman drainage of the Fen country), but the north had none of these except possibly the last, and then only in a small and irregular fashion. To the south there was also high taxation, requisition of goods, and conscription of men to fight battles far from their homes. In the north there were the goods paid to the local prince which were, in turn, used to maintain his household retinue and distributed among his subjects in public displays of gift-giving. South of Hadrian's Wall was a culture that borrowed from the great civilizations of the Mediterranean in its art, literature, and scholarship. In the north was the continuation of traditions that had endured for centuries, with an art that was admired by its southern neighbor and a warrior ethos that celebrated the individual. The division is apparent in the perception of Britain after the end of direct

---

⁶ Dio, *Roman History*, ed. and trans. Earnest Cary, 9 vols. (Cambridge, MA, 1914–27): IX, 262; the identification of the wall with Hadrian's Wall is confirmed by Dio's claim that it cut the island in half, which it almost did.

imperial administration. The sixth-century historian Procopius (*Historia Bellorum*, VIII.20) believed that Britain was actually two islands, with the northern part, called *Brittia*, lying opposite the mouth of the Rhine.[7]

Equally important was the change in physical geography. There is a greater percentage of arable lands south of Hadrian's Wall and comparatively fewer to the north. Unlike the broad sweep of the coastal shelf that extended from east to west on a gradually inclining trajectory in Roman Britain; north of Hadrian's Wall the land suitable for cultivation or prime grazing was confined to coastal strips; the most expansive were found along the eastern coast. Snaking their way round the great sea inlets now known as the firths of Forth, Tay, and Moray, these lands were home to most of the population and are where most of the surviving Pictish symbol stones are found. The lands north of the Wall are much balmier than they should be because of warm water flowing from the Gulf of Mexico known as the Gulf Stream. This current divides at the Pentland Firth with the flow along the eastern coast of Britain known as the North Atlantic Drift. The short growing season in the north meant that the main cereals were barley and oats while crops such as wheat could be grown only in small pockets. What was lacking in arable was compensated by grazing. Hills are prime land for raising livestock, and animals flourished on sloping pastures where their diet was enhanced by the minerals in the grass. There were also fish along the coasts and rivers such as salmon, while shellfish and seaweed were gathered along the shores. Last to be mentioned are the mineral deposits, the copper and iron in Galloway or the gold in Rhynie. But for centuries the single most impressive physical feature was the great Caledonian forest. Not only did it provide wood for building and fuel, but it was an effective defensive barrier because of the difficulty of traveling through it. Interspersed among the woods were wetlands of various types, and together they made any movement slow especially for large numbers of men such as formed the Roman armies.

Hadrian's Wall was a division in another way, and that was demographically. South of the Wall there had been changes in population as well as construction during the centuries of imperial rule. Population movement is often mentioned but is rarely studied. The Roman strategy of moving troops from one part of the empire to serve in another, the establishment of retirement communities (*coloniae*) for those troops in

---

[7] Procopius, *History of the Wars*, ed. and trans. H.B. Dewing, 7 vols. (Cambridge, MA, 1914–40): vi, 358.

disparate lands (Boadicea's rebellion was directed towards, in part, the veterans settled at the *colonia* at Colchester), and the general movement of people throughout the empire looking for work, profit, or safety meant that the population of Britain south of Hadrian's Wall by the fourth century was different from that north of the wall. Inscriptions give some indication of the diversity as they show that civil servants, military officers, and common soldiers upon whom the imperial administration relied were immigrants: Romans, Syrians, and Greeks as well as Gauls and Germans. A section of Hadrian's Wall from Carrawburgh to Brough on Noe was manned by the *cohors I Aquitanorum*.

The Picts Appear

The first reference to Picts in Britain comes at the end of the third century AD, three and a half centuries after the establishment of Roman rule in the island. Eumenius, a teacher of rhetoric in Augustodunum (now the city of Autun) in Gaul is believed to be the author of an oration, composed around 296, in praise of a Roman general named Constantius "the Pale" (*Chlorus*). Constantius had recently returned from Britain to Gaul in the wake of restoring imperial control after the island had fallen away from Rome's control and into the hands of independent rulers or usurpers in the later third century. His military campaigns from 293 to 296 began with the defeat of the usurper Carausius' army in Gaul, followed a few years later by the defeat and death of his subordinate Allectus. Eumenius' congratulations included an ungenerous assessment of the fighting skills of the Britons with reference to their enemies:

> In addition to that, a nation [i.e. the Britons] which was then primitive and accustomed to fight still half naked, only with Picts and Hiberni [i.e., the Irish], easily succumbed to Roman arms and standards, almost to the point that Caesar should have boasted about this one thing only on that expedition; that he had sailed across the ocean.[8]

This was not the end of Constantius' association with the Picts. After his death in 306 at York while preparing to lead an invasion north of Hadrian's Wall, a panegyric written around 310 remembered him: "For it was not he who had accomplished so many great feats thought it

---

[8] C.E.V. Nixon and Barbara Saylor Rodgers (eds.), *In Praise of the Later Roman Emperors*, the Panegyrici Latini (Berkeley, 1994): 126.

worthwhile to acquire – I won't mention the forests and swamps of the Caledonians and other Picts – either nearly Hibernia or Farthest Thule or the Isle of the Blest themselves, if they exist ..."[9] In these verses the name *Picti* clearly refers to peoples living beyond the imperial frontier of Britain. This was the same area where, less than a century earlier, the historian Herodian described the last campaign of the emperor Septimus Severus who had descended on Britain in order to deal with predations by the peoples beyond Hadrian's Wall. He noted that the mere fact of Severus' arrival so terrified the miscreants that they immediately sued for peace.[10] That conference was unsuccessful for the supplicants because the emperor was determined on a war for the moral well-being of his son. Worth recalling are two asides made by contemporary historians. First, Dio calls the people who lived beyond Hadrian's Wall Britons, who, he implies, were physically indistinguishable from the Britons living under Roman administration. Second, Herodian notes that they were tattooed and scantily dressed, wearing only iron bands round their necks and waists, from which they carried their weapons.

In order to understand the phrasing in the panegyrics on Constantius it is necessary to realize that Roman political control in Britain had been as chaotic as elsewhere in the empire in the previous half-century, popularly known as the "era of the barrack emperors." Prior to Constantius' deployment of his troops to the island, Britain had been for some time under the control of local rulers of whom the latest had been Allectus. Among his villainies, in the eyes of the imperial authorities, was to allow the northern defensive line of Hadrian's Wall to fall into disrepair. When Constantius was made a Caesar, or junior ruler and emperor-in-training, in 292, he was assigned the northwestern section of the empire as his area of operations. After regaining control of Britain, he had ordered the repair of Hadrian's Wall, but unfortunately, beyond his major achievements, almost no details survive for Constantius' expedition and its aftermath. Nevertheless, his elevation to the status of Augustus in 306 apparently was due in no small measure to his success against the Picts, among others.

Why does the word *Picti* abruptly appear at this time as the name for the people beyond the Roman frontier of Hadrian's Wall? The word is Latin and it derives from *pictus* (picture). Despite valiant efforts to make connections with earlier population or place names (and there is the

[9] Nixon and Rodgers, *In Praise of the Later Roman Emperors*: 226–227.
[10] Herodian, *History of the Empire*: i, 358.

possibility of a connection with the Pictones of Gaul), the choice of the word says as much about the men who were controlling the administration of the empire as about those they named. A good example is Constantius' superior, Emperor Diocletian, who halted the slide towards anarchy and oversaw the rescue operation in Britain. The new men were drawn from the provinces rather than from Italia and had risen to positions of eminence (often from extremely humble origins) through their own abilities. They were passionately proud of being Roman and contemptuous of anyone outside the empire. At the same time they were men in a hurry whose education was acquired "on the run," so to say. Not surprisingly the most popular form of historical writing among them was not elegant narratives such as those of Pliny, replete with literary allusion, but the *breviarum* or digest with its succinct information in which the essential facts were elaborated. The "new" Romans were quite blunt in their language; not for them the delicate nuances of their predecessors trained in classical literature. To take one example, they called the gold coin that was the standard currency of the age a *solidus*, "a solid bit."[11]

Similarly these new men had little knowledge of the ethnic diversity among the so-called savages beyond their northern frontier, but they knew what they read, and that included Caesar's *Gallic Wars* and Tacitus' *Agricola*. In their mind the northern peoples were the direct descendants of Caesar's Britons, whose heirs had challenged the great Agricola at the battle of *Mons Crampius*. Britain, of course, was famous for its painted people and no less an authority than the "Divine" Julius had noted in his *Gallic Wars* that the Britons painted themselves with the dye from woad. If Herodian is to be believed (and he was a contemporary of the events he described), then the practice of body decoration – whether painting or tattooing – had become a visible difference between the Britons living within and outside Roman control. The Romans had a horror of bodily disfigurement, believing that tattooing, body-painting, and body-piercing were the signs of barbarians or primitives. They did practice tattooing, but as a form of punishment. A captured runaway slave, for example, was tattooed on the face as a proclamation of his crime. In the eyes of the new men who staffed the imperial service, anyone outside the civilizing influence of Rome was no better than a slave. So the name *Picti* was clearly meant to differentiate between the civilized Britons (those within the bounds of the empire) and the barbarians who lurked beyond Hadrian's Wall.

[11] Peter Brown, *The World of Late Antiquity* (London, 1971): 28.

The name Pict was such a novelty when first used that it had to be paired with a more familiar appellation, hence "Caledonians and other Picts." The individual groups covered by the collective name *Picti* continued to be mentioned in the records. The name Caledonian, for example, was used by Roman writers, and writing almost a century later Ausonius (d. 395) used the names Caledonian and Briton when referring to people in Northern Britain, as in his *Mosella* (*Epistulae* XXVII.3.36) where he noted that "the Caledonian shore is under the Briton's gaze."[12] This is the only reference to Britons beyond Hadrian's Wall after the first appearance of the name Pict. The fifth-century poet Claudian used both *Caledonii* and *Picti* to describe the peoples outside Roman control in Britain.[13] Later in that century, Sidonius Apollinaris includes the Caledonians, Britons, Picts, Irish, and Anglo-Saxons as the inhabitants of Britain in one of his poems.[14]

The name Pict was only one of the various collective designations being coined at this time. The barbarians had been observing their successful, gigantic rival and during the late third/early fourth century they were coming together into large groups or confederacies when the situation demanded. In turn, the Romans were coining new names to describe these new situations. Just before the term *Picti* was employed to describe people living north of Hadrian's Wall, the term *Tervingi* (an early name for the Visigoths) is used as a collective term for several independent Germanic peoples who were cooperating against the Romans; it is used in a panegyric for the emperor Maximian delivered around 291. A generation after the panegyric about Constantius, the name *Scoti* ("Irish") appears for the first time in the fourth-century history of Ammianus Marcellinus. In a similar fashion the name Alemani has been shown to be a collective term for several distinct groups in a particular region.[15] These "unions of convenience" were not entirely new, as Julius Caesar

[12] Ausonius, *Decimi Magni Ausonii Opera*, ed. R.P.H. Green (Oxford, 1999): 217): "Sunt et Aremorici qui laudent ostrea ponti et quae Pictonici legit accola litoris, et quae mira Caledoniis nonnumquam detegit aestu" (it is not clear if his "Pictonic coast" means Britain or Atlantic Gaul); and 128 (*Mosella*, l. 68): "Tota Caledoniis talis patet ora Britannis."

[13] Claudian, *Panegyric on the Fourth Consulship of Honorius*, in *Clavdii Clavdiani Carmina*, ed. John Barrie Hall (Leipzig, 1985): 62.

[14] Sidonius, *Sidoine Apollinaire*, ed. André Loyen, 3 vols. (Paris, 2003): i, 57–58 (ll. 89–90).

[15] John Drinkwater, *The Alemani and Rome 213–496 (Caracalla to Clovis)* (Oxford, 2007): 45.

had discovered several centuries earlier when his invading legions arrived in Britain. On his first invasion a surprised Caesar saw his hopes of swiftly picking off individual kingdoms dashed when the Britons (with far more sophistication than the Romans were willing to credit to primitives) temporarily united and forced the Romans to retreat to the continent after penning the invaders in the southeastern corner of Britain. To prevent such unpleasant surprises the Romans had become masters of the tactic of divide and conquer, but the despised barbarians had learned the equally important lesson of cooperation.

The Barbarian Conspiracy of AD 367

During the period from late antiquity to the early Middle Ages, the Picts are frequently found in conjunction with another people called the *Scoti*, in other words the Irish. The panegyric on Constantius merely mentions them in the same passage as enemies of the Britons. A generation later, the Roman soldier and memoirist Ammianus Marcellinus describes the two peoples as allies.[16] In the hands of later writers it became a cliché, although it is not clear at this point if the Scots in question were colonists from the Irish kingdom of Dál Riata, later situated along the western Scottish coast and in some of the islands of the Hebrides, or were some other group of Irish settlers. They need not have been in northern Britain, for the tale "Expulsion of the Déisi" claims that at roughly this time an Irish clan from Meath emigrated and settled in southwest Wales under the leadership of an Eochaid Oversea.[17] Of course the *Scoti* need not have been in Britain at all, and they could have sailed directly from Ireland. What the panegyrics for Constantius the Pale do show is that the Picts had been added by the Romans to their list of enemies. More revealing is that the Roman writers are in no doubt that the Picts were the main adversary in Britain, with or without various allies.

This was merely one aspect of the increasing Roman paranoia throughout the fourth century about attacks on their borders. In Britain this was made worse by the island's apparent use as a semi-penal colony for troublemakers from other parts of the empire, who needed to be removed from their homes and put somewhere they would cause less trouble.

---

[16] Ammianus Marcellinus, *Rerum Gestarum Libri*, ed. John C. Rolfe, 3 vols. (Cambridge, MA: 1950–52): ii, 2.
[17] P.C. Bartrum, *Early Welsh Genealogical Tracts* (Cardiff, 1966): 4.

According to the fifth-century historian Zosimus, after the third-century emperor M. Aurelius Probus defeated the barbarians in Gaul, he deported captives from among the Burgundians and Vandals to Britain around 278.[18] Ammianus claims that the imperial administration in fourth-century Britain was disturbed by scoundrels such as Valentinus, the brother-in-law of the aforementioned Maximian, who had been placed on the island under the equivalent of police observation.[19] This might help to explain the unfortunate attitude that some people had towards anybody from Britain. Ausonius, for example, wrote the famous passage "there is nothing good in Britain," although the phrase was used in connection with one Silvius for whom he had a special dislike.[20]

Constantius the Pale's brief career had been unusually concerned with Britain. In light of his death at York while preparing an expedition to attack the area north of Hadrian's Wall, the restoration of imperial control in the last years of the third century might not have been as final as his eulogists claimed. Even in the comparatively benign years of the first half of the fourth century there are suggestions that in Britain, as elsewhere in the western provinces, all was not well. There was the constant danger of treason, for one, and Constantius' son Constantine "the Great" issued a law that anyone who allied with barbarians against Rome or even shared their loot was to be burned alive.[21] Legal threats within the empire were accompanied by negotiations outside it. Constantine's son Constans (emperor 337–350) tried diplomacy by treaty in 343 when he made a pact with the Picts and Scots to keep the peace. This was not necessarily a sign of weakness. As the empire was threatened by other more worrisome foes, the "buying off" of a nuisance on the extreme northwest frontier was a sensible course of action. Peace was kept for 17 years, but it was broken in 360 when the Picts ravaged the frontier lands, apparently the area immediately around Hadrian's Wall. Among the few scraps of information we have about this incident is the formation of an alliance among the Picts, the Scots, and the Attacotti. This raid, which must have been destructive in order to be

---

[18] Zosimus, *New History*, ed. and trans. Ronald I. Ridley (Sydney, 1982): 21 (I.68).
[19] Ammianus Marcellus, *Rerum Gestarum Libri*: ii, 132.
[20] Ausonius, *Decimi Magni Ausonii Opera*, ed. H.G.E. White, 2 vols. (Cambridge, MA, 1919–21), repr. 1985): ii, 216: "Nemo bonus Brito est."
[21] Clyde Pharr (ed.), *Theodosian Code and Novels and the Sirmondian Constitutions* (New York, 1952): 7.1.1 (*c.* 323).

recorded in Ammianus' history, was the beginning of warfare between the Picts (with or without their allies) and the Romans that was to last almost a century, continuing after the withdrawal of the legions from Britain. St. Jerome claimed that the Attacotti lived in Britain and were cannibals.[22] The suggestion has been offered that they were actually an Irish group who had settled round the Severn, encouraged by the Romans in order to enlist them as auxiliary troops, which would explain why they are found on the continent where they met St. Jerome.

The Romans were to learn that the Picts were formidable opponents not just in ferocity, but also in forming effective alliances, as their campaigns for the remainder of the century were to show. By mid-century the Romans were so concerned about what the Picts were preparing to do that they employed agents known as *arcani* to discover their plans. The sole reference to these individuals is found in a brief aside made by Ammianus, who reveals that the Romans had been using a spy network, called the Secret Service (Latin *arcanus*) to keep an eye on the Picts.[23] How members of the *arcanus* operated is suggested by the career of one Hariobudes who was sent by the emperor Julian to gather information about the Germanic King Horter.[24] Even though Horter was a staunch Roman ally, this did not spare him from the usual Roman mistrust of "barbarians." Hariobudes was chosen because he spoke the language fluently (his name suggests that he might have had some ties to the region). He roamed throughout Horter's realm and looked for any activity that might suggest a threat to Rome, but found none. There is no indication of Hariobudes' disguise, but one possible choice would have been a merchant. Since large groups of people such as battalions assembling for invasion, needed goods, it would be the obvious place for a traveling merchant. The clandestine career of Hariobudes matches Ammanius's brief account of the *arcani* in Britain, although he simply says that they spied on the barbarians by roaming over as much territory as possible and reporting any threatening movements to the Roman authorities.

This tactic seems to have gone badly wrong in Britain and the authorities were completely unprepared for the storm that broke in 367 in what the Romans described as a *barbarica conspirator* or Barbarian Conspiracy.

---

[22] Philip Rance, "Attacotti, Déisi and Magnus Maximus: The Case for Irish Federates in Later Roman Britain," Britannia 32 (2001): 243–270.
[23] Ammianus Marcellus, *Rerum Gestarum Libri*: ii, 132.
[24] Ammianus Marcellus, *Rerum Gestarum Libri*: i, 406.

Sometimes popularly known as the Pictish Revolt, Roman fears of a confederation of savages were justified when the Scots and Picts attacked south of Hadrian's Wall, where they were joined by the Attacotti, while the Franks and Saxons ravaged the north coasts of Gaul. At least one legion mutinied in order to join the rebel alliance and the imperial officials received a glimpse of how loyal were many of its subjects. One general named Nectaridus was slain and another named Fullofaudes was captured in an ambush. The rebellion succeeded, at least briefly, and for some time (now thought to be more a matter of months than years) the Picts and their allies were in control of Britain.[25] After other commanders had been unable to restore order, the emperor Valentinian dispatched Count Theodosius to put down the rebellion. Theodosius landed at Richborough and fought his way to London. Part of the difficulty was the Roman deserters/mutineers who either had joined the rebellion or decided to profit from the disorder by scavenging in irregular companies. That the Barbarian Conspiracy of 367 was a temporary rather than permanent success was due to the selection of Theodosius to lead the *reconquista*. Rather than executing summary justice on the malefactors from the garrisons, he simply gave them the opportunity to return to their barracks. Then he seems to have moved into the countryside where he systematically dealt with the chaos. His triumph was remembered and Claudian's panegyric on the third consulship of his grandson Honorius recalled how his ships had sailed the northern seas to conquer Picts and chase Scots with his sword.[26]

After imperial control was re-established under Theodosius' supervision, the hunt for scapegoats began. Among those who found fingers pointing at them were the *arcani*. The spies who had been sent out to the Picts were discovered to have changed sides, and instead of reporting to the Romans, they gave information to the enemy. Details about the charges are sketchy, but it seems that the barbarians were just as aware as the Romans of the usefulness of information about the plans of their enemies; and they had used their knowledge to plan both when and where they would attack. Whatever the specific details, Theodosius promptly disbanded the *arcani*. The sparse and vague information, which is capable of sustaining different interpretations, suggests that the Pictish invasion had been planned over a long period of time and the raiders

---

[25] Ammianus Marcellus, *Rerum Gestarum Libri*: ii, 50–56.
[26] Claudian, *Clavdii Clavdiani Carmina*, ed. John Barrie Hall (Leipzig, 1985): 55.

were not moving aimlessly around the countryside, but aiming for selected targets. This would explain why Roman resistance collapsed so quickly and also why one entire legion mutinied and joined the invaders. Little wonder that the Roman authorities were so panicked.

Late Fourth and Early Fifth Century

Within fifteen years the Picts felt sufficiently recovered to move against the Romans again. Once more the information is barely more than an announcement. One of Theodosius' officers named Magnus Maximus, who also hailed from what is now Spain, stopped another invasion by the Scots and Picts in 382.[27] His triumph encouraged him to declare himself emperor and lead troops from Britain to adventures on the continent. For five years he was successful, but was eventually defeated and slain. Magnus' connection with Britain might have been more than official. He reappears in Welsh literature as Macsen Wledig (the name means "Prince Magnus") in the tale called *The Dream of Macsen Wledig* where he is described as the emperor of Rome. The inscription on the pillar of Eliseg has a passage that seems to mean Magnus had a daughter named Severa, while he also appears in other genealogies.[28]

Sometime around the end of the fourth/beginning of the fifth century (the chronology is very vague at this point), the Picts, now in alliance only with the Scots, renewed their raids on Roman Britain. The Roman poet Claudian's eulogy of the great Vandal general Stilicho claims that large fleets were sailing from Ireland and that Stilicho gained a major victory over them on the western coast of Britain; a location has been suggested somewhere between Morecambe Bay and the Solway Firth.[29] This might be the same episode that the sixth-century author Gildas is referring to in his *Ruin of Britain* when he claimed that the Scots and Picts allied for attacks on Roman Britain.[30] There might have been more than a military aspect to these raids. While the debate continues on the period when the *Scoti* began making settlements on the western British

---

[27] For a helpful summary and discussion of the various records of his reign see Peter Salway, *Roman Britain* (Oxford, 1981): 401–409.
[28] P. Bartrum, *Early Welsh Genealogies* (Cardiff, 1966): 2; 10, 4.
[29] Salway, *Roman Britain*: 419 suggests a date *c.*398.
[30] Gildas, *The Ruin of Britain and Other Documents*, ed. Michael Winterbottom (Chichester, 1978): 21; 93, 14.

coast, from Brecknock to Argyllshire, the movement of troops to the continent in the late fourth and early fifth centuries would have been opportune times. In addition to the well-known settlements in what are now Wales and Scotland, place names suggest that smaller, less successful plantations were made.

Gildas claims that the Picts and *Scoti* were sailing to reach targets in Britain and he specifically mentions coracles.[31] These were light oval-shaped vessels with a wooden frame over which were stretched hides that had been treated to repel the water. Alliances between the Picts and Scots were military cooperation for commercial convenience. An aspect of these raids was the capture of slaves, and the best-known of these raiding parties came from Ireland to Britain and took captives including St. Patrick. Of course the raids were not new and had been going on for some time. A "Count of the Saxon Shore" had been set up more than a century earlier to guard eastern (imperial) Britain from raids. The danger from the west appears to have increased during the fourth century, as Ammianus Marcellinus suggests, and new fortresses had been built at Cardiff (to guard the passage from St. George's Channel into the Bristol Channel) and Lancaster (on the eastern side of the Irish Sea).[32]

In connection with raiding is the interesting problem of the "Pict" boat, which the Roman military historian Vegetius mentions as a special kind of boat used round Britain. The passage describing the boat (bk. IV, ch. 37) is not entirely clear and it will accommodate more than one translation, but it seems to refer to a vessel – the Pict boat – that was a scouting craft with 20 rowers on each side. If this number is correct, then this was a substantial vessel, similar in crew to the Viking raiding ships. The Pict boat was unique in its camouflage; everything – hull, crew's clothing, and tackle – was colored blue in order to blend in with the sea.[33] These Pict boats were used to find enemy craft and then take a report back to the main fleet, which could intercept the raiders. Of course there need not have been any connection of the boat with a people called Picts (setting aside the possibly that the original use of the boats by the Picts was copied by the Romans) and the name could simply refer to the painted (*picturatus*) vessel.

---

[31] Gildas, *Ruin of Britain*: 23; 94,19.
[32] James Campbell, *Anglo-Saxons* (London, 1982): 15.
[33] P. Flavius Vegetius Renatus, *Epitoma Rei Militaris*, ed. Alf Önnerfors (Leipzig, 1995): 240–241.

The Romans were using different ploys in their dealings with the peoples beyond their control in the British Isles or newly settled in imperial territory by the last decades of the fourth century. It was not just usurpers who were moving outside the island and troops from Britain were being recruited to serve both at home and abroad. St. Jerome met the cannibalistic Attacotti while the latter were serving in the Roman forces in Gaul. Recruitment was not restricted to the peoples within the imperial boundaries. This change is visible in the Old Welsh genealogies for the men living north of Hadrian's Wall. Genealogies contain sobriquets showing signs of service, such as the phrase *pes-rut* (scarlet cloak). A scarlet cloak was worn by Roman officers and the practice of using the trappings of command to incorporate their foes into imperial service (or at least flatter them) was an old one. A prince named Padarn Beisrud (for *pes-rut*, "red cloak"), is the ancestor of Cunedda, the king credited in later Welsh materials with leading the "Men of the North" (i.e., beyond Hadrian's Wall) to Gwynedd, and he is found in the genealogy of the famous eleventh-century Hiberno-Welsh prince Gruffudd son of Cynan.[34]

Roman interest in their northern neighbors was also changing as can be seen from geographical materials. Where to meet the barbarians, rather than niceties about their internal composition, was now the main consideration. This is clear when comparing Roman geographical texts of different ages.[35] Ptolemy's second-century *Geography* has the names of assembly places in connection with specific peoples, but both the *Ravenna Cosmography*, a seventh-century compilation based on materials later than Ptolemy's, and the third-century *Antonine Itinerary* gives merely lists of towns.[36] A reason why the *Ravenna Cosmography* and the *Antonine Itinerary* dispense with tribal names and merely recite "towns" in relation to geographical position is that the Roman officials had less interest in the internal organization north of Hadrian's Wall. It is interesting that both those documents used information composed either while or soon after the Antonine Wall was an active Roman outpost. The names of the "towns" are probably the names of *loci* or assembly places north of Hadrian's Wall where imperial officials would recruit or pay their "allies."

[34] Bartrum, *Early Welsh Genealogies*: 44 (Cuneda); 36 (Gruffudd).
[35] I.A. Richmond, "Fourth Century AD and After," in *Roman and Native*: 150–155.
[36] A.L.F. Rivet and Kenneth Jackson, "The British Section of the Antonine Itinerary," *Britannia* 1 (1970): 34–82.

One *locus* was the Tay, apparently the river Tay, and it is also mentioned in the sixth-century Irish devotional tract called *Columba's Breastplate*, which has a line that describes how kings shout round the Tay, apparently a reference to a meeting with an acclamation.[37] How to pay allies outside the imperial boundaries became more difficult after a fourth-century prohibition on melting down money for the purpose of selling the bullion out of the empire; the same edict also ordered that ships bound for foreign ports and roads leading to the borders were to be watched.[38] This required a flexible interpretation of the aforementioned law. One solution might be visible in the hoard of silver fragments from Roman objects found north of Hadrian's Wall at Norrie's Law in Fife, which had to be in pieces in order to circumvent the prohibition.[39]

Picts and the Last Days of Roman Britain

What can be seen in hindsight as a momentous decision was made in AD 408 when the emperor Honorius (grandson of the General Theodosius who had put down the Pictish Revolt) removed Roman troops from Britain. The decision to entrust the guarding of Britain to troops based in Gaul might have been seen at the time as a temporary expediency, but it would prove to be permanent. During the following decades there was a continued dwindling of imperial resources away from western Europe generally, and the fifth century is now regarded as the period of transition from classical antiquity to the Middle Ages in Europe. For Britain, this ushered in the an "heroic age," the era of men such as the missionary St. Patrick or the former-soldier-turned-bishop Germanus, or even the legendary Arthur. Despite the fame of individuals this is a difficult period for the historian. The scarce and often obscure documents from the fifth and sixth centuries are later supplemented by an avalanche of literary productions dealing with the period that might or might not contain scraps from genuine historical materials that have since disappeared.

By the end of the fourth century even the records maintained at Rome are vague about events in Britain; that is, of course, if Britain appears in

---

[37] P.L. Henry, *Saoithiúlacht na Sean-Ghaeilge* (Dublin, 1978): 195.
[38] Clyde Pharr, ed., *Theodosian Code and Novels and the Sirmondian Constitutions* (New York, 1952): 9, 23, 1.
[39] Lloyd Laing, "The Hoard of Pictish Silver from Norrie's Law, Fife," *Studia Celtica* 28 (1994): 11–38; he suggests that the metal was a votive offering (p. 35).

them at all. Little can be said for certain about what was happening in the south of Britain, much less beyond the frontiers of imperial control. The jostling for power among successful commanders such as Magnus Maximus, which led to local or regional civil wars, must have been as confusing to contemporaries outside the island as they are obscure to us. An example of how little is known comes from the aforementioned campaign in Britain of the great Roman general Stilicho. Stilicho was a Vandal, the son of a captain who had served Emperor Valens. He was one of Emperor Theodosius' leading generals, and after his master's death effectively administered the government of the teenage heir Honorius. Yet only in the verses of the poet Claudian do we learn that Stilicho had been in Britain where he defeated the Picts.[40] No date or place or any other detail is given. While current opinion places his campaign around 395 this is difficult to reconcile with his itinerary at that time, when he concentrated on dealing with the Goths under the leadership of his former comrade Alaric. Various other times can be put forward, such as the period after the defeat of Magnus in 387, when the imperial presence needed to be re-established. Nevertheless, all that is known about a campaign by the leading soldier of the Western Empire comes from an aside in verses composed by a court poet with the intention of flattering an emperor. The confusion increases when comparing the scattered accounts of local commanders defying imperial authorities with authors such as Claudian. The latter clearly had a confused idea of the geography and peoples of the British Isles. Referring back to his panegyric on the fourth consulship of the emperor Honorius (AD 398), for example, Claudian claims that the reconquest of Britain by Honorius' grandfather Theodosius caused the Orkney Islands to be stained with the blood of Saxons and that ice-bound Ireland wept for the slain Scots even as Thule was warmed by the slaughter of Picts.[41]

Setting aside the question of how much value the verses of Claudian have for official operations in Britain, he is a useful representative of how Britain was perceived in the imagination of the average "Roman on the street." He knew the island was surrounded by savages, with the Roman authorities (i.e., the military) holding back the swarms of Picts, Scots, and other barbarians. He remarks on the "tattooed life flowing out of the dying Pict" as an example of the success of Rome in dealing with the primitives who would dare to attack it. After the mid-fourth century more than mere paranoia was stoking the belief of Romano-Britons that

[40] Claudian, *Clavdii Clavdiani Carmina*: 215.
[41] Claudian, *Clavdii Clavdiani Carmina*: 62.

they were under concerted assault from the peoples beyond their borders. The imperial authorities had lost control of the island in the mid-fourth century due not just to turmoil within their own ranks, but also to invasions led by the despised peoples outside the frontier. For the "primitives" outside the imperial frontiers, Roman Britain must have seemed a promising location. Looking towards the south from the other side of Hadrian's Wall, the important point to Picts or Scots about the Revolt of 367 was that it had succeeded even if only very briefly. There was not as much loyalty among the population as the Romans liked to pretend and the imperial forces had to fight their way back into the island.

St. Germanus and the Picts

But was this a time of pandemonium in Britain? How damaging were the raids of the Picts? How quickly was the fabric of Roman Britain collapsing? While writers such as the later historian Gildas reinforce the idea of chaos, it is helpful to look at the different impression of life in Britain that is found in the *vita* (Latin for *Life*) of St. Germanus.[42] Germanus came from an aristocratic provincial family in Gaul and had served as a soldier before devoting himself to a religious life. His *Life* was written after his death by a man named Constantine who does not seem to have known Germanus personally, but who gathered his material from the saint's acquaintances. Constantine claims that Germanus visited Britain at least twice in order to put down the Pelagian heresy. Pelagius was a Briton who had studied at Rome around AD 380 and developed a doctrine of Christianity that argued for the essential goodness of humans, which meant that they could achieve a state of grace through their own efforts, a direct refutation of the doctrine of original sin. These views became very popular and St. Augustine of Hippo devoted much of his later career to fighting Pelagius' doctrine. During the second quarter of the fifth century, a synod was held in Britain about 429 at St. Albans (named after the first Christian martyr on the island) for the purpose of formulating plans to deal with the threat. In contrast with

---

[42] Constantinus of Lyon, "Life of Germanus of Auxerre," trans. F.R. Hoare, in T.F.X. Noble and T. Head (eds.), *Soldiers of Christ* (University Park, PA, 1994): 75–106; and Constance of Lyon, *Vie de Saint Germain d'Auxerre*, ed. René Borius, Sources Chrétiennes 112 (Paris, 1965). For discussion see E.A. Thompson, *St. Germanus* (Woodbridge, 1984).

the description of chaos implied by Claudian and Gildas, Germanus' travel to and through Britain shows a peaceful and prosperous land with wealthy individuals who could support an intellectual class. The idea of continuity with Rome can be seen in the best-known episode connected with his visit, the so-called Alleluia Victory.[43] An invading force of Picts and Scots were advancing against the native British levies who had replaced the Roman forces. Germanus had been a military officer before his entrance into religious life and he was asked to lead the Britons, who were some distance away and outnumbered. The British force was stationed in what had been a Roman army camp situated in a mountainous district with a river nearby; the *vita* specifically mentions that Germanus inspected its outer-works. The bishop traveled to meet the troops during Lent, and the actual battle was fought either on Easter Sunday or the next day. Germanus' military expertise is clearly apparent: he sent out scouts to report on the invaders' movement and when battle was imminent, he moved his troops out of camp in order to intercept the enemy in a valley. As the Picts and Scots attacked, Germanus ordered the troops to shout "alleluia." The sound of the collective roar as it echoed in the valley terrified the invaders (according to the *vita*) who fled. Setting aside the miraculous element, this might have been a standard military tactic. A similar episode is described by Tacitus during the campaign of his father-in-law Agricola in Galloway. Roman troops were preparing to move against the northern tribes at night when there was an attack on the lines. Agricola gave a command that was relayed along the ranks at such a volume that the attackers were led to believe their opponents were more numerous, and they retreated. Returning to Germanus, his battle took place roughly twenty years after the legions had been removed by Honorius, so it is just possible that the British troops included veterans from the *colonna* who could have been drafted into fighting the enemy as well as local levies.[44] The cultural significance of the battle for Constantine's audience is that the Picts and Scots are presented as an armed mob, while Germanus' Britons show proper military discipline by fighting in formation, most visibly by remaining in place as the enemy advanced towards them. The contrast between Roman-trained troops

---

[43] Michael Jones, "The Historicity of the Alleluia Victory," in J. France and K. deVries (eds.), *Warfare in the Dark Ages* (Aldershot, 2008): 209–219.

[44] There might be a religious aspect and this passage has been read as part of the orthodox victory over Pelagianism; see Gerald Bonner, "The Pelagian Controversy in Britain and Ireland," *Peritia* 16 (2002): 144–155 (at p. 147).

and their savage opponents was a staple of Roman military literature. The Alleluia Victory suggests some modification of popular opinions of this time. The incursions of the Picts and Scots were not always by small raiding parties, but instead could be significant invasions; the Britons were so certain of defeat that they were cowering within ancient fortresses. But several centuries of Roman rule had not disappeared. The Britain of Germanus was a civilized and intact society still preserving the structure of a Roman province. It was not destined to last long.

The *Life of Germanus* does not explain why the Picts and Scots were campaigning, but an active trade at this time was that in slaves. The Irish legend of Niall of the Nine Hostages, the eponymous ancestor of the Uí Néill, claims that his raiding took him as far as the English Channel (and later legends extended it farther south). Raiders from the Irish mentioned by Gildas probably had slaves as well as loot. St. Patrick was the most famous of the unfortunates captured by these bands. Although medieval accounts place his home along the Clyde in the vicinity of Dumbarton, he himself claims that he was born of British parents in Britain in the vicinity of *Bannavem Taburniae*, possibly Ravenglass in Cumbria.[45] His family were Christian and his grandfather had been a priest. At the age of 16, Patrick was carried off to Ireland before escaping and, eventually, returning to Britain. He returned as a missionary to Ireland, where he spent the rest of his days. All this information is supplied from his *Confession*, an autobiographical account of his spiritual development. Patrick is also our source of information that the slave traveled in both directions. His letter to Coroticus survives, complaining about his soldiers' capture of slaves that included Christians; Coroticus may have been the king of Strathclyde named Caratauc who appears in the genealogy in the British Library MS Harleian MS 3859.[46] By the seventh century, Muirchú, in his *vita* of Patrick, describes Coroticus as king of Aloo, apparently for Ail Cloithe or Strathclyde. Patrick's letter also shows that the identity of a Pict was changing. Now it ran along religious lines as well, and a Pict was not a Christian. Patrick makes clears that he does not regard Coroticus as a fellow citizen of the holy Romans (i.e. a Christian), but is counted among the Picts, Scots, and other apostates as allies of the demons.

---

[45] A.B.E. Hood (ed.), *St. Patrick, His Writings and Muirchu's Life* (Chichester, 1978): 23; 41, 1.
[46] Hood, *St. Patrick*: 35–38; Bartrum, *Early Welsh Genealogies*: 11 (section 16).

Summary

There were at least two groups of people in ancient Europe known as Picts, one in what is now Atlantic France and the other in Northern Britain. The former is mentioned in the last century BC and then fades from the historical record until the name Pictavia becomes common again with the career of the famous Bishop Hilary of Poitiers. Pictavia is found three centuries later and remains current until the final usage of it in a contemporary sense in the tenth century. In Britain the name Pict originally was applied to everyone living north of Hadrian's Wall by a writer living in Gaul at the end of the third century. The amount someone living in the center of Gaul knew about the geopolitical makeup of Britain in the late third century probably was not great, but he had heard about a group of people called Picts, most likely from returning soldiers. His informants almost certainly had fought in the British campaigns of Constantius the Pale. They had used a slang term "the tattooed" for their foes and that nickname for the barbarians who lived to the north of Hadrian's Wall had become popular. As the Romans made a practice of recruiting from throughout the empire, there is no reason to suspect that those soldiers had any specific information about the northern peoples. Their choice of the word Pict might have been based on observed similarities with another group of people, the Pictones of the Atlantic coast or based on the observation, made two generations earlier by Herodian, that those people were decorated with designs on their bodies. Regardless, the name was destined to endure both because of its easy retention and descriptive powers, and because of the bluntness of it. Novelty did not mean that it automatically replaced all the earlier terms and ancient names such as Caledonian or Maeatae continued to be used. Since the word Pict originally identified anyone who lived to the north of Hadrian's Wall, later English writers were correct when they spoke of the Picts of Galloway, an area that was beyond the boundary of Roman administration. So at its greatest extent, Pictland included not merely the kingdoms north of the Clyde–Forth line, but also the kingdoms that appear in later writing and are known as Gododdin, Strathclyde, and Rheged.

Returning to a purely British context, however, it is clear that the collective name Pict was a creation of the conditions that developed on the edges of the empire. Comparison with other "barbarians" in Europe (such as the Alemani) reveals that the Romans were attempting to understand how disparate groups could make common cause; an ability that did not fit the Roman idea of the savages beyond the imperial frontiers.

Certainly contemporary authors among the Romans such as the soldier/historian Ammianus saw them as more than just howling primitives, and he places the Picts among the leaders in assembling the famous Barbarian Conspiracy of the mid-fourth century. These contacts continued and when the Picts began to convert to Christianity, new ecclesiastical contacts led to creative exchanges with their former allies the *Scoti* whose missionaries labored among the Picts north of the Grampians, and these opened the way for connections with Irish churches.

There is little doubt that after Constantius the Pale had restored Britain to imperial control the *Picti* became the Roman's greatest problem in Britain. Whether acting alone on raids or in alliance with other "barbarians" the resulting unsteadiness culminated in the events of the year 367. Success against Rome must have emboldened all parties. Afterwards the Picts became almost a cliché as a foe whom the successful Roman commander defeated; and we would like to know the Picts' version of events. A new name for the northern peoples shows that the campaigns of Constantius were as important as the encomium claims. Despite efforts by Roman historians such as Ammianus to present a Britain firmly under imperial control, the reality was of a Rome facing foes capable of competing with them as equals. This was clearly demonstrated in 367 when the barbarians made common cause and temporarily took control of Britain. The timing could not have been worse for the imperial forces. Even though they reasserted control, the illusion of invincibility was gone, with too few forces to guard too much territory. Roman efforts to deal with the threat on their northern frontier show how important Britannia was to them. While the debate continues on the question "Why were the Roman troops withdrawn early in the fifth century?" it is clear that the activities of the Picts were making life very difficult for their enemies.

There are echoes here of the confrontations of the past. Oddity and ferocity were two legacies of late antiquity that survived long after the imperial troops were withdrawn from Britain. Tattooing, for example, was noteworthy. The seventh-century Bishop Isidore of Seville (*c*.560–636) associated it with everyone in the British Isles. He notes in his *Etymologies* (IX.2.103) that the Irish took their name from the practice of tattooing themselves with various figures, using an iron prick and black pigment.[47] He returns to the theme in his catalogue of characteristics,

[47] Isidore of Seville, *Isidori Hispalensis Episcopi; Tymologiarvm Sive Originvm Libri XX*, ed. W.M. Lindsay, 2 vols. (Oxford, 1911).

which includes the tattoos of the Britons and the Picts (XIX.23). He elaborates on the Picts by noting that an artisan uses a tiny point and juice from a native plant to give the nobility scars that were identifying marks.

A generation earlier the Byzantine historian Procopius (*c.*500–*c.*565) remembered the wall that separated the Roman world from the savages of the north. Procopius is a good example of how a well-informed individual could be confused about Britain, because he thought the island was actually two islands – Britain to the south and a second island called Britta that was opposite the mouth of the Rhine – and he also believed that the souls of the dead traveled to Britta. In his *History of the Gothic Wars* (VIII.20) he remarks on "the long wall" (i.e., Hadrian's Wall) that separated Britta into two parts.[48] Good land, civilized people, and an abundance of food were in the south (which Procopius reorients to the east). On the northern (Procopius' western) side, however, were savagery, snakes, and wild creatures. So pestilential was the air that a man or animal traveling from the civilized to the barbarous sides of the wall would die instantly, because the air was poisonous.

Whether as the land of the tattooed people or a pestilential wilderness, the regions outside of Roman control were rarely viewed in benign terms. Even someone such as Bishop Isidore who would be expected to have some reliable information cannot even decide who has body decoration and who does not. Little wonder that the Picts would hold their title of "mystery people" for such a long time.

---

[48] Procopius, *History of the Wars*: V, 264.

2
Myth and Reality

Other than some basic information about geography and tribes, at the end of the third century the Romans knew little about the parts of Britain beyond their control. This is clear from their coining of the word Pict as a convenient description. In the ensuing centuries we find more information available about the ethnicity, political geography, and language of the people beyond the Wall. There also grew up several legends that attempted to explain the origins of the Picts, not realizing that the name was an artificial term. This brief chapter will look at several controversial questions connected with the Picts. First, where did they live and how were they organized? Then what language did they speak? Finally what are some of the different legends about the Picts and what information do they contain?

Where were the Picts?

The brief examination of Romano-Pictish relations in the fourth century leads to the question "who and where were the Picts?" Knowledge of the configuration of the peoples in northern Britain outside the imperial frontiers was essential to the Romans although their method of getting information seems to have been in one of two ways: the use of spies (who could be anybody who had been in enemy territory), which included questioning people with whom they had dealings; and through forward camps, such as the fortress at High Rochester which seems to have been occupied after the abandonment of the Antonine Wall.

The Picts, First Edition. Benjamin Hudson.
© 2014 John Wiley & Sons, Ltd. Published 2014 by John Wiley & Sons, Ltd.

Study of Britain's peoples began with Julius Caesar who included a brief geography as well as ethnography for the southern portion in his *Gallic War* (bk. V, chs. 13–15). Later, Tacitus, in his *Agricola* (ch. X), quotes Livy on the shape of Britain resembling a two-headed axe, a verbal visualization which was followed by later geographers. Deliberate exploration of the island is mentioned by Tacitus' contemporary Pliny the Elder who wrote in his *Natural History* (IV.16) that an official Roman expedition had explored Britain as far as the Caledonian forest thirty years earlier. Since he completed his work around AD 77, the survey must have been commissioned a couple of years after the Claudian invasion of AD 43. As mentioned in the previous chapter, Dio Cassius, writing in the third century, claimed that the two main groups among the Britons beyond Hadrian's Wall were the *Caledones* and the *Maeatae*, and the names of others had been merged into them.[1] Both of the names continued in circulation for several centuries; the former by fifth-century authors such as Claudian, and the latter in the seventh-century hagiography of Columba of Iona composed by his successor, at several removes, Adomnán.

The coining of the term *Picti* two generations after Dio had written his history followed the chaos and temporary loss of Britain to the imperial authorities during the era of the Barracks Emperors. As mentioned in the previous chapter, the new men in control by the end of the third century had little time for the niceties of earlier centuries and "Pict" was a convenient general term for the people north of Hadrian's Wall. So the name *Picti* in a British context was a portmanteau term, a Roman creation of the late third century. Initially it was intended to be a generic, not a specific term. This type of blunt catch-all term is typical of the time as the powerful posts in the Roman army were occupied by talented but unsophisticated men who needed a simple term to describe a geopolitical situation the origins of which they had neither time nor training to investigate. In the verses of the early fifth-century poet Claudian, who never was anywhere near Britain, the new term is found together with the older ethnic name Caledonian, which continued to be used for centuries after the appearance of *Picti*; the final classical use of Caledonian is in the late fifth-century verses of Sidonius Apollinaris.

The people called *Picti* by the Romans did not apply that name to themselves. Among those who lived north of Hadrian's Wall were the inhabitants of the northern British kingdoms later known as Strathclyde

---

[1] Dio, *Roman Histories*, ed. Earnest Cary (New York, 1927): 262.

and Gododdin. As the decades passed there arose the problem of how to define "Picts" – who they were and where they lived – which seems to have depended to some extent on the individual writer. St. Patrick, as noted in the previous chapter, defined "Pict" by religion. In his *Letter to Coroticus*, he refuses to salute the recipient as a fellow-Roman, but as an enemy (i.e., non-Christian) like the Scots, Picts, and apostates (*socii Scottorum atque Pictorum apostatarumque*) who live in death.[2] Patrick's definition lies behind Adomnán's use of the term in his *Life of Columba*. Columba was a missionary to the non-Christian peoples north of the Scottish Highlands, so his Picts were distinct from the Christian Britons. Not everyone subscribed to that interpretation. In the sixth century Gildas retained the Roman geographical distinction. Because he knew there were no Picts in earlier Roman works, he had to make them into immigrants and claims that the Picts came from the north, from across the sea. They settle in Britain (after the withdrawal of the Roman legions) as far south as "the wall," which by this time meant Hadrian's Wall.[3]

Roman use of the name *Picti* as a collective designation for any group dwelling immediately to the north of Hadrian's Wall explains the insistence of later literature that there were Picts in what are now Lothian, Galloway, and Dumfriesshire. Moving ahead several centuries to material that will be treated in later chapters, according to the Laud manuscript version of the *Anglo-Saxon Chronicle*, about 711 an alderman called Bertfrid fought the Picts between the rivers Avon and Carron (in Linlithgow) which the Irish *Annals of Tigernach* places in Manau (see chapter 3). The Parker or A version of the *Anglo-Saxon Chronicle* uses the term "Pict" to describe the inhabitants of northern Britain in 875, when the Viking Halfdan settled his force on the Tyne, whence he raided the Picts and men of Strathclyde.[4] Whether the Tyne in question is the larger river that flows past Newcastle or the smaller one in Haddington is immaterial as neither is north of the Antonine Wall. The second and fourth bishops of the see of Whithorn, then under Anglian domination,

---

[2] A.B.E. Hood (ed.), *St. Patrick, His Writings and Muirchu's Life* (Chichester, 1978): 35.

[3] Gildas, *The Ruin of Britain and Other Works*, ed. Michael Winterbottom (Chichester, 1978): 93 "… gentibus transmarinis … Pictorum ab aquilone calcabilis …"; 95 "… omnem aquilonalem extremamque terrae partem pro indigenis muro tenus capessunt".

[4] John, Earle and Charles Plummer, *Two of the Saxon Chronicles, Parallel*, 2 vols. (Oxford, 1892–99), *sub anno* 875.

were named Pehthelm ("Pict Protector," died *c.*735) and Pehtwine ("Pict Friend," d.776 or 777). Alexander Neckham says much the same thing in his *De Laudibus Divinae Sapientiae Naturis* claiming that the Tweed was the boundary between the Anglo-Saxons and the Picts.[5] There was a belief in the twelfth century, in what had been the Old English kingdom (then province) of Northumbria, that the lands of the Picts included what is now Galloway. In 1164 Ailred of Rievaulx, the Cistercian writer and administrator, traveled into "the land of the Picts" to Kirkcudbright where he stayed for some time. Slightly later, Reginald of Durham told the story of badly behaved young members of the church who unwisely baited a bull on the festival of St. Cuthbert; he described them as clerks who were called *scollofthes* in the Pictish language.[6] *Scollofthes* is actually a Gaelic term to describe students attending a church school, which later came to mean a tenant on church lands. A western boundary is given in *Eulogium Historiarum* that claims the Solway Firth divided the Picts from the Britons, apparently meaning the Britons who lived to the south of Hadrian's Wall. Ranulph Higden in his *Polychronicon* stated that the Picts lived in Lothian as far south as the River Tweed.[7] Physical remains as well as literary remembrances show a culture that refused to obey an arbitrary barrier. A Class 1 Pictish symbol stone is at Roberton (in Lothian), while a stone at Trusty's Hill (a hill fort close by Gatehouse of Fleet overlooking the Solway Firth that is also known as Mote of Mark) has a double disk symbol with a decorated "Z-rod" – symbols that are considered "Pictish."

The people known as *Picti* to the Romans were called a different name in the vernacular of their neighbors, which was "Briton." This is clear from the Old Irish and Old Welsh names applied to the "Picts," respectively *Cruithne* and *Prydyn*, both of which translate simply as "Briton." *Cruithne* is simply an early Gaelic form of *Prydyn* or *Prythein*.[8] The religious division was retained, however, so that the people of Strathclyde and Gododdin, as well as the Britons living south of Hadrian's Wall, were called *Britones*. This could cause confusion as the Welsh did occasionally

---

[5] T. Wright, ed., *Alexandri Neckham de Naturis Rerum with Neckham's poem De Laudibus Divinae Sapientiae naturis*, Rolls Series 34 (London, 1863): 416.
[6] Reginald of Durham, *Libellus de admirandis Beati Cuthberti*, Surtees Society 1 (1835): 179 (ch. 85).
[7] *Polychronicon Ranulphi Higden*, eds. C. Babington and J.R. Lumby, 9 vols., Rolls Series 41 (London, 1865–86): i, 32.
[8] T.F. O'Rahilly, *Early Irish History and Mythology* (Dublin, 1946): 341.

use *Prydyn* to identify themselves and *Cruithne* was the name of one of the powerful Irish kingdoms known as Dál nAraide, which was located along the North Channel just south of Irish Dál Riata.[9] Similarity of names encouraged earlier generations of scholars erroneously to speak of "Irish Picts," implying that they were colonists from among the Picts of Britain. An Irish tract with the title *History of the Descendants of Ir* (*Senchus Síl hIr*), in a section composed in the tenth century, claims that 30 kings of the Cruithne ruled over Ireland and Britain, with seven of those kings coming from Britain.[10] That the term *Cruithne* translates as *Britones* is suggested by several entries from the Irish annals. Entries for the years 682, 697, 702, 703, and 709 describe the activities of Britons in northeastern Ireland, whose actions are similar to the Cruithne or Dál nAraide. A variety of chronicles are being amalgamated at this point, however, and the suggestion has been offered that the *Britones* were pirates from Rheged, based on the Isle of Man.[11] A defeat of the Cruithne or Dál nAraide at their stronghold of Rathmore is record for 682 as "The battle of Rathmore of the plane of Larne (went) against the Britons where Cathusach son of Máel Duin. King of the Cruithne, and Ultan son of Dicuil died" (*Bellum Ratha More Maighi Line contra Britones, ubi ceciderunt Cathusach mae Maeleduin ri Cruithne [ocus] Ultan filius Dicolla)*. Fifteen years later the Cruithne joined their neighbors the Ulstermen for a raid in County Louth: "The Cruithne and Ulad destroyed the plain of Murthemni" (*Britones et Ulaidh vastaverunt Campum Muiirteimhne)*. In 703 the allies were fighting each other when the Cruithne raided County Down. Population movement did not always proceed in one direction and this name indicates that peoples also traveled from east to west in the British Isles and that one group from Britain had settled in Ireland. Farther south along the Irish Sea, there were the *Laigin*, who gave their name to Leinster, and they reflect an origin in what is now Wales, taking their name from the Llŷn peninsula.

Most modern scholars have used the limitation of the term *Picti* following the Anglo-Saxon scholar the Venerable Bede. His *Ecclesiastical History* had been introduced and a reading of the section on Britain beyond the territory of Northumbria shows both the difficulty of writing

---

[9] Diarmuid Ó Murchadha, "Nationality Names in the Irish Annals" *Nomina* 16 (1991/92): 49–70 (at p. 57); he notes that the name appears in AD 446.
[10] M.E. Dobbs, "History of the Descendants of Ir," *Zeitschrift für celtische philologie* 13 (1921): 308–359; and 14 (1923): 43–144 (at 14: 64–69).
[11] G. Mac Niocaill, *Ireland before the Vikings* (Dublin, 1972): 114.

a history for the Picts and (a statement akin to heresy) that Bede was fallible. Bede lived in the neighborhood of Hadrian's Wall and he had read Gildas, who claimed that the Picts lived as far as the Wall. By the time Bede was an adult, however, the lands immediately north had been settled by the Anglo-Saxons for three generations and he knew that the native peoples called themselves Britons, not Picts. By this time it was four centuries since the term *Pict* seems to have been coined and it was two and a half centuries since Gildas had completed his *Ruin of Britain* (*De Excidio Britonum*). Bede's answer to the problem of reconciling his sources with his observations was simple. He decided that Gildas had not meant Hadrian's Wall, but had intended the Antonine Wall farther north, as the boundary for the Picts. The peoples in that region had already begun to make their own linguistic accommodations based on religion, and the Picts were the last to convert to Christianity. The two theories meshed.

Of course this was not without its difficulties as will be demonstrated in the following chapters. For example, how to explain Ninian of Whithorn as the missionary to the southern Picts even though his church at Whithorn was close to 100 miles south of the Antonine Wall across hilly terrain? Bede does not try. Nor does he explain why an Anglo-Saxon episcopal see for a bishop of the Picts was placed at Abercorn, south of the Antonine Wall. Nor does he explain why the incumbent named Trumwine was forced to flee after the Anglo-Saxons of Northumbria lost a battle fought two firths away. Earlier in a section called "A Description of Britain" (*De Situ Britanniae*), the first chapter of the first book, he had the Clyde separating the lands of the Picts from the Britons and also the lands of the Scots.[12] A problem is that Dumbarton Rock, which was the location of the capital, is on the north bank of the Firth of Clyde, in the territory Bede claimed was inhabited by either the Picts or Scots. One could argue that Bede was misled by the second-century geographer Claudius Ptolomeus, whose geography of the island of Britain erroneously has the lands north of the Clyde–Forth line at a pronounced 45° angle. Depending on how this was visualized (and the earliest maps, as distinct from texts, survive from the very end of the Middle Ages) this could place Dál Riata, the Scottish kingdom in Argyllshire and the southern Hebrides, immediately north of the Clyde and the Picts beyond the Clyde, but to the east. Bede notes that the Picts and Scots harassed

---

[12] Bede, *Historia Ecclesiastica* in *Venerabilis Baedae Opera Historica*, ed. Charles Plummer, 2 vols. (Oxford, 1896): i, 25.

the Britons by seaborne invasions and he notes that the Britons' territory extended as far north as the indentations of the sea (*duobus sinibus maris interiacentibus*) which on the western end had the city of Ail Cluathe, modern Dumbarton Rock, inconveniently (for Bede's argument) situated on the northern side. No one who had ever visited the region would have made such a mistake so either Bede was confused or he misunderstood his informant.[13] Less easy to explain is the geography of the eastern coast, where Gododdin held lands immediately north of the Firth of Forth in a region called *Manu* or *Manaw*, which is remembered in place names such as Clackmanann (Stone of Manu), east of Alloa. Bede's influence was considerable in his day and has continued to the present.

This leads to the question of a single state or multiple kingdoms of Picts. The idea of a single kingdom of the Picts in recent times goes back to a casual remark made by Sir Frank Stenton, the great historian of the Anglo-Saxons. In his seminal work *Anglo-Saxon England* he offered the passing remark: 'there is no doubt that the Picts with whom the English came into contact formed a definite kingdom, and not a mere congeries of tribes."[14] He offered no proof for his assertion, but this did not stop it from being eagerly taken as fact by his student F.T. Wainwright, and subsequently by other students of the era. The popularity is easy to understand. Not only does one all-inclusive name allow for endless speculation, but it also makes a "winner" in the race for the first kingdom of Europe. A reading of the sources indicates, to the contrary, that there was not a single Pictish kingdom, but several kingdoms that outsiders collectively referred to as kingdoms of the Picts. Even Bede claimed (*Historia*: II.4) that among the Picts were two main political confederations, north and south of the Grampians. He also knew that there were individual kingdoms within those regional groupings and his use of the term *provinciae* is his usual way of mentioning political divisions.[15]

For the geopolitical situation in northern Britain, a layout of sorts is suggested by an enumeration of kingdoms found in a fourteenth-century manuscript (the so-called Poppleton Manuscript now Paris Bibliothèque Nationale ms Latin 4126); the document was brought to general notice by the sixteenth-century antiquary William Camden who found it in

---

[13] On the problem of Bede's place name information see James Campbell, "Bede's Words for Places," in *Essays in Anglo-Saxon History* (London, 1986): 99–120.

[14] Sir Frank Stenton, *Anglo-Saxon England*, ed. Mary Stenton (Oxford, 3rd edn., 1971): 87.

[15] Campbell, "Bede's Words for Places."

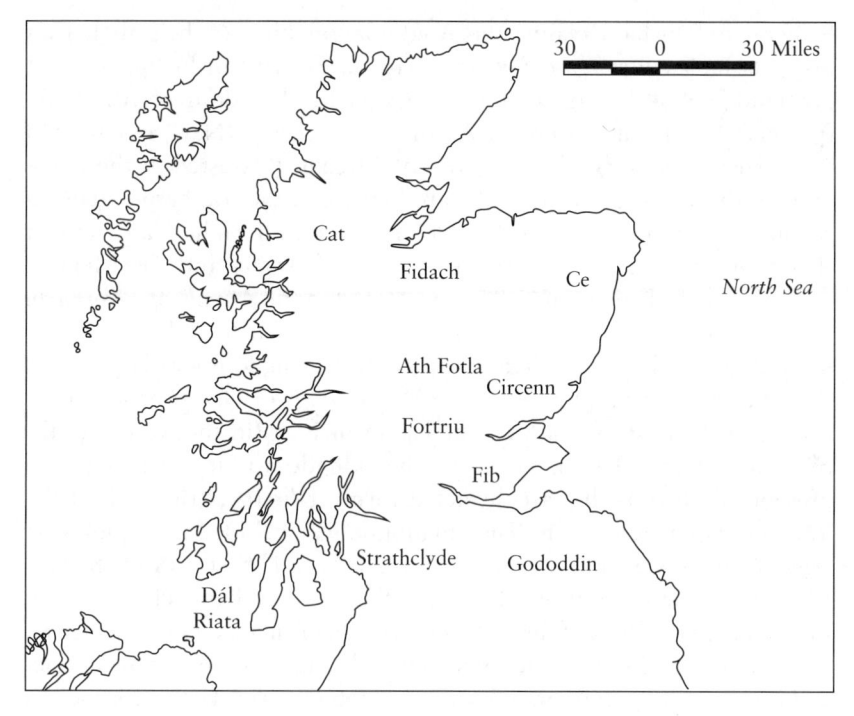

Map 2.1 Kingdoms of Northern Britain.

the library of Lord Burghley and who included some materials from it in his various editions of *Britannia*. A list of kings begins with Cruithen who divided his kingdom among his seven sons: Ce, Cat, Fib, Fidach, Fortriu, Fotla, and Circenn; their names subsequently were bestowed on the separate kingdoms (see Map 2.1).[16] This artificial explanation for the origin of kingdoms within a family was standard throughout medieval Europe and the names themselves seem to be Old Irish words. Among the individual kingdoms Fortriu (Strong) is the most frequently mentioned in the Irish annals, encompassing much of modern Stirlingshire and later possibly the lands of Manu of Gododdin. The name is a formation from *Verturiones*. Dunkeld was situated within Fortriu, and the *Annals of Ulster* for the year 865 have an obit for Abbot Tuathal of Dunkeld who was also the senior bishop of Fortriu. Later, in the tenth century, a note in the *Historia Regum* attributed to

[16] KES: 241–243.

Symeon of Durham claims the Anglo-Saxon king Aethelstan led an army as far as *Wertermorum* (the plain of Fortriu) in his invasion of Scotland in 934.[17] North of Fortriu was the kingdom of Ath Fotla (preserved in the modern name Atholl) which means (New) Ireland. On the eastern coast was the kingdom of Circenn ("Crested"); the name apparently refers to the crest-like appearance of the southern extension of the Highlands along the border of the coastal plain *Mag Circenn* (Plain of Circenn) in the modern region of Angus and the Mearns. A battle fought here about 598 is mentioned in the *Annals of Tigernach*. In the extreme north was Cat; the name means Battle and is preserved in modern Caithness. The extent of the early kingdom was larger than the modern region and notes in the *Martyrology of Óengus* concerning the martyrdom of Donnan on the island of Eigg (in the Moray Firth) place it in Cat.[18] The name of another kingdom that survives to the present is Fib (possibly a contracted form of *fir Ibe*, "the men of the Yew") now written as Fife. The kingdom of Ce included the region that now is called Mar and it appears in the title of two stories of the Old Irish learned tale tradition: the first is the battle of Bennachie (Peak of Ce) and the other tells of the destruction of the plain of Ce (see chapter 8). One name found in the list, Fidach (Woody), apparently is now extinct and it is a good description of northeast Scotland prior to the destruction of the Caledonian Forest. By the process of elimination, its location seems to have been along the southern shores of the Moray Firth and around the coast ending possibly in Aberdeenshire.

Were the Orkney and Shetland Islands considered a part of Britain? The eighth-century travelogue known as the 'Cosmography' of AEthicus Ister implies that the *Orcus*, apparently referring to the Orkneys, was separate from Britain.[19] On the other hand, the nearly contemporary *Life of Columba* by Adomnán mentions a king of the Orkneys at the court of Brude. Evidence comes from another saint's "life," in this case the *vita* of the Irish St. Findan. This text is especially interesting for information about Viking–Irish relations, although one of the many questions about it is the date of composition. The extant text survives in a late medieval manuscript, but the original seems to

---

[17] CPS: 68–69.
[18] Whitley Stokes, *Martyrology of Oengus the Culdee; Félire Óengusso Céli Dé* (Dublin, repr. 1984): 114; 116.
[19] Aethicus Ister, *The Cosmography of Aethicus Ister*, ed. Michael Herren (Turnhold, 2011): 26.

be ninth century in date. Findan's neighborhood is invaded by Vikings, who capture Findan and take him off in their ships. They are sailing round the northern tip of Britain, but stop somewhere in the Orkney Islands, where Findan escapes by swimming to "Pictland." Immigration from Scandinavia had changed the place of the Orkney Islands in the geopolitical scheme, but they seem to have been a special case for a considerable period.

Language

One part of understanding who the Picts were is their language. This has been a contentious topic and for more than two centuries there has been a debate about the speech of the Picts (see chapter 7). The beginning of the search for a "Pictish" language starts with Bede, who states (I.1) that the language of the Picts was different from any other language spoken in Britain during his lifetime.[20] He even gives an example (I.12) of a Pictish word when he explains that the end of the Antonine Wall was called *Peanfael* in the Pictish language.[21] A work known as *Cormac's Glossary* gives another example of a Pictish (*Cruithnech*) word with *cartit* meaning "chariot pin."[22] Modern scholars have added words or word forms that they believe are Pictish.[23] Irish literature claims that there were differences between Irish and Pictish. In the story of Conall Corc his inability to read the ogam inscription explains why the vengeful King Crimthann believed that he could orchestrate Conall's doom. Conall had been banished from Ireland and King Crimthann gave instructions to have the bearer murdered written in ogam script in "the language of the Cruithne" so that Conall was not able to understand them. He was saved, however, after falling asleep on the beach where a scholar whom he had rescued from captivity found him, and this friend understood the ogams. He altered the message so that it requested safety and honor for whoever carried the shield. The use of ogam script suggests that this form of communication

---

[20] Bede, *Historia Ecclesiastica*: i, 11.
[21] Bede, *Historia Ecclesiastica*: i, 26; for acknowledgment of its Brythonic base see ii, 24.
[22] Whitley Stokes, ed., *Three Irish Glossaries* (London, 1862): 12.
[23] See: Richard Cox, "Modern Scottish Gaelic Reflexes of two Pictish words; *pett and *lannerc," *Nomina* (1998): 47–58; Colman Etchingham and Catharine Swift, "English and Pictish Terms for a Brooch in an 8th-Century Irish Law-Text," *Medieval Archaeology* 48 (2004): 31–49.

was not limited to inscriptions on monuments. Confirmation that the language was unintelligible at least to the Irish is attested elsewhere, such as the *Life of Columba* where the saint converted an old man on the Isle of Skye after preaching through an interpreter.[24] But by the early twelfth century, as we have seen, Henry of Huntingdon could confidently claim that there was no trace of the language of the Picts.

Examination of the topic has been made more difficult by the fact that in different areas and at different times the languages spoken in northern Britain have included Latin, Welsh, Old English, Irish (in all its stages of development), Norse, French, and Scots. In practical terms this means, to take an example, that determining the type of language by a study of place names can have up to seven possibilities, depending on the location and the time period. As early as the eighteenth century there were different views (see chapter 8). John Pinkerton's advocacy of a Germanic speech cognate with Gothic (so far as he understood it) was met with a spirited rebuttal as other scholars believed that "Pictish" was related to Gaelic. By the late nineteenth century, Sir John Rhys believed that there was a non-Indo-European stratum in the Pictish language, following unsuccessful attempts to read the ogam inscriptions.[25]

The British/Welsh foundation, however, is clear from the study of place-name elements.[26] They are numerous, spread throughout northern Britain, and are clearly similar to, if not identical with, those found south of Hadrian's Wall. While the language spoken north of Hadrian's Wall was similar to that spoken to the south (i.e., similar to Old Welsh), there was the problem of the ogam inscriptions, and the possibility that two types of language were employed: a non-Celtic and possibly non-Indo-European tongue revealed mainly in ogam inscriptions as well as a Celtic language that showed affinities to P-Celtic or, in an insular context, Welsh.[27] The Indo-European element has come under close study: particularly important in this respect are the ogam inscriptions found throughout northern Britain, which have been the main examples produced in the argument. Recent studies have come to the conclusion that some of the inscriptions

---

[24] Adomnán, *Life of Columba*, ed. A.O. Anderson and M.O. Anderson (Oxford, 1991): 62.

[25] This was rebutted by Katherine Forsyth, *Language in Pictland: the Case Against Non-Indo European Pictish* (Utrecht, 1997).

[26] CPS: 339–424.

[27] K.H. Jackson, "The Pictish Language," in F.T. Wainwright, ed., *Problem of the Picts* (Edinburgh, 1955): 129–166.

are in different languages such as Old Irish or Old Norse.[28] There is no indication that Bede knew Welsh, while regional differences would account for the belief that he was dealing with a completely different tongue. Isolation of both fortification designations and geographical elements gives evidence of the survival of early British forms.

A word often associated with the language of the Picts is the place-name element *pit-* in one of its various forms. Although *pit* is often described as a Pictish word, this is mere guesswork. Only Gaelic- and Latin-language texts contain it and the name is found in the areas that later had the greatest concentration of Gaelic speakers, the eastern coastal districts. The earliest examples come from the *Book of Deer*, where the name is found in notices of grants of land given to the church's community; the originals seem to date to the tenth century. The church was located in Buchan, somewhere in the vicinity of the village of Old Deer, where it was refounded as a Cistercian monastery. Suggestions for *pit* have ranged from Welsh *peth* (thing) to Late Latin *petia terrae*, although for the latter term it is not explained why people who lived well beyond the area of Roman administration would adapt an obscure term from a language never current among them. If one is willing to think outside of a British context, there is the possibility that *pit* is cognate with Old Norse *beit* meaning "pasturage." The *pit* names are located within easy access of the coast and the waterways leading to the Scandinavian lands, and there is a correspondence of the area where the name *pit-* is found with the Class 2 symbol stones possessing stylistic arrangements similar to those found on the Götland picture stones. So it is possible that language developed in parallel fashion on either side of the North Sea.

After their conversion to Christianity one language that was spoken among the Picts was Latin, the language of the Christian Church. Clergy could travel widely within the Christian lands because they could find other clergy. This tongue was employed for worship, record keeping, and memorial inscriptions. An example of the last is the Latin inscription found at Tarbat.[29] Latin was spoken only by a minority among any of the peoples in Britain, and of the many controversies connected with the

---

[28] Richard Cox, *The Language of the Ogam Inscriptions of Scotland* (Aberdeen, 1999) and Katherine Forsyth, "The Ogham-Inscribe Spindle Whorl from Buckquoy: Evidence for the Irish Language in Pre-Viking Orkney?" PSAS 125 (1995): 677–696.

[29] CIIC: I, 489, no. 518.

study of the Picts perhaps none has been as contentious as efforts to identify their vernacular language.

Creating Legends

The coining of the name Pict for the peoples living north of Hadrian's Wall after the reassertion of imperial power in Britain in the late third century became a methodological problem for later writers. From their reading of Julius Caesar and Tacitus, medieval scholars knew the names of some of the peoples living beyond Rome's frontier in Britain. They also knew that neither Caesar nor Tacitus mentioned Picts. Medieval writers did not understand the process whereby the name *Picti* was created, so they assumed that the word referred to an entirely new population who had arrived in northern Britain sometime between the first and third centuries AD. That led to the need for an explanation of who these supposedly new people were and where they originated. One of the reasons why a later observer should have arrived at the conclusion that the name Pict meant an immigrant is that there had been population movement in the north of Britain as had happened in the southern part of the island. The immigration from Ireland, for example, was not confined to the well-known kingdom of Dál Riata. As mentioned above, another group is claimed to have settled in Wales, supposedly led by a captain named Eochaid Oversea (*Allmuir*). Traces of lesser known or smaller movements can be found along the western coast of Britain, and it has been proposed that some of these settlements were encouraged, or at least tolerated, by the Roman authorities who recruited troops from them.

Throughout the Middle Ages there were different versions of the beginnings of the Picts. More will be said later (in chapter 7) about the literary interest in the Picts after the conquest of the Scots, but here it is useful to look at brief accounts of four different legends connected with the question "who were the Picts and what was their origin?" These four versions are used as representative samples because they were composed before the mid-ninth century, before the Scottish victory of Kenneth son of Alpin, the famous Kenneth MacAlpin of popular history. The texts from which the accounts are taken range in date from the mid-sixth to the early ninth centuries and represent all the major population groups of the British Isles – Anglo-Saxon, Irish, and Welsh – with the exception, of course, of the Picts themselves. Possibly the earliest attempt to explain the appearance of the Picts is mid-sixth century and comes from Gildas' *Ruin of Britain*. In an aside placed amid the account of a second Roman withdrawal from Britain in the fifth century, Gildas notes that this event was followed by the arrival of larger raiding fleets from the Scots and Picts. He returns to the topic later and claims both Scots and Picts seized the whole of the northern part of the island of Britain from the inhabitants, as far as Hadrian's Wall. Since he had previously noted that the Picts came from the north and the Scots from the northwest, he seems to have assumed that they were resident in Britain during the later fourth century.[30]

Another attempt to explain the origins of the Picts, which is more definite about its information than Gildas, comes a century later in the prologue to the Old Irish legal text known as *Senchus Mar*, which was set down in writing around 700. The prologue grafts the history of the *Scoti* onto Biblical history as a prelude to the invasion of Ireland. The passage begins with them in Egypt where they refused to accompany Pharaoh's army as it pursued the Israelites.[31] Instead, they fled across the Mediterranean. While resting in eastern Germany (one assumes in the broadest geographical application of the word), the Irish were sought out by 36 great warriors from Thrace who joined their company. Later, when they arrived in the British Isles, the Thracian champions are forcibly settled in the country of the Cruithne who are descended from them. This story, like many origin legends begs a number of questions, not least who was in northern Britain before the Thracian warriors. A similar story is found in the *History of the Descendants of Ir* with the additional information that the Thracians settled in the plains of Fortriu and Circenn and that these were seized from Britons.[32]

The best known of all origin legends concerning the Picts is that given by the Venerable Bede. According to this tale, the Picts sailed from Scythia to Ireland. The Irish were unwilling to allow them to settle permanently, so they offered to support the Picts militarily if they would

---

[30] Gildas, *The Ruin of Britain*: 93, 14 "... gentibus transmarinis ... Pictorum ab aquilone calcabilis ..."; 95, 19.2 "... omnem aquilonalem extremamque terrae partem pro indigenis muro tenus capessunt."

[31] D.A. Binchy, *Corpus Iuris Hibernici: ad fidem codicum manuscriptorum*, 6 vols. (Dublin, 1978): v, 1653.40–1654.4, which supersedes the earlier *Ancient Laws of Ireland*, 6 vols. (Dublin, 1865–1901): i, 21–23.

[32] Dobbs, "History of the Descendants of Ir," *Zeitschrift für celtische philologie* 14: 65.

carve out kingdoms for themselves in Britain. The Picts agreed and were successful, but discovered that the native Britons refused to intermarry with them. So they requested wives from the Irish, who were willing to provide them, but on condition that henceforth their kings were to be selected from the mother's lineage when the succession to the kingship was in doubt, a practice that Bede claims continued to his own day. This legend is later retold in various Irish texts, such as the twelfth-century synthetic history called *The Book of Invasions (Lebor Gabála Érenn)* where the Picts are called *Cruithne*, together with certain elaborations and refinements. One of these is that Leinster is identified as the place where the Picts settled in Ireland.[33] The Irish were glad to employ their skill as healers after a Pictish druid used a vat of milk from white-polled cattle that cured any wounded warrior. After the battle of Ard Lemnacht, the Irish become uneasy about the continued presence of the Picts, so they sent them to Britain with the promise of military aid. Once again there was the request from the Picts for wives, whom the Irish supplied with the provision that the succession to the kingship will be from the mother's line; the Picts agreed, invoking the sun, moon, and stars as their guarantors.

The final version of the legend concerning the origins of the Picts to be examined here is found in the *History of the Britons* attributed to a ninth-century Welsh writer called Nennius. He claims that the Picts came from Scythia, but their landfall (unassisted) was the Orkney Islands, whence they moved south. There is no mention of the Irish nor is there any suggestion that they had lived elsewhere in the British Isles prior to their settlement in the north of Britain. There seems to be a conflation of the origin story known to Bede with a cross-reference to classical sources. In his *Agricola*, Tacitus suggests origins for some of the peoples of Britain and points out that the Caledonians resembled the Northern Germans in appearance and physique. Nennius has nothing to say about Irish wives or inheritance/succession through the female line.

These statements on the origins of the Picts show some similar aspects. First, all the accounts believe that the Picts came from somewhere outside Britain, but they have little indication of how long ago that had occurred and there is little agreement about precisely where they originated. The only writer who gives any guide as to the time when the Picts arrived in Britain is Gildas and his account is vague, although he sees the Picts as

---

[33] R.A.S. Macalister, *Lebor Gabála Érenn*, 6 vols., Irish Text Society 34, 35, 39, 41, 44, and 63 (London, 1938–56): v, 174–176.

arriving in Britain almost a century and a half after they are first mentioned in the panegyric for Constantius the Pale. Neither of the places offered as the homeland of the Picts – Thrace or Scythia – is sensible, although elsewhere in his *Ecclesiastical History* Bede implies that Scythia was Scandinavia. Then only Bede, and his Irish admirers, believed that the Picts spent any time in Ireland. Even the earlier Irish work, the *Senchus Mar*, does not place them in Ireland, but has them deposited directly in Britain. Finally, only Bede is aware of any unusual succession practice. None of the others has any comment, although Gildas does say that the Scots and Picts had different customs together with their joint savagery.

The different legends of the Picts show how historians in the early Middle Ages dealt with a methodological problem, and how little they knew about people any distance away. The different authors were all familiar with Latin literature and they had read classical accounts of the Roman conquests in Britain, especially those of Julius Caesar and Tacitus. They also knew that there were no Picts mentioned in their works, but later there were peoples, called Picts by outsiders, who lived in northern Britain. Since Britain was an island, the Picts (so the reasoning might have gone) had to sail to it. Writers in Britain such as Gildas and Nennius apparently failed to see an obvious connection with Caesar's Pictones and instead brought them from the north, with Nennius giving them a landfall in the Orkney Islands. Irish writers knew the Picts as *Cruithne* and they also knew that there were people called that on their island. So they had to account for the appearance of these new peoples. Since the Irish believed themselves to be immigrants, the Cruithne must have been incomers, too. The Irish had to fit the Picts into their own merger of Irish origins and Biblical exegesis as well as account for the arrival of the Picts in Britain. So they had the Picts come to Ireland and then onto Britain, in the same northern part of the island where *Scoti* were settled. In short, their method was a familiar mixture of potted antiquarianism and speculation.

Summary

To the question "what's in a name?" the answer for the Picts is "much confusion." The Roman application of a single name for the British population in the northern part of the island beyond their control led to a belief among medieval scholars that a new people had entered Britain. The panegyrics for Constantius show that for the people living outside the imperial boundaries, the older population names such as Caledonians are being given a new collective designation of Pict. The numerous place names of British origin confirm that the same language continued to be spoken. The following century Ammianus Marcellinus, in the discussion of the Barbarian Conspiracy of 367 noted that the Picts were divided into two groups: the Dicalydones and the Verturiones; the first name means "the two Caledonians."[34] This is part of the same political geography used by the third-century writer Dio, while his contemporary Herodian states bluntly that the people living north of Hadrian's Wall who met with the Emperor Septimus Severus were Britons even though they were barbarians reveling in their nudity and skin decoration. The changes in the use of the name through the centuries show increasing awareness on the part of the Irish and Anglo-Saxons of the people and political configurations that were obscure to the Romans. The replacement of tribal designations with kingdoms occurred by the seventh century and represents a cultural shift towards a centralized government.

---

[34] Ammianus Marcellus, *Rerum Gestarum Libri*, ed. John C. Rolfe, 3 vols. (Cambridge, MA, 1935–39): ii, 52.

3

The Early Middle Ages

The *Life* of Germanus gives the last glimpse of Roman society flourishing in Britain. Idealized a picture as it might be – with its productive farms, prosperous towns, and officials – there is also the shadow of a new reality, the return to a warrior society. This accompanied a subtle shift in the perception of the Picts: their competence. Earlier writers considered their military prowess secondary to that of Rome; therefore any success they enjoyed was expected to be temporary and due more to good fortune than any actual ability. Certainly that was Ammianus Marcellinus' interpretation of the events of the year 367. As the decades passed, however, it became clear that ability was not lacking. Beginning with Germanus' visit and continuing into the ninth century the Picts were recognized as one of the premiere fighting forces on the island. Their military competence did not lead to respect, however, and an aspect that remained was cultural condensation. Roman writers had presented the Picts as colorful savages, who were to be contrasted with those enjoying the benefits of civilization (courtesy of Rome). There still was little interest in the peoples themselves, merely how they fit into the author's larger theme.

This peaceful scene was to change very quickly. While modern writers like to use phrases such as "the heroic age" for the period from AD 400 to 600, a more apt description could be 'the obscure age." Even though modern historians bristle at the name Dark Ages applied to this period and prefer the term Early Medieval, there is no denying the fitness of the former so far as understanding the period is concerned. The removal of the Roman administration opened the way for ambitious leaders to

The Picts, First Edition. Benjamin Hudson.
© 2014 John Wiley & Sons, Ltd. Published 2014 by John Wiley & Sons, Ltd.

come to the fore. Some of these are more legend than fact, while others were important, and for many the debate continues, such as Cunedda of Gododdin from the region round the firth of Forth, who features prominently in Welsh genealogies. We are not always certain when legend is masquerading as history or history is being remembered in the form of legend.

Immigrants and Natives

Very soon after Germanus' visit, a group of successful warriors arrived in Britain. This was the emigration of Germanic peoples from the regions of southern Denmark and northern Germany, a population movement now known as the Coming of the Saxons (*Adventu Saxonum*), which marked the first permanent settlements of the Angles, Saxons, and Jutes. The precise date is unknown – even Bede with his interest in chronology was unable to assign a specific year – but scholarly opinion places it in the mid-fifth century, slightly after the St. Albans synod. Whether this was a massive movement of settlers or merely a few boatloads of warriors remains unclear, but the effect was the introduction of a another ethnic stratum into an island that was witnessing the ebbing of a Mediterranean culture. The presence of Germanic peoples in Britain was not new. Ammianus Marcellinus claims that the Alemanni were among the Roman auxiliaries there, while the Barbarian Conspiracy of the mid-fourth century saw the Picts collaborating (or so the Romans believed) with the Franks. The *Adventu Saxonum* was different, however, and these Germans were coming to stay.

Gildas and Nennius both point to the Picts as one of the reasons why Germanic mercenaries were invited into Britain. According to Gildas, as the Roman forces withdrew from Britain, the attacks by Picts and Scots increased. So the Britons tried a Roman strategy, one that would fail miserably for them: hiring a savage to fight a savage.[1] Several centuries later in the *History of the Britons* Nennius expanded Gildas' explanation, claiming that a British tyrant named Vortigern hired Germanic mercenaries led by chieftains named Hengist and Horsa to guard Britain. Vortigern married the daughter of one of the newcomers and the mercenaries turned on the British. They were driving all before them until there

---

[1] Gildas, *The Ruin of Britain and Other Works*, ed. Michael Winterbottom (Chichester, 1978): 26; 97, section 23.

appeared a British champion named Arthur. In a series of battles, the last at a *mons Badonis* (Mt Badon), the invaders were conquered.[2] While the debate about the historicity of Arthur continues, the battle was genuine and Gildas claims that he was born in that year.[3] This is, of course, the basic legend of King Arthur familiar to students of early British history from its more literary treatment in Geoffrey of Monmouth's *History of the Kings of Britain*.

North of Hadrian's Wall there was another population movement taking place at roughly the same time. Immigrants from Ireland had been moving to Britain and settling on the western coasts for decades. The later history/legends of some of these claimed that they moved in groups led by members of their royalty, such as Eochu OverSea leading the Déisi into southwest Wales.[4] This time it came from the west as the aristocracy from the Irish kingdom of Dál Riata moved from their base in County Antrim to establish themselves in the southern Hebrides and Argyllshire. Sometime round the end of the fifth century a Fergus son of Erc moved his capital to Britain and led his clan the 13 miles across the North Channel to Kintyre. Exactly who went with him is unclear, although later traditions claim that his five brothers and their families accompanied him. The families of Dál Riata were looking for a refuge and were moving to stay ahead of the new power, the clans who called themselves O'Neill (Uí Néill) and who were pushing in from the western region round Sligo Bay. Dál Riata was not alone in their flight; St. Patrick's patrons the Ulstermen (*Ulaid*) were forced to abandon Armagh and the saint died at Saul on the eastern coast.

One question concerns the circumstances of Dál Riata's movement into Britain. Were they conquerors who carved out a kingdom from the territory of their defeated foes? Or were they settlers living at the sufferance of a patron? Unlike the usually elaborate legends that grew up around such population movements there are only a couple of mentions of Dál Riata moving into Britain and they are very brief. The earliest comes from the tract called *The History of the Men of Britain* (*Senchus Fer nAlban*). This is a miscellany of origin legend, genealogy, political geography, and naval muster roll; the speculation that it was assembled

---

[2] Nennius, *The British History and Annals*, ed. John Morris (London, 1980): 76, section 56.
[3] Gildas, *Ruin of Britain*: 26, 98, section 26.
[4] P.C. Bartrum, *Early Welsh Genealogical Tracts* (Cardiff, 1966): 4.

around 700 still seems the most probable.[5] Much later, in the tenth-century collection of materials concerning St. Patrick now known as the *Tripartite Life*, the saint directs Fergus to lead his people to the east.[6] The brevity is interesting. Not until the late medieval period is there extensive discussion by Scottish historians, who clumsily amalgamate various legends.

The first Pictish king to appear in contact with the Irish settlers of Dál Riata was Brude son of Maelcon, who appears in Adomnán's *Life of Columba* in several episodes in which the saint demonstrates the power of Christianity or gains safe passage for his monks. There could have been a political aspect to Columba's association with Brude that might underlie the relations between the two men. Before the arrival of Columba on Iona there had been warfare between Brude and Dál Riata. Sometime after mid-century (the *Annals of Ulster* gives alternative dates of 558 and 560) Brude attacked Dál Riata and in the general rout killed their king Gabran. Into this tense region came Columba who sailed to Iona a few years later; the usual date given for the foundation of the community is 562.[7] The reason for the hostilities is unknown, but empire building by kingdoms along the Atlantic was a process of decades rather than simply one or two years. From northeast Ireland the Ulstermen attempted to imitate the westward expansion of Dál Riata. Under the leadership of King Báetan son of Cairill, the Ulster fleet moved into the Irish Sea around 578 and captured the Isle of Man. Although the occupation did not last more than a few years (if that), it showed what could be done.

Slightly later, around 580 or 581 (according to the record consulted) Dál Riata went on the offensive again. Led by a son of Gabran named

---

[5] This tract and the later attached genealogies were edited and translated by John Banner, *Studies in the History of Dalriada* (Edinburgh, 1974): 41–49. The additional genealogies probably were added in the tenth century. For an alternative suggestion that the entire tract is a tenth-century compilation see D. Dumville, "Ireland and Britain in the Earlier Middle Ages: Contexts for *Miniugud Senchusa Fher nAlban*," in Colm Ó Baoill and Nancy McGuire (eds.), *Rannsachadh na Gàidhlig 2000* (Aberdeen, 2002): 185–211.

[6] Whitley Stokes, *The Tripartite Life of Patrick*, Rolls Series 89, 2 vols. (London, 1888). A more recent edition is by K. Mulchrone, *Bethu Phatraic* (Dublin, 1939), but it does not have a translation.

[7] There is the possibility that the Irish annals calculated the date based on Adomnán's claim that the church on Iona was founded two years after the battle of Cúl Drebene: Adomnán, *Life of Columba*, ed. A.O. Anderson and M.O. Anderson (Oxford, 1991): xxviii.

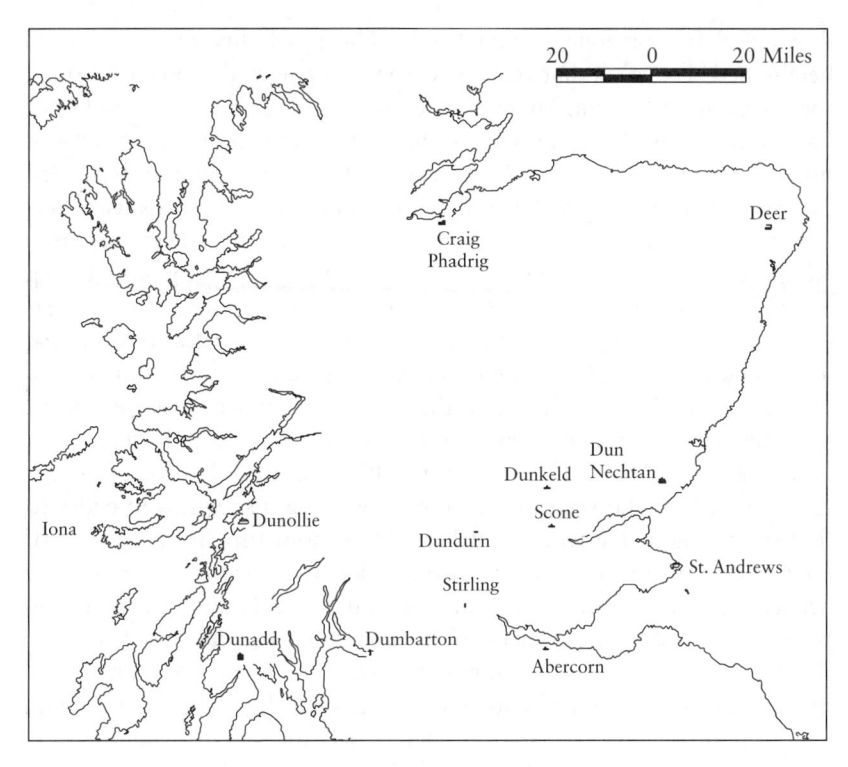

Map 3.1 Churches and Fortresses.

Áedan, the fleet sailed along the western coast of Britain for an invasion of the Orkney Islands. Nothing more is stated beyond an announcement of the event, although the notice of the death of a Cennaláth, king of Picts, in the same year might indicate he ruled in the Orkneys (or it might be coincidence). Once again it is possible to speculate on another connection with an episode in Adomnán's *Life of Columba*, and Áedan might not have been alone in his designs on the Orkney Islands. The saint traveled up the Great Glen to the fortress of King Brude, perhaps somewhere in the vicinity of modern Inverness – Craig Phadraig is one possible site (see Map 3.1), where he found another visitor, who was a king from the Orkney Islands conferring with Brude. The saint seized the opportunity to secure a guarantee of safety for a fellow missionary, which Adomnán notes would have meant death for him without that protection (see chapter 5). A record of Brude's attack on the Orkneys might be misplaced in the Irish annals, which note that in 682 the Orkneys were devastated by someone named Brude. The possibility of confusion is heightened because in that year there was a king named Brude, who ruled the kingdom of Fortriu. There is, of course, no reason why he could not have been involved in islands far to the north. Nevertheless, we have seen how there are alternative dates offered for events, and it has been observed that the Irish annals reflect the combining of records using different cycles, transferring rotations as mentioned in Ceolfrid's letter to King Nechtan.[8] This might be another instance of information falling victim to the efforts by later writers to synchronize material from different records that employed dissimilar chronological cycles. If Columba was counting on Brude's influence to secure the compliance of his vassal, the latter was short-lived; within three years Brude was dead and there is no mention of any later *rex Pictorum* in Adomnán's narrative.

The attacks from Dál Riata on the Picts continued throughout the reign of Áedan who seems to have been varying his victims in order to find the weakest. He won a battle in *Manu* sometime in the period of Baetan's death (the year before by one calculation or the very next year according to another record). This presents a problem of interpretation because there were two places where this could be: the Isle of Man or the area round the Forth. Adomnán might be referring to it in one of his stories about Columba as a prophet. One day, without warning, Columba ordered his attendant to ring a bell and summon the brothers to the church so they could pray for the success of Áedan's army in a battle after which Columba announced that the barbarians had fled, but it was an unhappy victory. A few sentences later the barbarians are identified as the Miathi, who killed Áedan's sons Artuir and Eochoid Find.[9] Miathi is a variant spelling of the earlier Maeatae, mentioned by Dio in the third century as living south of the Antonine Wall. So in this instance it seems that Áedan was active along the Forth rather than the Isle of Man, which is called *Eumania* in the entry for the previous year in the Irish annals. This is an area where, according to Bede, the people were Christians, but this did not prevent Columba from calling them barbarians, which reveals how flexible nomenclature was depending on the writer consulted.

Success between the firths of Clyde and Forth as well as the expedition to the Orkneys may have encouraged Áedan to further expeditions against the Picts. His next battle was at an unknown place called *Leth*

---

[8] T.F. O'Rahilly, *Early Irish History and Mythology* (Dublin, 1946): 235–259.
[9] Adomnán, *Life of Columba*: 32; discussion of the location is at pp. xix–xx.

Reid (the name means "smooth side" or "smooth slope") around 590. About the time of Columba's death in 595 Áedan led an unsuccessful campaign against the kingdom of Circenn where he was defeated with the loss of several of his sons. Since Circenn was on the eastern coast and farther north than the previous attacks on Manau, one can conjecture that this campaign was more than a casual slap at a neighboring rival. The severity of that defeat might be reflected in the silence of the sources where there is no indication that Áedan ever led another campaign to the north or east. He did, however, turn south where more defeat awaited him in a battle that seems to have been fought somewhere between the Antonine and Hadrian Walls. The Scots discovered that they were not alone in their expansionist interests when they confronted the Angles of Northumbria in a battle fought at a location known only as *Degsastan* (Stone of Degsa) in 603. The most that can be suggested for the location of the conflict is a possible site somewhere in Dumfriesshire, perhaps modern Dawstone. If the battle were fought between the firths of Clyde and Solway, then there is the distinct possibility that the men of Dál Riata were being used by Strathclyde in imitation of the Roman practice of using a barbarian to fight a barbarian. The clash was more famous in its day than now and few details are known. The king-lists known as "I" include the battle among the events of Brude son of Maelcon's reign, although they do not make a connection with him.[10] The English records are clear that it was a victory for the Angles under the leadership of Aethelfrith, while the Irish records are less certain. What seems to be a story connected with the battle is the earliest version of an Irish tale known as *The Conception of Mongan (Compert Mongáin)*.[11] An Irish prince named Fiachna Lurga, the king of Dál nAraide (the people also known as Cruithne) allied with Áedan and went to Britain to fight against the Saxons. In his absence the pagan Irish deity of the sea, Manannán mac Lír, visited Fiachna's wife and begat a son named Mongan. In compensation for this trespass, Manannán traveled to Britain where he saved Fiachna's life and won the battle for the Irish.

The recitation above gives the impression that the northern peoples were completely on the defensive, but this was not so. A generation

---

[10] See, for example, Oxford, Bodleian manuscript Latin Misc. C75, f. 53vb. and KES 280.
[11] K. Meyer, *Voyage of Bran son of Febal* (London, 1895): 42–45. A broader discussion of this period is H. Moisl, "The Bernician Royal Dynasty and the Irish in the Seventh Century," *Peritia* 2 (1983): 103–126.

after the death of Gildas and sometime round the death of Columba, a new and important document comes to hand from Old Welsh poetry and is now known as *The Gododdin* (*Y Gododdin*).[12] Gododdin was the name both of the peoples and of the kingdom situated northeast from Hadrian's Wall as far as the Firth of Forth and west by northwest from Lothian into what is now Stirlingshire.[13] In classical records the people are known as the *Votadini*. According to the demographics of the late Roman Empire, the Gododdin were Picts since they lived north of Hadrian's Wall. They referred to themselves as *Prydyn* or *Prydein* which are variant spellings of a name that simply means "Britons."[14] Their western district was known as *Manau* (the precise meaning is unclear but it seems to be "plain") and the element is preserved in the names of the towns Clackmannan (the Stone of Manau) north of the Forth and Sliabmannan (the Hill of Manau) south of the river. By the late sixth century the capital of Gododdin seems to have been Dun Edin, apparently Edinburgh, but a major fortress had been at Traprain Law (known as Dunpedlar in some records) to the southeast, where a major hoard of mostly mutilated late Roman coins has been discovered together with other goods such as jewelry inscribed with designs that have been considered "Pictish." The people known as Gododdin are mentioned in other works, and verses ascribed to the Welsh poet Taliesin tell of preparations for a raid on Manau.[15]

All the details concerning this raid come from *Y Gododdin* in the form of an extended eulogy for the aristocratic warriors who fought and died on the campaign. Understanding the verses is difficult because the language of the poem is obscure and the identification of some of

---

[12] The modern scholarly edition is by Sir Ifor Williams, *Canu Aneirin* (Cardiff, 1938); later translations/paraphrases based on his work are Kenneth Jackson, *The Gododdin* (Edinburgh, 1969) and John T. Koch, *The Celtic Heroic Age* (Andover, 1997): 296–337.

[13] For a survey see Christopher Snyder, *The Britons* (Oxford, 2003): 217–219.

[14] There is not the space here to enter into a detailed discussion of the problem, yet students of early Welsh accept the following: 1) *Prydyn* and *Prydein* are often confused; and 2) that the former specifically indicates the north of Britain sometimes is based on editorial convenience rather than historical investigation; see J.E. Caerwyn-Williams' notes to Sir Ifor Williams, *Poems of Taliesin* (Dublin, 1975): 120; and Sir Ifor Williams, *Armes Prydein* (Dublin, 1972): 21–22.

[15] Williams, *Poems of Taliesin*: 5.

the places is uncertain. While an exact translation of *Y Gododdin* is still to come, in broad outline the verses tell of an expedition undertaken about 600 when a force from Gododdin traveled south to join a British coalition in an attack on a new group of immigrants, the Angles, in north Yorkshire. The poem gives an impression, but no more, of the warrior culture beyond the Wall. They departed from their fortress at what is now thought to be Edinburgh Castle, and rode south to *Catraeth* (usually identified as Catterick in North Yorkshire, south of Darlington), about 160 miles away. Since a man on horseback, with remounts, can cover about 70 miles per day, then there would have been two and a half days of riding prior to the actual battle. The force consisted of 300 mounted men and one version of the poem claims that the entire army from Gododdin was killed with the exception of one survivor. Among the details in the narrative is that the warriors rode to the battlefield, but apparently they fought on foot in the manner found throughout European battlefields of the time. Once battle began, the men of Gododdin used swords, spears, and long knives together with shields for protection.

The Romans had been worried about the "barbarians" around them, organizing alliances during the fourth century (always considered conspiracies by the paranoid officials of the Empire), but they were right to be worried if the poem *Y Gododdin* is an accurate guide. The verses give an unexpected insight into the diplomacy that preceded major military alliances. The army that faced the Angles at *Catraeth* consisted of troops from several kingdoms, some of them as distant from Gododdin as northern Wales. These assemblies show communication among distant groups which allowed for the planning of complex military operations that involved fighting some distance from their home bases. Nevertheless, the men of Gododdin and their allies were defeated and it marked the beginning of the end for the kingdom of Gododdin. The kingdom does not seem to have collapsed all at one time, but Anglo-Saxons settlers began to move into the lands beyond Hadrian's Wall very soon after the battle. The Anglo-Saxon St. Cuthbert was born near Melrose about 634. If the Dun Etain that was besieged around 641 is the same as Edinburgh Rock and the capital of Gododdin, then its destruction marked the end of independent Gododdin. The Angles established a major fortress at Bamburgh to safeguard their territory; later a bishopric was established at Abercorn (within the territory of Gododdin) in 681 with Trumwine as the bishop.

Soldiers of Fortune

Mercenaries, either individually or in groups, were a part of this early medieval world. They could be men of no significant birth who were adept with a sword or noble exiles who traded their fighting prowess for hospitality. Mercenaries were employed throughout the British Isles and it has been suggested that the collapse of the British kingdoms beyond the Humber such as the kingdom of Gododdin led to the appearance of Irish babies named Llewellyn in the late sixth/early seventh century as aristocrats from North Britain became mercenaries in Ireland where they married Irish women.[16] Well-born soldiers of fortune might or might not have been commonplace on the battlefield, but they were a staple character in literature. The legend of the Picts in the Irish *Senchus Már*, for example, claim that they were mercenaries.

There are soldiers of fortune in some of the earliest texts. *Y Gododdin* names the warrior Bubbon who came from a kingdom across the Firth of Forth. The verse inserted in the poem that celebrates the victory of the men of Strathclyde against Freckled Domnall the king of Dál Riata might mean that mercenaries from Gododdin were present. There was Llifiau son of Cian who led a force of a hundred men and came from beyond Bannog (the mountainous hills that extend from Stirling to Dumbarton), while the Gwid son of Peithan might have been the Fid or Faoith (from *Wid*) of the Pictish king lists.[17] The Pictish aristocrat named Tarain who fled for refuge to St. Columba, who in turn sent him to join the retinue of a noble named Feradach, illustrates one of the ways an exiled noble earned a living.

Mercenaries from among the Picts or Cruithne are in a tale that was originally written prior to the supremacy of the Scots and comes from the Old Irish story known as *The Destruction of Da Derga's Hostel* (*Togail Bruidne Dá Derga*), which seems to be based on an eighth-century original.[18] The earliest (incomplete) copy is in the *Book of the Dun Cow* (*Lebor na hUidre*) which has a version that was compiled from an original of the ninth century.[19] The story tells about the accession to the

---

[16] Eoin Mac Neill, *Phases of Irish History* (Dublin, 1919): 203.
[17] Jackson, *Gododdin*: respectively pages 107, 99, 103, and 131.
[18] Eleanor Knott (ed.), *Togail Bruidne Dá Derga*, Medieval and Modern Irish Series 8 (Dublin, repr. 1975): 22–23.
[19] R.I. Best and Osborn Bergan (eds.) *Lebor na Huidre* (Dublin, 1929): 207–245 (f. 83a–99a); the Cruithne are at f. 88a, p. 219; R. Thurneysen, *Die irische Helden- und Königsage* (Halle, 1921): 24.

kingship and subsequent destruction of a man named Conaire whose mother was human and father was a bird-man. The literary elements of the story are an interesting study of Irish society in the period before the conversion to Christianity, and the taboos placed upon Conaire when he is made king reveal some of the supernatural and physical restrictions placed on rulers. His employment of three warriors, in this instance from Cruithentúath, is a commonplace in these tales, where mercenaries add an exotic element to the narrative. The individuals are no more than part of the scenery, but their appearance, clothes, and weapons are all intended to be part of the general air of foreboding that permeates the tale. In particular, the repetition of the color black heightens the idea of doom, as catastrophe awaits King Connor after he gave an unjust judgment, thus violating one of his taboos. The men are called Dub Longes son of Trebuat (which translates into English as Dark-Ship son of the Terrible-Folk), Trebaut son of O'Lonsce (Terrible-Folk, great-grandson of the Fierce-Thorn) and Curnach son of O'Fiach (the Horned-One, great grandson of the Raven). The use of *dub* (black) or *dond* (brown) is employed throughout their description. They are large brown men whose hair is cut in a circular pattern round their heads and each is wearing a cowl with a long hood.

The legend of a royal Irish exile among the Picts is in the Irish tale known as The Finding of Cashel.[20] The tale is an interesting mix of origin legends and folk-tale motifs that was composed in the interests of the Éognachta dynasties that dominated southwestern Ireland. The hero is named Conall Corc and he was the son of King Luigthech and Bolce *Ben-bretnach* ("the British woman"), shedding a light on diplomatic contacts between the islands. Conall's foster-mother was Fedelm the witch, and one night when a coven was meeting at Fedelm's house, he was hidden under a cauldron, but was burned after one of the witches sent a flame where the child was hidden. Later the boy was adopted by his cousin King Crimthann, but was slandered by Crimthann's wife whose advances he spurned. The furious king plotted Conall's destruction by sending him on a mission to the king of the Picts. His instructions to have the bearer murdered were written in ogam script in "the language of the Cruithne" so that Conall was not able to understand them. He was

---

[20] Vernon Hull, "Conall Corc and the Corco Luigde," PMLA 62 (1947): 887–909; and Kuno Meyer, *Anecdota from Irish Manuscripts*, iii (1910); for discussion see Myles Dillon, "The Story of the Finding of Cashel," *Ériu* 16 (1952): 61–73.

saved, however, after falling asleep on the beach where he was found by a scholar whom he had rescued from captivity, and who understood the ogams. His friend altered the message so that instead it requested safety and honor for whoever carried the shield. The scholar's alteration was so successful that Conall was welcomed by the Pictish king and given his daughter as a wife. Conall's son by his Pictish wife was known as Coirpre Cruithnechán (the Little Cruithne). The name Cruithnechan is found on a memorial slab at Clonmacnoise.[21] Conall remained in Pictland until the death of Crimthann, when he returned to Ireland.

What turns this formulaic tale into an interesting comment on northern Britain comes in an aside in a genealogy from the twelfth-century manuscript that is now Bodleian Rawlinson B. 502 (folio 148a31), where it is claimed that among the descendants of Conall's son Coirpre were the Éoganachta of Mag Circenn (*Eoganachta Maigi Dergind*) in Britain, among whom was King Angus.[22] This Angus has been identified as the eighth-century prince Angus son of Fergus and the question has been whether literature is being deployed in the service of political expediency or is historical belief being presented as literature. This section of genealogies was composed in the eighth century and it is preserved in an early twelfth-century manuscript, so Angus son of Fergus is the one intended. How did emigrants from southwest Ireland end up in northeastern Britain? One answer is that they had been recruited by the Britons as auxiliaries, in imitation of the Romans, and had moved north. The twelfth-century Irish synthetic history *Lebor Gabála* claims that swordland (i.e., conquered territory) was taken on the eastern Scottish coast in the "plain of Circenn" (roughly the area from Stonehaven to Forfar) by people from the Eóganachta. The distance from the southern Irish region to this eastern area of Scotland is roughly 420 miles; by comparison the distance from Forfar to London is over 480 miles. We have already seen that a people in southern Wales traced their ancestry to the midlands of Ireland, so population movement could occur over vast distances, especially if those moving were warriors who subsequently intermarried with the people employing them.

Enemies could become friends very quickly. An aristocratic mercenary apparently was suitable marriage material for a princess. In the story of Conall Corc, one married the daughter of the king while he was at her father's court. Even though this story is fiction, the situation must have

---

[21] CIIC: ii, 46.
[22] Michael O'Brien, *Corpus Genealogiarum Hiberniae* (Dublin, 1962): 196.

been familiar and believable to an audience of warrior aristocrats where such unions could not have been unknown. When King Edwin, one of Bede's heroes because of his Christianity, took control of Northumbria he expelled the sons of his rival Aethelfrith from the kingdom.[23] The brothers – Eanfrith, Oswald, and Oswy – fled north to the Picts and Scots: Eanfrith went to an unidentified Pictish kingdom while Oswald and Oswy fled to Iona. Eanfrith married a member of one of the royal families and their son, Talorgan, succeeded his grandfather as king. There is certainly evidence that royal families were intermarrying. Marriage could be temporary, a feature of aristocratic life throughout the British Isles as is testified by the numerous scoldings from the clergy. *Senchus Fer nAlban* notes that a dynast of Cenél nAngusa in Dál Riata named Galán was the son of a Pictish mother. Kinship was no guarantee of peace. The victor of the battle of Dun Nechtan in 685, Brude, was the cousin of his vanquished foe, the Anglo-Saxon prince Ecgfrith.

Weapons were the tools of their trade for soldiers of fortune. In the story of Conall Corc, for example, his shield was used to carry the message from his malevolent king to his counterpart in Britain. Returning to the mercenaries from Cruithentúaith in the Old Irish tale *The Destruction of Da Derga's Hostel*, they are described as big men with everything about them dark, wearing short cowls with long hoods and carrying huge swords, shields and broad javelins. Particularly interesting is the implication that mercenaries were hired because they were generally believed to be superior fighters. The episode ends with a prophecy that the fighters will be wounded, but will escape.[24] One can compare the descriptions of clothes and weapons in the story with the images found on the symbol stones. The description of the Pictish weapons in *The Destruction of Da Derga's Hostel* match the type of implements carved on the Class 2 Pictish stones and they were in the basic armory of any warrior in early Britain. The one different feature is the large, black sword. The color could be irrelevant and simply continues the scene's element of menace, but the size of the sword is quite different from the shorter thrusting weapon common during the early Middle Ages. The literary description might indicate that the Picts were using an early version of what would later become the claymore (Gaelic *cliabh mór*) the great sword that came to prominence several centuries later.

[23] Bede, *Historia Ecclesiastica* in *Venerabilis Baedae Opera Historica*, ed. Charles Plummer, 2 vols. (Oxford, 1896): i, 127 (III.1).
[24] *Togail Bruidne Da Derga*: 22–23.

News from the Picts

The battle of Degsastan marks the end of one relatively informative period. Most of the information from that period was connected with Columba and Áedan son of Gabran. This shows again why so much early medieval history seems to revolve around a handful of individuals or events, and why other expanses of time and distance are unnoticed. The survival of the poem Y *Gododdin* allows us possibly to make too much of the collapse of one northern British kingdom. Competition, alliance, victory, and defeat can only occasionally be identified for this period. In order to make some sense of the isolated pieces of information, it is occasionally necessary to combine items. For example, there is a man named Gartnat whose death is recorded about 601 and he is probably the same as the Gartnan son of Domelch found in the king-lists among other names of the early seventh century. Sometimes the names found in the annals simply seem to be Pictish, such as the Talorcan who died around 617, while others are specifically connected with northern Britain, as is the Cinedon son of Lugthren (or Luchtren), styled King of Picts, whose obit appears among the events of 631. Occasionally a sequence of names suggests kinship. For example, around 635 a man named Angus son of Nechtan died. His father might be the same man as the Nechtan son of Uerb who is found in the king-lists. At about the same time was fought the battle of Sequise where the deaths of three men were recorded: Lochene son of Rechtan "Longhead," Cumuseach son of Angus and Gartnan son of Fid (whose death is recorded a second time under the same year entry). There is a Sequise in County Roscommon, but the personal names from this entry are not found in any of the local genealogies. A British location is suggested upon discovering a Gartnan son of Fid in the king-lists. This leads to the question, was Cumuseach the son of Angus son of Nechtan? To continue the link with the battle of Sequise, a Brude son of Fid died in 641 while a Iarnboidh son of Gartnan was burned to death in 643; was Brude the brother of, and Iarnboidh the son of, Gartnan son of Fid? Without the guidance of other records combining names remains speculation, but the fact that the chronicles tend to follow family units suggests the connection. The list of names continues with the war of the sons of Gartnat son of Accidan in 649, followed in 653 by the deaths of Ferith son of Totholan and Tolarg son of Fid, styled king of Picts. This was followed ten years later by the death of Gartnan son of Domnall, styled king of the Cruithne in the *Annals of Tigernach*. The next year was fought the battle of *Lutho Feirnn* (Marsh of the Alder) that was located somewhere in Fortriu. We would like to know more about the circumstances surrounding the expulsion from the kingship of Drust in 671, whose death is noticed among the events of 678.

The perception of the kingdoms in the north of Britain as victims after the establishment of the Angles might need modification. Were the royal families of Strathclyde, like those of Dál Riata, attempting to move into the lands north of the Forth and having some success? Dál Riata and the Angles of Northumbria might have had their expansionist interests matched by Strathclyde.[25] To begin, the poem *Y Gododdin* has a verse about the foreign warrior Wid son of Peithan. Variant spellings of *Wid* would be *Fid*, *Gwid*, or *Gwyd*. He might be the same individual as the *Fid* in the so-called Pictish king-lists, whose three sons – Garnard, Brude, and Talorg – are listed and two of whom have already been introduced; depending on the list consulted, there is an additional son named *Nechtan filius Fide*.[26] Moving on, the death of King Gureit of Strathclyde occurred in 658 and, in the middle of the seventh century, the king over Fortriu was Brude son of Bile. The medieval hagiographical text *Life of Adomnán* claims that he was the son of the king of Strathclyde; a recent study of the text has suggested that it was composed in the tenth century.[27] In the genealogy for the kings of Strathclyde preserved in the twelfth-century British Library Harleian MS 3859 Bile's father is named Neithon son of Gwyddno.[28] This leads to a question: was the Nechtan son of Gwyddno who is the father of Beli the same man as the Nechtan son of Gwyd (Fid) who is found in the king-lists? The difference in spelling between *Wid* and *Widno*, which would be a variation of *Gwydnno*, becomes less worrisome when realizing the late date of the king-lists, and that their orthography gives unusual forms of names. In the Irish annals the father of Garnard and Talorg is spelled *Foith*, which replicates the *dd* of the *Gododdin*.

Suddenly, during the final two decades of the century, notices of attacks on strongholds or efforts to reduce them through a siege appear in the annals. Once again we don't know if this was a new development or merely that the incidents were considered important enough to warrant inclusion in the annals. This does show, however, the reliance that was

---

[25] For a brief survey of Strathclyde see: Snyder, *Britons*: 219–221.
[26] Jackson, *Gododdin*: 130.
[27] Máire Herbert and Pádraig O Riain (eds.), *Betha Adamnáin*, Irish Texts Society 54 (London, 1988).
[28] Bartrum, *Early Welsh Genealogical Tracts*:10.

Figure 3.1 Dunnottar Castle. Photo Robert Hudson.

being placed on defensive sites and that they were so effective that their reduction was necessary. The first record is in 680 with the siege of an unidentified place called Dunbaitte. The only reason for assuming that it was located in Britain is that no place of that name is known in Ireland. The following year (681) a place that is well known is the location of a siege at *Dun Foither* (Fort of the Thicket) now known as Dunnottar (see Figure 3.1), for which a second siege is recorded in 694. Two years later, in 683, there were sieges of Dunadd in Dál Riata and Dundurn in Perthshire. The attack on Dundurn might explain the destruction of the defenses and their subsequent rebuilding that was found during excavations in 1976–77.[29] In 692 there was the siege of an unidentified place described as *dun deauae dibsi*, possibly Dundaff south of Stirling.[30]

[29] Leslie Alcock, Elizabeth A. Alcock, and Stephen T. Driscoll, "Reconnaisance Excavations on Early Historical Fortifications and Other Royal Sites in Scotland, 1974–84: 3, Excavations at Dundurn, Strathearn, Perthshire, 1976–77," PSAS 119 (1989): 189–226 (at p. 203).

[30] *The Life of Columba, Founder of Hy, Written by Adamnan*, ed. William Reeves (Dublin, 1857): 378nE.

The last name for the seventh century is the burning of Dunolly (near Oban) in the territory of Dál Riata in 698; early in the eighth century is recorded the siege of an unidentified place called *Rithe*, which is usually assumed to be somewhere in northern Britain.

How powerful or influential a prince might have been is one of the basic questions asked by historians. Great leaders can arise and extend their empires widely, only for it all to vanish after their death. For example, was Brude son of Maelcon as powerful a ruler as suggested by the Irish annals and Adomnán's *Life of Columba*, or is this merely a reflection of his association with Columba of Iona? One suggestion is that he was as powerful as Adomnán implies, and that his empire building was done so well that for a generation afterwards Dál Riata's attacks had been forced south of the Grampians. His successors might not have had his ability and in the second quarter of the seventh century attacks from the immigrant Scots now shifted to the north of the Grampians, despite their apparent setback at the battle of *Degsastan*. There is an obit for a son of Áedan mac Gabrain named Eochaid *Buide* (The Blond) who died in 629 and is styled "king of the Picts." Was this merely a miscopying on the part of a scribe or is it accurate, suggesting that he was overlord of some territory among the Picts?[31] The record is preserved in the *Annals of Ulster* where it is noted that the information comes from the *Book of Cuanu* (*Liber Cuanach*), a frequently cited record. One reason for not dismissing the item as a simple error is that Eochaid's son Domnall Brecc (the Speckled) was defeated in the battle of Glen Morison in 640. There is a Glen Morison (or Moriston) about 30 miles west of Loch Ness and this could be yet more evidence of attempts by the princes of Dál Riata to expand into the territory of their neighbors. Another battle against Dál Riata was in 654 when Talorgan son of Ainfrith defeated Dunchad son of Conaing and Congal son of Ronan at Srath Ethairt (another unidentified place). Talorgan enjoyed his victory only briefly as he died in 657. Collaboration of a very uncertain variety around efforts to annex territory towards the north, in this instance the Isle of Skye, comes from the Old Irish romance *The Tale of Cano the son of Gartnan* (*Scéla Cano meic Gartnáin*). The tale is actually a romance about the love of a mercenary from Dál Riata named Cano son of Gartnan for Créd, the wife of a king named Marcus. The first part of

---

[31] J.M.P. Calise, "Genealogies and History: A Reassessment of Cenél nGabráin," in Benjamin Hudson (ed.), *Familia and Household in the Medieval Atlantic World* (Tempe, AR, 2011): 19–50 (at pp. 27–28).

the story concerns the reason why Cano was a wandering warrior: he was forced to flee from Britain as noble families from Cenél nGabráin were moving onto the Isle of Skye and fighting for control of the island.[32] What might or might not be connected is the notice in the annals that the sons of Gartnan led the people of Skye to Ireland in 668 and returned, apparently to Skye, in 670. Movement against the Picts may have continued and the mystery deepens when in 669 two men named Itharnan and Corindu die among the Picts. Dál Riata once again raided the Orkneys in 709 when the son of Artabláir was slain.

Battle of Dun Nechtan

The obscurity of northern British affairs in the annals is relieved temporarily in the last quarter of the seventh century with one of the best known events in early British history, the battle of Dun Nechtan (also known as Nechtan's Mere) fought on Saturday, May 20, 685. At this battle the myth of Northumbrian invincibility crumbled. Some idea of the battle of Dun Nechtan's importance can be gauged by the detailed information attached to it in Irish and Anglo-Saxon records. The battle took place as increasing demands on the king of Northumbria by both the laity and the church forced King Ecgfrith to encroach on his neighbors. Although Bede presents him as a failure, his greatest weakness probably was trying to balance the claims of an increasingly demanding clergy with the need to reward his aristocratic followers.[33] One of his first moves, in 681, was to establish a bishopric for the Picts at Abercorn on the southern shore of the firth of Forth (west of Edinburgh) for which the first (and only) bishop was named Trumwine or Tumma. This might have been in the aftermath of a victory that the *vita* of Wilfred by Eddius Stephanus claims Ecgfrith won early in his career with the assistance of a nobleman named Beornhaeth. While popular wisdom places this diocese north of the Firth of Forth, there is absolutely no evidence for its bounds, although Trumwine's seat at Abercorn must mean that at least one boundary was south of it. Despite this visible sign of his dominance in the region, financial demands on a prince continued to make necessary a predatory attitude toward his

---

[32] D.A. Binchy (ed.), *Scéla Cano meic Gartnáin* (Dublin, 1975): 1.
[33] Patrick Wormald, "The Age of Bede and Aethelbald," in James Campbell (ed.), *The Anglo-Saxons* (London, 1991): 94.

neighbors. Any action in Britain, however, had immediate and unpleasant consequences. So in 684 Ecgfrith ordered an invading force across the Irish Sea to attack on the eastern coast of Ireland; the force was commanded by a noble named Berht or Bercth, apparently a son of Beornhaeth.[34] According to the Irish annals the invaders landed in the vicinity of the river Boyne, within the region called Brega (north of modern Dublin).

The raid, a foretaste of the Viking incursions of the following century, may have proved to be profitable and encouraged the Northumbrian prince into the venture that claimed his life. Regardless of how this profited the king financially, it earned him the lasting rebuke of Bede, who saw his death a year later as divine retribution. In 685 Ecgfrith personally led an invading force north across the Forth. His reasons are unclear. Bede, in his *Life of Cuthbert* describes his foray as "rashly daring" (*ausu temerario*) and continues with the observation that with cruel and savage fury he devastated the kingdoms of the Picts.[35] Later, in the *Ecclesiastical History*, Bede claims that Ecgfrith undertook the expedition against the advice of his friends (who included Cuthbert). This report also has the precise date of the battle (the king's 40th year, the 15th year of his reign on the 13th day of the Ides of June, which is May 20).[36] The Irish and later English records give the location and his adversary: the *Annals of Ulster* place the battle at Dun Nechtan, (Nechtan's Fort); which is echoed by the *Annals of Tigernach* with the additional information that Ecgfrith's opponent was Brude son of Bile the king of Fortriu. Bede gives a brief account of the battle in his *Ecclesiastical History*, when the advancing Anglo-Saxons were lured by the (seemingly retreating) Picts into a narrow mountain pass. There the Picts counterattacked and Ecgfrith, surrounded by his bodyguard, was slain.

The tactics employed by Brude were part of the ancient strategy for the peoples in the north of Britain. Both Dio and Herodian claim that the Caledonians and Maeatae used similar strategy against the Romans

---

[34] Eddius Stephanus, *The Life of Bishop Wilfrid*, ed. Bertram Colgrave (Cambridge, repr. 1985): 166.
[35] Bede, *Vita Sancti Cuthberti*, in Bertram Colgrave, *Two Lives of Saint Cuthbert* (Cambridge, 1940): 242. A comparison of this version with that of the *Anonymous Life* (p. 120), shows that Bede incorporated into his account an eyewitness remembrance with an expanded version of events.
[36] Bede, *Historia Ecclesiastica*: I, 266–267.

during the third-century campaign of the emperor Septimus Severus.[37] The Britons frequently employed the tactic of luring their opponents into a trap by feigning retreat into a wood or marsh. Dio mentions that the heavy armor of the Roman troops inspired their enemies to refuse pitch battle, but instead they attempted to lure the Romans into water, where the southerners would sink into the mire. Herodian gives the additional information that the "barbarians" hid in the woods and marshes, but their plans were foiled, in part, by the Roman construction of pontoons to move troops across the wetlands. A battle scene between cavalry and infantry carved on a stone in the churchyard at Aberlemno has been interpreted as a memorial to the battle, with the added assumption that the cavalry were the invaders from the south.

It is usually assumed that Ecgfrith's forces traveled overland to Dun Nechtan. There is a reason to look again at the assumption of a land route, because of the historical problem of a slow speed for an army moving in the lands north of the Antonine Wall. Only in the later Middle Ages is there enough information to calculate travel times. To take an example, the rate of speed for Edward I's army in Scotland during the campaign of 1296 was slow. His troops took four days to cover the 40 miles between Montrose and Aberdeen, but traveled the 20 miles from Strathdon to Deeside in one day.[38] Averaging the two gives a rate of 15 miles per day; this comes close to the Roman standard of 14 miles per day for an army on the march. An additional factor is that an army moving by land from Northumbria had to cross both the river Forth and the river Tay, unless they sailed across the respective firths, and that is a distance of about 170 miles. So using the faster of the two speeds from Edward's army gives eight and a half days' travel while the slower speed gives 17 days and the Roman figure suggests 12 days. Bede, however, claims that the battle took place on a Saturday but the outcome was announced at the English court the following Monday. He is unlikely to be incorrect, as this was the type of information that interested Bede and about which he was precise. The battle was fought during his lifetime (he was probably about 12 years old at the time) and Ecgfrith was a patron of his monastery; moreover there were plenty of older people he could have consulted and apparently did consult in order to obtain the

---

[37] Dio, *Roman Histories*, ed. Earnest Cary (New York, 1927): 266, and Herodian, *History of the Empire from the time of Marcus Aurelius*, ed. C.R. Whittaker (Cambridge, MA, 1969): 362.
[38] Richard Muir, *Shell Guide to Reading the Celtic Landscape* (London, 1985): 266.

Figure 3.2 The countryside round Dunnichen. Photo Robert Hudson.

information in his *Life of Cuthbert*. One solution to the apparent contradiction is that the Anglo-Saxon army sailed to the battlefield rather than marched. The Northumbrians had undertaken one maritime campaign recently – to Ireland – and the location of their royal fortress as well as the battle site were in easy communication with the sea (Dunnichen is about 10 miles west of the coast). Sailing was not unusual, and that is how St. Cuthbert traveled when he made his interrupted journey to the land of the Picts. If Bede's chronology is accepted, and assuming that the landing place was somewhere in the vicinity of Arbroath (to take one of a number of candidates) while the news was announced at Bamburgh then the sailing distance was 70 miles (113 km). At 5 knots the sailing time was about 20 hours; adding on the time it took to travel 10 miles (15 km) from the coast to the battlefield. In average conditions then, two days would be ample to travel.

As the foregoing discussion assumes, the traditional location of the battle of Nechtan's Fort has been placed somewhere in Forfarshire possibly in the vicinity of modern Dunnichen (see Figure 3.2) and the battle scene on the carved stone in Aberlemno churchyard has been proposed

Figure 3.3 Battle scene from Aberlemno Cross-slab no. 2. Photo Robert Hudson.

as a memorial to the conflict (see Figure 3.3). An alternative location has been proposed that places the battle farther north at Dunachton (which also means Nechtan's Fort) southeast of Inverness in the Badenoch and Strathspey region.[39] Bede describes the battle as taking place in a mountainous region, terrain not found today in the gently rolling farmland round Dunnichen, but it is found in the more northerly location. The topography, however, is not an insurmountable problem because centuries of land management have transformed the area dramatically, especially during the era of agricultural improvement beginning in the eighteenth century. The wetlands that dotted the landscape even two centuries ago have been drained or linked into larger bodies of water. Still remaining, however, are the startlingly abrupt peaks that one encounters barely 10 miles from Dunnichen, the southeastern part of the Grampians. Bede is clear that the Anglo-Saxon army was lured into the hills and depending on the initial contact between the forces, such movement

[39] Alex Woolf, "Dun Nechtain, Fortriu and the Geography of the Picts," SHR 85 (2006): 182–201.

would be expected in the course of battle. Bede does not give the name of the battle site, which is supplied by the Irish annals, and a fortress would be a recognizable landmark although not necessarily the exact location of the fight.

A location for the battle south of Forfar rather than south of Inverness is suggested by a reading of Bede's *vita* of St. Cuthbert of Lindisfarne.[40] He gives a long description, beginning with the departure of the king's force and the queen visiting her sister, who was a nun in Carlisle. Cuthbert goes to visit her on the Friday before the battle and on the day of the conflict (Saturday) has a vision of the king's death while touring the Roman antiquities with the queen. He urges her to return to the royal fortress on Monday and he will join her after dedicating a church on Sunday. Bede gives a summary of his sermon, which his audience believed was a warning about the return of a plague that had devastated the neighborhood. He was actually referring to the destruction of Ecgfrith and his army, which became obvious the next day, Monday, when a fugitive from the battle arrived at the royal court and confirmed that the king had died at the very time that Cuthbert had his vision. So 48 hours after the battle, a survivor had returned to give the news. At this point it is useful to return to the discussion above, on the rate of travel of an army. Admittedly one man traveling on his own can make faster time than an army. The distance overland between Bamburgh and Dunachton is about 200 miles over mountainous terrain. A horseman can cover between 35 and 50 miles per day over open country without remounts. If the faster rate is used, then it would have been impossible for someone to have fought at Dunachton on Saturday and arrived at the royal court by Monday; he would not have arrived until Wednesday at the very earliest. Going by sea is not much better even if the conditions were favorable, because the sailing distance is more than 200 miles alone, and then the distance overland (about 60 miles depending on where along the coast one landed) must be added to it. So Bede's chronology rules out a location north of the Grampians.

The battle of Dun Nechtan took place in the kingdom of Circenn, but the victor Brude son of Bile was styled king of Fortriu. There are two interpretations for his presence on the east coast. One is that he held some lordship over Circenn and was defending his satellite kingdom. The other explanation is that he and Ecgfrith were fighting for control of

---

[40] Bede, *Vita Sancti Cuthberti*, i: 240–248.

Circenn. Curiously, the profit for either adversary is not obvious. Bede saw Ecgfrith's defeat as the beginning of the end for Northumbria. The victor fared little better in the records, and the only certain further reference to Brude is his obit in 693. Repercussions from the defeat at Dunnichen echoed for years. Bede writes that the subjugated peoples won their release from Anglo-Saxon domination; in particular he claims that some of the Picts recovered their independence. Who were they? Bede notes that Ecgfrith's expedition to Circenn was an attack, not the defense of a sub-kingdom. If he is correct in stating that Ecgfrith attacked multiple kingdoms, then the kingdom of Fife would be another logical victim. Bede gives some indications that the liberated Picts included those in the territory south of the Forth. He notes that Bishop Trumwine of Abercorn was forced to flee his episcopal seat, and enter retirement at Whitby, while nuns fled from their village for fear of the barbarian army, which might mean that Brude seized his advantage and pressed southwards.[41] If this region was temporarily lost to the Angles, and they were fleeing to safety, it would explain why in 698 (*Annals of Ulster*) or 699 (*Anglo-Saxon Chronicle*) the Northumbrians under the leadership of ealdorman Berct or Berctfrid (also called Bernith in the Irish annals), apparently the same man who led the raid on eastern Ireland in June 684, were defeated by the Picts possibly around Manau and the ealdorman was slain. This was not the end of the story, because there was another clash between the Picts and Northumbrians in 711 in a battle fought in "the plain of Manau" according to the Irish annals, which the *Anglo-Saxon Chronicle* places more specifically between the rivers Avon and Carron.[42] Among the slain was a young warrior named Finnguine son of Deileroth.

Competition and Kingdoms

Immediately after the battle of Dun Nechtan the source materials temporarily return to their laconic habits. When the victor Brude son of Bile died in 693 so, too, did an Alpin son of Nechtan of whom nothing is known beyond his name, which appears to place him among the Picts. Four years later, in 697 a Tarain was expelled from his kingship, but he returned in 699. Another obscure individual, Fergussan son of Maelcon, died in 703.

---

[41] Bede, *Vita Sancti Cuthberti*: 254.
[42] The battle is mentioned in the earlier Parker version of the *Anglo-Saxon Chronicle* while the later Laud version gives the names of the rivers.

At this point there is a change as a pronounced Irish element appears. Princes with Irish names such as Angus, Fergus, and Deirile competed for supremacy among the Picts. Also at this time there begins to appear in the Irish annals not only more reports about northern Britain, but more specific information, especially for the period 693 to 741. Competition among the various peoples becomes visible as specific kingdoms – Fortriu, Atholl, and Circenn – are named in the records. Unfortunately this does not mean that all becomes transparent. Individual kingdoms are not consistently identified in the annals and the late medieval lists of kings simply give names without connecting them with any specific kingdom.

Dynasty of Deirili

Names found in the king-lists can be used in connection with the annals to identify three dynasties by the beginning of the eighth century.[43] The first appears at the end of the seventh century in the persons of the three sons of Deirili (see Lineage 3.1). Deirili is a form of Old Irish *Deróil[e]*, which has the general meaning of "humble" (in the Würzberg Glosses it is closer to "insignificance," translating Latin *contemptibilis*) and is found usually as a sobriquet.[44] That might be its meaning in the garbled form

```
            Deirili
              |
              |
      |------------------|------------------|
    Cináed            Brude            Nechtan
    (d.713)          (d.706)          (d.732)
```

Lineage 3.1   Family of Deirili.

---

[43] KCS: 23–29.
[44] *Contributions to a Dictionary of the Irish Language, degra-dodelbtha*, arranged by Mary E. Byrne and Maud Joynt (Dublin, 1959): col. 41; W. Stokes and J. Strachan, *Thesaurus Palaeohibernicus*, 2 vols. (Dublin, repr. 1975): i, 611. An interesting interpretation of the name has been Der-Ilei, "daughter of Ilei": see T. Clanchy, "Philosopher-King: Nechtan mac Der-Ilei," SHR 83 (2004): 135–149, but a problem is that the form *der* for "daughter" first appears in Middle Irish (i.e., after late ninth century) texts, so it is not obvious that an Irish writer in the eighth century would have been familiar with it. The form is also found in Welsh, but, again, the dating is difficult.

that survives in the late manuscripts that preserve the king list, although it could be used as a form of Christian humbleness, in the same way that *Moel-* "slave" was used in Máel Coluim, the name of several Scots kings. The first of that dynasty was a Brude who died in 706 and is described as a king in his obit. Brude was a witness to the famous *Law of Adomnán (Cáin Adomnáin)* also known as the *Law of Innocents*, which was circulated among kings and ecclesiastics in Ireland and Northern Britain in 697.[45] The author was Adomnán, abbot of Iona and the hagiographer of Columba. The law prohibits attacks on noncombatants in times of warfare. Brude is the last of the 91 subscribers and is styled "king of the Cruithne" (*Ri Cruithintuathi*). After his death he was succeeded immediately by his brother Kenneth (Cináed) who died violently (his throat was cut, a polite way of saying "beheaded") in 713. The last of the brothers was Nechtan who was captured and imprisoned by a neighboring prince named Drust in 726. Drust was expelled from his kingship the following year by another rival named Alpin. Nechtan had regained his freedom, probably soon after his capture, and took lordship over Alpin son of Feret who was defeated in a major battle in 728 round "the Fortress of Belief" (Caislen Credhi). The fortress was at Scone, apparently the same place where the *Scottish Chronicle* notes in 908 that the Scots king Constantine made a proclamation at the "Hill of Belief." Nechtan eliminated his rivals just in time to face a far more successful rival in Angus son of Fergus. In 729 Nechtan's tax collectors – spelled *exactatores* in one manuscript but corrected to *exactores* in a second version; the word is the plural of *exactor*, (tax collector) with the extended meaning of oppression by being forced to pay – were defeated in a battle with the army of Angus near Tyndrum.[46] Tyndrum is in Strathfillan, on the edge of Rannoch Moor, and it has gold and silver deposits, explaining why control of the region was coveted and rival groups of tax collectors contested for it. The domination of Fortriu by Angus may have sufficiently weakened its kingly families so that the province would be among the first to be conquered by the Dál Riatan dynasty of Cenél nGabráin and would be used as their early center of power in the lands of the Picts.

---

[45] Máirín Ní Dhonnchadha, "The Guarantor List of *Cáin Adomnáin*, 697," *Peritia* 1 (1982): 178–215 (at p. 214).
[46] For a different interpretation of the passage see Alex Woolf, "AU 729.2 and the last years of Nechtan mac Der-Ilei," SHR 85 (2006): 131–137.

Dynasty of Drostan

A second dynasty was that of Atholl, and the identification is made with Talorgan the son of Drostan. He is styled king of Atholl in the notice of his death in 739, which helps to locate the family. The names are useful examples of how scribes could interchange forms such as the name of Talorgan's father whose name can be spelled various ways: Dru(i)st, Drost, and Dru(i)sten (Drostan) are types that scribes used while Drostan is a diminutive of Drost/Drust.[47] Continuing the hypothesis on mere names, Drust son of Donald died in 679 and his father's name might be an Irish rendering of the Welsh name Dumnagual. Gartnan son of Donald precedes Drust in the king lists and died in 663. Talorgan had a brother named Nechtan who, in 713 according to the *Annals of Ulster*, had him clapped in irons. There is some confusion about him because he shared the same first name with his contemporary Nechtan son of Deirili who was defeated by Angus son of Fergus.[48] The confusion extends further when the king-list designated D makes him the brother of Talorgan son

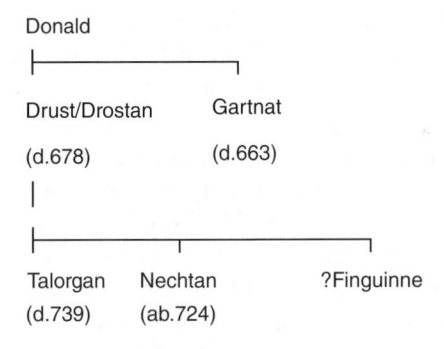

```
Donald
├──────────────────┐
Drust/Drostan      Gartnat
(d.678)            (d.663)
│
├──────────┬────────────┐
Talorgan   Nechtan      ?Finguinne
(d.739)    (ab.724)
```

Lineage 3.2 Family of Drostan.

---

[47] Kenneth Jackson, "The Language of the Picts," in F.T. Wainwright (ed.), *The Problem of the Picts*: 161.

[48] One solution was offered by Duncan, "Bede, Iona and the Picts," in R.H.C. Davis and J. M. Wallace-Hadrill (eds.),*The Writing of History in the Middle Ages: Essays Presented to Richard William Southern* (Oxford, 1981): 36n1; but see KES: 85–89, for a discussion that reaches different conclusions.

of Ainfrith. He seems to be the Nechtan whom Bede claims (*Historia*, V.21) solicited advice from Abbot Ceolfrid of Wearmouth/Jarrow on the calculation of the date of Easter and the organization of the churches in his kingdom. The placement of that letter in the *Ecclesiastical History* is about 710, but this should not be interpreted too strictly; since the next date is Ecgbert's conversion of the community of Iona to the Roman calculation of Easter in 716, then it must have been somewhere between the two dates. He expelled the clergy from Iona in 717, across the Dorsum Britanniae, which was the boundary between Dál Riata and Atholl. That was a year after the community had changed its method of calculating the date of Easter, so the expulsion was clearly political rather than ecclesiastical. Bede saw it as a sign of the declining influence of the Columban federation in Britain. The expulsion of the Iona clergy is one way of distinguishing between the two Nechtans, for the family of Nechtan son of Deirili would not be expected to expel members of that church because of their connections with Iona. There might be a connection with the conflict this year between the men of Strathclyde and Dál Riata, who fought a battle at the rock called Minuirc (possibly Clach na Breatan in Glen Falloch), where Strathclyde was defeated. Nechtan abdicated in 724 to live in religious retirement. Talorgan apparently ascended to the kingship upon the abdication of his brother and seems to have been content with his limited rule, for he did not participate in the contests for supremacy among the Picts during the period 726–729. He was not completely successful in rising above the fray, and in 739 he was captured and executed, by drowning, by Angus son of Fergus. Poor Talorgan seems to have had difficulty in staying out of close confinement; several years before his death, in 734, he had been chained in the tower of Dunollie, a prisoner of the Dál Riatan dynasty of Cenél Loairn.

The history of the family of Drostan is difficult to discern after the death of Talorgan. If the Druist son of Talorgan who appears in the late eighth century is the son of the Talorgan who was slain in 739, then the family may have survived the attacks of Angus son of Fergus.[49] It is equally likely that Druist was the son of Angus' brother Talorgan (see below). Moving ahead several centuries, the fate of [Ath]Fotla/Atholl gives a clear indication of how the rise to supremacy of the family of Kenneth mac Ailpín came at the expense of more kingdoms than Fortriu. The next time an official is directly linked to this area is in the tenth century and he is styled *satraps*, that is, a provincial governor.

[49] ESSH: i, 253 n2.

Dynasty of Angus son of Fergus

Machinations and triumphs of the previous princes pale in comparison with the career of the most successful northern British prince of the eighth century, and a case can be made to extend that back to the sixth century. With the possible exception of Áedan son of Gabran of Dál Riata, no one extended his power over a wider area than Angus son of Fergus; his neighbors in Dál Riata and Strathclyde would suffer from his attentions. In common with many great leaders of this period of European history, Angus appears apparently out of nowhere. Nothing is known of his immediate ancestry beyond his patronymic, although the Fergussan son of Maelcon whose death is recorded in 703 might be a variation on his father's name. Whether it is simply a quirk of the historical records or a genuine reflection of his power, from 728 to about 781 affairs north of the Forth were dominated by Angus and his family. Their successes may have provided the model for the later conquests made by the man popularly credited with the union of the Picts and Scots, Kenneth I (or Kenneth son of Alpin), and his dynasty. Some indication of Angus' importance is reflected by the Irish chronicles. In the *Annals of Ulster*, for example, almost half of the northern British notices for more than 50 years mention either Angus or someone who appears to be a member of his family. The amount of detail about Angus' career during the second quarter of the eighth century suggests that the influence of Bede on historical writing was expanding during his lifetime and immediately after his death. Exact dates, exact locations, and specific individuals make a brief appearance in connection with affairs north of the Forth. The early medieval world was less disconnected than is popularly believed, and in addition to intellectual or spiritual contacts carried on via the churches, there was also political contact. As will be seen, contacts between northern Britain and the Irish and Anglo-Saxons were important politically and militarily.

The location of Angus' family is fixed on the eastern coast in Circenn (modern Angus) by the aforementioned contemporary record embedded in the genealogical collections in Oxford, Bodleian MS Rawlinson B. 502, where a connection is made between his family and the Eóganacht of Munster.[50] The surprise at finding a king on the northeastern coast of Britain tracing his ancestry back to Ireland is surpassed only by finding

---

[50] In the same manuscript an Angus son of Fergus (Óengus mac Fergusa) also appears as the father of Eochu Muinremar (f. 144g; see: O'Brien, *Corpus*: 165), but that is probably a confusion with Óengus Fir found in the genealogies of the

that the connection was in the southwest of the island. That connection might explain the eighth-century Irish lines of verse on the ales of sovereignty: "Round the fields of the Cruithne, round Circenn, red ales like wine."[51] There have been efforts to ignore or discard this information by viewing it as an effort to connect with the aforementioned Conall Corc or an acknowledgment of the undoubted power of Angus, but these reasons simply don't fit with the construction of contemporary genealogies where fabrication on a scale such as this would be immediately detected and questioned. As has been asked, why would an Irish group be found in eastern Britain? One reason that was suggested earlier is that they were mercenaries. Gildas' Britons might not have been the only ones imitating the Romans in using a barbarian to fight a barbarian. While legends are not necessarily historical memories, they can give a context for past events. One legend claims that the semi-historical Irish king Nath-í, whose death is placed in the Alps, battled in Circenn and cleared sword-land among the Picts; a variation on this legend claims that the Picts hired mercenaries from among the Gaels and settled them on sword-land.[52]

Angus appears in the Irish annals for the first time in the year 728 when he defeated Alpín son of Feret, and killed his son, in a battle fought at Moncrieff Hill (also known as Moredun Hill), which is a prominence 725 ft (220 m) above sea level about three miles south of Perth. The location of this battle both shows how communication lines were secured and also gives an indication of strategy. The hill is on a peninsula between the rivers Tay and Earn, and it is a passage between the Sidlaw and Ochil Hills; the high road from Edinburgh to Perth ran along the western shoulder. There are the remains of a fortress on the summit, which commands a panoramic view of the region. Whoever controlled this hill effectively controlled the movement of troops along the waterways and by the land routes. Little wonder that a note in the *Annals of Tigernach* claims that with his victory Angus took power, with the unspoken fact that Alpin was forced to submitted to Angus' overlordship. This

---

Scottish kings (f. 162c, see: O'Brien, *Corpus*: 328). On genealogies as a product of a literate scholarly class see Donnchadh Ó Corráin, "Creating the Past: The Early Irish Genealogical Tradition," *Peritia* 12 (1998): 177–208.

[51] Daniel A. Binchy (ed.), *Scéla Cano meic Gartnáin*: 18 and 38.

[52] For Dathí's battle in Circenn see *Yellow Book of Lecan* (Trinity College, Dublin, MS 1318): 192b25ff; the question of early Gaelic settlement on the eastern Scottish coast and its connection with place names is discussed in CPS: 217–220.

submission meant the payment of tribute (i.e. taxes), which left the vanquished with fewer resources. His reversal at Moncrieff Hill clearly contributed to Alpín's subsequent defeat later that year by Angus son of Fergus at the Fortress of Belief (Castellum Credi), which is probably the same place as the Hill of Belief at Scone; Nechtan took power. Angus' campaign for power south of the Grampians continued the next year, this time at the western end of what is now Perthshire when his army fought the *exactores* of Nechtan mac Deirili at *Monit Carno iuxta Stagnum Loogdae*, which has been identified as the vicinity of Lochan na Bí, near Tyndrum.[53] The battle must have been significant because the annalistic entry of it in the *Annals of Ulster* gives some of the names of the fallen in Nechtan's force and they included Bicoet son of Monet together with his son, Finguine son of Drostan, and Ferot son of Finguinne among others. Angus' army apparently drove Nechtan's forces up Strathearn and into Glen Drochet.[54] This is high country (the town of Tyndrum is situated 700 ft or 210 m above sea level) with little agricultural value other than grazing in the era before improvement, so why was there such an important confrontation in what appears to be a marginal district? As noted, there are mines in this area, especially of gold and lead, from which silver is extracted. In short, empire building in the north of Britain, as elsewhere in Europe, was driven more by long-term goals than is suggested by the brusque entries in the surviving records. This battle is the last record of Nechtan other than the notice of his death in 732.

Angus' success alarmed his neighbors and in 729 another rival, named Drust, attacked Angus in a battle at the Ridge of the Red Flowers (*Drum Derg Blathuug*), now Druim Dearg, about 20 miles west by northwest from Forfar in a river valley west of the river Isla in Forfarshire. This might have been on the border of the kingdom of Circenn, where a steep path, dropping from approximately 1200 ft (325 m) above sea level, comes into a level plain by the river. One interpretation is that Drust was deliberately choosing to approach Angus from the north because the defenders might expect an army to take the more southerly and easier route. Whatever his reasons, Drust was slain and, once more, Angus was victorious. By this time it was clear to everyone that Angus was the power north of the Forth. He had defended his home kingdom and had won victories as far west as the Ridge of Britain (*Druim Alban*) that marked the boundary with the lands of Dál Riata. He might not have been

[53] CPS: 50.
[54] CPS: 401–402.

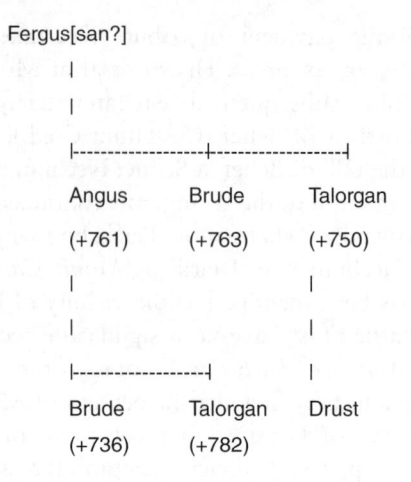

```
              Fergus[san?]
                   |
                   |
        |----------+----------|
      Angus      Brude     Talorgan
      (+761)     (+763)     (+750)
        |                     |
        |                     |
    |---------|               |
   Brude   Talorgan          Drust
   (+736)   (+782)
```

Lineage 3.3 Family of Angus Son of Fergus.

present at the battle fought near Tyndrum, for the annal entry is careful to say that it was Angus' army that was victorious. By this time, however, his ambitions might have been even greater. The *Annals of Tigernach* notice in the same year as his victory at Drum Derg that a fleet of 60 Pictish ships was lost off Ross Cussine (which seems to be Troup Head in Banffshire, nine miles east of Banff, between Macduff and Fraserburgh). This action might or might not have any connection with Angus, but if this fleet had been engaged in hostilities, the number of ships suggests more than a mere raid. The only notice of this fleet is in the so-called *Annals of Tigernach* and they give no indication of how the fleet met its end, but the choice of verb could indicate that it was shipwreck because of rough seas rather than interception by a defending force.

Having dismissed his rivals east of Druim Alban, Angus turned his attentions toward Dál Riata. He must have been a mature warrior by this time, for on those campaigns he was assisted by his son Brude in addition to his brother Talorgan (see Lineage 3.3). Another benefit for Angus was the dynastic battles within Dál Riata. The two main dynasties – Cenél Loairn and Cenél nGabráin – had been fighting each other for generations, a pastime that left both easy prey for any rival outside their kingdom. With the despatch of his rivals in the east, Angus turned his forces against Dál Riata in 731. Brude son of Angus defeated, first, Talorgan mac Congusso of Cenél nGabráin and then turned his attention to the rival dynasty of Cenél Loairn, now led by sons of the seventh-century prince Ferchar Fota (the Tall). Unsurprisingly in a society that glorified violence, Ferchar's sons

Selbach and Ainfcellach were each other's greatest rival and had devoted much of their energies to sibling destruction. Ainfcellach's son Muiredach had assumed the kingship of Cenél Loairn by 733, but Selbach's family remained in a position of power and his son Dungal waged a feud with Brude, the son of Angus. Initially Dungal had the better of it, and to escape his opponent, Brude fled to sanctuary in Ireland, first at Tory Island (off the coast of Donegal) and then at *insula Cuilén rígi* (possibly Inch, off the Inishowen peninsula). Both islands were in the territory of the powerful O'Neill kingdoms; the former in Cenél Conaill and the latter in Cenél nEógain, who earlier had defeated the forces of Dál Riata and may have been viewed by Brude as a safe haven; the suggestion has been offered that this reflects an alliance.[55] He was mistaken and Dungal violated both sanctuaries in pursuit of his foe. Fortunes were reversed the next year. A brusque entry in the Annals of Ulster claims that an unidentified force destroyed the Fort of the White Hill (Dun Lethfinn) in retaliation for Dungal's violation; he was forced to flee to Ireland to escape (as eloquently stated in the *Annals of Ulster*) from the power of Angus. Nevertheless, Ferchar's family proved to be less easy to overcome than Angus' eastern rivals; they even enjoyed some success against their opponents. One of these was the capture in 734 of Talorgan son of Drostan of Atholl who was chained in the tower at Dunollie, the main fortress of Cenél Loairn located just to the north of Oban. His capture might have been a result of border raiding or, as had been the case for the men of Gododdin at the battle of Catterick, Angus seems to have been campaigning with the help of allies, one of which was the unfortunate Talorgan. Two years later, in 736, Angus personally invaded Dál Riata and carried out a campaign of devastation. He destroyed whatever was at the ceremonial site at Dunadd, burned the fortress of Creic and captured Dungal together with his brother Feradach; both men were dragged off in chains. Despite these losses, Cenél Loairn was powerful and its forces did not stand idly by. They intercepted a force under the command of Angus' brother Talorgan at Cnuicc Coirpri in Calatros at Eddarlind where they were defeated. The location is uncertain and arguments have been made for the site of the battle in the area of Loch Awe, although other possibilities exist.[56] Angus' triumph was bitter-sweet, however, as his son Brude died that year. The ill-fated Talorgan

---

[55] Brian Lacey, "Fahan, Tory, Cenél nEógain and the Picts," *Peritia* 20 (2008): 331–345.
[56] The location of these sites is not clear despite Watson's arguments in favor of the area round Loch Awe; see CPS: 105–106.

of Atholl was released from captivity but sooner or later fell into the hands of Angus who had him drowned in 739. The defeat of Cenél Loairn by Angus' brother Talorgan brings up an interesting question: how did an empire-builder administer his domain? Talorgan was leading the army of Fortriu, which suggests that Angus was using a tactic common throughout the British Isles, that of setting up a family member in the kingship. Their powers must have been extensive and clearly Angus had confidence in his brother's ability as a field commander

His effort to conquer Dál Riata was still incomplete, so Angus launched a massive campaign in the west that the *Annals of Ulster* described as a *percussio* (hammering) of Dál Riata in 741. There is, however, no record of any capitulation. Furthermore, there is no further notice of Angus in Dál Riata, nor is there any further mention of Cenél Loairn for the eighth century. These two silences could be related, and the renewed supremacy in Dál Riata of Cenél nGabráin after 736 may be connected with Angus' campaigns, which seem to have been directed primarily against Cenél Loairn. If one were to suggest a date for the beginning of the move by at least some of Cenél Loairn forces up the Great Glen to the lands round the Moray Firth, then the mid-eighth century should be considered. The tenth-century *vita* of St. Catroe claims that the Scots moved into Ross as they expanded towards the east, and this might be a remembrance of the path taken by the people of Cenél Loairn as they moved out of Dál Riata.[57] Interestingly, the one dynasty that seems not to have faced Angus' army was the one that would dominate Dál Riata for the remainder of the century and produce the kings of the medieval Scottish kingdom – the family of Eochaid son of Echdach. Their location in the Kintyre peninsula may have ensured their future success. Angus' attacks on Dál Riata may have had an influence on Irish affairs. By the early eighth century there seems to have been an alliance between Dál Riata and the northern Uí Néill kingdom of Cenél Conaill. The latter suffered serious reverses and began its descent into obscurity until briefly re-emerging in the tenth century. Major attacks on Cenél Conaill's power in the Foyle basin were made by the Cenél nEógain prince Áed Allan between 732 and 734; and the absence of any provocation in Ireland has been explained by the impetus coming from Britain, with the attacks on Dál Riata by the forces of Angus son of Fergus at that time.[58]

[57] ESSH: i, 44n.
[58] T.M.O. Charles-Edwards, "The Ui Neill 695–743: the Rise and Fall of Dynasties," *Peritia* 16 (2002): 396–418 (pp. 408, 412, and 416).

After 741 Angus turned his attentions towards Strathclyde. For the year 744, the twelfth-century *Historia Regum* of Symeon of Durham, following an older northern chronicle, notes a battle with the men of Strathclyde that may be a misdated notice of the battle of *Cato* found in the *Annals of Ulster* among the events of 750, when Angus' army was led once again by his brother Talorgan.[59] This time, however, Angus' troops were defeated and Talorgan was slain. The defeat must have been overwhelming and possibly Angus was badly injured because there is a note in the *Annals of Ulster* claiming the "end of Angus' reign," while the continuation of Bede's history claims, erroneously, that Angus died.[60] His rivals may have been encouraged by this setback and two years later, in 752, there was an invasion of Angus' province of Circenn. A battle was fought at an unidentified place known only as *Asreith* where among the slain was a Brude son of Maelcon. Apparently Angus was the victor, because four years later he settled a remaining score, and he did it in the company of a new ally, Eadberht of Northumbria. Since the conclusion of Bede' *History* there had been a brief resurgence of Northumbrian power under the leadership of King Eadberht. Now, for the first time since the seventh century, the Northumbrians were annexing territory, this time along the coast of the North Channel in the region of Kyle, where Ayr is now located. In the year that Angus' army was defeated in the battle of Cato, Eadberht moved north from his lands in Galloway, in southwestern Scotland, to capture the Plain of Kyle in 750, completely encircling the southern bounds of Strathclyde. His ambitions were greater and, according to the *Historia Regum*, Eadberht allied with Angus in 756 for an attack on the Strathclyde fortress at Dumbarton. Nothing is known of the campaign other than its success for Eadberht and Angus; the men of Strathclyde were forced to surrender on August 1.[61] The entry continues with an obscure notice that, on the 10th of the same month, his army perished after moving from "Ovania" to Newburgh. The question of who moved and perished is uncertain, although a possible identification of the place names is that Ovania is Loch Owel and Newburgh is the

---

[59] See *Historia Regum*, in *Symeonis Monachi Opera Omnia*, ed. Thomas Arnold, 2 vols. (London, 1883–85): ii, 38. The battle is called Gueith Mocetauc in the *Annales Cambriae*, ed. J. Ab Ithel (London, 1860): 9; there Talorgan is styled king.
[60] *Baedae Continuatio*, s.a. 750, in *Venerabilis Baedae Opera Historica*: i, 362.
[61] *Historia Regum*: ii, 40–41.

town of the name on the western end of Fife. Angus died five years later in 760.[62]

If the information from Irish and English records is to be trusted, Angus was the most powerful monarch north of the Forth for almost a generation. Even though he had his setbacks, his empire stretched from the North Sea to the Hebrides. A question that needs to be asked is: how did Angus accomplish his empire-building? Any answer must be speculative, but the sheer magnitude of his achievement is impressive. He came from almost obscure circumstances, although, as noted above, the Fergussan son of Maelcon who died in 703 might be his father. One wonders if Angus had an ally who is revealed only tangentially, that is, Northumbria. Was the alliance between Angus and Eadberht in the last decade of the former's career merely a collaboration of convenience or was this a longer-standing arrangement? The *Book of Life* (*Liber Vitae*) that was maintained by the community of St. Cuthbert, then at Lindisfarne, has among the names of the mid-eighth century Ungus, the Old English rendition of Angus' name. What makes this significant is that Angus was not loved by the Northumbrians and the continuation to Bede's *History* calls him a murderer whose career was one of crime. The presence of Angus is significant because casual or occasional political allies were not included, only those who had some involvement with the church. To take the speculation farther, this could be another instance of the alliance building that so worried the Romans, and that is visible in the attack of Gododdin on the Angles of Northumbria, which was accomplished with individual warriors from outside the kingdom as well as with the cooperation of the kingdoms in what is now northern Wales. Like many empire-builders, his successors were not men of his caliber and Angus' domain fell apart quickly. As will be discussed in another chapter, three years later in 763 died a Brude who is styled King of Fortriu, showing that at least one of Angus' satellites had regained its independence. We would like to know more about the Cinadon who died in 774 and was, according to Symeon of Durham, the host of the exiled Northumbrian prince Alhred of Bernicia. The last of Angus' children, called Dubtholargg (Dark Talorg) died in 782 and his obit in the *Annals of Ulster* styles him "king of the Picts on this side of the mountains [*citra Month*]."

---

[62] The *Annals of Tigernach* have two announcements of his death, once in 758 where he is styled *rí Alban* (which at this date means "a king of Britain") and the other among the events of 760 where he is styled *rex Pictorum*.

Summary

Combining the admittedly few and not always informative source materials gives a picture of northern Britain as a busy place by the sixth century. Immigrants were settling and challenging the existing order. On the eastern coast the Angles were pushing into the lands north of the river Humber. By the end of the sixth century they would be fighting for the lands from Hadrian's Wall as far north as the Firth of Forth. In the next century they moved west to the Solway Firth and occupied the lands round the northeastern shores of the Irish Sea. On the other shore of Britain were immigrants from Ireland in the kingdom known as Dál Riata. The Irish homeland, also known as Dál Riata, was opposite the lands they inhabited in Britain, 13 miles (21 km) across the North Channel, and the British branch continued to be involved in Irish affairs. While the circumstances, dates, and even composition of the immigration remain areas for speculation, later materials claim that the royal dynasties moved to Britain sometime during the fifth century. This was only one of several groups of peoples who took lands in Britain during what seems to have been a series of population movements from Ireland. Why they emigrated is a question that is answered in various ways according to the legend consulted. One reason among several is they might have been settled in Britain by the northern kingdoms as mercenaries or allies against the foreign foes such as the Romans or hereditary enemies. As noted earlier, Bede writes that Iona was given to Columba by Brude son of Maelcon. While he ties the grant to the conversion of Brude and his people, since the island was actually within the territory of Dál Riata this could be an indication that the church was within Brude's territory and that he was adapting the Roman tactic of using mercenaries.

By the end of the sixth century the savages of the Roman imagination emerge as individuals of sophistication and nuance. When Columba visited the court of King Brude he found a prince who could be tolerant and diplomatically minded. Even though the king's foster-father, the *magus* Broichan, was the saint's spiritual adversary, the two men met as intellectual equals. Any study of political affairs at this date is tentative and speculation too often must substitute for definitive statements. Only for a brief period is there sufficient material to allow even for conjecture and this is largely connected with the career of Angus son of Fergus. What is clear is how fluid the political situation was in northern Britain. Alliances were made and broken as circumstances or opportunity dictated. Through much of the seventh century the power broker in the north was Strathclyde. While the Northumbrians were able to dismantle the kingdoms of Gododdin and Rheged, they were unable to disturb Strathclyde until the mid-eighth century, and then only in a general rising of the north.

The career of Angus brings into focus the Irish expansion across the north of Britain. The appearance of men with Irish names and the identification of a kingdom called Ath Fotla or New Ireland, now spelled Atholl, remind us that not all the Irish were on the west coast in Dál Riata. The movement of people that accompanied the decline of Roman power in northern Europe occurred beyond Hadrian's Wall and the establishment of the Irish colony from Dál Riata was merely one of several settlements in Britain made from Ireland. The expansion of Christianity through the missionary efforts of Columba of Iona might have had a political aspect, but this is hard to justify using the *Life of Columba* by Adomnán. What becomes abundantly clear is that the sixth to eighth centuries were a period of political shifting and population movement. Much of the movement was by the political elites, and any changes would have been slow. The son of a king of Strathclyde ruling Fortriu or the appearance of a kingdom called New Ireland are warnings against complacency about "racial purity" in northern Britain. Whether or not one was a Pict was largely a matter of location and local culture. The Scots would implement legislation in the ninth and early tenth centuries to bring the local laws and the church into line with the administration with which they were familiar, even though individuals descended from Gaels had held power in Pictland for generations.

4

People and Work

A memorable episode in Adomnán's *Life of Columba* is the saint's visit to the court of the King Brude son of Maelcon, probably located somewhere near modern Inverness Castle. There he learned that the *magus* Broichan, the king's foster-father, had a slave girl who was a Christian. Columba requested that she be released, but this bid for her freedom, made purely on humanitarian terms, was refused. Columba warned Broichan that he would repent his decision and seek out his aid before he had returned to his boats. All happened as the saint predicted. Immediately after the departure of Columba, Broichan apparently suffered a seizure and messengers were sent to find the company from Iona before they began their trip home, offering to free the girl if the saint would cure the *magus*. Columba produced a white stone and prescribed that it be dropped into water that Broichan drank; the instructions were obeyed and the *magus* recovered.

A common episode in Christian literature – saintly power mocked and subsequently publicly acknowledged – usefully begins the topic of people and society. Society in the north of Britain, like all societies in Europe, was status-conscious, based primarily on ancestry. The status of one's parents determined the class into which one was born, which determined whether one's life would be characterized by relative comfort or ceaseless toil. The three orders in the familiar division of medieval society – those who pray (*oratores*), those who fight (*bellatores*), and those who work (*laboratores*) – are all embodied in this episode. The *oratores* are represented by Columba as a member of the clergy, and they are discussed in the following chapter. The *bellatores* are Brude and Broichan as members

The Picts, First Edition. Benjamin Hudson.
© 2014 John Wiley & Sons, Ltd. Published 2014 by John Wiley & Sons, Ltd.

of the aristocracy. Brude represents the apex of society, the king, who is the head of an inwardly mobile tier of society, as demonstrated by Broichan's fosterage of him. At the bottom of society were the unfree peasants and slaves, such as the unnamed Christian slave girl. With her, this passage illustrates the problem of attempting to study the great mass of individuals, those who work. Although the slave girl is the subject of the episode, nothing is known about her: no name, no history, and no idea of what happened after she was freed.

Kinds of People: Royalty and Aristocracy

The people for whom most information remains were the ones who ruled society, the aristocrats such as the nobles and kings. The records of western European societies during the early Middle Ages are dominated by those at the pinnacle, be they kings, emperors, or chieftains. Whether it was the invader interested in his foe, the cleric seeking a patron to donate land and materials or the poet looking for a generous sponsor, all turned their gaze towards the leader of the community. The earliest information about society's organization in Britain comes from two treatises by Roman writers: Julius Caesar's *Gallic Wars*, the carefully edited account of his campaigns in Britain in 55 and 54 BC; and Tacitus' history of his father-in-law Agricola. Tacitus habitually refers to the British princes as "kings" (*reges*); both he and Caesar note that they are independent, but in times of war could unite under a single leader. Moving to northern Britain, Tacitus singles out Calgacus who commanded the forces of the northern peoples in their unsuccessful attempt to defeat the Romans at *Mons Craupius*, and gives him one of the most stirring speeches made against the Romans. For the inhabitants of the north of Britain he mentioned that there were two main divisions – the Caledonians and the Maeatae – which suggests that these were the groupings that appeared in times of war when the smaller kingdoms needed to cooperate. Even though the name of only one female war leader – Boadicea – is known, Tacitus claims that either men or women could succeed to the kingship.

Chronicles and historical narratives show that there were various grades of kings among the Picts similar to those found among the Irish and the Welsh. These different levels of status explain why there were sub-kings as well as kings. Within individual kingdoms the nature of the office of kingship had the same sacral and political aspects. Between realms, however, the relationship of one prince to another could vary.

So an "under-king," such as the client-king (*regulus*) ruling in the Orkneys who was in attendance on Brude when Columba was present, had all the sacred and secular attributes of his overlord even though he had less political power. The difference in power could be major. A brutal demonstration is visible in 739 when Angus son of Fergus ordered the drowning of his *subregulus*, the king of *Athfotla*.

Unlike the later Middle Ages when some idea of the early life of an aristocrat can be gleaned from household accounts or personal memoirs, very little can be said about the childhood or training of even royalty for the earlier period, other than the occasional anecdote. As was common in other northern European societies, such as the Irish, the Picts practiced fosterage, in which a child was raised by a family other than the biological one. Fosterage was used, at least in part, as a diplomatic tool, uniting families through the agency of a child. In Ireland, the emotional ties between child and foster-parent frequently were closer than those with his or her biological parents. Adomnán refers to Broichan's fosterage of Brude, which explains why the former had such a prominent position at the royal court. The *vita* of St. Cainnech has the story of the daughter of a king of Picts who was blind, deaf, and dumb. Her foster-parents (*nutritores*) brought the child to the saint who healed her.[1]

Duties of a prince consisted of defending his people and maintaining order within the kingdom. The military aspect is the usual fodder of traditional history, with its emphasis on battles. Kings led their troops not just to defend their realm, but also to expand its borders or their influence with campaigns of conquest, domination, or simply to raid their neighbors in order to enrich their followers. The last is the usual explanation for the attack on the Picts leading to the expedition to Dun Nechtan led by the Northumbrian king Ecgfrith in 685; his earlier expedition to Ireland apparently was undertaken for the same purpose. In a less aggressive method of paying for his government, the lord levied dues, usually described as taxes. One incident suggests the collection was a sign of lordship in a particular area when, in 729, the *exactores* (tax collectors) of Nechtan were slain by his rival Angus son of Fergus. Collection was considered a sign of power, and the *Prophecy of Berchán* gives the sobriquet of "tax-collector" to Kenneth son of Alpin, the man credited with the union of the Picts and Scots in medieval records.[2] The mode of payment of dues probably varied, but if the types of goods paid to the

---

[1] *Vita Sanctorum Hiberniae*, ed. Charles Plummer, 2 vols. (Oxford, 1910): i, 159.
[2] Benjamin Hudson, *Prophecy of Berchan* (Westport, 1996): 42.

Scots kings in the twelfth century was similar to those paid in the eighth, then livestock and processed foods were used. King David I received cheese, wheat, and swine as his taxes.[3]

Taxes paid for the support of the prince and his court in a public display of hospitality or largess. These were visual reminders that the prince was socially different from his subjects and, consequently, was able to live and interact with them in a certain way. One of these ways was the public exhibition of status when a subordinate visited the court of the overlord and there, in view of the community, demonstrated his inferior position. An informative illustration comes from the famous speech of St. Columba to King Brude, asking him to entrust (*commendare*) to his subordinate, the king of the Orkney Islands, the safety of a missionary named Cormac if he happened to land into that king's domain.[4] Since the Orcadian king was present at the time, that public performance both acknowledged Brude's power and also made clear to his under-king what was being requested. The choice of the Latin word *commendare* is important, because it implies that Brude could command his sub-king to see that it was done, but did not need to enforce it himself. So he passed to the king of the Orkney Islands responsibility for the well-being of any of Columba's monks.

A further aspect to this meeting was the right of a prince to regulate his borders, to say who could and who could not enter his domain. Adomnán includes the aside that Columba was wise to act as he did, otherwise Cormac would have been slain if he had been found on the islands without the king's permission. A stranger was especially vulnerable because he had no kindred to oversee his safety. In the story of Conall Corc the ogams on his shield were a letter of introduction, initially deadly but, after they were altered, beneficial. Later in the Middle Ages the prince's protection of a particular class of stranger – the merchant or trader – became a standard feature of commercial treaties and the royal court undertook to hear any complaints. The right to control admission extended to communities as well as individuals. When King Nechtan expelled the Columban community in 717 across the Ridge of Britain he was simply exercising his prerogative to allow or forbid residence within his realm.

---

[3] ESC: 82.
[4] Adomnán, *Life of Columba*, ed. A.O. Anderson and M.O. Anderson (Oxford, 1991): 166.

Display of status, personal safety, and the reception of visitors had to be in a suitable locale in a fortress or some type of defensive work safe from predators. There were various types of stronghold. One of these is the hill fort, which begins to appear about the fifth century BC; their remains are found throughout Atlantic Europe north of the Pyrenees. Caesar remarked on these hilltop enclosures, calling them *oppida* (sing. *oppidum*). The defensive benefits are obvious. A prominent hill fortress was Dundurn, which was built after the withdrawal of the Roman administration from Britain and later was used by the Scots; the ninth-century prince Giric is associated with it.[5] This type of fort used to be known as a "nuclear" fort, in which the construction used the existing land formations in order to secure the defenses, which were usually a series of earthen walls and ditches. The same idea is also found in a simpler type of construction from post-Roman period, such as the stronghold at the Mote of Mark, in Galloway. There was also re-use of earlier forts, in which an inner secure place or dun was built within an earlier series of fortifications. The construction of these buildings could be intricate. Timber, for example, could be used in addition to earth and stone in the building of the forts. The fortress of Dumbarton used upright timbers that were tied to horizontal beams to secure the face of the wall, while at other places the wooden pieces were nailed together to hold them in place, as at Dundurn and Burghead.[6] This type of wall is called a Gallic Wall (*Muris Gallicus*). Less elaborate in construction is the dun, a small compact fortified structure usually made of stone, in which boulders form the outer part of the wall surrounding an inner core of rubble. Examples of this fortress are found at Dumyat and King's Seat, Dunkeld.[7] The physical geography also influenced the type of fortress, such as the peninsular fort. A peninsular fortress stood on ground that was surrounded on several sides by water, a natural defense. While usually limited in space, some could cover an extensive area of land. A good example is Burghead jutting into the Moray Firth, which was extensively damaged

---

[5] L. Alcock, E.A. Alcock, and S. Driscoll, "Reconnaissance Excavations on Early Historic Fortifications and Other Royal Sites in Scotland 1974–84, 3: Excavations at Dundurn, St. Fillians, Perthshire," PSAS 119 (1989): 189–220.

[6] L. Alcock and E.A. Alcock, "Reconnaissance Excavations on Early Historic fortifications and Other Royal Sites in Scotland 1974–84, 4: Excavations at Alt Clut, Clyde Rock, Strathclyde, 1974–75," PSAS 120 (1990): 108–110; K.J. Edwards and I.B.M. Ralston, *Scotland after the Ice Age* (Edinburgh, 2003): 225.

[7] R.W. Feachem, "Hill-forts of Northern Britain," in A.L.F. Rivet (ed.), *The Iron Age in Northern Britain* (Edinburgh, 1966): 70.

in the nineteenth century, but clearly covered at least six acres. Another example is Dunnottar castle (see Figure 3.1), just south of Stonehaven, extending into the North Sea. The population within these forts might have been dense and they would have depended on a reliable source of water. Burghead has a subterranean well/cistern measuring roughly 16×12 ft (4.9×3.6 m).

Whether or not a fortress contained the permanent residence of a lord is not always clear because many of these strongholds appear to be uncomfortable and restricted. Nonetheless, possession of the fortress was a visible sign of lordship, and ease could have been sacrificed to expediency. According to Adomnán's *Life of Columba*, Brude's royal court was inside the fortress and the king left his house (*domus*) to greet Columba after the latter had forced open the doors in the fortress' gates, which were secured with crossbars.[8] Another personal residence inside a fortress is suggested when St. Buite supposedly resurrected a king named Nechtan at his fortress, possibly Kirkbuddo near Forfar.[9]

The building of a fortress, and its occupation, might take place over a long period of time. One example is at Traprain Law where the original fort was built in the Neolithic Age, after which it was modified, then gradually enlarged to an open settlement of about 40 acres during the Roman period. When the Votadini (i.e., the Gododdin) made it their capital they built a wall around it early in the fifth century before abandoning it.[10] Sometimes the habitation of a site varied, such as the now-destroyed fortress at Clatchard Craig where Neolithic and Iron Age pottery were found, but the buildings seem to have been begun in the sixth century AD.[11] Construction or refurbishment could go on for a long time. Building at Burghead, for example, seems to have begun in the fifth or sixth century and continued into the seventh.[12] There is an even longer time frame for Dunnottar, which continued to be used as a military installation into the seventeenth century. Some of these fortifications could have dense populations by the standards of the day. The main fortress or *caput*

---

[8] Adomnán, *Life of Columba*: 146.
[9] *Vita Sanctorum Hiberniae*: i, 88–89; and Benjamin Hudson, "Kings and Church in Early Scotland," SHR 73 (1994): 145–170 (at p. 147).
[10] Richard Muir, *Shell Guide to Reading the Celtic Landscape* (London, 1985): 199.
[11] Joanna Close-Brooks, "Excavations at Clatchard Craig, Fife" PSAS 116 (1986): 117–184.
[12] Muir, *Reading the Celtic Landscape*: 200.

of the people known as the Segovae near Melrose at Elidon Hill North was enlarged twice and eventually contained 300 houses.[13]

The lord presided over the hall or court, referred to in Latin sources as the *aula*. This might be the residence within the fortress or it might be a separate structure, where he entertained his retinue and visitors, using the food taxes that he collected from his subjects. The remains of two timbered halls have been uncovered at Doon Hill in East Lothian; the earlier structure, Hall A, is dated to the sixth century, contemporary with the events described in the poem Y *Gododdin*.[14] What remains of the layout of this hall is reminiscent of the plan of the king's hall that is preserved in the twelfth-century Irish *Book of Leinster* with its stylized placement of individuals by function and status.[15] Entertainment was usually in the form of performances either in verses recited by poets or the telling of stories; among the Irish was a canon of stories that were appropriate for recitation, of which a list of titles is preserved in the *Book of Leinster* (see chapter 8). Y *Gododdin* has a line of verse where the poet recited the *Lay of the son of Dwywai* and continues with the complaint that poetry and the men of Gododdin have been parted since the death of Aneirin.[16] Music was also part of the expected entertainment, and there are images of different instruments on the decorated stones. The harp seems to have been a popular instrument, such as the one on the symbol stone at Brechin (see Figure 4.1). Earliest representations of true harps are found on the symbol stones, both small harps that rested on the leg and larger instruments that sat upon the floor such as that on the Dupplin Cross. The triple pipe was found throughout the British Isles and a Pictish example is found on a stone at Lethendy. A cymbal on the stone at Nigg might have been copied from an exemplar, but there is no reason why it was not used as a musical instrument. Also at the court were the visible rewards of domination, as the prince dispensed gifts, bestowed favors or was available to hear the petitions of his subjects. At one time or another most luxury goods passed through the court. Broichan the *magus* was drinking from a glass vessel when he suffered his seizure and sent a request for help from Columba. Within these halls took place the ritual gift-exchange that bound

---

[13] Muir, *Reading the Celtic Landscape*: 200.
[14] Edwards and Ralston, *Scotland after the Ice Age*: 227.
[15] R.I. Best, Osborn Bergin, M.A. O'Brien, and Anne O'Sullivan (eds.), *Book of Leinster, formerly Lebar na Núachongbála*, 6 vols. (Dublin, 1954–83): i, 116, with facing fascsimile of *Tech Midchúarda*.
[16] Kenneth Jackson, *The Gododdin* (Edinburgh, 1969): 99.

102 People and Work

Figure 4.1 A harp from Brechin Stone. Photo Robert Hudson.

individuals and were a sign of one's place in the community. King Brude had a treasury (*thesauris regis*) where he kept treasures such as the floating white stone that Columba sent to revive the *magus* Broichan after his seizure.[17] Inventories might have been kept of these goods, because the stone was sought after Brude's death, but not found.

Succession to High Office

Associated with lordship are the sites where the inauguration or king-making took place. A well-known example in northern Britain is the "moot-hill" of Scone that is situated on a hill overlooking the river Tay adjacent to the confluence with the river Almond. Here were conducted the ceremonies for the making of the Scots king certainly by the later Middle Ages and this seems to have been a continuation since a much earlier period. A place known as *Taba* (i.e., the river Tay) is included

[17] Adomnán, *Life of Columba*: 142.

among a diverse list of place names in the Roman geographical guide known as the *Ravenna Cosmography*, a seventh-century compilation of names taken from various sources such as Roman road books, and it has been suggested that the names outside Roman jurisdiction are those of assembly areas.[18] A verse in the Old Irish poem *Columba's Breastplate* (*Amra Coluim Chille*) refers to the kings of tribes shouting round the river Tay, possibly a reference to a king-making ceremony in which the nobility assent to the selection of the newly made king.[19] Present during inaugural ceremonies would have been an assembly of warriors. Prior to the emigration of the Scots into Argyllshire it is possible that the local peoples used a mound more famously connected with the Scots, the hill of Dunadd in the Moss of Crinan. On top of the hill is the outline of a foot in stone and the image of a boar; later tales claim that the prince placed his foot within the stone outline to show that he would walk in the way of his ancestors. The idea of placing a foot on a sacred or special stone is elaborated in an Irish pseudo-prophecy now known as the *Phantom's Frenzy* (*Baile in Scáil*) where the prehistoric King Conn "of the Hundred Battles" steps on a stone that screeches the number of his descendants who will be king. Magic stones could be big or small and they are often found in Irish legends. The most famous was Lia Fail, the pillar at Tara that supposedly screamed when a true king placed his chariot wheel against it. The tale *Fled Dúin na nGéd* has a stone that refuses to be moved if a falsehood is said.[20]

Ceremonial drinks as a part of the inaugural ceremony were used by the Irish and there is some evidence that they were used in northern Britain as well. *Cuirm* was the name of the ale that conferred kingship among the Irish. In Leinster, for example, *cuirm* was brewed in the region of Cuála, an area round the river Dodder (in what is now the south of Dublin city) and drinking it bestowed on a prince the legitimacy of rule. Returning to the *Phantom's Frenzy*, the Phantom's request for a list of the kings is answered by a woman representing the sovereign spirit of Ireland who prefaces the name of the individual prince with the statement that she pours for him "a portion of the red ale" of lordship.

---

[18] I.A. Richmond, "Ancient Geographical Sources for Britain North of Cheviot," in I.A. Richmond (ed.), *Roman and Native in North Britain* (London, 1958): 131–149 (at p. 148); a transcript of the relevant section is at p. 155.

[19] A version is printed in P.L. Henry, *Saoithiúlacht na Sean-Ghaeilge* (Dublin, 1978): 195.

[20] R. Lehman, *Fled Dúin na nGéd*, *Lochlann* 4 (1969): 131–159 (at p. 158).

Sometime in the eighth century a poet made a tour of Ireland and northern Britain. As a remembrance of his journey he composed a poem on the different ales that he consumed and the resulting Old Irish poem is now embedded in *The Tale of Cano the Son of Gartnan (Scéla Cano meic Gartnáin)*.[21] The different ales represent different kingdoms and the poet's journey took him to northern Britain where, during his visit to eastern Scotland, in the kingdom of Circenn he was given a drink that tasted like wine: "Bitter ales of the Saxons round Inber in Rí; round the fields of the Cruithne of Circenn, red ale like wine."[22] There were various ingredients used for making ales in northern Britain, one of which was the sap of birch trees that required only a quarter allowance of malt, while another recipe used the aleberry.[23] Drinking utensils might have been similar to the drinking horn of which an image is found on a slab from Bullion (Invergowrie) as a mounted man drinks from a horn that ends with a bird's head.[24]

A question that has dominated the discussion of succession to the lordship among the Picts is: how was a king selected? The question needs to be asked because of a comment made by the Venerable Bede. At the very beginning of his *Ecclesiastical History* (I.i) he relates a legend explaining the origins of the Picts. After the Picts left their homeland in Scythia, they arrived in the British Isles and settled in Ireland. The Irish were unwilling to allow them to remain so they advised the Picts to win land for themselves in Britain, a conquest that the Irish would support. After the Picts followed that advice and won land for themselves in the north of Britain, they sent a request for wives to the Irish, which the latter provided on the condition that whenever the succession to the kingship was in doubt (*ut ubi res veniret in dubium*), the king should be selected from the female rather than male line. Bede concludes by noting that the custom continued to his own day. Speculation on the precise meaning of his words has ranged from the measured to the lunatic together with efforts to rearrange early eighth-century history to accommodate his words. Interpretations of this passage have generally followed one of three lines of reasoning. The first is that the Picts practiced matriliny,

[21] D.L. Binchy (ed.), *Scéla Cano meic Gartnáin* (Dublin, 1975): 18.
[22] Binchy, *Scéla Cano meic Gartnáin*: 18.
[23] C. Anne Wilson, *Food and Drink in Britain* (Harmondsworth, 1976): 342 and 348.
[24] R.B.K. Stevenson, "The Inchyra Stone and Other Unpublished Early Christian Monuments," PSAS 92 (1958/59): 33–55 (at p. 44).

which means that they consistently chose a ruler from the female rather than male line. Those who believe that the Picts practiced strict matrilineal succession point to the king-lists, with the observation that no man in that list has his name used as a patronymic by his successor.[25] The trust reposed in the king-lists must be tempered with the recognition that they are collections of materials that, in their present form, were composed centuries after the collapse of the Pictish kingdoms (the earliest surviving manuscript dates from the fourteenth century) and that they contain the rulers of several kingdoms. The second argument, that this practice was occasional, relies on the phrase "when the matter was in doubt." This has led to the close scrutiny of specific times and particular reigns, such as that of Bede's contemporary Nechtan; in support there have been compiled intricate charts to show that the statement was concerned with a couple of particular examples.[26] The third view is that Bede meant what he said, but that he was referring to something that was also used by other insular societies – Irish and Welsh – at that time (except the Anglo-Saxons), where the candidate with the better maternal connections had an advantage if all else was equal.[27]

Bede's statement must be given serious consideration as he claims that the practice was being used even as he wrote. While most of the discussion has revolved round the interpretation of Bede's somewhat cryptic comment, there has been little interest in placing it into some type of context. No one before Bede has anything to say about the succession to high office among the Picts, and after him there is mere repetition of his statement with the elaboration increasing with the chronological distance of the writer.[28] When reading the verses emanating from peoples south of the Forth or Clyde (such as *Y Gododdin* or the material connected with the shadowy King Urien of Rheged) the implication is of a patriarchal society. The same is true for Bede's contemporary Abbot Adomnán of Iona, whose description of the Picts in his *Life of Columba*

---

[25] Molly Miller, "Matriliny by Treaty: The Pictish Foundation Legend," in Dorothy Whitelock, Rosamond McKitterick, and David Dumville (eds.), *Ireland in Early Mediaeval Europe: Studies in Memory of Kathleen Hughes* (Cambridge, 1981): 133–161.
[26] T.O. Clanchy, "Philosopher-King: Nechtan mac Der-Ilei," SHR 83 (2004): 135–149.
[27] KCS: 10–11.
[28] G. Mac Eoin, "On the Irish Legend of the Origin of the Picts," *Studia Hibernica* 4 (1964): 138–154.

has no information concerning any unusual method(s) of succession to the kingship. The description of the origins of the Picts found in the contemporary prologue to *Senchus Mar* has the Picts making their journey from Thrace rather than Bede's Scythia, but their alliance with the Irish does not lead to any stipulations. The only writer who suggests anything is Gildas and he merely states that the Picts and Irish were united in villainy although they had different customs.

A useful approach might be to reverse the inquiry and look at what was normal among the Anglo-Saxons during Bede's lifetime. There was an increasing interest in the status of a king's mother among the Anglo-Saxons during the eighth century as the church attempted to encourage princes to behave according to biblical strictures, a difficult quest that was not entirely successful anywhere throughout the Middle Ages. Pope Gregory II (r.715–731) sent a letter to the Anglo-Saxon missionary Boniface in 726 which discusses both the permissible degrees of wedlock and whether or not a man might put away a wife who was too ill to allow him his marriage rights; he returns to the topic of second marriages in his announcement of investing Boniface with the *pallium*.[29] A letter of 743 from Pope Zacharias to Boniface addresses the complicated problem of a nephew who wanted to marry his aunt who previously had been married to her cousin.[30] This helps to explain why, in his letter to King Aethelbald of Mercia, Boniface begins his list of complaints with the king's irregular union, which led to the insistence that Anglo-Saxon kings had to be selected from the children of legitimate marriages, rather than casual liaisons.[31] While worries about illegitimate unions were not new, prohibitions must have been difficult to enforce and would explain Bede's sensitivity to the role of the mother in succession among the Picts. An indication of the difficulty is suggested by an illuminating example from one of the clauses in a report of papal legates to Pope Hadrian in 786. In a meeting with King Aelfwold of Northumbria and Archbishop Eanbald of York, Bishop George of Ostia produced documents containing various regulations to be observed, among which there was a regulation concerning the succession to the kingship. Here the instruction is that kings were to be chosen by priests and elders of the people (i.e., the aristocracy), but a specific direction is that kings were not to be born in

---

[29] English translations are printed by C.H. Talbot, *Anglo-Saxon Missionaries in Germany* (New York, 1954): 80–83 and 84–87.
[30] Talbot, *Anglo-Saxon Missionaries*: 102–106.
[31] Talbot, *Anglo-Saxon Missionaries*: 120–126.

adultery or incest; only men from lawful marriages were to be made kings.[32] Although the mother's status among the Anglo-Saxons seems to have been casual, in Irish and British societies the more elevated a woman's personal rank, the more it ensured her son's success in claiming the kingship. This was a practical matter because a woman whose family was wealthy and held high position could devote more resources to her son than a woman who had been a slave. In polygamous societies there could be two or more male competitors, both children of the preceding king, who were of equal age and ability; in that situation the son whose mother had the higher status was chosen. In addition, other close male relatives could also be eligible and the so-called Laws of Hywel Dda go so far as to claim that the *edling* or heir could be a son or brother or nephew.[33] A study of contemporary Welsh practice concludes that if a male heir was not old enough, then a man maternally related to the royal family could be selected.[34] Both societies had customs similar to Bede's description of succession among the Picts – that is, if two men were sons of the same father, then the son of the woman with higher rank would have precedence; in other words, the son of a princess was to be preferred to the son of a slave.[35] There is no indication that in either Strathclyde or Gododdin was matrilineal succession practiced. As mentioned above, the mother did have an influence, but the main consideration was a candidate's male forebears.

Finally, customs often are more honored in the breach than in the observance. Ambitious men in a society that glorified confrontation and violence were unlikely to be too fastidious in their observance of inconvenient traditions, which could be adjusted to fit new circumstances. There were many in any society who might desire a share of the wealth and power of an office such as king and be willing to throw

---

[32] Arthur Haddan and William Stubbs, *Councils and Ecclesiastical Documents Relating to Great Britain and Ireland*, 3 vols. (Oxford, 1869–78): iii, 447–462; and E. Dümmler, "*Alcuini Epistolae*," in MGH, *Epistolae Karl. Aevi*: II, 3.

[33] A.W. Wade-Evans, *Welsh Medieval Law* (Oxford, 1909): 3 and 148 (V2a23–V2b1). On the matter of Welsh eligibility see T.M.O. Charles-Edwards, *Early Irish and Welsh Kinship* (Oxford, 1993): 216–225.

[34] Charles-Edwards, *Early Irish and Welsh Kinship*: 99–100.

[35] See Norah Chadwick, *Celtic Britain* (Newcastle, CA, repr. 1989): 82, where she cites the Laws of Hywel Dda that a king could nominate his successor, be he brother, son, or nephew. See also the observations of James Hogan, "The Irish Law of Kingship, with Special Reference to Ailech and Cenél Eoghain," *Proceedings of the Royal Irish Academy* 40 C (1932): 186–254 (p. 254).

Figure 4.2 Detail of weapons on Aberlemno Cross-slab no. 2. Photo Robert Hudson.

in their lot with anyone who offered a change that could profit them. Apart from (one interpretation of) Bede's comment there is no reason to believe that the Picts practiced matrilineal succession. In short, a strict reading of Bede implies that the female lineage was brought into play only in unusual circumstances, which was true among the Irish and British. Bede was in a better position to know the truth of the matter than modern writers.

Below the kings were the aristocrats who governed the smaller divisions of the kingdom. The nobles constituted local government and they were the king's representatives. In addition, from their ranks came the higher church officials who administered the spiritual life of the neighborhood. Military service was expected and battles were commemorated in verse, such as the description of the individual combats at the battle of Catterick in *Y Gododdin*. Commemoration also extended to art, and aristocratic patronage explains why there is the attention to detail in weapons and horses on, for example, the battle-scene carving on the stone in Aberlemno churchyard (see Figure 4.2). As was not unusual for a class that justified its existence through fighting, war was not the only

Figure 4.3 Two men fighting, Glamis no. 2. Photo Robert Hudson.

opportunity for violence. There were personal rivalries and another stone from Glamis shows two men fighting a duel (see Figure 4.3). Unlike the peasants whose labor on the land was essential to the community, the nobles were more easily, and profitably, expelled. There is the example of the unfortunate Tarain, a noble whose flight to Columba was remembered by Adomnán in his *Life of Columba*.[36] The reason why Tarain fled to Columba is never specifically stated, but the saint sent him to join the entourage of a noble of Dál Riata named Feradach of Islay. Feradach, in turn, caused him to be murdered. There is little reason to doubt the essential truth of the story; it has too many details for a casual fabrication and no obvious reason for it. Finding protection with a powerful

[36] Adomnán, *Life of Columba*: 126.

warrior was not uncommon nor was that sanctuary's violation. Returning to the events of the year 733, the trust placed in sanctuary on Tory Island by Brude son of the powerful Angus son of Fergus was unfortunate since it was ignored by his rival Dungal the son of Selbach of Dál Riata, according to the *Annals of Ulster*. Unsuccessful in his first attempt, Dungal also violated sanctuary at the island of *Culenrigi* or Inch Island off Inishowen (County Donegal).

Kinds of People: Commoners

The majority of people belonged to the class about which we know the least: the peasants, commoners, or ordinary folk. They did not lead armies or endow churches or pay for works of art, so they usually lived and died in obscurity, unnamed and unmourned in any historical record. All is not lost, however, and the common folk did leave remembrances of themselves in traces of their homes and the debris from their daily lives. Nor are they completely absent from the written records, although when they do appear it is perhaps as an unnamed character in a hagiographical episode or possibly an incidental figure in a carving such as one of the huntsmen in the panel on the Shandwick stone.[37]

Unlike the settlements round churches or the strongholds of the powerful, identifying the dwellings of the humble is more difficult and one of the many problems of studying the early Middle Ages. Although much has been done in recent decades, compared with the numerically fewer clergy and aristocracy combined there are relatively few of their homes found. Even after they have been located, without the happy discovery of some artifact or material that can be assigned a date, it is often difficult, if not impossible, to assign them to a specific century, much less a precise period of years. There is the additional problem of datable materials that were not native to the region. Driftwood, for example, was incorporated into buildings in the Northern Isles and Outer Hebrides beyond the time span of this enquiry, from possibly as early as the late Neolithic to the Viking Age.[38] Architectural style is less help than might be thought, because there is a variation in construction that reflects the

---

[37] ECMS: ii, 72.
[38] N. Fojut, *Guide to Prehistoric and Viking Shetland* (Lerwick, 1993): 22; A. Small, "Excavations at Underhoull, Unst, Shetland," PSAS 98 (1966): 225–248.

available materials. The smaller flagstones suitable for building in the Shetland Islands, for example, reflect the geology of the area.[39]

Sometimes a building popularly associated with the Picts had passed out of use by the medieval period. The prime example is the broch, a tall, circular, fortified structure with an interior courtyard usually found above an imaginary line of 45° extending from the Hebrides to the Moray Firth. Defense appears to have been its primary purpose; a family could safely stable their livestock inside the broch while remaining above the herd or flock on a wooden platform. These structures appear initially in the Hebrides in the first century AD and are found mainly in a line north of the Great Glen. Many of the brochs were built on the coasts near havens. They seem to have been abandoned as dwellings about the year 300, although homes later were built close to them, and apparently they continued to be used as "bolt-holes." So the end of the broch era coincides with the first references to Picts. The brochs' communication with the sea might explain why some of the remains found inside them are reminiscent of those found in the south of Britain. For example, the inhabitants of the broch made their clothes using equipment similar to that found in Glastonbury and relaxed by playing dice with cubes like those found in Somerset. Farming and metal-working were the trades of the broch-dwellers. Since the soils are better at sea-inlets than the surrounding areas, these were prized farms where barley was grown and short-horned cattle, pigs, goats, sheep, and horses raised.[40]

Found in the same general area as the broch is another type of subterranean or semi-subterranean home called a "wheel house." These are structures of great antiquity and an example is the famous house at Skara Brae. Farther north, and inhabited into the Middle Ages, is Jarlshof in the Shetland Islands; the name is not historical but reflects the popularity of the nineteenth-century writer Sir Walter Scott. The rooms or chambers radiate from a common central area, and the structure is stone-built. The same general design is found again in the round houses that were built of wood and thatch, and are found from northern Britain to Ireland. Jarlshof was inhabited to the ninth century and for the last century of its existence there was a Viking settlement in the same area.

[39] J.R.C. Hamilton, *Excavations at Clickhimin, Shetland* (London, 1968).
[40] E.C. Bowen, *Britain and the Western Seaways* (London, 1972): 66; J. M. Bond, "Pictish Pigs and Celtic Cowboys: Food and Farming in the Atlantic Iron Age," in B. Ballin Smith and I. Banks (eds.), *In the Shadow of the Brochs: the Iron Age in Scotland* (Stroud, 2002): 177–184.

Other types of dwellings come from farther south and are sometimes called "cellular houses" because they were built in a manner roughly resembling a figure 8. This building could be rectangular with semicircular ends or have a large rounded main area to which is attached a smaller circular area. They are often found in western and northern Scotland; remains have been found, for example, at Gurness in the Orkney Islands.[41] They can also be found in a more easterly location such as the "Picts House" (sic) found in Aberdeenshire whose layout is recorded on the back of a grazing agreement.[42] A variation is known as a Pitcarmick house, which differs by having only a single entrance. The name came from an excavated building in Perthshire and a date of the eighth to ninth century has been seen for their flourishing.[43]

Occasionally associated with the cellular house is a subterranean structure known as the souterrain, sometimes described in literature as "Picts' houses." These subterranean structures are found across northern Europe, from Scandinavia to the British Isles to continental Atlantic Europe.[44] Tacitus (*Germania*, ch. 16) describes the Germanic peoples digging underground caves which they used as winter retreats (because of the warmth) and granaries. The northern British examples are found in a zone that begins in the north of Ireland and then travels into what Sir Cyril Fox famously described as the "Highland Zone" from the Shetland Islands to central Scotland; another zone is in the southwest from Cornwall into Brittany.[45] The function of these spaces is not clear. If the examples given by Tacitus are any indication, they might have been refuges and/or food storage places. The souterrains seem to have appeared about 500 BC and continued for almost a millennium – possibly as late as the ninth century; they continued to be used into the twelfth century in Ireland. The greatest concentration of them is found in Angus and Fife, although they are found as far north as the Shetland Islands where an impressive one is at Jarlshof.

---

[41] Edwards and Ralston, *Scotland after the Ice Age*: 225–226.
[42] Aberdeen Uni. Lib. MS 3759/1/148, with the title "Picts' House at Glenkindie opposite Culquoiche."
[43] Edwards and Ralston, *Scotland after the Ice Age*: 229–230.
[44] Cornelia Weinmann, *Der Hausbau in Skandinavien vom Neolithikum bis zum Mittelatler* (Berlin, 1994): 73–80.
[45] Much work on this was done by F.T. Wainwright in two studies: "Souterrains in Scotland,"*Antiquity* 27 (1952): 219–232; and *The Souterrains of Southern Pictland* (London, 1963).

Earning a Living: Agriculture

The Picts, like many other peoples of medieval Europe, were overwhelmingly farmers. In an age of subsistence agriculture, a huge workforce was required to produce the food that would feed the population. Most farms would have been a combination of some livestock and some arable cultivation, which was the usual arrangement in temperate zones until recent times. The extent of individual landholdings would have been much smaller than modern farms, again a customary feature of farming prior to the revolutions in mechanization that occurred in the eighteenth and nineteenth centuries. Since so many of the records and stories were concerned with the activities of the élites, there is little information specifically about the people who grew the food. In an oblique reference to the prestige of the farmer, a line of verse in the *Prophecy of Berchán* describes the Scots king Constantine (styled King of the Picts) as the herdsman of the cattle byre of the Picts, a poetic way of saying that he had charge of the wealth of his subjects.[46] Although a farmer was socially far below a nobleman, farming was a respected profession. The materials in the *Aberdeen Breviary* for the feast of St. Nechtan (January 8) remark that he humbled himself by abandoning his aristocratic life for that of a farmer because the latter profession came closest to divine contemplation.[47]

While both livestock and crops played important roles in agriculture, they were also consumed in different quantities by different types of people. Meat, whether from domesticated or wild animals, was largely consumed by the wealthy and high-status individuals. Such comestibles were a luxury and a sign of one's place in society; in the eleventh-century Welsh tale *How Culwuch Won Olwen* the hero Culwuch is refused entrance into Arthur's hall, because "knife had gone into meat," but he is consoled with the assurance that "hot peppered chops" would be prepared for him.[48] Was the "Pictish" boar on the mound at Dunadd destined for the same fate? The less exalted dined primarily on plant products and those foodstuffs that were available locally.

---

[46] Benjamin Hudson (ed. and trans.), *Prophecy of Berchán: Irish and Scottish High-kings of the Early Middle Ages* (Westport, 1996): 84, section 127.
[47] Alan Macquarrie, *Legends of Scottish Saints* (Dublin, 2012): 20.
[48] Thomas Jones (trans.), *The Mabinogion* (London, 1949): 98.

Arable farming

Those who grew the crops were important in society. Even the élites were concerned about the agriculture that fed them and provided their wealth. A story preserved in the Irish historical compilation known as the *Fragmentary Annals of Ireland* has a man named Fiachna contemplating his possible succession to the kingship while inspecting the plowing on his land.[49] Along the eastern coast of modern Scotland stretches a plain of varying width suitable for the cultivation of crops. Wheat, for example, can be cultivated in that plain occasionally as far north as the Moray Firth.[50] A piece of visual evidence might be the celebrated picture stone now known as Rhynie Man found near the town of the same name, where there are several other important carved stones. This is a figure of an unprepossessing individual whose purpose and identity have been the subject of various theories. There is nothing extraordinary about him. He seems to be dressed in what could be working clothes and is carrying an implement that appears to be an adze over his shoulder, apparently to break up the clods of earth in preparation for planting. For less exalted individuals, and for ordinary meals of the élites, plants provided most of the diet. The average person ate far more cereal grains during the Middle Ages than today. The main grains were oats and barley often prepared as a meal-porridge; an example, from the later Middle Ages, is the dish known in Gaelic as *brochan*. Another type of preparation, again known from later medieval records, was a small round cake baked on flat stones; it was the ancestor of the scone griddle of more recent memory. These cakes are found throughout Britain; in Wales (mentioned in the Laws of Hywel Dda), as well as through the north of England and into Scotland.[51] They were the one cooking implement carried by Scots troops in the later Middle Ages and they so intrigued the chronicler John Froissart that he recorded the cooking stone and the actual baking in his chronicle.

The clergy had lands for growing crops, and kept stores of seed for their own use. The late medieval *Aberdeen Breviary* has an anecdote in which St. Machar requested rye and barley seed from Bishop Ternan.[52] Ternan had none, but filled several sacks with sand and sent them to

---

[49] Joan Radnor, *Fragmentary Annals of Ireland* (Dublin, 1976): 10.
[50] L. Dudley Stamp, *Man and the Land*, New Naturalist Series (London, 1955): 110.
[51] C. Anne Wilson, *Food and Drink in Britain* (London, 1976): 232.
[52] Macquarrie, *Legends of Scottish Saints*: 142.

Machar, who grew a harvest from it. A similar story is told of the aforementioned Nechtan, who gave away all his seed and sowed sand, which yielded an abundant crop. Grain seed was also a suitable medium for paying compensation. A story from Adomnán's *Life of Columba* relates an episode when the saint sent his monks in a boat to collect wattles from a field in a place called *Delcros* (Prickle-point) in order to construct a new guesthouse. The owner of the field, named Findchán, complained that the monks were robbing him. Columba ordered that six *modii* (roughly 6 pecks) of barley be given to him as compensation, and he was to plant the crop immediately. He did so, even though it was past midsummer (June 21), much later than the time when barley should be planted. Nevertheless, the crop sprouted and he harvested a fully ripe crop at the beginning of August.[53] The location of Delcros is unknown, but there are several places in Scotland with a similar name, Dealganros, also meaning "prickle-point," such as Dalcross near Inverness, site of the airport on the Moray Firth.[54]

The land most suitable for growing crops was, and remains, the eastern coast from the Firth of Forth to the Black Isle, and this region is still intensively cultivated. Less contiguous areas could be cultivated, and fields on uplands where there was less forest. Most early medieval fields were square in form.[55] In contrast with the occasional evidence of wheat cultivation, oats are well represented. For example, oat cultivation flourished in the Orkney Islands as has been seen at Pool.[56] Flax was also cultivated in the Orkneys, for both cloth and oil. Both oats and barley were grown at Scalloway from the fifth century to the eighth with oats eventually predominating, and the same mixture is found at Dundurn. For most crops a problem was the short growing season. Returning to the story of Findchán, the miraculous element in that story is the short space of time needed by the grain to ripen. Apparently seed that had not been sown before midsummer was believed not to have a sufficient season for ripening before the autumnal frosts, a point that Findchán makes to his wife. The crucial part of the grain harvest was the threshing, in which the kernels are separated from the stalk. In the early Middle Ages one method of harvesting the grain was to cut off the stalks close to the ears of grain with a sickle. The grain was separated

[53] Adomnán, *Life of Columba*: 96–98.
[54] CPS: 93.
[55] Stamp, *Man and the Land*: 19.
[56] Edwards and Ralston, *Scotland after the Ice Age*: 251.

from the stalks either by a flail that pummeled the stalks or simply by throwing it into the air and allowing the chaff to blow away. One method of doing this was in threshing barns that were constructed so that the kernels separated from the stalks and fell through openings in the floor where they were collected from a hole in the ground. Such a building is suggested by another story from the *Life of Columba*, where the saint prophesies that a certain wealthy miser would be killed in a trench of a threshing floor.[57]

Connected with agriculture is the place name *pit/pett* which is found on the eastern coast from the Firth of Forth to the Moray Firth. There is much controversy about this word, not least on its origin, which would give some insight into its meaning (see chapter 2). The earliest occurrence of the word is in the *Book of Deer* where it is found four times; thrice in connection with individuals – Maldub's *pett*, Mac Garnait's *pett*, and Mac Gobraig's *pett* – and once with a building, the *pett* of the mill (*Pett in Muilinn*).[58] As records increase during the later Middle Ages, *pit-* is found as a place-name element, usually with a Gaelic second element. Even a cursory glance through documents that deal with land, such as charters or financial materials, give many more examples. A study of the actual sites with *pit-* names that covered only a selected area of Fife revealed some interesting features.[59] First all the *pit-* sites are between 50 and 650 ft (15–200 m) above sea level. The soils are almost exclusively of the Brown Forest Group, that is loamy to sandy loam clay. The *pit-* names are not found in areas where flooding and waterlogging occur. The *pit-* element does appear in sheltered areas with good drainage and without any military advantage or evidence of fortification (i.e., they were unlikely to have been fortified). Although the very limited nature of the study must be emphasized, these *pit*-sites show all the characteristics of land that is used for growing crops. The drainage would have prevented seeds or plant roots from rotting, while the loamy soil is good for growing cereals. Equally important is the shelter, for non-hybrid varieties of grains had taller stalks than modern, hybrid plants. Wind damage was, and still is, a concern. Since these crops would have been harvested by sickle, taking off the heads of the plants, the need for standing crops was great.

[57] Adomnán, *Life of Columba*: 122.
[58] Kenneth Jackson, *Gaelic Notes in the Book of Deer* (Cambridge, 1972): 39–40.
[59] G. Whittingdon and J.A. Soulsby, "A Preliminary Report on an Investigation into Pit Place-names," *Scottish Geographical Magazine* 84 (1968): 117–125.

So what does *pit* signify? One idea is that *pit* refers to a farmstead because it was later translated as Gaelic *baile*, and covered approximately 100 acres, both grazing and arable.[60] If so, comparison with the classical Anglo-Saxon hide of approximately 120 acres is worth considering, since the theoretical justification for it was the amount of land needed to support one peasant family for one year. Another suggestion is that both *pit-* and *baile* were equivalent to the English "townships" found in eighteenth-century rentals.[61] Both theories encounter a problem in that some names now with *pit-* are earlier found as names using *baile*, as well as vice versa. In addition so many *pit-* names survive that there must have been some difference. Using the study from Fife, the answer to the question "what was a *pit?*" seems to be that it was the most valuable part of the farm, often associated with arable cultivation. This could explain why parcels of land with *pit-* names are often expressly named in land grants; these were especially desired tracts of land.

Livestock

For early societies, the most luxurious foodstuffs were provided by animals. These came in the forms of meat and dairy products. Meat was a staple of feasts and other status displays where it was considered an appropriate ration for the diet of a warrior or king. There were three ways of obtaining animal protein. The first was through domesticated or semi-domesticated animals; these include cattle, sheep, and domesticated pigs. Their theft was a standard story-line in literature, as in the Irish *Cattle Raid of Cooley* (*Táin Bó Cuailgne*), and cattle raiding seems to have been known among the Picts as elsewhere. The *Rennes Dindshenchas* (*History of Place Names*) preserves a story about an Irish noble whose herd consisted of cows that he had taken from the Highlands (Irish s*liab monaid*) in Britain.[62] How prized were livestock is revealed by the aforementioned verse on King Constantine who is the herdsman of the cattle byre. This was not unique to the Picts and the twelfth-century charters of the Scots kings refer to their taxes (*cáin*) paid in animals.[63] Grazing

---

[60] Jackson, *Gaelic Notes in the Book of Deer*: 114–116.
[61] Andrew Mckerral, "The Lesser Land and Administrative Divisions in Celtic Scotland," PSAS 85 (1950–51): 52–64 (at p. 54).
[62] Whitley Stokes, "*Rennes Dindshenchas*," *Revue Celtique* 15 (1894): 272–484 (at p. 412).
[63] King David gave his *can* of pigs and cattle due from Fife, Forthrif, and Clachmanan to the Church of Dunfermline around 1133 (ESC 103: 81–82).

Figure 4.4 Hunting scene, Aberlemno Stone no. 2. Photo Robert Hudson.

rights were jealously guarded. One version of the story of the martyrdom of Donnán of Eigg claims that his community settled, without permission, on the lands that were reserved for the grazing of a queen's flock of sheep. She had her servants kill the intruders in fury at the infringement upon her rights to the grasslands.[64] Apparently the queen's hostility was not one of religious orientation, but at Donnán's usurpation of her right to use the land. A settled community would consume the local resources that were considered the property of another. The second way of obtaining protein was through hunting, which in a Scottish context included deer and wild boar. These animals are represented on the decorated stones together with hunting scenes (see Figure 4.4). The third way was fishing with salmon prized as the most desired fish, to be discussed later in this chapter.

Pride of place for meat in Pictish society was given to beef. Excavations at both Buckquoy (Orkney) and Dundurn show that half the remaining animal bones came from cattle. After this the percentage of pigs and sheep vary. Pigs were preferred at Dundurn, where more than 30 percent

[64] ESSH: i, 143.

of the bones were from swine, while mutton or lamb was preferred in the Orkneys with 30 percent of the bones found at Buckquoy. The Picts probably boiled their meat. One method would be to use pot boilers, stones that were heated and then dropped into a vat to cook the meat.[65] This was also the method preferred in Ireland. An alternative was to boil the meat in the animal's hide, which was done in the Hebrides. The blood was boiled into cakes in the Highlands.[66]

While beef probably was reserved for special occasions or for the élites, milk and its byproducts were ubiquitous. Evidence of dairy products comes from bog butter, a name given to butter or lard stored in a wooden cask and then buried in peat, which acted both as a refrigerant and a hygienic method of preserving the butter. How ancient was the practice is uncertain; in Scotland there is evidence of it as far back as two millennia, and possibly there might be much older evidence from Ireland.[67] The severe weather in northern Britain would have aided dairying because the stabling of cattle would have helped with milking and preparation of milk products. Cheeses from Wales or Scotland during the later Middle Ages were noted for having hairs in them. A healthy and convenient way of consuming milk was as sour or buttermilk, known in the Highlands as "sourdook."

Cattle in northern Britain are descended from animals of one of two types: *Bos primigenius* or *Bos longifron*.[68] The latter seem to have occurred in the east and had a moderately thick body and broad frame with a short-horned head. These are the bulls that feature on the symbol stones found at Burghead. There has been some speculation that they were black in color, as is commonly found with other "Celtic" breeds such as the Welsh Black and the Kerry. In the west the *Bos primigenius* seems to have been the ancestor of cattle such as the Highland, Longhorn, and White Park. As well as their unusually long horns, they have double-hair coats that keep out the damp and insulate against the cold. At the end of the Pictish period, the Scandinavians who settled in the

---

[65] Wilson, *Food and Drink in Britain*: 62; for a different assemblage see Ewan Campbell, "The Raw, the Cooked and the Burnt: Interpretations of Food and Animals in the Hebridean Iron Age," *Archaeological Dialogues* 7 (2000): 184–198.

[66] Wilson, *Food and Drink in Britain*: 94.

[67] "Bog Butter Test," New Scientist (March 20, 2004) at http://www.*newscientist*.com/article/mg18124392.400 (accessed October 10, 2013).

[68] F.H. Garner, *The Cattle of Britain* (London, 1944).

Hebrides, the Orkneys, and the Shetland Islands brought polled (hornless) cattle, the ancestors of now-extinct breeds such as the Polled Sutherlands and the Skye Polls.

Cattle require a large acreage of land for grazing although the exact acreage varies. So much of the cattle rearing might have taken place away from the main farming area. After the crops had been gathered, livestock would be moved back to the arable fields to consume the gleanings of the harvest and fertilize the fields. Cattle might have been moved into forests in order to clear land by eating some seedlings and trampling others, which turned parts of the forests in rough grazing.[69]

Lower in status than cattle were sheep, although they had equally varied uses. Many of the early medieval breeds of sheep in Britain were little changed from their Neolithic ancestors. Some of these ancient types can still be found today, such as the Soay sheep of St. Kilda or the Shetland sheep. Improved breeds that are good examples of earlier types are the Cheviots (so named after their home in the Cheviot Hills) prior to their international export. Where the sheep were raised might be indicated by surviving bones. Only 8 percent of the bones at Dundurn were from sheep, but, as noted above, almost a third of the bone remains at Buckquoy. Sheep's wool was the main material for cloth in the medieval British Isles. Unlike modern practice, sheep were not shorn in order to obtain their wool. Instead, wool was collected as sheep lost it when the animals molted in the summer. The wool was gathered either by plucking it from the animal or by collecting bunches where it had been rubbed off on some object such as a tree or rock. Wool might have been one of the commodities exported by the peoples of northern Britain. The votive woolen bale that was found in a brooch on the Isle of Skye suggests that it was an ancient trade commodity.[70]

Wool was probably the most common material for clothing. What clothes looked like can be indicated from the symbol stones and from a couple of items that have been unearthed.[71] A child's hood, radiocarbon-dated between AD 250 and 615, has been salvaged from a peat bog in

---

[69] Stamp, *Man and the Land*: 40.
[70] T.C. Lethbridge, *Herdsmen and Hermits, Celtic Seafarers in the Northern Seas* (Cambridge, 1950): 65.
[71] On this topic see Anna Ritchie, "Clothing among the Picts," *Costume* 39 (2005): 28–42; Alice Blackwell, "Dressed Bodies," in David Clarke, Alice Blackwell, and Martin Goldberg (eds.), *Early Medieval Scotland: Individuals, Communities and Ideas* (Edinburgh, 2012): 7–10.

the Orkneys, and it was made of reused fabric. This is probably a smaller version of the short hooded cloak worn by an archer on the St.Vigeans (number 1) stone. Plaids were worn around the shoulders and baggy trousers by the warrior on the Kirriemuir (number 2) stone. Some warriors wore tunics that extended below their knees and were belted, as in the battle scene from the Aberlemno Stone (see Figure 3.3). The men fighting a duel on the Glamis symbol stone are wearing sleeveless tunics that end above the knees (see Figure 4.3 above).

The European wild pig or *sus scrofa scrofa* is found in early art in Britain as well as represented on symbol stones.[72] Pigs are more effective than cattle in clearing forests and since they were rarely enclosed, it seems that their maintenance was designed both to feed the animal and to convert forest areas into rough grazing. Once again using bone percentages, it seems that pork was more often consumed in the south than the north; roughly 30 percent of the bones from Dundurn were pigs as compared with only 20 percent from Buckquoy. Its undomesticated cousin, the wild boar, would have been one of the animals hunted, and representations of the boar appear on the symbol stones. Also found on the symbol stones are chickens. The birds were a source of meat and the hens produced eggs. An interesting way of preserving eggs has been found in eastern Scotland, the Hebrides and the northern islands, where the eggs were placed in ash deposits.[73]

The horse in Pictish society, as in all European societies, was a high-status animal. The horse was the luxury animal of the late antique/early medieval world, whether a draft animal pulling a load or the riding steed of a wealthy individual. The Picts used harnesses and some sort of saddle or pad for riding as can be seen in the hunting scene on a symbol stone at Aberlemno (see Figure 4.4 above). In the Hebrides, the Highlands, and the Shetland Islands were animals now classified as "ponies." They are the descendants of *equus caballus*. A pure form of this animal survives on the island of Barra, while the Shetland and Highland ponies are closely related.[74] The horse was used in hunting, although all the surviving evidence for it shows the packs of the wealthy. Dio claims that the northern peoples who fought Septimus Severus used chariots pulled by ponies. With

---

[72] B. Cunliffe, *The Ancient Celts* (London, 1997): 85; the figures of two boars found at Hounslow in Middlesex might have been decoration on a helmet.
[73] Wilson, *Food and Drink in Britain*: 126.
[74] Irene Hughson, "Pictish Horse Carvings," *Glasgow Archaeological Journal* 17 (1991–92): 53ff.

protein at a premium, harvesting the beasts of the forest was one way of supplementing the little that was produced by farmers. There are pictures of deer and boar on the symbol stones as well as different birds. One stone shows a huntsman with his pack of hounds after a deer.

Earning a Living: Trade and Industry

Trade and manufacturing are difficult topics for the history of the early Middle Ages and one is reduced to dependence on stray references in written works and the possibility of material survivals uncovered in archaeological excavations. Adding to the uncertainty is the imprecision with which we can attempt to assign a date to inorganic materials such as metals or stone. In ancient times there were important trade routes through northern Britain. One Bronze Age route went across northern Britain, from Northern Ireland to the Firth of Lorne, then up the Great Glen to Inverness and across the North Sea.[75] Another with even greater longevity ran from Ireland along the Hebrides to the Pentland Firth and then into the North Sea. This was the route taken in the ninth century by the Viking captors of St. Findan, who was abducted in Leinster, and carried from the Irish Sea to the Orkney Islands, where he escaped and hid until the ships sailed away. He was given refuge by a priest who had studied in Ireland. Subsequently Findan made his way to the Continent where he lived the rest of his days as a hermit on an island.[76] A possible earlier allusion to this route might come from Ausonius' poem *Libra*, which discusses equilibrium in nature: "libra Caledonio sine litore continet aestus."[77]

[75] Lethbridge, *Herdsmen and Hermits*,: 31; Jonathan Wooding, *Communication and commerce along the Western Sealanes AD 400–800* (Oxford: Tempus Reparatum, 1996): 107. For a different view see two essays by Ewan Campbell: "The Archaeological Evidence for Contacts: Imports, Trade and Economy in Celtic Britain AD 400–800," in K.R. Dark (ed.), *External Contacts and the Economy of Late Roman and Post-Roman Britain* (Woodbridge, 1996): 83–96; and "Trade in the Dark-Age West," in Barbara Crawford (ed.), *Scotland in Dark Age Britain* (St. Andrews, 1996): 79–91.

[76] H. Lowe, "Findan von Rheinau: Eine Irische Peregrinatio im 9. Jahrhundert," *Deutsches Archiv für Erforschung des mittelalters* 42 (1986): 25–85; W.P.L. Thomson, "St. Findan and the Pictish–Norse Transition," *in* R.J. Berry and H. Firth (eds.), *The People of Orkney* (Kirkwall, 1986): 279–287.

[77] Ausonius, *Decimi Magni Ausonii Opera*, ed. R.P.H. Green (Oxford, 1999): *Eclogue* vi.

One of the most important commoners was the smith or artificer. Not only did the smith with his anvil, hammer, and tongs operate the local metallurgical installation, the smithy, but he was also well compensated for his trouble.[78] The smith's hammer is one of the figures found on carved stones such as at the Mote of Mark. Smiths made the metal objects for agriculture such as harness fittings, weapons like swords and spearheads, and he also made locks (for example, the barrel padlocks found at Dundurn and Buiston). The smith made the snaffle bits found at the Mote of Mark and Whithorn, which are represented on symbol stone 8 from Meigle. Not surprisingly a smith could be wealthy. An example from Irish literature is the story of Cú Chulainn, who got his name when he accidently killed the watchdog of a smith named Nechtan, who was giving a dinner in honor of the king. Even though Nechtan was concerned about the size of the royal retinue, the fact that he had riches enough to be the host of royalty, and was considered an acceptable individual to extend an invitation to royal guests, shows the esteem in which these individuals were held by society.

There are mineral deposits within northern Britain, among which are gold deposits. When the eleventh-century king Malcolm Canmore sent his brother-in-law Edgar on what proved to be an aborted mission to the Continent, among the gifts that he sent were vessels made of gold.[79] As many as 24 of the 42 gold-bearing sites in Britain are north of Hadrian's Wall and 14 of them are north of the firths of Clyde and Forth.[80] Among their locations are Helmsdale (Sutherland), Knock (Banff), Rhynie (Aberdeenshire), Glen Clova (Forfarshire), and Comrie (Strathearn). An important deposit is at Cononish in the lead-mining district of Tyndrum. This is also the region where a major battle was fought in the eighth century between the *exactores* (tax collectors) of two rival princes; the battle might have been for establishing jurisdiction over the region's mineral wealth. Gold was being paid as a tax to the king in the twelfth century, when King David I assigned his gold revenues from Fife and Fothrif to the church of Dunfermline.[81]

[78] The following examples are supplied from Lloyd Laing, *Archaeology of Celtic Britain and Ireland c. AD 400–1200* (Cambridge, 2006): 99–102.
[79] A.O. Anderson, *Scottish Annals from English Chroniclers* (London: David Nutt, 1908): 98, after the *Anglo-Saxon Chronicle*, D version, for 1074.
[80] British Geological Survey, *Minerals in Britain: Gold* (London, 1999).
[81] ESC 65, from the *Register of Dunfermline*, no. 28. The payment of gold is omitted from Malcolm IV's confirmation of December 19, 1154/1159 (RRS: I, 182–185, no. 118), but it is reinserted in his brother William the Lion's confirmation *c.* 1166 (RRS: II, 140–142 at 140), no. 30.

A puzzling reference to a trade in copper comes from the text known as the *Cosmography of Aethicus Ister*. This is a travelogue of the world, compiled essentially from the Bible and scholarly readings, especially Isidore of Seville, by someone living in the realm of the Franks during the eighth century. He might or might not be the same man as Virgilius Maro Grammaticus, an Irish grammarian of the seventh century. He specifically names the Orkney Islands as one of the places where ships call and later claims that it is one of the main places for metals, particularly copper, and metalworking.[82] Unfortunately he is not more specific, and it is possible that he might have confused this with mainland Britain, in a passage very similar to one in Isidore of Seville (XIV.vi) who mentions the rich metals.[83] If one interprets Aethicus Ister's "Orkney Islands" as encompassing the entire archipelago as far as the Shetland Islands, then this is accurate, as there is evidence of mining there from prehistoric times, both iron and copper. Gold is not found in the Orkney Islands, but farther south in Sutherland or farther north at Unst in the Shetland Islands, which also have copper – for which there is also no evidence in the Orkney Islands. In addition there are soapstone (steatite) quarries in the Shetland Islands. Orkney may have been the mart for those wares, however, and the Lammas Fair continued to bring in a widely ranging group of people.[84]

Another artisan-cum-workman was the leatherworker who made the reins for the horses and the shoes for their riders. They kept their tools in boxes and one such box was found in the Orkney Islands at Birsay, which held leatherworking tools. Leatherworking is seen in the example of a decorated shoe from Dundurn.[85] There is evidence of hide tanning at the excavated site at Portmahomack, where the remains of cattle hooves, which would have been removed from the hides to be worked, have been found in what seems to be a pattern design.[86]

[82] Aethicus Ister, *Cosmography of Aethicus Ister*, ed. Michael Herren (Turnholt, 2012): 26, 27.
[83] Isidore of Seville, *Etymologiarvm Sive Originvm*, ed. W.M. Lindsay, 2 vols. (Oxford, 1811): ii, 132.
[84] Robert Van de Noort, *North Sea Archaeologies: A Maritime Biography, 10,000 BC–AD 1500* (Oxford, 2011): 129.
[85] Laing, *Archaeology of Celtic Britain and Ireland*: 146.
[86] Martin Carver, *Portmahomack, Monastery of the Picts* (Edinburgh, 2008): 122–125.

Earning a Living: The Sea

Popular imagination has many images of the Picts, as John White's watercolor paintings testify, but rarely are they remembered as sailors. There has been so little consideration of a maritime people that the aforementioned study on the element *pit-* in place names suggests that one reason why so few are found along the coast is that the Picts were terrified of the sea.[87] The Picts did sail, however. While there is no indication that they traveled as far afield as the Carthaginians or Vikings, they did move beyond their coasts. Gildas describes the Picts as an "overseas nation," a seaborne enemy, and specifically mentions the armada of coracles sailing across the sea, carrying the Picts and Scots.[88] He also describes the invaders as worms slithering out of the fissures of rocks when they disembark from the coracles.

The Picts need to be placed within an Atlantic context in order to understand the maritime aspect of their culture. In the northeast Atlantic there were two types of boats, those made of animal skins and those made of wood. When they first appear in a British Isles context is difficult to determine, not least because of the fragile nature of the materials and modern reliance on fortunate finds of evidence. Although the earliest identifiable wooden craft in Europe date from around 7000 BC, both types of vessel appear to have been in use somewhere in the British Isles by the fifth millennium BC.[89] The skin boat is the less easy to identify because of its more fragile components and the date of its appearance has to be extrapolated from the discovery of what appear to be oars rather than any remains of the craft itself. Skin boats are found among all peoples, largely because of the simplicity of their construction. For skin boats of the British Isles, modern writers make a distinction between the coracle, used in inland waters, and the curragh,

---

[87] G. Whittington and J.A. Soulsby, "A Preliminary Report on an Investigation into Pit Place-names," *Scottish Geographical Magazine* 84 (1968): 123.

[88] *Ruin of Britain*, 94, section 19: "Itaque illis ad sua remeantibus emergunt certatim de curucis, quibus sunt trans Tithicam vallem evecti, quasi in alto Titane incalescenteque caumate de artissimis foraminum caverniculis fusci vermiculorum cunei, tetri Scottorum Pictorumques greges"; and 93, section 14 "... gentibus transmarinis ..."

[89] Van de Noort, *North Sea Archaeologies*: 147; J.N. Lanting, "Dates for the Origin and Diffusion of the European Log Boat," *Palaeohistoria* 39/40 (1997/98): 627–650.

suitable for ocean sailing.[90] These distinctions were not noted in the Middle Ages, and Gildas uses the word *curuces* to describe the vessels sailed by the Picts. The craft's wooden frame was frequently made of willow, over which was stretched a waterproof covering of cattle hides sealed with tallow or beeswax. The building techniques seemed not to have changed for millennia. Comparison of the river coracle used on the Boyne early in the twentieth century with the miniature golden boat found in a hoard that was buried in the second century BC at Broighter, on Lough Foyle near Derry, in 1896 reveals that the two craft were very similar.[91] Although seemingly fragile, it was actually a very stout vessel and was one of the premier Atlantic transports. So seaworthy were these apparently delicate craft that they continued to be used well into the twentieth century. There is a picture of this type of boat on the wall of Jonathan's Cave at East Wemyss (Fife). Another illustration of a boat comes from farther north on the famous Cossans Stone (north of Glamis) even though the carving is very decrepit, the boat seems to be a skin boat (see Figure 4.5). The naval raids mentioned by Gildas have an echo in the Irish *Life of St. Comgall* (partly composed in the tenth century). Comgall was resident on the Isle of *Heth* when a Pictish raiding party sailed to the island and looted it.[92] The saint prayed for divine retaliation, which arrived in the form of a huge wave that battered the villains' fleet.

The skin boats were not the only type of vessel; there were also boats made of wood. Originally the log boat was a canoe made from the hollowed trunk of a tree. These were used in inland waters or along the coast, unless fitted with some type of stabilizer to keep them upright. Later developments led to building of larger and more seaworthy craft through the use of multiple boards for the hull such as tied- and, later, clinker-built construction. There is some indication that these craft were introduced to Britain from Ireland and one found at Locharbriggs (Dumfries) has been dated to about 2600 BC.[93] A famous incident connected with a log boat

[90] David Tilson, "The Teifi Coracle," *Material Culture Review/Revue de la culture matérielle*, 37 (1993), at http://journals.hil.unb.ca/index.php/MCR/article/view/17560/22442 (accessed October 10, 201).

[91] Bowen, *Britain and the Western Seaways*: 186–187. On the topic as a whole see Sean McGrail, *Ancient Boats in North-West Europe: The Archaeology of Water Transport to AD 1500* (London, 1998).

[92] Charles Plummer (ed.), *Vitae Sanctorum Hiberniae*, 2 vols. (Dublin, 1910): ii, 11.

[93] Van de Noort, *North Sea Archaeologies*: 157.

Figure 4.5 Boat on St. Orland's Stone, Cossans. Photo Robert Hudson.

occurs in Adomnán's *Life of Columba*. The island community on Iona used boats from necessity and their missionary labors north of the Grampians followed a water route that went up the Great Glen. During one voyage, the saint and his entourage encountered a water monster, which later in the popular imagination is identified with the Loch Ness monster. The monster had already attacked and killed one of the local men before his companions could reach him in a boat built out of alder.[94] This description fits the wooden canoe that has been found in submerged contexts. Scotland has the Black or Common Alder, which is a birch found throughout Europe that grows along water courses. The wood can be carved easily and it bends readily; it is also waterproof and has been used to make water pipes. This wood is not resistant to rot, however, and

[94] Adomnán, *Life of Columba*: 132.

decays very quickly. So it can be used to make a boat speedily, but not one that lasts long. By the early Middle Ages the use of alder was also outdated, which may explain why the wood was specified; oak had been the preferred variety since the Neolithic period. A wooden canoe might have been the type of small craft (*nauicula*) that features in another episode in Adomnán's *Life of Columba*, when Columba foretells that a virtuous pagan would be brought to Skye for baptism before he died.[95]

One type of patrol boat, as mentioned in an earlier chapter, is described in the late fourth-century *Epitoma Rei Militaris* by the Roman military theorist P. Flavius Vegetius Renatus, popularly known as Vegetius. He describes a type of boat that was called by the Britons a "Pict boat" and acted as a scout boat for a fleet.[96] They were also used for surprise attacks on enemy shipping, giving the flotilla commander the opportunity to observe his foe's strategy. According to Vegetius' brief description they carried 40 rowers and were camouflaged with blue paint, even down to the sails and blue clothing for the crew, so that the vessel blended into the color of the sea. The fact that the craft could be painted suggests that it was a wooden vessel rather than a skin boat.

Gildas is the first writer to connect the Pictish raids with sea travel, and his (admittedly difficult) chronology suggests that these amphibious assaults were occurring at least by the reign of Theodosius in the late fourth century. The constructions of Roman shore forts on the eastern and western coasts have given the impression that there was little concern about attacks from the north. Laws that prohibited giving instruction in boat building to barbarians from the late fourth and fifth century suggest, however, that transmarine foes such as, for instance, the Franks, Saxons, and Irish were not the only ones of concern to the Romans.[97] The wording of the prohibitions makes more sense if the foe could attack by land or sea. Imperial need for revenue from international commerce was matched by official fears that hostile military ventures were being made possible by Roman coins and technological expertise. So merchants were to be watched. In addition there was the stipulation that they were to live in towns where taxes were collected. A limit was placed on the amount of

---

[95] Adomnán, *Life of Columba*: 62.
[96] Vegetius, *P. Flavii Vegeti Renati, Epitoma Rei Militaris*, ed. Alf Önnerfors (Leipzig, 1995): 240–241.
[97] Clyde Pharr (ed.), *Theodosian Code and the Sirmondian Constitutions* (New York, 1952); the numbers in round brackets refer to the appropriate section (9.40.24).

money traders could carry for their commercial ventures, and officials were to watch the ports and roads to ensure that coin didn't leave the Empire in order to be melted down for bullion.[98] Gildas' Picts and Scots might have been deliberately attacking Roman ports; legislation enacted during the reign of Honorius ordered boats to patrol the harbors in order to prevent attacks.[99] The date of that legislation (*c*.410), has a special relevance because the legions stationed in Britain had been withdrawn by that time and the seas were vital for the imperial troops to travel from Gaul.

The maritime abilities of at least some of the princes among the Picts is suggested by an incident recorded in Adomnán's *Life of Columba* where the saint requests that King Brude order his under-king of the Orkney Islands to give safe passage to any Christian missionaries that might land in his domain.[100] Apparently Brude carried out the request, because the episode ends with the statement that Cormac, one of Columba's monks, was saved from death because of this safe-conduct. We can assume that the battle fought in the Orkney Islands in the year 709, which resulted in the death of a man named Artabláir, involved a naval attack from outside the islands, but there is also the possibility that the conflict was an internal skirmish.

Sailing was quicker when compared with traveling great distances over land, but it was not without its perils. Even inland waterways were hazardous, and we assume that the *Annals of Ulster*'s notice of the drowning of many Picts on *Loch Abac* (possibly Loch Awe) in 676 was due to shipwreck, caused by either violent weather or a battle. Returning to Columba's colleague Cormac in the Orkney Islands, there is an account of his survival of almost certain shipwreck. He was caught in a gale blowing from the south and it carried him north for 14 days. On the 14th day his coracle was attacked by a sea-swarm of stinging creatures that damaged the oars and threatened to puncture the hide of the coracle. Only fervent prayer for a breeze from the north, which was answered, saved the distressed mariners.[101] Storms were a constant danger, and once Columba's effort to bail out the vessel was stopped by the crew who asked him to pray instead.[102] Just between Ireland and Scotland is the whirlpool known as Breccan's Cauldron (Coire Breccáin), the second

---

[98] Pharr, *Theodosian Code* (24.1, promulgated *c*.447 and 9.23.1, from *c*.356).
[99] Pharr, *Theodosian Code* (7.14.2).
[100] Adomnán, *Life of Columba*: 166.
[101] Adomnán, *Life of Columba*: 168–170.
[102] Adomnán, *Life of Columba*: 110.

largest in Europe, which is subject to tidal activity. Coire Breccáin was famous and remembered in the Irish collection of geographical lore known as the *Metrical Dindshenchas*: "From east and west – no passing gust – the sea of Orkney and the sea of the cold Britons meet for fierce eager fame betwixt Britain and Ireland."[103] Columba claimed that a certain Colmán had been caught in it as a divine prompting towards more fervent prayer.[104] The verses in the *Metrical Dindshenchas* imply that a trade route ran along this whirlpool and the mention of the "sea of Orkney" combined with Aethicus Ister's particular mention of the islands in the context of metals could indicate that it extended along the Hebrides and then past the Orkney Islands.

Although there is little evidence of a taste for seafood among the Picts, there are hints from the verses of the late fourth-century poet Ausonius that a trade in items from the sea was being carried out with Gaul. In his poem on the river Moselle, he mentions the seaweed, coral, and pearls found along the Caledonian shore.[105] Ausonius was also a gourmand with a partiality for oysters. He includes a catalogue of oysters in a letter to his friend Paulus, in which he mentions those of Caledonia.[106] Ausonius notes that there are some people who prefer the oysters gathered on the "Pictonic coast," left by the tide for the Caledonian to look upon in wonder. All of these are mere asides in verses, but the sum of them suggests that during the last years of the Imperial administration in Britain there was a trade in pearls, coral, and oysters between the peoples beyond Hadrian's Wall and the Romans. This trade might have been directly with Gaul if the reference to the Caledonian tide can be extended. There is no difficulty with placing any of the trade items in a northern British context. The pearls and coral were used for jewelry and this might have been the reason why they are specifically mentioned, for Ausonius continues by remarking on the waves that mimic necklaces, an unusual choice for comparison. His comments are supported by the earlier comments of Tacitus in his *Agricola* (ch. 12) in which he notes that in Britain pearls are collected from the animals that are thrown up by the sea. He gives that as the reason why the pearls in Britain are cloudy in color, because

[103] E. Gwynn, *Metrical Dindshenchas*, 5 parts (Dublin, 1903–35): iv, 81.
[104] Adomnán, *Life of Columba*: 28.
[105] Ausonius, *Opera*: 117; the editor would see the use of Caledonia as a special effect (p. 472), but Ausonius is being quite specific at this line.
[106] Ausonius, *Opera*: 194–195; the editor suggests that this refers to the entire island (p. 610).

the clear ones need to be plucked from the living oysters in the sea. Pearls were prized for jewelry into the Middle Ages and beyond. Bede mentions the variety and beauty of British pearls in "De Situ Brittaniae et Hiberniae," the introductory section of the *Ecclesiastical History*. They continued to be harvested from Scottish rivers well into the twentieth century; "pearl-fishing" was one way the "traveling folk" earned cash. Ausonius may have had as informants sailors who worked the trade routes between northern Britain and Gaul. As noted above, in his verses on the *libra*, usually translated "pound" but meaning here "equilibrium" he mentions the moderation of nature that, unaided by the shore, prevents the Caledonian tide from reaching the shores of Gaul.[107] There might have been harbors and trading areas. The *vita* of Boecius claims that the saint sailed from Germania to the shores of the Picts (*ad finibus Pictorum*). After resurrecting King Nechtan in his *castrum*, the saint traveled to Dál Riata in order to sail back to Ireland.[108]

This leads to the question: was much fish actually eaten by the Picts during the early Middle Ages? There is little evidence of any significant consumption of fish that required catching far from land; most of the bone assemblages imply limited fishing that could be done close to shore.[109] This assessment is supported by the pictorial evidence. Accurate representations of fish can be found on the decorated stones such as the stone at Kintore with it salmon from the nearby river Don (see Figure 4.6). Among small fish are the herring shoals that appear off the Shetland Islands in early June and continue throughout the summer. Haddock and cod are found on the eastern coast while on the west coast there are crabs (traditionally caught in plaited baskets) as well as conger, sea bream, skate, and sharks.

Boats were also used to transport livestock for grazing on islands. Returning to the martyrdom of Donnán of Eigg, the pagan Pictish queen who was responsible for his "red martyrdom" (i.e., death by violence) was moved to violence because Donnán and his monastic community had established themselves on the island where she was accustomed to have her sheep grazed in the summer. This implies that the animals were not present when the clerics had arrived on the island, but were transported there in the proper season.

[107] Ausonius, *Opera*: 109.
[108] Plummer, *Vitae Sanctorum Hiberniae*: i, 88.
[109] J.H. Barret, A.M. Locker, and C.M. Roberts, "'Dark Age Economics' Revisited: The English Fish Bone Evidence 600–1600," *Antiquity* 78 (2004): 618–636.

Figure 4.6 Salmon on a stone at Kintore. Photo Robert Hudson.

Summary

The few scraps of information about society in northern Britain show many similarities with life throughout Europe. In the organization of society there was a hierarchy with a numerically small élite, both secular and ecclesiastical, supported by a large, and largely invisible, population of workers. Even for those who wrote the records (the clergy) or their patrons (the aristocracy) the information tells less than would be hoped. One's place in society was displayed visually by dress and accoutrements as exhibited by princes with magic stones or clerics with their tonsure. There was also an acknowledgment of the importance of all members of society and even the mightiest king knew that he enjoyed his feasts through the labors of those who worked the fields.

In providing for the necessities of life, use had to be made of the raw materials close to hand. Too little information survives to make more than the most general of comments, but farming was the main occupation of the vast majority of people. There was some manufacturing, but this was usually in the form of blacksmithing or leatherworking. Even though the evidence for this is found in connection with church or royal sites, it is possible that further archaeological investigations will yield a wider range of locations for those activities. Perhaps the least expected aspect of life is the seemingly limited nature of harvesting the products from the sea, especially in the context of the later Scottish fishing industry.

One aspect of this society is how little it differed from its neighbors in goods. Other than luxury goods, there was conformity of raw materials throughout physical regions regardless of the political allegiances of the people. Crops and livestock demanded particular types of climate and soil to prosper, and the great age of agricultural improvement was still in the future. This could lead to pronounced changes in a very short distance as the physical geography made dramatic changes. At the same time certain types of industry were required to sustain even so basic a standard of living as was found in the early medieval period. Metalworking for the horseshoes, weapons, and implements was practiced by a class of professional smiths. The artificers included the leatherworkers and joiners as well as the shipwrights. There must have been variations in status among the workers, and the huntsman who appears on the symbol stones would probably have considered himself on a higher level than the peasant resting from tilling his fields in order to watch the hunt pass by.

5

Spirituality

Spiritual beliefs and religious practices provide a window into a society. They show what people consider to be their relationship with a greater power beyond this world (however it is defined) as well as helping to explain customs and hierarchy. The topic of Christianity among the peoples of northern Britain has an added importance, because the clergy were the record-keeping class in the early Middle Ages. So the information that has been preserved in those documents is mainly what interested the officials of the church. The conversion of the peoples of northern Britain to Christianity together with the use of written records was a change from earlier times, for which much of the information about spirituality is archaeological or anecdotal. Objects survive, but the theology behind them must be guessed or deduced. Remains of idols, votive offerings, shrines, and graves are all testimonies to beliefs, and changes in them. The evidence is found buried in extinct ponds, carved as images on stones, and as names given to places or regions. Most of the written information about Christianity and conversion to it is found in two sources that have provided so many of the examples in earlier chapters: Adomnán's *Life of Columba* and Bede's *Ecclesiastical History*, which are supplemented by stray items of information from a few *Lives* of the saints and the chronological listing of deaths of the religious that is found in the annals or chronicles. Like the earlier period, traces of early Christianity remain in place names and in physical materials such as stone crosses or the remnants of monastic and church buildings. While later works claim to have information about particular individuals or churches, rarely can this be verified by comparison with any other source

The Picts, First Edition. Benjamin Hudson.
© 2014 John Wiley & Sons, Ltd. Published 2014 by John Wiley & Sons, Ltd.

of materials. So much of what can be said about spirituality is tentative and deduction must substitute for certainty.

Pre-Christian Belief

Medieval writings on religion in northern Britain overwhelmingly concentrate on Christianity, its progress and adaptation. The practice and the leaders of the local non-Christian cults are for the most part unknown. Little more than acknowledgment of its existence is given to non-Christian belief. One reason for this is the lack of information. Even the recovery of items that appear to be connected with worship often cannot be definitively related to a particular ceremony. Another reason for the lack of information from Christian writing is cultural condensation of the word *pagan*. The term comes from Latin *paganus* and originally was used for someone who lived in the countryside and was remote from the latest changes. Throughout history the image of the rustic has been synonymous with "primitive." In Christian writings the meaning was extended to include one who was easily deceived. A persistent character in hagiography is the rustic who was beguiled by devilish tricks until his "eyes are opened" by the Christian missionary who is the opponent of the local cult leaders.

One of the oldest surviving vestiges of spiritual belief or worship, or so we assume, are represented by some of the stone monuments that are found throughout Britain. Although most attention is given to famous structures such as Stonehenge, the lands of northern Britain are particularly rich in these monuments. We can only guess at the exact purpose(s) of circles such as the recumbent stone circle at Loanhead of Daviot, or what seem to be the mixed funerary and ceremonial functions of the tombs and stone structures known as the Clava cairns in Invernesshire. Although the stones themselves were set in place thousands of years before the word Pict was ever used, they mark areas of spiritual use that, in some instances, extend into the present. An example is the church at Midmar in Aberdeenshire (the first element of Midmar is from Old British *mig-*, "marsh") where there is a stone circle in the churchyard with a recumbent stone. Although the present church was built in the eighteenth century, its predecessor was to the south of the circle and dedicated to St Ninian.[1]

---

[1] For coordinates and dimensions of the stone circles see Aubrey Burl, *A Guide to the Stone Circles of Britain, Ireland and Brittany* (New Haven, CT, revised ed., 2005): 101–102 (Loanhead of Daviot); 104 (Midmar); 127–135 (the Clava cairns).

One aspect of religious activity associated with pre-Christian divine worship in the region round the British Isles and Atlantic France was the building of a wicker structure. Strabo and Pomponius Mela mention sacred isles where there was the ritual thatching of a structure. This was carried out by a community of women who were believed to have the power of prophecy. A wooden female idol at Ballachulish in Argyllshire was discovered with remains of wickerwork, possibly connected with the ritual thatching and dethatching of houses; a stone shrine uncovered at Glenlyon in Perthshire might have had a similar function.[2] Island retreats for religious use continued after the conversion of people to Christianity. In addition to churches on coastal islands such as Iona and Lindisfarne, there was use of uninhabited islands as burial grounds, for example the Isle of May in the Firth of Forth where a monastery with a cemetery had been in use from the sixth century; a church was constructed there in the ninth century and it was a place of pilgrimage by the twelfth.[3]

Religious beliefs traveled and one of these migrants was the cult of the horned god popularly known as Cernunnos. A well-known representation of this mysterious figure is situated on the Gundestrup Cauldron found in a peat bog in Denmark (made sometime between 200 BC and AD 300) where the deity is depicted with horns, holding a serpent, and wearing a torque around his neck. Emulation of this deity might explain the damaged head found near Perth with a ram's horn on the undamaged side.[4] A pony-cap with horns, which appears to have been a votive offering connected with a cult of a horned deity has been found at Torrs (Kirkcudbrightshire); and the remains of cauldrons with tools have been found at Carlingwark Loch (Kirkcudbrightshire), Eckford (Roxburghshire), and Blackburn Mill (Berwickshire).[5] The cauldron or container is found in connection with Irish legends of the Picts/Cruithne in Ireland prior to their settlement in Britain. In the poems *Ard Lemnacht in This Land in the South* (*Ard Leanmachta is tir sear theas*) and *What brought the Picts*

---

[2] Anne Ross, *Pagan Celtic Britain* (London, 1974): 66. For a possible visit by an imperial official to sacred isles round Britain, see I.A. Richmond, "A Forgotten Exploration of the Western Isles," *Antiquity* 14 (1940): 193–195.

[3] Robert Van de Noort, *North Sea Archaeologies: A Maritime Biography, 10,000 BC–AD 1500* (Oxford, 2011): 135.

[4] Anne Ross, "A Celtic (?) Stone Head from Perthshire," *Transactions and Proceedings of the Perthshire Society of Natural Science* 11 (1966): 31.

[5] S. Piggott, "Three Metalwork Hoards in Southern Scotland," PSAS 82 (1952–53): 68–123; S. Piggott and R.J.C. Atkinson, "The Torrs Chamfrein," *Archaeologia* 94 (1955): 197–235.

to marvellous Britain (*Cruithnig cid dos-forglam i niat Alban amra*), there is the story that they were successful in the battle because 150 (hornless) cows were milked into a magical container and wounded men were placed in it to soak the poison out of their blood.[6] The horned god is occasionally described as the "lord of the animals" for his mastery over them. A similar agent, whose power comes from God, is the Christian saint. Columba demonstrated his power in the famous episode on the river Ness. He wanted a boat that was secured to the other bank and a monk named Lugne swam across to retrieve it. This disturbed a monster which tried to attack the swimmer. Columba, however, made the sign of the cross and invoked the name of God, telling the beast to go no farther and not to harm Lugne; a command that was swiftly obeyed.[7]

The horned god or "lord of the animals" represents a transitional link between human and animal cults. As mentioned earlier, the second-century geographer Ptolemy places a people known as Cornavii in the region of what is now Caithness. While the name might mean simply "people of the promontory" an alternative interpretation is Horned Ones or people who worship a horned god.[8] To the south, in the vicinity of modern Sutherland, were the Caereni "Sheep People" and beyond them in Kintyre were the Epidii, a name which might be connected with the great horse deity Epona.[9] A possible remembrance of an animal cult might lie behind an item in the so-called Wonders of Britain appended to versions of the *History of the Britons*. The first "wonder" is the eagles of Loch Leven, where, it is claimed, there are 60 islands in the loch and 60 rocks around it, each with an eagle's nest.[10] This is repeated by Geoffrey of Monmouth in the *History of the Kings of Britain*, where the eagles gain an additional talent as they shriek whenever a portentous

---

[6] The various versions with translations are in J.M.P. Calise, *Pictish Sourcebook. Documents of Medieval Legend and Dark-Age History* (Westport, 2002): 48–79.

[7] Adomnán, *Life of Columba*, ed. A.O. Anderson and M.O. Anderson (Oxford, 1991): f. 75b (p. 132); see also Jacqueline Borsje, "The Monster in the River Ness in *Vita Sancti Columbae*: A Study of a Miracle," *Peritia* 8 (1994): 27–34; Charles Thomas, "The 'Monster' Episode in Adomnan's Life of St. Columba," *Cryptozoology* 7 (1988): 38–45.

[8] C. Thomas, "Animal Art of the Scottish Iron Age and its Origins," *Archaeological Journal* 118 (1963): 14–16.

[9] Ross, *Pagan Celtic Britain*: 189.

[10] Nennius, *British History and Annals*, ed. John Morris (London, 1980): 81.

event occurs.[11] Once again there is a reference to a similar action in literature and the poem *What Brought the Picts to Marvellous Britain* claims that one of their traits was "heeding bird voices" (*gotha en da fhariri*).[12] Divination from the calls of birds is found throughout northern Europe and the sixth-century historian Procopius claims that a king of the *Varni* (a people originally located on the Baltic coast) named Hermegisclus changed the marriage plans for his son after a bird had croaked (what he believed to be) a prophecy to him.[13]

Cult leaders are difficult to identify. One of these leaders is, however, better served in popular literature than historical sources. Latin records describe him as a *magus* and he has attracted a great deal of attention. The word is Persian in origin and means "magician," with the extended sense of someone who was "learned." The Bible uses this word for the three *magi* (translated "wise men" in some English bibles) who sought the Christ-child (Matthew 2:1–13). In medieval insular hagiography the *magus* or "magician" is a standard villain. From his appearance in the sources, he is similar to the description of the druid as given by Julius Caesar and Tacitus. They described the druids as one of the two most important classes of men, almost equal in power with the king. A sensational aspect of these holy men according to Roman writers was that they propitiated their deities with the sacrifice of living creatures, including humans, in wicker constructions in the form of men. That was one of the reasons (another was their success at fomenting rebellion) why the druids were outlawed by the Romans.

One of St. Columba's rivals/tormentors at the court of King Brude was a *magus* named Broichan who had been the king's foster-father and was his advisor. The little that is known about him shows that life for the élite of the priestly class was little different from the aristocracy. Broichan owned slaves, one of whom was a Christian woman whose release had been requested by Columba. Owning female slaves implies the possession of livestock, for women traditionally carried out the feeding and milking of cattle which produced the "white foods" that were a dietary staple among the peoples of the British Isles. Irish hagiography claims that St. Brigit of Kildare's father was a druid and one of

[11] Geoffrey of Monmouth, *History of the Kings of Britain*, trans. L. Thorpe (London, 1966): 219 (bk. 9, ch. 6).
[12] The various versions with translations are in Calise, *Pictish Sourcebook*: 56–79.
[13] Procopius, *History of the Wars*, ed. Dewing, v, 255–257 (book VIII.xx).

her miracles was the replenishing of a milk pail that her slave mother had spilled. Broichan was not the only *magus* at Brude's court and Adomnán's *Life of Columba* has an episode where the other *magi* attempt to drown out the singing at Vespers by the saint and his party outside the royal fortress. To counteract this, the saint began singing the 44th Psalm in a voice like thunder, which frightened the king and his court.[14] *Magi* were believed to have control over the elements and it is implied that they conjured up contrary winds to delay the saint and his companions on their return to Iona.[15]

What precise cults the *magi* led can only be surmised, but one of them seems to have been a water cult. Their location occasionally can be deduced from votive offerings such as the cauldron in the extinct pond in Kirkcudbright. A direct reference to one comes, once again, from Adomnán's *Life of Columba*. The saint was in the land of the Picts and he heard of a diabolical well which was worshiped because it poisoned anyone who drank from it. Skin rashes, blinding, and crippling were visible manifestations of the evil spirit who maimed anyone drinking from the well. A priesthood appears to have served the place because when Columba approached the well, the "magicians" watched what they hoped would be his injury. True to hagiography, however, the saint raised his hand and after blessing the waters in order to drive away the demons, he drank safely. So thoroughly had the well been cleansed that instead of disease, cures were affected.[16] Death-dealing wells or springs were venerated by non-Christians throughout northern Europe well into the early Middle Ages. The Anglo-Saxon missionary Willibrord, to give one example, was stranded on an island on the boundary between the Danes and Frisians where the only source of water was a sacred spring, and when he and his company drank the water, the inhabitants were astonished that they neither died nor became insane.[17]

Evidence for cults is also suggested by personal names and an intriguing one is the previously introduced Tarain. Tarain is a form of the name Taranis, the thunder god of Gaul who was the equivalent of Jupiter; the name is inscribed on a stone found at Chester where there seems to be

---

[14] Adomnán, *Life of Columba*: 70. For an analysis of this episode see John Purser, *Scotland's Music* (Edinburgh, 1992): 33–34.
[15] Adomnán, *Life of Columba*: 12.
[16] Adomnán, *Life of Columba*: 108–110.
[17] C.H. Talbot, *Anglo-Saxon Missionaries in Germany* (New York, 1954): 10. An interesting side-note is that the king was expected to take action against anyone who profaned the site.

an equivalence – Jupiter Taranis.[18] Three items associated with Taranis are the wheel, the eagle, and the serpent; an altar fragment from Alzey shows Taranis flanked by a wheel and an eagle holding a ring in its beak, while another altar fragment has his torso again flanked by the wheel (with a serpent beneath it) and an eagle.[19] As one of the war deities, the Gauls dedicated the heads of the slain to Taranis, and his cult also seems to have had an association with the druids.[20] Eagles, serpents, and circles in some instances are found on the symbol stones. The name Tarain is found in various contexts throughout the island; the Welsh tale *How Culwuch won Olwen*, for example, gives a Tarain as one of the heroes of the Britons. Turning again to Adomnán's *Life of Columba*, a Pictish noble named Tarain (Tarainus) fled to St. Columba for protection and was treacherously slain by Feradach, a wealthy man who lived on Islay to whom he was entrusted.[21] The same name is also found among princes and a Tarain son of Anfrith (Latin *filius Entifidich* or *Amfredech*) was expelled from the kingship in 697 and fled to Ireland in 699.

Christianity

The date of the first introduction of Christianity among the peoples north of Hadrian's Wall is uncertain. Unlike those living within the Empire, there was no compulsion for any of the "barbarians" to accept Christianity in the late fourth century when it became the sole subsidized religion. This does not mean that there were not Christians among them. The late second-/early third-century Christian apologist from Carthage named Tertullian claimed in his *Adversus Judaeos* that there were Christians in Britain in the area beyond Roman control, which can only be read as indicating to the north of Hadrian's Wall. In a passage on the expansion of Christianity he notes that it extended as far as the region of the Britons inaccessible to the Romans.[22] Similar information comes from Tertullian's

[18] Ernst Hübner, *Inscriptiones Britanniae latinae: consilio et auctoritate Academiae litterarum regiae borussicae* (Berlin, 1959): 168.
[19] E. (Lantier-)Espérandieu, *Recueil General des Bas-Reliefs, Statues et Bustes de la Gaule Romaine*, 10 vols. (Paris, 1910), nos. 7749 and 299 respectively.
[20] Paul-Marie Duval, "Teutates, Esus, Taranis," *Études Celtiques* 8 (1958–59): 41–58 (at p. 44).
[21] Adomnán, *Life of Columba*: 126.
[22] Tertullian, *Adversus Iudaeos* §7.3 in *Corpus Christianorum Series Latinae* II. 1354: ... *et Britannorum inacessa Romanis loca*. This tract was written c.195.

contemporary Origen who, in his homily on Luke 1: 24–32, remarks "The power of the Lord and Saviour is with those who are in Britain, separated from our world..."[23] The Christian mission north of the Wall was closely connected with the community to the south. St. Patrick's birthplace seems to have been almost on the northern frontier of Imperial Britain. He stated that he was born a Christian and that his father Calpornius was a deacon and his grandfather Potitus was a priest. The Christian message of equality explains why in one of his letters he addresses a powerful ruler named Coroticus, probably the king of Strathclyde, as an equal and refuses to salute him as a fellow citizen of the holy Romans (i.e., a Christian). There is little doubt that there were Christian communities north of Hadrian's Wall by the sixth century. The poem Y Gododdin, for example, has references to Christian imagery and ritual among the descriptions of the warrior, such as the reflection that warriors died in battle without the opportunity to go to church to do penance.[24] The (probably) sixth-century memorials to the bishops Nicolaus (?) and Naiton found at Pebbles (the former at Cross Kirk) have been cited as evidence of a diocese in the Upper Tweed Valley.[25]

Ninian: Apostle to the Southern Picts

Establishment of Christianity as the "official" religion of the Roman Empire by the end of the fourth century made it a base for missionaries who wished to proselytize among the peoples beyond its boundaries. A man associated with this obscure period was Ninian or Ninnius. Bede (who writes his name as Nynias) implies that he was the first known

---

[23] Origen, *Homilies on Luke, Fragments on Luke*, trans. Joseph Lienhard SJ (Washington, DC, 1996): 27. The passage is connected with a diversion on I Corinthians 5: 4: "You are gathered together, in my spirit also, with the power of the Lord Jesus."

[24] Kenneth Jackson, *The Gododdin* (Edinburgh, 1969): 118. On the question of the impact and spread of Christianity, see: Ian Smith, "The Origins and Development of Christianity in North England and Southern Pictland," in John Blair and Carol Pyrah (eds.), *Church Archaeology: Research Directions for the Future* (York, 1996): 19–37; Sally Foster, "The Strength of Belief: The Impact of Christianity on Early Historic Scotland," in Guy de Boe and Frans Verhaeghe (eds.), *Religion and Belief in Medieval Europe* (Zellik, 1997): 229–240.

[25] Charles Thomas, *The Early Christian Archaeology of North Britain* (Oxford, 1971): 15–17.

Christian missionary north of Hadrian's Wall. Ninnius is a familiar Latin forename (the man who translated the *Iliad* into Latin was called Ninnius Crassus). Almost all that is known about him (other than the stray reference in Irish materials) comes from the Venerable Bede (III.4).[26] He claims that Ninian (*Nynias*) was a Briton (*virus de natione Brettonum*) who studied at Rome and built a church of stone that was popularly known as the White House (*Ad Candida Casa*) upon his return to Britain, which was dedicated to St. Martin of Tours; there Ninian and other saints are buried.[27] He was a missionary among the Picts "on this side of the mountains" (*qui intra eosdem montes habent sedes*) many years before the mission of Columba of Iona. Later Anglo-Saxon sources follow Bede's outline. The interest by Anglo-Saxons reflects their conquest of the region extending from Carlisle to what is now Stranraer by the kings of Northumbria shortly before the time Bede was composing his history. Two generations afterwards the eighth-century scholar Alcuin (the director of Charlemagne's schools) received poems concerning Ninian from two of his former students at York who were then living at Whithorn. The poems (surviving in a tenth-century manuscript) are the *Miracles of Bishop Ninian (Miracula Nynie Episcopi)* and the *Hymn of Holy Bishop Ninian (Hymnus sancti Nynie episcopi)*.[28] Ninian became famous among the Irish as a schoolmaster as well as missionary, and several Irish saints – such as Finnian of Clonard – are said to have been his pupils.[29] Anglo-Norman interest in Ninian appears in the twelfth century when his *vita* was written by the Cistercian scholar Ailred of Rievaulx (the name Ailred is a francophone rendering of Aethelraed).[30] Later materials expand on this information with claims that Ninian was the son of a king who

---

[26] See the *Ecclesiastical History*, in *Venerabilis Baedae Opera Historica*, ed. Charles Plummer, 2 vols. (Oxford, 1896): i, 133.

[27] On the question of St. Martin see Juliet Mullins, "Trouble at the White House: Anglo-Irish Relations and the Cult of St. Martin," *Proceedings of the British Academy* 157 (2009): 113–127.

[28] The poems were edited by Karl Strecker in MGH, *Poetae Latini aevi Carolini*, IV (fasc ii–iii): 943–962, and discussed by him in "Zu den Quellen für das Leben des hl. Ninian," *Neues Archiv der Gesellschaft für ältere deutsche Geshichstunde* xliii (1920–22): 1–26. See also Wilhelm Levison, "An Eighth-Century Poem on St. Ninian," *Antiquity* xiv (1940): 280–291 (at p. 283).

[29] For Finnian, see Whitley Stokes (ed.), *The Martyrology of Oengus the Culdee: Félire Óengusso Céli Dé, Kalendar of Oengus* (Dublin, repr. 1984): 212.

[30] Ailred's *vita* of St. Ninian was edited by Alexander Penrose Forbes, *Lives of S. Ninian and S. Kentigern*, Historians of Scotland 5 (Edinburgh, 1874): 137–157,

actually met St. Martin, and imported builders to build his church. How much the later materials depend on now-lost historical materials and how much on learned speculation is uncertain, but Bede, who says he is merely repeating common report, probably has the older details.

The White House or *Ad Candida Casa*, which the Irish called *Futerna*, was built at the southern end of the Whithorn peninsula, at the edge of what is now the town of Whithorn. The Whithorn peninsula juts into the Irish Sea, and the site of Ninian's church is only a couple of miles from the coast. Immediately on the beach is a cave where the saint supposedly retired for contemplation, which contains some Christian graffiti. The Irish Sea put Ninian on a convenient route for the lands south of Hadrian's Wall, the western coast of Scotland, and eastern Ireland. The priests (*sacerdotes*) Viventius and Mavorius who are commemorated on a stone at Kirkmadine (in the Rhinns of Galloway) that is no later than the late fifth century may have been a part of a mission attached to Whithorn. Stories about Irish students at his church make sense in light of its easy accessibility. By the later Middle Ages its fame had passed into literature. A story that Ailred of Rievaulx preserved in his *Life* of Ninian is the tale of a boy who was studying with the saint, but had been disobedient and was about to be punished. So he ran off with the saint's staff and tried to sail away in a coracle, which had not been given its protective leather covering. The writer remarks that the vessel moved at the slightest touch and was soon in the sea, where the water began to pour in. Afraid of drowning, the boy place the staff in a hole and the sea miraculously reversed its submergence of the vessel.[31]

Bede's statement that Ninian was responsible for the conversion of the Southern Picts to Christianity is regrettably vague, merely noting that those people lived on his side – that is south – of the mountains. Since the location of Whithorn is in lands that are believed to have been part of the kingdom of Rheged, and were south of Strathclyde, which Bede declared to be south of the kingdoms of the Picts, this leads to a mystery, especially since two bishops of Whithorn had names with *Pict-* as an element: Pehthelm (Pict Protector, d.735), and Pehtwine (Pict Friend, d.776). Like all historians, Bede was dependent on his source materials. If he was using

---

with preceding translation. See also G.W.S. Barrow, "The Childhood of Scottish Christianity: A Note on Some Place-Name Evidence," *Scottish Studies* 27 (1983): 1–15; John MacQueen, *St. Nynia* (Edinburgh, 1961).
[31] *Vita* of Ninian, in Forbes, *Lives of S. Ninian and S. Kentigern*: 151–152 (ch. 10).

materials that applied the term *Pict* in the older Roman sense (e.g., as Gildas used it) for anyone who lived north of Hadrian's Wall, then Ninian could have been active in the region between the Antonine and Hadrian Walls while still credited with the conversion of the southernmost Picts.

When Ninian flourished is also uncertain, although the traditional late fourth-/early fifth-century date has been challenged.[32] Evidence that there was a Christian community at Whithorn in the fourth century is suggested by the Whithorn Stone from the first half of the fifth century commemorating a Christian named Latinus which also includes the name of his grandfather, implying that he, too, was a Christian.[33] Remaining with the earlier date for Ninian's career makes intriguing an item of information in the chronicle of Prosper of Aquitaine. He claims that about 431 Pope Honorius sent a Bishop Palladius to the Scots. The home of Palladius has been placed in what is now Poitou.[34] Much of the controversy has revolved around two questions: first, is he the real St. Patrick; and, second, if not, then should his mission be placed before or after Patrick's?[35] Neither of those questions is relevant here, but one that *is* relevant is the area(s) of his activities. According to the *vita* of Patrick by Muirchú (a contemporary of Adomnán) Palladius preceded Patrick but accomplished nothing; he left Ireland to return home, but died in the land of the Britons (*in Britonum finibus vita functus*).[36] Where were those Britons? An aside in the Irish version of Nennius' *History of the Britons* preserved in the Irish *Book of the Dun*

---

[32] See two essays by Thomas Clancy, "The Real St. Ninian," *Innes Review* 52 (2001): 1–26; and "Saints' Cults and National Identities in the Early Middle Ages," in Alan Thacker and Richard Sharpe (eds.), *Local Saints and Local Churches in the Early Medieval West* (Oxford, 2002): 397–421.

[33] Katherine Forsyth, "The Latinus Stone: Whithorn's Earliest Christian Monument," in J. Murray (ed.), *St Ninian and the Earliest Christianity in Scotland: Papers from the Conference Held by the Friends of the Whithorn Trust in Whithorn on September 15th, 2007*, BAR British series 483 (Oxford, 2009): 19–41.

[34] Dáibhí Ó Cróinín, "Who was Palladius 'First Bishop of the Irish'?," *Peritia* 12 (2000): 205–237.

[35] Both questions were sparked by T.F. O'Rahilly's controversial lecture published as *The Two Patricks: A Lecture on the History of Christianity in Fifth-Century Ireland* (Dublin, 1942); for an overview of the controversy see D.A. Binchy, "Patrick and his Biographers, Ancient and Modern," *Studia Hibernica* 2 (1962): 7–173.

[36] Muirchu's *vita* is printed by Ludwig Bieler, *The Patrician Texts in the Book of Armagh* (Dublin, 1979): 72.

Cow (*Lebor na hUidre*), written about 1100, notes Palladius had a church "in Fordun in the Mearns" (*i Fordun isin Mairne*), now thought to be Fordun, 11 miles (17 km) southwest of Stonehaven.[37] Another note, this time a comment from a fifteenth-century Irish manuscript of the ninth-century *Martyrology of Oengus* (*Félire Óengusso*) claims that Palladius was also known as Torannán and an earlier, fourteenth-century Irish manuscript *Lebar Brecc* (*Speckled Book*) repeats Muirchú in saying that he was not well received in Ireland, so he went to Britain. The editor of the *Martyrology of Oengus* speculates that this might be evidence that Torannán is to be identified with Ternan who is found in later Scottish calendars as one of the early laborers for Christianity in northern Britain.[38]

Columba: Apostle to the Northern Picts

Compared with the sparcity of information remaining about earlier or contemporary missionaries, there is a flood of material connected with the sixth-century Columba of Iona. Thanks to the *vita* composed by his successor of a century later, Adomnán, more is revealed in his hagiography about the cultural, spiritual, and social life in the Highlands and farther north than in any other record. Columba (the name is Latin for *dove*) was known to the Irish as Colum Chille (Dove of the Church), but his name in the world was Crimthann. Columba came from royal stock in the north of Ireland; his kingdom of Cenél Conaill was part of the powerful Uí Néill confederation. Setting aside the various stories concerning the circumstances of his emigration from Ireland, he established a church on Iona in the mid-sixth century. The name Iona is actually a misspelling of the island's name Iova (Sheep) Island. There are two different accounts of who allowed Columba to set up a church on that island (which is tiny, only about one mile by two). Bede claims that the donor was Brude son of Maelcon, the king of Picts known from Adomnán's *Life of Columba*.[39] The *Annals of Ulster*, however, mention

---

[37] R.I. Best and Osborne Bergin (eds.), *Lebor Na Huidre, Book of the Dun Cow* (Dublin, 1929): 10 (f. 4a): "Ro innarbad Pledias a Hérind [ocus] tánic coro fogain do Dia i Fordun isin Mairne."

[38] Stokes, *Félire Óengusso Céli Dé*: 148.

[39] Bede, *Ecclesiastical History*, in *Venerabilis Baedae Opera Historica*, ed. Charles Plummer, 2 vols. (Oxford, 1896): 133. The controversy continues; see Thomas Clancy, "Iona in the Kingdom of the Picts, a Note," *Innes Review* 55 (2004): 55–57.

an alternative donor in Conall son of Comgall, the king of Dál Riata who is awarded the honor in his obituary in 574. Supporting Bede's information is a passage from the preface to *Altus Prositor*, which claims that messengers from Pope Gregory I visited Columba and that Brude son of Maelcon gave Iona to Columba.[40] Since *Altus Prositor* is an eleventh-century work, that might reflect nothing more than that the writer had read Bede. Possibly both Bede and the *Annals of Ulster* are correct. Brude's territory might have run down the Great Glen to the Hebrides; if Iona was in a borderland, the good will of both princes would be desirable to insure the community's survival. Even a cursory reading of his *vita* shows that Columba was a diplomat. He had to negotiate some difficult issues, such as his mission to Brude's court in order to gain safety for missionaries. For reasons such as these Columba became the patron saint of the Irish in Britain, and Bede claims that at least some of the Picts looked on him in much the same way.

One of the many problems with using Adomnán's *Life of Columba* is that he intended it as a devotional text, so any historical information was included to provide examples to support his thesis. This is clear from the division of the book into three sections which had as their themes angels, miracles, and prophecy. His themes give some insight into the mentality of the Christian missionaries who labored among the Picts.[41] Unlike the administrative concerns found south of Hadrian's Wall or on the Continent within the bounds of the empire, these men were involved with the mystical aspects of Christianity, which emphasized the visible manifestations of the divine. The mentality of the individuals who brought a new religion is reflected in the art on the carved stones that include angels, humans, animals, and fantasy creatures around crucifixes.

Adomnán's account has much unique information that has been cited in earlier chapters, and it leaves no doubt that the saint's main area of action was in the Outer Hebrides and along the Great Glen as far as Inverness, and possibly as far west as Buchan, where the legend of the foundation of the church of Deer claims that Columba was directly responsible. Some indication of his success can be gauged by the prominence of the churches connected with Iona, sometimes called simply the Columban *paruchia* or parish. Bede claims that during his lifetime the

---

[40] ESSH: i, 98.
[41] For opinions on this point, see: Thomas Clancy, "Columba, Adomnán, and the Cult of Saints in Scotland," *Innes Review* 48 (1997): 1–26; James Fraser, "Adomnán, Cumméne Ailbe and the Picts," *Peritia* 17–18 (2004): 183–198.

Columban *paruchia* was dominant in northern Britain from the Scottish Highlands to the river Forth. Columban missions throughout the north were more than mere outposts of Christianity; they were also transmitters of Gaelic culture and the arts. The roles of missionary and teacher occasionally were seen as one and the same. In the poem known as *Columba's Breastplate (Amhra Coluim Chille)* there is a listing of church fathers who influenced him together with the line that notes his blessing was on the fierce ones of the Tay – referring to Columba, but meaning that monks from Iona were active in that region.[42]

Saints and Missions

The church of Iona was not alone in sending its missions among the peoples of northern Britain. Sometimes these missionaries are memorialized in lists or asides found in later medieval works. The more extensive claims can be set aside as elaboration, but they show that by the twelfth century missionary work among the Picts was considered crucial for any saint venerated in what was then the Scottish kingdom. John of Fordun gives a summary of sorts that includes Kentigern, Ninian, Palladius, Servanus, and Ternan; in other chapters are mentioned Regulus, Brendan and Machar, Columba, and Drostan.[43] Slightly later than Ninian was Kentigern, also known as Mungo, the patron saint of Glasgow although his home was farther east in Gododdin. What is known of his career comes largely from two twelfth-century works. The earlier was written by an unknown cleric at the order of Bishop Herbert of Glasgow and only a fragment of it survives, while the later, apparently complete, *vita* was composed by Jocelin of Furness.[44] This claims that credit for the conversion of the Picts to Christianity was due to Kentigern as well as Ninian and Columba; in what seems to be an awkwardly added postscript,

---

[42] T.O. Clancy and Gilbert Márkus (ed. and trans.), *Iona, the Earliest Poetry of a Celtic Monastery* (Edinburgh, 1995): 104–115 (at p. 112).

[43] William Forbes Skene (ed.), *Johannis de Fordun, Chronica Gentis Scotorum*, Historians of Scotland 1 and 2 (Edinburgh, 1871–72): i, 77, 94–95, 108, 113, and 117. For studies of individuals see Alan MacQuarrie, "*Vita Sancti Servani*: The Life of St. Serf," *Innes Review* 44 (1993): 122–152 and Alexander Boyle, "Notes on Scottish Saints," *Innes Review* 32 (1981): 59–82.

[44] Forbes, *Lives*: 159–242 (Jocelin) and 243–252 (Anonymous), with preceding translations. See also John Durkan, "A 'Lost' Manuscript Life of St. Kentigern," *Innes Review* 54 (2003): 227–229.

it is explained that the Picts apostatized and their reconversion was solely the work of Kentigern, who also converted the *Scoti*.[45] Royal gratitude to a saintly patron expressed in the donation of lands is found in the foundation legend of Abernethy (see below), which claims that King Nechton son of Erp gave the land for the building of a church dedicated to St. Brigit of Kildare after his return from exile in Ireland.[46] Little is known of Curitan of Rosemarkie, although he has been identified as the *Curetán epscop* who, with King Brude son of Derili, subscribed to the Law of Innocents, also known as the Law of Adomnán (Old Irish *Cáin Adomnáin*); he is number 22 in the list.[47] Another possible subscriber is Ioain of Eigg (no. 38) who died in 725.

More ambiguous is the mission of Máel Ruba of Bangor, who founded a church at Applecross around 671. Applecross is well to the north of the traditional early boundary of the Irish colony of Dál Riata at Ardnamurchan and it is opposite the Isle of Skye. Just off the southern end of the island is the island of Rum and a Beccan of Rum died in 677. Their missions might have some connection with the expansion of Dál Riata northwards into the lands of the Picts. According to Adomnán, when Columba went to the Isle of Skye for solitude and when he gave the last rites there to a pagan named Artbranán, he had to speak to him through an interpreter.[48] The romance known as *The Tale of Cano son of Gartnan* claims that dynasts from Dál Riata were settled on Skye by the mid-seventh century; and the story begins with Cano's expulsion from the island.[49] This should be compared with the account of the movement from Skye to Ireland and back to Skye of the three sons of

---

[45] Forbes, *Lives*: 209; the elaboration becomes more extensive later when Kentigern is credited with sending missions to the Orkney Islands, Norway, and Iceland (p. 220). See also Alan MacQuarrie, "The Career of Saint Kentigern of Glasgow: *Vitae, Lectiones* and Gimpses of Fact," *Innes Review* 37 (1984): 3–24.

[46] This is found in the so-called king-lists; the earliest episode is in the famous Poppleton Manuscript, printed in KES, p. 247; for comment see E.G. Bowen, "Cult of St. Brigit," *Studia Celtica* 8/9 (1973/74): 41.

[47] *Ad Acta Sanctorum*, March, ii, 444–445, where he is called Kiritinus of the Picts; Máirín Ní Dhonnchadha, 'The Guarantor List of *Cáin Adomnáin*, 697," *Peritia* 1 (1982): 178–215 (p. 191).

[48] Adomnán, *Life of Columba*: 63 and 133–135.

[49] Adomnán, *Life of Columba*: 62 (i, 33) and D.A. Binchy (ed.), *Scéla Cano meic Gartnáin* (Dublin, 1975): 1; Cano's home was actually nearby Skye on Inis moccu Chein.

Gartnaith and their followers. So the question is simply: were the missions of Máel Ruba and Beccan to convert the pagans or were they to serve the needs of colonists from Dál Riata?

Other saints had brief contacts with the Picts. The *vita* of Comgall of Bangor claims that he founded a monastery "in regione Heth," which is usually identified as the island of Tiree, which was attacked by a fleet of Picts. The saint sought divine vengeance for the attack, which took the form of a tremendous percussion.[50] The *vita* of St. Cainnech (*Cainnicus*) claims that his journey across *Druim Alban* (the Ridge of Britain) was interrupted so that he could heal the daughter of an unnamed king of Picts.[51] Even more dramatic is the episode in the *vita* of St. Buite, who travels through the kingdoms of the Picts when he returned to Ireland from a pilgrimage to Rome. He resurrects a king named Nechtan and is given the fortress where the event occurred, which has tentatively been identified with Kirkbuddo, near Forfar.[52]

Throughout northern Britain the sending out of missions from a church which acted as a base of operations appears to have been the standard method of operation. This may have extended to the Orkney Islands with the church at Birsay as the principal church.[53] This is exactly the method described by Adomnán for clergy from the Iona community. Without urban centers, much of the pastoral work would have been away from churches and necessitated the use of portable equipment, such as the portable stone altar similar to that found at Wick, probably of a seventh- to eighth-century date. The sedimentary stone is 4 ins × 3½ ins (10 × 8.8 cm) and about ¾ in (2 cm) thick with a central cross and four crosses at the corners.[54] These would have been carried by the clergy and a representation of this might be on the symbol stone from Papil, Shetland, in what are usually identified as book satchels.

Ecclesiastical relations between the Picts and the Anglo-Saxons preceded the inquiry into the date of Easter made in the eighth century by King Nechtan of Abbot Ceolfrid of Wearmouth and Jarrow that is mentioned by Bede (V.21).[55] After the Synod of Whitby in 664, in which the

---

[50] *Vita Sancti Comgalli*, in Charles Plummer (ed.), *Vita Sanctorum Hiberniae* (Oxford, 1910): ii, 11.
[51] Plummer, *Vita Sanctorum Hiberniae*: i, 159.
[52] Plummer, *Vita Sanctorum Hiberniae*: i, 88–89.
[53] S.E. Crudden, "Excavations at Birsay, Orkney," in A. Small (ed.), *The Fourth Viking Conference* (Edinburgh, 1965): 22–31.
[54] Thomas, *Early Christian Archaeology of North Britain*: 194.
[55] Bede, *Historia Ecclesiastica*: 332–346.

Northumbrian king Oswy chose to follow continental Christian practices rather than the older rituals used by the Irish, Columban influence began to decline outside northern Britain, and probably within the lands north of the Forth as Northumbrian influence spread into the region north of Hadrian's Wall by the early eighth century. During this period of Northumbrian ascendancy, the Angles set up a bishop named Trumwine with a seat at Abercorn on the southwestern side of the Firth of Forth, in the lands of the former British kingdom of Gododdin, and he is called the bishop of the Picts. There was casual and friendly contact between the clergy of the Picts and the Northumbrians. The *vita* of St. Cuthbert has an episode where the saint made a journey to Pictavia which was interrupted by tempestuous seas and Cuthbert's party was saved from starvation by the finding of a stranded beast.[56] The location for this adventure has been proposed as Nith on the coast of Fife which makes sense of the party's expectation of a quick journey, although it fails to explain why the stranded wayfarers did not seek shelter with the local inhabitants.[57] The distance by water is approximately 60 miles (100 km), measuring from Fife Ness to Lindisfarne; assuming that the craft sailed at an average of 5 knots then the voyage would have taken approximately 10 hours, which explains why Cuthbert and his companions did not pack ample provisions. Perhaps their return was interrupted by the inclement weather, and they took shelter on one of the islands in the Firth of Forth.

Soon after Adomnán had composed his *vita* of Columba, and while Bede was writing his *Ecclesiastical History*, there were two popes who had special interest in Britain. Both of them took the name Gregory and they were the opponents of the Byzantine emperor Leo III, whose support for iconoclasm (the destruction of images) was to precipitate a controversy that would rage in the eastern churches for a long time. Pope Gregory II (r.715–731) was the host of the West Saxon king Ine on his pilgrimage to Rome in 729 as well as being the patron of the Anglo-Saxon missions to the Germanic kingdoms led by Boniface, who seems to have been a native of the region round Exeter. In 721 he called a synod to discuss the problem of illegitimate marriages. The strictures of that synod led to the insistence later urged on the Anglo-Saxons that their

---

[56] The story is found in the "Anonymous Life of St. Cuthbert," in Bertram Colgrave (ed.), *Two Lives of St. Cuthbert* (Cambridge, 1940): 82.
[57] A. Breeze, "St. Cuthbert, Bede, and the Niduari of Pictland," *Northern History* 40 (2003): 365–368.

kings had to be selected from the children of legitimate marriages, rather than casual liaisons.[58] This might have been one of the reasons for Bede's sensitivity to the role of the mother in succession among the Picts. Gregory II's successor Gregory III (r.731–741) continued the campaign against iconoclasm and was more immediately involved in affairs in Britain. He elevated York to archiepiscopal status in 735 at the request of King Ceolwulf, to whom Bede dedicated his history. This might have been the time when the churches north of Hadrian's Wall were assigned to York, a submission that Scottish bishops from the twelfth century onwards would attempt to overturn. Extending York's area of authority into northern Britain was in keeping with Gregory's concerns about orthodoxy, particularly in Britain. He warned his clergy against purveyors of false doctrine, especially the Britons (i.e., Welsh) who had not yet accepted the Roman calculation of the date of Easter. In a letter to the bishops of the Alans and of the Bavarians, Pope Gregory III condemns the British clergy by name: *Vel venientium Britonum, vel falsorum sacerdotum*.[59] The pope's uneasiness extended to some of the Irish, with whom his protégé Boniface clashed in his dealing with the Germanic peoples. If Pope Gregory III did add all the churches in northern Britain to York's care, it was the final act in a process of extension that had begun decades earlier. An interesting side note to Gregory III and Britain is a forgery that continues to be cited as evidence that a Sedulius, described as a bishop of Britain and Irish by birth, was present at a papal council in the company of another bishop called Fergustus who is described as a Pict and bishop of Scotia.[60] Unfortunately the document was believed to be genuine by the mid-nineteenth-century scholar A.W. Haddan who included it in the collection popularly known as *Councils and Ecclesiastical Documents relating to Great Britain and Ireland* and it occasionally resurfaces.[61]

The introduction of Christianity did not mean that paganism abruptly disappeared. This coexistence of religions was common throughout

---

[58] This was the subject of a letter from the Anglo-Saxon St. Boniface to King Aethelbald of Mercia in 746/47, printed in Arthur Haddan and William Stubbs, *Councils and Ecclesiastical Documents Relating to Great Britain and Ireland*, 3 vols. (Oxford, 1869–78): iii, 350–356.

[59] Haddan and Stubbs, *Councils and Ecclesiastical Documents*: i, 203.

[60] MGH, *Epistolae*, III: 704–707 (at p. 706). The eleventh-century forgery reads: "Fergustus episcopus Scotia Pictus huic constituto a nobis promugato subscripsit et Sedulus episcopus Britanniae de genere Scotorum subscriptsit."

[61] Haddan and Stubbs, *Councils and Ecclesiastical Documents*: ii, 7.

Europe, and magical charms based on the older non-Christian faith were used for centuries, often with the addition of a Christian tag. Sometimes artifacts suggest that pagan cult centers continued long after Christianity is believed to have swept all before it. A representation of the horned god Cernunnos has been found in Meigle in an eighth-century AD context.[62] There might be a literary preservation of an animal totem in the sixteenth-century *Breviary of Aberdeen* where, in the *vita* of St. Machar, the saint turns a boar into stone.[63] During the actual conversion phase there was a great deal of hostility, especially from the local holy men whose cults were being discarded. Adomnán tells a story about a family living somewhere along or near the Great Glen who had converted to Christianity after which their son died. The "magicians" hailed the incident as evidence of the feebleness of the Christian God compared with the strength of their own gods. When the saint prayed at the body of the dead child, the boy came back to life and was escorted to his parents in a clear triumph for Christianity.[64]

Kings, Nobles, and the Church

A generation after the death of King Ecgfrith in the battle of Dun Nechtan, Bede reports (*Historia*: IV.21) that the Pictish king Naiton or Nechtan, after meditating about the scriptures, came to realize the error among the churches in his realm in calculating the date of Easter. So he sent an appeal to Abbot Ceolfrid of Wearmouth and Jarrow, sometime before 716, asking him for help in bringing the churches in his lands into conformity with those of the Northumbrians.[65] He also asked for the services of builders who worked in stone in order to build a church. The bulk of the chapter is taken up with Ceolfrid's reply, in which he gives

---

[62] Ross, *Pagan Celtic Britain*: 185.
[63] ESSH: i, 41.
[64] Adomnán, *Life of Columba*: 138.
[65] Bede, *Historia Ecclesiastica*: 332–346. An interesting discussion of this exchange and its influence on Bede's writings is A.A.M. Duncan, "Bede, Iona and the Picts," in R.H.C. Davis and J. M. Wallace-Hadrill (eds.), *The Writing of History in the Middle Ages: Essays Presented to Richard William Southern* (Oxford, 1981): 20–27. See also Julianna Grigg, "Pascal Dating in Pictland: Abbot Ceolfrid's Letter to King Nechtan," *Journal of the Australian Early Medieval Association* 2 (2006): 85–101.

the necessary calculations as well as the justifications for them. The chapter concludes with the king ordering the publication of the information. There seems to be a postscript to that episode. In 717, members of the Iona community were expelled across the Ridge of Britain by Nechtan. Such good relations help explain why traces of Anglo-Saxon artistic influence are found along the eastern Scottish coasts. Evidence can be found as far north as Ross, where a Latin inscription found at Tarbat has lettering that has been cited as evidence of Northumbrian influence at the end of the eighth century.[66] When John of Fordun and other late medieval Scottish writers claimed that the Anglo-Saxons were the allies of the Picts in the fight against the Scots, they may have been remembering the association between the Picts and Angles that, after the end of Northumbrian domination, evolved into ecclesiastical cooperation.

Disagreements within the Christian community about doctrine and ritual were occasionally more serious than calculation of feast days. Some of these non-orthodox dogmas were so distinct that they were classified as heresies. A particularly persistent one was associated with Britain, and Germanus' visit to the Synod of St. Albans was in response to Pelagianism, the belief that humans are essentially good and can achieve salvation without the need for intervention on the part of the church or even divine grace. This might have been present outside Romanized Britain. The Irish *Life of Columba*, in its present form a late medieval production, has two bishops trying to send Columba away from Iona, but the text claims that they were not really bishops.[67] Without making too much of an obscure item in a very late production, this is an odd item to put in a saint's life and it might be a memory of bishops espousing the Pelagian view who were attempting to assert their right to this area.

There are many stories about the establishment of churches among the Picts, but most are preserved in documents composed centuries after the supposed event. The association of Nechtan son of Erp with St. Brigit is linked to the church of Abernethy. The story is mentioned in most king-lists, but the most fulsome version (in a somewhat jumbled account) claims that early in his career Nechtan had been an exile in Ireland.[68] There he prayed to St. Brigit who answered his prayer by

[66] John Higgitt, "The Pictish Latin Inscription at Tarbat in Ross-shire," PSAS 112 (1982): 300–321 (p. 318).
[67] ESSH: i, 45.
[68] KES: 247 and ESSH: i, cxx–cxxi; this is from the famous Poppleton Manuscript (see chapter 8) and for comment see Bowen, Cult of St. Brigit: 41.

promising that if he returned home, then he would be king. So the second year after Abbess Dairlugdach of Kildare came to Britain, Nechtan gave Abernethy to St. Brigit until Domesday. Another story that is possibly connected with this Nechtan is found in the *Aberdeen Breviary* concerning St. Boniface and his followers at Restennet.[69] The saint and his companions were residing near Restennet, but King Nechtan led an army to send them away. There the king was inspired to accept baptism and gave the land to the saint in perpetuity. The name Nechtan is found throughout Britain and Ireland. A bishop named Naiton is commemorated on a stone found at Peebles, while a famous saint of Devon and Cornwall was named Nechtan, often found in association with a Winnoc.[70] In a secular context, Nechtan was the name of the craftsman who made the crozier found in 1814 walled up in Lismore castle.[71] A form of the name came from the Mediterranean, from Egypt, and it could be a remnant of Roman contact. Another (dubious) memorial of a royal donation is preserved in the *Register of the Priory of St. Andrews* where a Brude son of Dergard, "qui ultimus regum Pictorum," is credited with the donation of land to the community of St. Serf's of Loch Leven.[72] There is a Brude son of Dergard in the "X" group of king-lists while there is a Brude son of Derili in the "Y" group; the former is credited with a reign of 30 years while the latter is given only six years. Neither man was the last king of the Picts and both names are among the princes of the late seventh/early eighth century; Brude son of Derili died in 706 (see chapter 3).

A somewhat different foundation legend, with a noble as the donor this time, is the story concerning the foundation of the church of Deer, which is preserved in the surviving Gospels known as *The Book of*

---

[69] Alan Macquarrie (ed.), *Legends of the Scottish Saints ... in the Aberdeen Breviary* (Dublin, 2012): 86, under March 16.

[70] Thomas, *Early Christian Archaeology of North Britain*: 17; and G.H. Doble, *Lives of the Welsh Saints*, ed. D. Simon Evans (Cardiff, 1971): 145n154.

[71] CIIC: ii, 109; the bishop, Niall mac meic Áeducáin, might be twelfth century.

[72] This item has been printed several times, with some slight differences in orthography, first in *Liber cartarum prioratus Sancti Andree in Scotia*, ed. Thomas Thomson, Bannatyne Club 69 (Edinburgh, 1841): 113, then in Haddan and Stubbs, *Councils and Ecclesiastical Documents*: ii, 147 and in ESC: 4: "Brude filius Dergard, qui ultimus regum Pictorum secundum antiquas traditiones fuisse recolitur, contulit insulam Lochleuine Deo Omnipotenti et Sancto Servano et keledeis heremetis ibidem commorantibus et Deo servientibus et servituris in illa insula."

Deer.[73] According to this legend, Columba and his disciple Drostan visited Aberdour (Abbordoboir) and were given the land by the local noble (called a *mormaer*) named Bede. Then they came to the vicinity of what is now Old Deer and the clerics asked for that land as well. Bede refused to surrender it, but when his son fell ill, he asked for their prayers and in return gave an offering of land extending from "the rock of the spring" (*cloch in tiprat*) to the "rock of the *pit* of the son of Garnat" (*cloch pette mic Garnait*). The child recovered and Drostan remained there; he wept when Columba departed and so the name "tears" (*deara*) was given to it. Even though this type of story is a staple of saintly literature, to a modern reader it does not reflect well on either Columba or Bede. Nonetheless, the basic premise, that Columba visited the area and was given a grant of land, is not impossible. Adomnán states that King Brude gave Columba permission to proselytize in his lands, which could have extended as far as Buchan. The distance from the vicinity of Old Deer to Inverness is about 90 miles (145 km). The *Annals of Ulster* note that a Vineus abbot of Ner died in 623 and, in 679, the death of a Nechtan, who seems to be the same man as the "Nechtan of Ner from Britain" who is commemorated by the ninth-century ecclesiastical calendar known as the *Martyrology of Oengus the Culdee* (*Félire Óengusso Céli Dé*).[74] The phonetic equivalence of *Nér/nDér* has been noted and the extension of time necessary to begin Vineus' term of office during the lifetime of Columba is not excessive.[75]

Just before the middle of the eighth century there is the first mention of the church Cindrigmonaid (Head of the Royal Mound?) that would become the church of St. Andrews and, centuries later, archiepiscopal see for the Scots. Tuathalan, the abbot of the church of Cindrigmonath, died in 743. One school of thought sees its foundation as a counter to the

---

[73] The Gaelic charter notes, including the foundation legend, are edited by Kenneth Jackson, *Gaelic Notes in the Book of Deer* (Cambridge, 1971). For studies on this manuscript, see: Kathleen Hughes, "The Book of Deer (Cambridge University Library MS. Ii.6.32)," in D. Dumville (ed.), *Celtic Britain in the Early Middle Ages, Studies in Scottish and Welsh Sources* (Woodbridge, 1980): 22–37; and Katherine Forsyth (ed.), *Studies on the Book of Deer* (Dublin, 2008).
[74] Stokes, *Félire Óengusso Céli Dé*: 14, where the editor hypercorrects the *ner* of the manuscripts to *nár* (noble).
[75] T.F. O'Rahilly, *Early Irish History and Mythology* (Dublin, 1946): 373n1; and Jackson, *Gaelic Notes in the Book of Deer*: 6.

influence of Iona, which might have been seen as benefiting Dál Riata.[76] Various legends about the church circulated during the Middle Ages, which claim that the church was endowed by a king named Hungus (i.e., Angus) the son of Fergus.[77] A curious legend is preserved by the fourteenth-century historian John of Fordun who claimed that a church founded at Muckros had its name changed to Kilremont (for Cindrigmonath) after Hungus gave to it a tenth of his kingdom; he subsequently built St. Andrews cathedral.[78] Most scholars identify him with the eighth-century prince. If the church was not dedicated to St. Andrew until later, then is it possible that the ninth-century Angus son of Fergus was the patron of the new foundation? The story of the foundation of the church, in a fourteenth-century copy of a twelfth-century legend, claims that he established it after a battle with an Anglo-Saxon king named Aethelstan. The story of the church's foundation is obviously confused if not a complete fabrication; there was no king in Britain named Aethelstan during the reign of either the eighth- or ninth-century King Angus. One simple explanation is that the tenth-century King Aethelstan, who did lead an army into Scotland in 934, became incorporated into the legend, which borrows from the *vita* of John of Beverly. Precisely when the church was dedicated to St. Andrew is not clear. An item in the Irish *Chronicon Scotorum* claims that the eastern Irish prince Aed son of Maelmithig, a tenth-century descendant of Kenneth I, died on his pilgrimage to Cindrigmonath. The first appearance of the name is in two charter notes preserved in the *Register of the Priory of St. Andrews* with the grants of two bishops named Máel Duin (MS *Maldunus*) and Tuathal (MS *Tuadal*); both men are described as "bishop of St. Andrews."[79]

An interesting statement connected with Angus' grant together with a listing of the relevant properties is preserved in the *Register of the Priory*

[76] T.M.O. Charles-Edwards, "The Ui Neill 695–743: The Rise and Fall of Dynasties," *Peritia* 16 (2002): 410.

[77] M.O. Anderson, "St. Andrews before Alexander I," in G.W.S. Barrow (ed.), *The Scottish Tradition: Essays in Honour of Ronald Gordon Cant* (Edinburgh, 1974): 1–2; "The Celtic Church in Kinrimund," in David Roberts (ed.), *The Medieval Church of St Andrews* (Glasgow, 1976): 1–10; Davuit Broun, "The Church of St Andrews and its Foundation Legend in the Early Twelfth Century: Recovering the Full Text of Version A of the Foundation Legend," in Simon Taylor (ed.), *Kings, Clerics and Chronicles in Scotland 500–1297: Essays in Honour of Marjorie Ogilvie Anderson on the Occasion of her Ninetieth Birthday* (Dublin, 2000): 108–114.

[78] Skene, *Johannis de Fordun*: i, 77.

[79] ESC: 6–7.

Figure 5.1 Dunkeld from *Theatrum Scotiae* (1693). Source: Francis H. Groome, *Ordnance Gazetteer of Scotland: A Survey of Scottish Topography*, 6 vols. (Edinburgh: Thomas Jacek, 1882–1885): II, plate XII.

of St. Andrews.[80] A list of witnesses to the grant includes names such as Talarg son of Ythernbuithib, Nechtan son of Chelturan, and Sinan son of Lutheren. With the exception of Ythernbuithib all the names are found in some text concerned with the Picts. Then there follows a list of seven churches at Cindrigmonad, including dedications to St. Regulus, Michael Archangel, the Blessed Virgin Mary, St. Damianus, St. Brigid, and St. Muren, the last is a community of fifty women of royal birth. The transcriber of the text, Thana son of Dubabrach, claims to have written it in the villa of Meigel (Migdele) at the direction of the king "Pherath filius Bergeth," who seems to be the same as the *Vered f. Bargot* of the later king lists. The entire tract can be dismissed as mere fabrication, a pseudo-foundation story designed to give authenticity to the legend of Angus' foundation of the church. At the same time, the admission that in its form the text is a copy and the names themselves might be an indication that there is something more than mere invention behind the story.

The claim of a ninth-century founding of an ecclesiastical community at Dunkeld (see Figure 5.1) is credited to Constantine son of Fergus in

---

[80] Taken from John Pinkerton, *An Enquiry into the History of Scotland Preceding the Reign of Malcolm III or the Year 1052 Including the Authentic History of that Period*, 2 vols. (London, 1789): i, 460.

the early thirteenth-century (X) group of king-lists; if that is accurate then its foundation was sometime between the end of the eighth and beginning of the ninth century.[81] No foundation legend survives and little is known about it until a generation later during the reign of the Scots king Kenneth I. According to the *Scottish Chronicle* (see chapter 8), he had transferred the relics of Colum Cille to a church which he ordered to be constructed; a later Anglo-Saxon list of saintly resting places locates the relics of Columba at Dunkeld. By the second half of the century the church seems to have been the head of the Columban federation in Britain when an entry in the *Annals of Ulster* is the obit in 865 for Tuathal son of Artgusso, who is referred to as chief bishop of Fortriu and abbot of Dunkeld. Tuathal's titles indicate episcopal administration of the churches, but, if so, the office of bishop might not have been connected with a particular house because Tuathal's successor Flaithbertach son of Muichertaich, is styled *princeps* on his death in 873, the usual Irish designation for an abbot although it could mean a bishop. By the tenth and eleventh century there are references only to abbots of Dunkeld.

One church which is still being studied is at Portmahomack on the Tarbat peninsula, jutting into the Moray Firth. Excavations were made at the church owing to the desire of the local population to establish a tourist center. An older church was found under the foundations of the existing building with an adjacent cemetery. Also nearby were found the remains of various commercial enterprises including a mill and tannery.[82] The site was used for centuries and shows that religious centers were retained for long periods of time.

One aspect of missionary work that was as true for northern Britain as anywhere else was the need to secure the permission, if not the active participation, of the élites. The importance of these permissions was crucial. When Columba asked for safety for his missionaries in the Orkney Islands during an audience with Brude and the king of the Orkneys, he was not engaging in mere histrionics. That cooperation was vital and, as Adomnán's narrative points out, would have resulted in

---

[81] One opinion on the importance of Dunkeld is John Bannerman, "The Scottish Takeover of Pictland and the Relics of Columba," *Innes Review* 48 (1997): 27–44.
[82] An interim report is Martin Carver, *Portmahomack: Monastery of the Picts* (Edinburgh, 2008); a broader view is Isabel Henderson, "Monasteries and Sculpture in the Insular Pre-Viking Ages: The Pictish Evidence," in Benjamin Thompson (ed.), *Monasteries and Society in Medieval Britain: Proceedings of the 1994 Harlaxton Symposium* (Stamford, 1999): 75–96.

death if permission had not been obtained. Even at the local level the same concern is visible in the story concerning the circumstances of the founding of the church at Deer. Even though Columba had received a grant of land from the nobleman named Bede, his request for additional territory is refused. There is recourse to the formula of "saint saving sick child" to convince the father to relent. As already seen in the instance of Iona, great care was taken to name the donor. There was an aspect of pious gratitude, but also safety, indicating the quarter whence protection could be expected. The danger of not getting the necessary permission or protection is graphically illustrated in the "martyrdom" of Donnán of Eigg in 617. This is now Eigg Island, off Inverness, and the death of Donnán had become famous by the ninth century when it was commemorated on April 17 in the *Martyrology of Oengus*.[83] The notes to the main text, which were added in the eleventh century, are a combination from several sources in both Latin and Irish; the place of his martyrdom, for example, is located from Caithness to Galloway. The stories essentially agree that a a high-status woman objected to the presence of Donnán and his community, so soldiers were called in to kill them. The Irish version claims that the perpetrator was a queen and that the community had appropriated land where her sheep customarily grazed. The moral of either story is clear; taking or using land without permission could lead to death.

An interesting deficiency in the material connected with Christianity is the conversion story at the highest levels of society. Columba was a visitor at the court of King Brude and important enough to treat with his foster-father Broichan as an equal. At no point in his narrative, however, does Adomnán claim that the saint converted the prince. The saint causes the doors of his fortress to open, he cures Broichan, and controls river monsters, but he does not convert Brude. Of course it is possible that Brude was already a Christian, but then his apparent friendliness with "magicians" becomes difficult to explain, especially in light of their supposed antics in opposition to Columba and his companions. In the story of Deer's foundation, there is not the expected conclusion with the conversion of Bede the Mormaer. He gives the land apparently as payment rather than piety and the name supposedly comes from the tears shed by Drostan, Columba's companion.

---

[83] Stokes, *Martyrology of Oengus*: the main entry is on p. 107 and the explanation is pp. 114–116.

As these episodes have shown, the clergy were the mobile class of their day. Peasants were expected to remain in their communities. The aristocracy moved usually in connection with war or politics. Only the clerics traveled throughout kingdoms, as well as farther afield in Britain and Ireland. This was possible because the Christian community shared a common language, Latin. An example is Iogenan the Pict, a priest in Ireland, whose book of hymns written by St. Columba was lost by his student while crossing a river in Leinster, the great southeastern province of Ireland. After six months the satchel and volume were discovered washed up on the riverbank. The satchel was rotten from the water damage, but the hymnal was dry and in perfect condition.

Summary

In conclusion, like much else about the Picts the history of Christianity among them is obscure, as is the period before their conversion. One hagiography written by an Irish abbot and a history composed by an Anglo-Saxon monk are the two main sources, supplemented by materials whose usefulness to the historian is not always easy to gauge. Archaeological remains are few and difficult to date. Not surprisingly, the main missionaries who are named in the historical sources are foreign, such as Columba or Donnán of Eigg. The native ones, such as Ninian of Whithorn and Kentigern, are remembered in little more than a few incidents that later become expanded by writers in the twelfth century. Clearly the combination of spiritual conversion and education were dual aspects of their missions. The school at Whithorn credited to Ninian and the foundation at Glasgow by Kentigern show them both orthodox in their belief and imperial in their organization, in which the church becomes the center from which the missions are sent. In contrast is the activity of Columba and his monks, who labor and found churches among their converts.

The introduction of Christianity to the people living north of Hadrian's Wall began at least by the second century. By the end of the Roman era in Britain missionaries were actively proselytizing among the "Picts." Men such as Ninian were commemorated by remembrance at their churches or in written memorials. Perhaps there were efforts to introduce a diocesan organization in the lands between the Antonine and Hadrian Walls. Certainly by the sixth century the kingdoms of Strathclyde, Gododdin, and Rheged had been converted to the new faith. The work of a mission from Ireland and based on the island of Iona oversaw the conversion of the northernmost peoples. While Columba became the best known of the missionaries thanks to the writing of Adomnán, memories of other laborers were preserved, again in connection with specific churches.

The importance of individual churches began to supersede that of missionaries by the eighth century. These churches were focal points for the entire community and their multiplicity of purposes are remembered in stories of sand yielding crops and saintly miracles. Unlike individuals, the churches required the active participation of the local élites. With the inclusion of the powerful members of society, the churches in northern Britain became part of a structure found throughout Western Europe.

6

Art

An aspect of Pictish society which continues to fascinate and intrigue both the scholar and the layman is their art. In Pictish art, as in the art of any culture, native inspiration was complemented by the work of their neighbors, objects brought in from distant lands, mythological and religious typologies, as well as the scenes of everyday life around them. Another part of the fascination is the mystery of the art. Despite generations of study the meaning of much of it remains disputed. Pictish art fits into two broad categories: objects which were intended to be moved, such as jewelry; and objects not intended to be moved, at least not after being put in place, such as stone sculptures. A feature of both categories is technical competence. This competence went beyond mere craftsmanship to composition and inspiration in the use of borrowed motifs and designs. Silver chains found from Peebleshire to Aberdeenshire, for example, have delicate designs cut into the metal clasps. Rock carving was both incised and relief, the latter including elaborate knot-work. While the former are on display in museum exhibitions, many of the latter still can be seen by traveling through the countryside. Huge rocks, occasionally six or seven feet (about 2 meters) tall, with images and designs cut into them, are found in fields or along the side of the road. Ornamental stones have been found from the Northern Isles to the land south of the Firth of Forth. A great variety of images have survived. Some are from the animal world with birds, salmon, bulls, and horses. Others are of people fighting, working, or hunting. Particularly striking are the abstract or nonfigurative designs such as "Z-rods," double discs connected with parallel lines, and geometric figures.

The Picts, First Edition. Benjamin Hudson.
© 2014 John Wiley & Sons, Ltd. Published 2014 by John Wiley & Sons, Ltd.

While there are variations in designs and execution, the basic forms and motifs that are considered Pictish can be found on objects from the Shetland Islands to Galloway. These designs were produced by artisans who were part of a wider artistic community, borrowing from and influenced by works both earlier and contemporary. The geographical range for borrowing was broad and its range can be seen in comparison with objects throughout the British Isles and beyond. This was not limited just to symbols or scenes connected with Christianity, but also involved the presentation of ideas. The study of art is very much the province of specialists, many of whom are trained artists themselves. Voluminous studies on almost every aspect of detail, style, motif, and execution of the images and objects found in northern Britain have been composed through the decades. So only a few of the numerous aspects of art in the north of Britain during the fifth through the tenth centuries are discussed here, and then only in a very general way; a comprehensive study of the topic would take volumes rather than a brief chapter.[1]

Rock Art

One of the most commented-upon features of this art has been the rock carvings found north of Hadrian's Wall. While most art must be viewed indoors – museums or galleries – many of the stone or rock carvings are still situated outdoors. They vary in size from small rocks to massive blocks to the walls of caves, and have been found in different contexts such as open fields, churchyards, in rubble, and buried in the ground. Sometimes the stones were used as building materials and occasionally all that remains are fragments. The main concentrations of them are found round the eastern coast from the Moray Firth to the Firth of Tay. New stones or parts of stones continue to be discovered, sometimes accidently in buildings and sometimes in archaeological excavations, such as the one at Portmahomack on the Tarbat peninsula.[2] The technical skill employed in making the stones varied greatly. Some images are little more than lines intersecting at 90°, representing a Christian cross. Other

---

[1] An important study is by George Henderson and Isabel Henderson, *The Art of the Picts, Sculpture and Metalwork in Early Medieval Scotland* (New York, 2004).
[2] Described in Martin Carver, *Portmahomack, Monastery of the Picts* (Edinburgh, 2008).

sculptures have two or three different scenes, with a great amount of detail and thought given to composition.

The stones have been a curiosity for centuries and there are records of them in different accounts. A possible mention comes from the *Book of Deer*, the now-fragmentary Gospel written probably in the tenth century with notes concerning land and other donations made to the church of Deer added as late as the second quarter of the twelfth century. According to one charter-note a Comgell son of Cainnech, who was the toísech of Clann Chanann, gave a plot of land with one boundary that was "the large pillar stone at the end of the thicket" (*gonige in gorthe mór i gginn in fris*).[3] Late in the eighteenth century, the collection of material for what would become known as the *Statistical Account* (with reports supplied mainly by local ministers) gives casual descriptions of the stones and their carvings, together with speculation about their purpose. The late eighteenth-century description of Aberlemno composed by William Mitchell in the *Statistical Account* mentions: "Two obelisks remain, one in the churchyard and another on the highway from Brechin to Forfar, about 8 or 9 feet high; there were erected in memory of the total defeat of the Danes and have some rude hieroglyphical sculptures."[4] Occasionally the speculation is more specific, and James Lyon, minister of Glamis, noted that

> within a few yards of the manse of Glammiss [sic] is an obelisk, of rude erected design as generally supposed in memory of the murder of Malcolm II king of Scotland. On one side of the monument, there are figures of two men who, by their attributes, seem to be forming the bloody conspiracy. A lion and centaur, on the upper part, represent the shocking barbarity of the crime. On the reverse, several sorts of fishes [sic] are engraven, a symbolic representation of the lake in which, missing their way, the assassins were drowned.[5]

Greater precision was employed in describing the carved stones during the cataloguing of them in the nineteenth century. The most important effort to introduce some order into the mass of material was made by Joseph Anderson whose 1892 Rhind Lectures were used as the foundation for the massive *Early Christian Monuments of Scotland* (ECMS) with a catalogue of artifacts, a project in which he was joined by

---

[3] Kenneth Jackson, *Gaelic Notes in the Book of Deer* (Cambridge, 1972): 32, no. V.
[4] John Sinclair of Ulbster (ed.), *Statistical Account of Scotland*, 21 vols. (Edinburgh, 1791–99): xiii, 4.
[5] Sinclair, *Statistical Account of Scotland*: xiii, 276.

J. Romilly Allen. While it now must be supplemented with more recent discoveries, clearer (in some cases) reproductions, and the occasional change of location for some objects, it remains a treasure of information. In addition to its importance as a pioneering piece of scholarship, *Early Christian Monuments of Scotland* preserves some material that subsequently has gone missing or has been destroyed. Allen and Anderson also devised the threefold classification scheme for the stones that, with modifications, remains the accepted division of the sculpted stones.[6] In explaining why these works of art are found in certain places, they employed chronology, suggesting that the making of these carvings began after the settlement of the Scots in Dál Riata and the Anglo-Saxons in the region between the Firth of Forth and Hadrian's Wall, followed by their movement to the west into Dumfriesshire and Galloway.

Class 1 stones are unshaped rocks (not carved into a rectangle or a cross) upon which have been carved geometric designs and figures. The majority of stones of this first class have been found in northern Scotland with a concentration in Aberdeenshire, Banff, and Buchan. Most of the Class 1 symbol stones have incised designs, that is, the lines were cut into the stone. This is a simple method of carving and an illustration of the process comes from the *vita* of St. Samson of Dol. He had made a visit to Ireland and on his return journey to the continent he stopped in Cornwall, where he carved a cross in the face of a rock using an iron bar and a mallet. The result was probably similar to the rudimentary cross that is found on a stone now in the churchyard of St. Fergus, Dyce (see Figure 6.1). Other stones have more extensive decoration. The amount of attention given to the stylistic composition seems to have been haphazard, and some images occasionally give the appearance of having been carved randomly on the surface. Some of these images are recognizable animals, although the purpose or message they intend to convey is not agreed to the satisfaction of everyone. In addition there is the problem of chronology, a fiercely debated topic. The customary date of carving for these stones is the seventh and eighth centuries, but challenges to that chronology have been made ever since the dates were proposed. An example of a Class 1 stone with both elaborate symbols and script is the reconstructed Brandsbutt Stone at Inverurie (see Figure 6.2). This is a squat whinstone

---

[6] ECMS: i, xi; the following classification includes the modifications proposed by R.B.K. Stevenson, "Pictish Art," in F.T. Wainwright (ed.), *Problem of the Picts* (Edinburgh, 1955): 97. Lloyd Laing, "The Chronology and Context of Pictish Relief Sculpture," *Medieval Archaeology* 44 (2000): 81–114.

166 Art

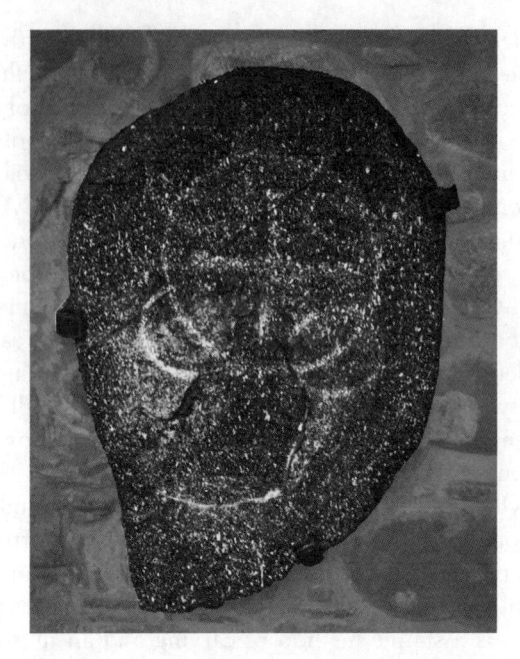

Figure 6.1 Rudimentary cross at St. Fergus', Dyce. Photo Robert Hudson.

boulder that had been broken up and used as part of a dyke, but five pieces were retrieved and reassembled. The stone is part of a circle, consisting of possibly a dozen stones. What remains of the decorations on the stone are a crescent with V-rod and, below it, a serpent on top of a Z-rod. On the side is an ogam inscription that, reading the customary direction from bottom to top, has been transliterated: *irataddoarens*.

Technically more ambitious are the Class 2 stones, where the actual rock has been shaped, usually carved into a rectangular or pillar form. These stones are found predominantly south of Aberdeen with an important cluster in Angus, especially the area from the vicinity of Forfar to Glamis and then northwest to Meigle. Upon this fashioned rock face have been chiseled geometric designs and figures in relief (i.e., the stone is chipped away from the design so that it protrudes beyond the surface). Since the rock has been shaped, it can give the appearance of being framed and the images on it seem to be grouped in specific episodes, such as the angels adoring the cross on a stone at Aberlemno (see Figure 6.3). These sculptures have been dated from the eighth to the ninth centuries, and occasionally as late as the tenth century in the case of the so-called

Figure 6.2 Symbols and ogams on Brandsbutt Stone. Photo Robert Hudson.

Sueno's Stone at Forres. There are also relief versions of some symbols that are incised on Class 1 stone, such as the semicircle with V-rod that is found above a hunting scene on another stone at Aberlemno (see Figure 6.4). Some of the images are obviously connected with Christian theology, such as crosses or scenes from Bible stories. The interpretation of other images is much more difficult as many are geometric designs. Unlike the Class 1 stones, however, many of the panels in the Class 2 stones are deliberating telling a story, such as the symbol stone in Aberlemno churchyard with its depiction of a battle scene that some believe to be a commemoration of the battle of Dun Nechtan, fought in May 685. This may be part of a tradition in northern Europe, especially in ancient Scandinavia, of carvings showing specific scenes.[7]

---

[7] Knut Helskog, "Landscapes in Rock-Art: Rock-Carving and Ritual in the Old European North," in Christopher Chippindale and George Nash (eds.), *The Figured Landscapes of Rock-Art* (Cambridge, 2004): 265–288 (at p. 273).

168   Art

Figure 6.3   Angels adoring the cross, Aberlemno Stone no. 3.
Photo Robert Hudson.

The final group are the Class 3 stones, which have only Christian religious symbols. They are found throughout Scotland, usually in connection with a religious house or area.[8] Since the iconography is Christian, there is little debate about the meaning of most, but not all, of it. For example a stone now in Brechin Cathedral has an image of a man holding an animal, which might or might not represent Samson killing the lion (Judges 14: 5–6; see Figure 6.5). This is the easiest class of material for comparative purposes and for the identification of specific saintly cults. The Class 3 stones are believed to begin concurrently with Class 2 stones, but continue to the twelfth century. They are often neglected in discussions of this early period of art because of the well-known religious iconography. The presumed familiarity with the images

[8]   On this topic see Isabel Henderson, "Monasteries and Sculpture in the Insular Pre-Viking Ages," in Benjamin Thompson (ed.), *Monasteries and Society in Medieval Britain: Proceedings of the 1994 Harlaxton Symposium* (Stamford, 1999): 75–96.

Figure 6.4   V-rod design at top of Aberlemno Stone no. 2.
Photo Robert Hudson.

had led them to be set aside in favor of the mysteries of the other two classes, but they span the period from the Pictish to Scottish kingdoms. They usually have images of the cross, often decorated with knot-work that has parallels with sculptures throughout the British Isles.[9] They also show that orthodox Christianity was found among the peoples of northern Britain, which is clear from a comparison with religious iconography throughout the British Isles.[10]

Various reasons are offered for the erection of these decorated stones. The Class 3 stones, for example, were clearly statements of religious orientation and Christian belief. Examples are found throughout Christendom, although there are numerous local variations or adaptations. Those stones found outside the confines of a churchyard might have been markers of lands that belonged to or had been given to a

[9]   Brett Garrett, *Celtic Knots with and beyond J. Romilly Allen* (Zürich, 2009).
[10] Charles Thomas, *The Early Christian Archaeology of North Britain* (Oxford, 1971).

Figure 6.5   Samson wrestling a lion?, from Brechin. Photo Robert Hudson.

church. The purpose(s) of the Class 1 and Class 2 stones are less easy to discern and they seem to have been varied. One could have been to commemorate an individual, although not necessarily as a grave marker. The *Fragmentary Life of St. Kentigern* has an interesting story concerning the raising of such a stone.[11] The grandfather of the saint was killed by a javelin thrown by a swineherd. Thereafter his friends set up a royal stone with a carved stone on top of it about a mile south of Traprain Law. In a different way, the use of stone carving as funerary monument can be seen on the St. Andrews sarcophagus, which is believed to date from the late eighth century, where biblical and classical images are both used.[12] They

[11]   Alexander Penrose Forbes, *Lives of S. Ninian and S. Kentigern*, Historians of Scotland 5 (Edinburgh, 1874): 249: "Amici vero Regis, in loco ubi occubuit, erexerunt in signum regale lapidem grandem, imposito illi desuper saxo minore arte cauatoria, qui adhuc ibi permanet distans a monte Drumpelder in parte austrina, quasi uno miliario."
[12]   On this monument see: Sally M. Foster (ed.), *The St Andrews Sarcophagus: A Pictish Masterpiece and its International Connections* (Dublin, 1998).

seem also to have been used as boundary markers and the passage from the *Book of Deer* is quoted above. Another example is the bounds of the lands granted to the church at Abernethy, ascribed to King Nechtan son of Erp, which extended in part from "the stone in Apurfeirt to the stone in Ceirfuill, that is Lethfoss" (*que posite sunt a lapide in Apurfeirc usque ad lapidem iuzta Cairfuill id est Lethfoss*)."[13]

Images found on the stones range from the abstract to the pedestrian. Depending on how strictly one divides the different figures into groups there are about four dozen distinct forms. About thirty of those images appear to be abstract objects or geometric forms while the remainder are animals and mythological creatures.[14] The most frequently found image is an upside down crescent with a *v* upon it that resembles a broken arrow, as on the Brandsbutt stone. This appears more than four dozen times, carved both in relief and incised. The next most recurrent image is another abstract form, in this instance a figure that resembles a *z* (also with terminals suggesting a broken arrow) on which is placed a figure consisting of two circles joined with lines. While there are some large examples, a modest representation is from a stone now in the churchyard of St. Fergus, Dyce (see Figure 6.6). Only with the third most repeated design, of a mirror and comb, are the images easily recognizable. An example of this is another stone from Aberlemno where the mirror and comb are at the bottom right (see Figure 6.7). Other geometric forms include stepped rectangles, various types of circular forms and connected circular shapes. Among the fantastic designs are monstrous fish (such as the so-called "Pictish water-beast" on the St. Fergus stone), decorated serpents, and centaurs; while the animals are represented by familiar creatures such as bulls, hounds, wolves, birds, and elk. Intriguing and useful to the historian are the scenes that show people in identifiable activities such as hunting, fighting and riding. There are variations on the basic forms and an interesting collection of examples is found for the "crescent with V-rod," for which there are more than 30 different forms.[15]

---

[13] Transcribed in KES: 247.

[14] An old, but useful, catalogue is in ECMS: i, 57–128; while a more recent and detailed list is Anthony Jackson, *The Symbol Stones of Scotland* (Stromness, 1984); he reduces the symbols to 28 basic groups (pp. 68–78).

[15] Stevenson, "Pictish Art," 102–103; Craig Cessford, "The Multiple Crescent and V-rod – an Anomalous Symbol Grouping," *Pictish Arts Society Journal* 11 (1997): 31–32.

Figure 6.6 Geometric designs from a stone at St. Fergus', Dyce. Photo Robert Hudson.

Figure 6.7 Mirror and comb from Aberlemno Stone no. 1. Photo Robert Hudson.

Attempts to "discover" the meaning of the Pictish symbols have employed different approaches, which usually satisfy few people beyond the proposer.[16] One method is a frequency count, in which the number of times a symbol appears is tabulated either individually or as part of a set.[17] A second scheme is cartographic, in which the symbols are divided into groups, which are then plotted on maps.[18] Finally there is one school of thought that reads the images as pictographs or some other form of communication. A problem common to all these schemes is not knowing the purpose of the stones. Of course, the meanings of those with Christian iconography are fairly clear, especially the ones found in churchyards or the vicinity of churches. The symbols are sometimes found on the back of crosses and this might be interpreted as the commemoration of some event. Such a purpose has been proposed for the symbol stone in the churchyard at Aberlemno with its battle scene on one side of a stone, on the other side of which is a cross (see chapter 4). But many others are obscure. They have been seen as boundary markers, kinship statements, and statements of non-Christian religions. All the suggestions might be correct, since it is very possible that there were different purposes behind different carvings.

Some of the symbols on the stones can be interpreted in several contexts.[19] Take the representation of the eagle as one example. For the Romans, an eagle was a symbol of Imperial power, carried by every legion into battle; and this might have been borrowed by the Picts.[20] In a Christian context it is the symbol for John the Evangelist or, remaining

---

[16] For some comments see: Lloyd Laing and Jennifer Laing, "The Date and Origin of the Pictish Symbols," PSAS 114 (1984): 261–278; Katherine Forsyth, "Some Thoughts on Pictish Symbols as a Formal Writing System," in David Henry (ed.), *The Worm, the Germ, and the Thorn: Pictish and Related Studies Presented to Isabel Henderson* (Balgavies, 1997): 85–98; Ross Samson, "The Reinterpretation of the Pictish Symbols," *Journal of the British Archaeological Association* 145 (1992): 29–65; Stuart Kermack, "An Attempt on the Meaning of the Pictish Symbols – Part 1," *Pictish Arts Society Journal* 11 (1997): 9–18.

[17] For examples see Stevenson, "Pictish Art": 98; Jackson, *Symbol Stones of Scotland*: 109–110.

[18] Stevenson, "Pictish Art": 100 and 124; Jackson, *Symbol Stones of Scotland*: 93–96; and a more extensive British Isles map is in Henderson and Henderson, *Art of the Picts*: 32.

[19] On the animals see C.A. Gordon, "The Pictish Animals Observed," PSAS 98 (1967): 215–224.

[20] Ross, *Pagan Celtic Britain*: 348.

Figure 6.8 Carrion bird from Aberlemno Cross-slab no. 3. Photo Robert Hudson.

in the same context, also a symbol of power and victory; the eagle is one of the four beasts around the throne of heaven at the Last Day (Revelation 4:7).[21] In a British context, the eagle is the companion of the warrior, who feasts on the corpses left after the battle; in *Y Gododdin* the poet announces "before the barrier of Aeron [a warrior named Cynon son of Clydno] had passed away the beaks of eagles praised his hand."[22] An illustration of this comes from the battle scene on the stone in Aberlemno churchyard where a bird pecks at a recumbent figure (see Figure 6.8). The importation of foreign ideas in the image of the snake or serpent is one of the starkest contrasts. For Christians, the serpent was

[21] On this matter see George Henderson, "The Representations of the Apostles in Insular Art with Special Reference to the New Apostles Frieze at Tarbat, Ross-shire," in Alastair Minnis and Jane Roberts (eds.), *Text, Image, Interpretation: Studies in Anglo-Saxon Literature and its Insular Context in Honour of Éamonn Ó Carragái* (Turnhout, 2007): 437–494.

[22] Kenneth Jackson, *The Gododdin* (Edinburgh, 1969): 113.

an image of evil, the form of the devil when he tempted Eve in the Garden of Eden.[23] In a classical context, the serpent was a figure of knowledge and wealth; and he is often found in conjunction with the Celtic horned god Cernunnos as in the scene on the Gundestrup Cauldron where Cernunnos holds a serpent with one hand and a torque with the other. Even after their conversion to Christianity, some peoples used the serpent in the latter sense; returning to *Y Gododdin* and Cynon son of Clydno, he is called "the serpent on the trail of the enemy."[24] A serpent features prominently on the Class 1 stones from Brandsbutt and Aberlemno. The lion had an equally varied background. For Christians he was the symbol for the Evangelist St. Mark as well as being the sign for the resurrection. In a non-religious context, there was a military inference as the lion's hide was worn by the standard bearer of the Roman legions. Creatures of the water apparently were important to the sculptors. In a Christian context, the fish was the sign of a Christian individual, while the dolphin was a sign of faith. Celtic literature, however, used the fish, particularly the salmon, as a symbol of knowledge. In the Welsh tale *How Culwuch won Olwen*, the salmon was sought out because he was one of the oldest and wisest creatures of the world and a comparison of the episode in the story has been made with the eagle on a salmon on a stone at St. Vigean.[25] There might also be an ethnic or political aspect, and the salmon, for example, was also the totem for the Christian kingdom of Dál Cais, located in what is now southern County Clare in Ireland. Christian iconography uses the fish as a symbol of a believer, and there are several incidents in which fish have a prominent role, such as Jesus' division of the loaves and fish or the eating of a fish by the resurrected Christ. This might be the context for the salmon representation on a stone in Kintore churchyard. Finally, the "Pictish water-beast" has a parallel with the mythical hippocampus, which could also be used for the "great fish" or whale that swallowed Jonah to English speakers.

Of course, one can hypothesize a great deal. For example, the double discs on the stones might be intended as multiple suns, an optical illusion that is seen occasionally in the British Isles, like those seen by the future King Edward IV prior to the battle of Mortimer's Cross. Rays of the sun

---

[23] Douglas Maclean, "Snake-bosses and Redemption at Iona and in Pictland," in R.M. Spearman and John Higgitt (eds.), *The Age of Migrating Ideas: Early Medieval Art in Northern Britain and Ireland* (Stroud, 1993): 244–253.
[24] Jackson, *Gododdin*: 123.
[25] Ross, *Pagan Celtic Britain*: 350–351.

are illustrated as lines while the moon is usually depicted in the form of a crescent. The semicircle with two lines in the form of a *v* could be a sign for the moon through which lines emanating upwards from a single point are rays of the sun; both are found on medieval crucifixion scenes and, in early Christian art, they represent baptism. A sun and moon are found on a ninth-century grave marker from Lindisfarne, where they are separate and on either side of a crucifix.[26] The rod with a distinctive termination might be the sign of the Archangel Gabriel.

Some of the figures suggest a higher level of literacy or more classical influence than is usually credited to the Picts. A possible Roman and/or British context for the eagle and lion have already been mentioned, and other animals also found in classical contexts, such as the boar or deer, are part of a general European heritage. The bull is interesting especially in light of the limited area in which it has been found, primarily around Burghead on the Moray coast. Little of the older construction survives as much of it was demolished in the nineteenth century during the building of the modern town. The bull stones might have been part of the ramparts that greeted arrivals to the settlement. There might have been a religious component to the bull stones and the animal had a prominent role to play, for comparison, in the cult of Mithra, one of the deities popular among Roman troops where the initiate was "baptized" when a sacred bull had its throat slit and the blood washed him. As a form of sympathetic magic, the attributes of the beast – strength and ferocity – were to descend to the recipient. The bull, together with the boar, is used as a figure of battle prowess in the *Gododdin* when a warrior named Grugyn is described as a "bull of battle."[27] Together with the commonplace, such as the bull, there were also completely fictitious figures such as the centaur, which is carved into the Maiden Stane at Chapel of Gairoch in Aberdeenshire. There are no centaurs in the British Isles, but the idea of them may have come from literature. One of the best known is Ovid's *Metamorphosis* (12: 210–535), while the other is a Christian context in Anathasius' *Life of St. Antony*, the desert father. Another image that might have a connection with the Mediterranean world is that of two discs connected by parallel lines. The same design is found in England on a tenth-century cross-shaft at Bilton in Ainsty; there it is

---

[26] Rosemary Cramp (gen. ed.), *Corpus of Anglo-Saxon Stone Sculpture in England* (Oxford, 1984–): *Durham and Northumberland*; the photograph is no. 1132 and the discussion is at i, 206.

[27] Jackson, *Gododdin*: 107.

Figure 6.9 Sueno's Stone from a nineteenth-century print.
From the author's private collection.

being held by a man, which has prompted the suggestion that it is a representation of a scroll.[28]

One of the most intriguing monuments in this context is the famous Sueno's Stone outside the town of Forres (see Figure 6.9).[29] The stone is tall and one side has a series of warriors both standing and horizontal. Suggestions for this stone have ranged from a battle commemoration of the defeat of Vikings to the defeat of the army of King Dub son of Malcolm (d. July 966) whose body, according to legend, was hidden under a bridge at Kinloss and removed only because the sun refused to shine until it was

---

[28] Cramp, *Corpus of Anglo-Saxon Stone Sculpture in England*, 8: West Yorkshire, the photograph is figure 40 and a discussion is on p. 97.

[29] The title of the image is "Pillar at Forres" and the legend "I. Ingleby Sc." is at the bottom left corner. This print seems to be listed in Alfred Russell Smith's *Catalogue of Ten Thousand Tracts and Pamphlets and Fifty Thousand Prints* (London, 1878), item no.818, p. 17 of the section of the work "Prints and Drawings Relating to Scotland"; here the title is "Forres, Sculptured Pillar, Two Views," and the artist is identified simply as Ingleby.

revealed.[30] An interesting feature of Sueno's Stone is the line of fighters, known as the warrior procession. This feature is rarely found in the British Isles and occurs only twice on surviving monuments there; both are in Cumbria.[31] The first is on the tenth-century hogback tomb at Gosforth which has a line of warriors with shields and spears. The other representation comes from Lowther, where eight warriors are in a boat. Both of these are from an area with intense Scandinavian colonization and it has been suggested that they were the product of the immigrants' workshops. The motif is old and the warrior line is found on the Gundestrup Cauldron.[32] The Cumbrian examples apparently reflect Scandinavian influence and there is no reason not to place Sueno's Stone in the same context.

This suggests that in addition to influences from the south or west, there might have been influences from Scandinavia and the lands round the Baltic. This is an idea that has prompted speculation since the late nineteenth century and is worth reconsidering. An interesting point of comparison is that some Class 2 stones have similarities with the picture stones of Gotland, especially the middle groups designated C and D.[33] There are divisions into scenic panels with recognizable figures. While the Gotland stones feature more ships, the position of riders on horses, far forward on their mounts, together with the presentation of the figures, gives some interesting parallels. The boat and figures on the Cossans Stone (see Figure 4.5) have a parallel with a plaque from Germany. Does this represent influence from northern Britain moving to the Baltic regions, or vice versa, or no contact at all? If current chronologies are accepted, however, then it would seem that the designs were moving from east to west.[34]

Images on the stones also suggest some of the social contexts of Pictish society. For example, among the images found on both Class 1 and Class 2 stones are blacksmithing tools such as a mallet, tongs, and symbols that

[30] W.D.H. Sellar, "Sueno's Stone and its Interpreters," in W.D.H. Sellar (ed.), *Moray: Province and People* (Edinburgh, 1993): 97–116.
[31] Cramp, *Corpus of Anglo-Saxon Stone Sculpture in England*, 2: Cumbria, i, 105 (Gosforth) and 130 (Lowther).
[32] Ruth Megaw and Vincent Megaw, *Celtic Art* (London, 1990): 176.
[33] The Gotland stones are comprehensively studied in Sune Lindqvist's old, but still valuable *Gotlands Bildsteine*, 2 vols. (Stockholm, 1941–42).
[34] Others have seen the movement in the opposite direction, see Alexander Bugge, *Vesterlandenes Inflydelse paa Nordboernes og saerlig Normandenes ydre Kultur, Lovesaet og Samfundsforhold i Vikingetiden*, Videnskabs-Selskabets Skrifter 2, Historisk-Filosofisk Klass, 1904, no. 1 (Christiana, 1905): 323–330.

seem to represent a chisel and an anvil. The smith was an important individual in early medieval societies since he was the fabricator of any iron object including the tools that would carve the designs on stones; he also made the metal objects on which designs could be placed. Possibly many of the artists were smiths. Some idea of his importance comes from the Old Irish tale known as *The Cattle Raid of Cooley* in an episode connected with the childhood of the hero Cú Chulainn where a blacksmith and artificer named Culann invited a king named Conchobar to dine with him. He asked the king to include a small retinue since he did not have land but only the profits from his trade. There are two aspects of that story which are interesting in connection with the carvings. First, a smith had high enough status to be able to invite a king to dine with him and, second, the profits from his trade were sufficient to pay for a party which would satisfy a prince and even a limited number in his retinue.[35] Other cultures similarly held smiths in high regard and the Isle of Man has a stone with a runic memorial to Akan the smith. Analogous to the blacksmith's skill in fashioning an object from metal was the sculptor's skill in carving stone. The appearance on the stones of a chisel and hammer might have some connection with the people who made the images.

Movable Art

Among the impressive pieces of Pictish art are massive silver chains, some as much as 18 ins (45 cm) in length. Chains were a coveted item of gift exchange throughout northern Europe. Tacitus notes that the Germans particularly prized gold chains as presents (*Germania*, ch. 15). A dozen have been found, so far, and their real purpose is unknown – anything from personal adornment to ceremonial regalia is possible.[36] Only three of them have been found north of the Clyde–Forth line, but they are assumed to have been manufactured in the Pictish region because two chains, one found in Lanarkshire and the other at Parkhill in Aberdeenshire, have symbols on a broad link (possibly the fastener) which are similar to those found on the symbol stones. They may be a link (no pun intended) with the heroic age of warrior chieftains rewarding their followers with

---

[35] Cecile O'Rahilly (ed.), *The Stowe Version of Táin Bó Cuailnge* (Dublin, 1973): 29 (l.852).
[36] Andrew Breeze, "Pictish Chains and Welsh Forgeries," PSAS 121 (1998): 481–484.

treasure in public displays of gift-giving. Alternatively, they might be just an article of apparel. Another example of what seems to be intended as apparel comes from the Norrie Law treasure from Fife, where two silver plaques with Z-rod designs were unearthed.

An important collection was uncovered on July 4, 1958 in the nave of the ruined church on St. Ninian's Isle: 28 pieces of decorated silver were found in the decayed remains of a Larchwood box, and they were deposited sometime in the late eighth or early ninth century. Among the objects are seven silver bowls, a silver hanging bowl, a silver spoon, and 11 silver-gilt penannular brooches.[37] Clay forms for casting brooches that were similar to the St. Ninian brooches, except smaller, were discovered at the Broch of Birsay. The deposit seems to have constituted the treasures of families in the vicinity rather than the property of clergy serving the church, although the secularized clergy at this period in Ireland could well have kept these types of materials.[38] Fine dining also gives examples of art. The hanging silver bowl found at St. Ninians seems to have been a finger bowl while other bowls were probably drinking bowls. Curiously, the nearest example for comparison with the silver bowl comes from Scandinavia.

Finally, a particular type of object that has been the subject of much study is the penannular brooch. These are found throughout the north Atlantic. Many of these brooches survive only in fragments. The main distinction between the Pictish and Irish varieties seems to be that the Pictish are true brooches, while the Irish are actually ring-pins.

Summary

Even in this very brief survey the richness and variety of Pictish art can be glimpsed. The production of those pieces was not in isolation and one of the many interests in northern British art is the evidence of borrowing

---

[37] For a detailed survey see Alan Small, Charles Thomas, and David Wilson, *St. Ninian's Isle and Its Treasure*, 2 vols. (Oxford, 1973). On the hanging bowl, a context is given in Susan Youngs, "Anglo-Saxon, Irish and British Relations: Hanging Bowls Reconsidered," *Proceedings of the British Academy* 157 (2009): 205–230.

[38] For discussions, see: David MacRoberts, "The Ecclesiastical Character of the St. Ninian's Isle Treasure," in A. Small (ed.), *Proceedings of the Fourth Viking Conference* (Aberdeen, 1965): 224–246; David Clarke, "Communities," in David Clarke, Alice Blackwell, and Martin Goldberg (eds.), *Early Medieval Scotland: Individuals, Communities, and Ideas* (Edinburgh, 2012): 69–139 (at pp. 125–129).

and copying, with the inference for the orientation of society. There is clear evidence of the influence of Irish and Anglo-Saxon art in the items produced in Angus or Fife, in addition to Mediterranean designs that must have been either observed or found in illustrations. Nevertheless, it is clear that a particular style was being developed and a particular application for it in the symbols found on the stone sculptures.

For the historian, art gives an insight into the wealth as well as social organization and belief of a society. To take the example of the symbol stones, sculpture on that scale was (and is) expensive. The people who paid for it (in whatever way) had disposable wealth that could be used for such an enterprise. Silver chains are another type of expensive commodity. Both are examples of art that was intended to be seen by more than the recipient and therefore the designs or symbols employed were part of a cultural vocabulary, in the same manner as the Christian images of a cross or angels were obvious to any observer. The structure of society is visible in the scenes on the stones, with an aristocracy pursuing such pastimes as hunting, which was a practice for the war-scenes found on other stones.[39] There is a glimpse of recreation, with the harps and pipes. This art shows a society which shared many of the concerns and motivations of its neighbors. Worship, status, and activity are all represented and we can glimpse the people as they saw themselves.

---

[39] Lloyd Laing and Jennifer Laing, "Archaeological Notes on Some Scottish Early Christian Sculptures," PSAS 114 (1984): 277–287.

7

Conquest and Obscurity

Pictavia, moreover, was named after the Picts ... For God condescended, as a reward for their wickedness, to make them alien from, and dead to, their heritage – they who not only spurned the Lord's mass and precept, but also did not wish to be placed equal to others in the law of justice.

This brief passage from the *Scottish Chronicle* is the medieval eulogy for the Picts.[1] The explanation for the end of their ascendancy is the sin of pride, the deadliest of the deadly sins, and the price of their transgression was to become strangers in their own land. While this morality tale was explanation enough for the monkish historians of the Middle Ages, it is not nearly enough for later scholars.

The collapse of kingdoms is a fascinating topic. Why does it happen when it does? Too often speculation must be employed for this remote time and place. For northern Britain the few records encourage questions rather than providing answers. By the last quarter of the eighth century Britain north of Hadrian's Wall returns to obscurity in the surviving records. The Irish chronicles give occasional and laconic notices of events, often little more than isolated names, while the absence of a Bede deprives us of a narrator who can elaborate on the scraps of information from the annals. Yet this was one of the most important eras for northern Britain. The wheel of fortune swung around and the hunters became the prey as immigrants from the kingdom of Dál Riata annexed territory to the east and began the end of the separate Pictish

[1] Benjamin Hudson, "The Scottish Chronicle," SHR 77 (1998): 129–161.

The Picts, First Edition. Benjamin Hudson.
© 2014 John Wiley & Sons, Ltd. Published 2014 by John Wiley & Sons, Ltd.

kingdoms in a process that would culminate in the creation of the kingdom of Scotland. Immigrants also came from another direction and there was the arrival of settlers from Scandinavia and the beginning of the Viking Age. At the same time the serious threat from the Angles of Northumbria began to ebb as they became occupied with their own feuds and civil war. By the end of the century the kingdom of Northumbria appears to be in political chaos and a new power, the Frankish monarch Charles the Great, or Charlemagne, was extending his influence into the region. Finally, there was climatic change as the late eighth/early ninth century reached the nadir of the climatic cooling that had been continuing since the fifth century and would begin to reverse in the early tenth century.

New Political Order

Perhaps the least expected development was the political collapse of the dynasty of Angus son of Fergus. After dominating affairs in northern Britain for almost a generation Angus' achievements seemed to have assured the supremacy of his dynasty by the mid-eighth century. Even though not all his enterprises had been successful, his foes (and they were many) had been unable to challenge him. While Angus' successors were not able to extend his legacy, they maintained his gains for at least half a generation. Into this situation an old entity re-emerged with a new vigor. The rising power in the north by the last years of the eighth century was Dál Riata. Despite the battering by Angus, described as a *percussio* in the *Annals of Ulster*, Dál Riata had kept its independence and in the ensuing half-century it had recovered its ability to project power outside its bounds, as demonstrated by two brothers named Áed *Find* (the Fair, d.778), and Fergus (d.781), the sons of Eochaid son of Echdach and, therefore, the descendants of Áedan son of Gabran. Their attacks on the Picts in the last quarter of the eighth century laid the foundation for the better known triumphs of Kenneth MacAlpin. Without taking away from the latter's personal triumph, his path to power appears to have been a culmination of gradual Scottish movement.[2]

During the mid-eighth century one of the main dynasties of Dál Riata – Cenél Loairn, located round what is now the town of Oban

[2] Many of the arguments made here reflect earlier work, from a Scots rather than Picts perspective, in KCS: 17–36.

and the Isle of Mull – seems to have begun to move northeast into the lands of the Picts round the Moray Firth. The last time the annals mention them in Dál Riata is in the second quarter of the eighth century in the year 736. When they reappear in the chronicles they are located along the Moray Firth and in northeast Scotland.[3] Tracing from their location in Dál Riata to their later region suggests that they traveled up the Great Glen and took lands initially in what was the kingdom of Cat, the realm of Columba's host King Brude. The movement might not have been accomplished in a single action. The tenth-century *vita* of the celebrated church reformer St. Catroe refers to this movement into the "lands of the Picts." Prefaced to the account of his career are a couple of sentences briefly describing the movement of an unspecified group of Scots into what is now Rosshire followed by a later additional progress eastwards to St Andrews and "Bellethor."[4] The passage is difficult to interpret and it seems to combine the movements of Cenél Loairn and their rivals Cenél nGabráin; but a movement into what became Rosshire is sensible for Cenél Loairn in light of their subsequent settlement. Additional support for this date comes from the form of the Gaelic name element *kil-* (church), which suggests a late eighth-/early ninth-century introduction.[5]

Cenél Loairn were not the only ones looking eastwards, and their southern rivals of Cenél nGabráin had a history of efforts to move across the Ridge of Britain, the mountain chain that had been one of the boundaries of Dál Riata. Áedan son of Gabran, it will be remembered, had devoted much of his career to campaigns against his eastern neighbors, as had his descendants. A couple of events illustrate how the currents of power were shifting. The first occurred in 768 when Aed the Fair, son of Eochaid of Dál Riata, invaded Fortriu. This was a generation after the *percussio* of Angus son of Fergus and it is an eloquent indication of the severity of his attacks. Nevertheless, the passing of his foe emboldened Aed to lead an attack to the east. His opponent was a prince named Kenneth (spelled variously Cinadhon or Cinaed). He is found in the king-lists as *Ciniod filius Wredech* and is assigned a reign of 12 years. Kenneth seems to have successfully

---

[3] KCS: 133–134.
[4] J. Bollandus et al., *Acta Sanctorum* ... (Brussels 1642–), March 6: 495: "per Rosim amnen Rossiam regionem manserunt."
[5] W.F.H. Nicolaisen, *Scottish Place-Names* (London, 1975): 129–130; a distribution map is provided on p. 142.

defended his kingdom because he was still ruling in 774 when he gave sanctuary to King Alhred of Northumbria.[6] His reception of Alhred continued the goodwill between the Anglo-Saxons and the peoples north of the Forth that Bede implies was begun by Nechtan. Alhred needed a powerful friend because his own nobles had deposed him, even though (or perhaps because of) his support of Anglo-Saxon missionary efforts among the Germans. He had presided over the synod that sent abroad the missionary Willehard, who became the acquaintance of Charlemagne and whose labors led to the foundation of the archbishopric of Bremen. Kenneth died in 775 "gathered from the abyss of this dirty life," as stated in one eloquent eulogy.[7] He was followed in death three years later, in 778, by his daughter Eithne, one of the few female names in the annals, a forename which in this instance was popular in Ireland. Dying in the same year as Eithne was her father's adversary Áed the Fair.

According to the king-list two years later died an Elpin son of Wroid, who might be the same man as the Eilpin *rex Saxonum* found in the Annals of Ulster; the usual supposition is that *Saxonum* is a mistake for *Pictorum*. The next year, in 781, died Áed's successor and brother Fergus. At this point the collective nature of the king-lists is seen because a Drest son of Wroid is listed as king for four years, but in 782 is the notice of the death of Dubtolarg (Dark Talorg), who is described in his obit as "king of Picts on this side of the mountain" and given a reign of two years in the lists. So, once again, rulers of different kingdoms are being included in one list. The "dark" element is apparently a sobriquet, because he is called Talorgan son of Angus in the king-lists. The cryptic phrase "this side of the mountain" (*citra Monoth*) returns to the problem posed earlier in connection with Bede's comment on the location of Ninian's missionary labors "among the southern Picts, who live on this side of the mountain" (*Namque ipsi australes picti, qui intra eosdem montes habent sedes*). Which mountain and which side of it are intended? As has been seen, the mountains in question are not necessarily the Grampians, although that seems to be most logical choice.

---

[6] Symeon of Durham, *Historia Regum*, in *Symeonis monachi opera omnia*, ed. Thomas Arnold, 2 vols. (London, 1883–85): ii, 45: "... postea ad regem Pictorum nomine Cynoht cum paucis fugae comitibus secessit."

[7] Symeon of Durham, *Historia Regum*: ii, 46: "Rex Pictorum Cynoth ex voragine huius coenulentis vitae eripitur."

Constantine Son of Fergus

The lack of details connected with those princes who lived in obscurity and whose deaths get the barest of mentions is typical for this period. This is even true for an event that would have repercussions throughout the Middle Ages, the permanent political establishment of the *Scoti* in the lands that were described as those of the Picts. In either the year 789 or 790 a battle was fought in which, according to the *Annals of Ulster*, a Constantine defeated a rival named Conall son of Tadc somewhere "among the Picts." The annalist had two different sources with slightly dissimilar dates. The earlier entry notes "a battle among the Picts [*inter Pictorum*] where Conall son of Tadg was defeated; and he fled and Constantine was the victor" and the second entry notes "the battle of Conall and Constantine is written here in other books." The phrase *inter Pictorum* has often been translated as "between the Picts," but *inter* referring to a specific group or place has the meaning "amid" or "within"; the entry therefore means that the battle was fought in the territory of the Picts. Who were Conall and Constantine? If names are any indication, then Conall son of Tadg appears not to be a Pict; his name is purely Gaelic and he appears again in the *Annals of Ulster* when he was slain by another rival named Conall son of Áedán in Kintyre in 807.

Returning to Constantine, his name is Latin in origin and it appears in various contexts, often with some connection with Roman Britain. There was the famous fourth-century Roman emperor Constantine the Great, in addition to a fifth-century usurper from Britain (the so-called Constantine III), as well as the fifth-century author of St. Germanus' *vita*, and an eighth-century pope. Constantine in diverse forms also appears in British genealogies and pseudo-histories.[8] The name seems to have enjoyed some popularity at an earlier date; the Abbot Constantine, "tyrant whelp of the foul lioness of Devon" was a contemporary of Gildas who claims that he murdered two youths in church in front of the altar.[9] The Constantine who was victorious among the Picts about 790 does not have a patronymic, but the *Annals of Ulster* have among the events for the year 820 an obit for a Constantine son of Fergus who

---

[8] To take two examples see: P.C. Bartrum, *Early Welsh Genealogical Tracts* (Cardiff, 1966): 58 and 109; a full list is given in the index.

[9] Gildas, *Ruin of Britain and Other Documents*, ed. Michael Winterbottom (Chichester, 1978): 99: "... inmundae leaenae Damnoniae tyrannicus catulus Constantinus."

is styled King of Fortriu. There is general agreement that this is the same man who defeated Conall and their battle appears to have been for control of Fortriu. What was Constantine's ancestry? The matter is made more uncertain because simply being styled "king of Fortriu" need not be a comment on his ancestry. To move into the next generation, the Scots king Kenneth I (the "unifier of the Picts and Scots," according to medieval records), his brother, and his sons were all styled "king of the Picts," but their ancestors came from Dál Riata. Chronologically it is highly improbable, if not impossible, that Constantine was the brother of the mid-eighth century Angus son of Fergus. There is also the possibility that his father was an otherwise unknown individual. This leaves the possibility that he was the son of the Fergus who was king of Dál Riata and died in 781. There are two reasons for suggesting this last identification. First, Constantine is included among the kings of Dál Riata in the Irish synchronized texts of the eleventh century.[10] These lists gathered together princes who ruled during a specific period and for the historic period they list only those men who were Gaels from what were considered Irish kingdoms, one of which was Dál Riata.[11] The second reason is that verses apparently referring to Constantine in the eleventh-century historical prophecy known as the *Prophecy of Berchán*, expanding on a ninth-century original, describe him as the first of the Scots to rule among the Picts while Kenneth son of Alpin, popularly known as the unifier of Picts and Scots, is described in the next set of verses.[12] The verses claim that this prince, who is one of the few without a sobriquet, begins his career after a period of oppression by the Cruithne; he attacks when they are threatening to subjugate his kingdom. He will conquer them in battle and his cavalry will range along the river Earn. Finally, he will not be king when he dies in Kintyre. As will be seen, the details appear to match what can be discovered about Constantine's reign.

After establishing himself in Fortriu, Constantine seems to have been a continuator rather than an innovator. One possible example of the alliances he continued was with the Northumbrians. When another

---

[10] This argument follows H.M. Chadwick, *Early Scotland* (Cambridge, 1949): 129–132, and KES: 194.

[11] There are two modern editions: R. Thurneysen, "Synchronismen der irischen Könige," *Zeitschrift für celtische Philologie* 19 (1933): 81–99; A. Boyle, "The Edinburgh Synchronisms of Irish Kings," *Celtica* 9 (1971): 169–179.

[12] Benjamin Hudson (ed. and trans.), *Prophecy of Berchán: Irish and Scottish High-kings of the Early Middle Ages* (Westport, 1996): 41.

Northumbrian king named Osbald (known as *patricius*, the Patrician) was forced to flee his kingdom in 796, after a reign of 27 days, he sailed to the "land of the Picts" for sanctuary after a brief stay at the holy island of Lindisfarne.[13] Perhaps it was there he received a letter from Alcuin urging him to enter a religious house, which he eventually did before his death. The identity of Osbald's host is suggested by the aforementioned work known as the *Book of Life (Liber Vita)* belonging to the community of St. Cuthbert, which was kept originally at Lindisfarne and is now at Durham. Books of Life are rolls of individuals who were visitors to or benefactors of a particular religious house. Three interesting names appear in the Durham *Liber Vitae* in the section for kings: Angus, Constantine, and Eóganán.[14] The position of the names implies that the men are Angus son of Fergus, Constantine son of Fergus, and his nephew Eóganán, the son of his brother and successor Angus. A logical assumption is that Constantine did give sanctuary to Osbald and he was more involved with the Angles of Northumbria than is seen in the surviving scraps of written materials. While there is much that is not known about why certain individuals were included in Books of Life, it seems unlikely that merely providing sanctuary to one exile would have been quite enough for a foreign prince to be included.

There are other indications that Constantine was famed for his piety. In the so-called *Dunkeld Litany* there is a section for the holy martyrs, where is found the name Constantine Rex.[15] There were various levels

---

[13] Symeon of Durham, *Historia Regum*: ii, 57: "... et inde ad regem Pictorum cum quibusdam e fratribus navigio pervenit."

[14] The older edition, *Liber Vitae*, was edited by Henry Sweet in *The Oldest English Texts* (Early English Text Society, no. 83, 1885): 154 and facsimile *Liber Vitae Ecclesiae Dunelmensis. A Collotype Facsimile of the Original Manuscript, with Introductory Essay and Notes*, ed. A. Hamilton Thompson (Surtees Society, vol. 136, 1923); they have been superseded by David and Lynda Rollason (eds.), *Durham Liber vitae: London, British Library, MS Cotton Domitian A.VII: edition and digital facsimile with introduction, codicological, prosopographical and linguistic commentary, and indexes including the Biographical Register of Durham Cathedral Priory (1083–1539)* by A. J. Piper (London, 2007), 3 vols., I: Óengus (*Unist*) is at f. 12r.a; Constantine (*Custantin*) at f.12v.a; and Eóganán (*Uoenaen*) at f.12v.b.

[15] Arthur Haddan and William Stubbs, *Councils and Ecclesiastical Documents Relating to Great Britain and Ireland*, 3 vols. (Oxford 1869–78): ii 279; Patrick Wormald, "The Emergence of the *Regnum Scottorum*: A Carolingian Hegemony?" in B. Crawford (ed.), *Scotland in Dark Age Britain* (St. Andrews, 1996): 131–147

of martyrdom and only one – red martyrdom – was coupled with violent death. While this litany was preserved in an early modern manuscript, it appears to have been maintained from at least the ninth century because there is a prayer for the success of King Giric and his army; and the only King Giric died about 889. This type of preservation of information is not unique and examples of survival in undiluted form for centuries due to a liturgical nature have been demonstrated for French materials. Other contemporary or near-contemporary Gaelic royal individuals are found in the *Dunkeld Litany* such as the aforementioned Giric, and an Armkillach (i.e., Ainfcellach) who ruled Dál Riata briefly in 697–698 before being exiled and who was killed in 718 while battling his brother Selbach. Why might Constantine have been included in the *Dunkeld Litany*? By the fourteenth century, at the latest, Constantine was regarded as the founder of the church of Dunkeld. This appears in the so-called king-lists designated as Group X, such as List K (Corpus Christi College, Cambridge MS 133) embedded in a copy of the *Scalacronica* where Constantine is given a reign of 40 years with the added information that he was the founder of Dunkeld.[16] Another list, also from this X group, credits him with a reign of 42 years and the building of St. Andrews.

The final piece of material is the appearance of a Constantine son of Fergus, "king of Alba," in the Middle Irish text *The Expulsion of Mochuda from Raithen (Indarba Mochuda a rRaithe)*.[17] Mo Chuada was an Irish saint in Leinster and the story is concerned with his expulsion from the church at Raithen (near Tullamore, Ireland). One of the pilgrims at the church is a devout, but slow-witted, prince named Constantine son of Fergus. He had abdicated his kingship in order to end his days in religious retirement. Constantine is assigned a plot of land called "Constantine's field." His capacity for hard labor, an immense appetite,

---

(at p. 142); for the retention of ninth-century materials in later calenders see Susan Boynton, "Prayer as Liturgical Performance in Eleventh- and Twelfth-Century Monastic Psalters," *Speculum* 82 (2007): 896–931 (at p. 898).

[16] KES: 287 (for Dunkeld): "Costantín fits Fergus .xl. aunz. Cesti fist edifier Dunkeldyn"; and Oxford, Bodleian MS Latin misc. c75, f. 53 (for St. Andrews): "Constantinus filius Fergus xlii. annis, Iste primo edificvuit ecclesiam sancti andree."

[17] Charles Plummer (ed.), *Indarba Mochuda a rRaithen* in *Bethada Náem nÉrenn*, 2 vols. (Oxford, 1922): i, 300–311; and ii, 291–302. For the connections between Leinster and Dál Riata see Douglas Maclean, "Knapdale Dedications to a Leinster Saint: Sculpture, Hagiography and Oral Tradition," *Scottish Studies* 27 (1983): 49–65.

and an almost comic propensity to perspire are all noted, and they share some similarities with the behavior of the pagan Irish deity known as the Dagda (the Good God). If this Constantine is intended for the ninth-century prince, then the story cannot be genuine, since Mo Chuda died several centuries before Constantine; another version has a Constantine who apparently was a prince in Devon.[18] Nonetheless, the story is making a connection with a church dedicated to Mo Chuda, and there was one in Kintyre, in Knapdale. This is the region where the *Prophecy of Berchán* claims that the victor over the Picts would die. There is an interesting aspect to this tale in that it suggests how much of a sacrifice a prince had to make in order to enter religious retirement. One episode has a group of local nobles attempting to expel the saint and his followers. Constantine is sent to turn them from their purpose, but after being refused a greeting by members of the mob, he warns them against the sin of pride. In a statement that could have been echoed by any prince who had abandoned the world for religious retirement, Constantine remarks that he was once a powerful king, but traded worldly splendor for salvation: "Seven men were under my domination, everyone a king and each with gold, silver, flocks of sheep and herds of cattle; all was in my power, but now I am here in slavery for the love of God."

Constantine was a contemporary of Charlemagne whose biographer Einhard claims in the *Vita Karoli Magni Imperatoris* that the emperor was in contact with princes of the *Scoti*.[19] This appears to have been the starting point, first mentioned in the *Scotichronicon* of John of Fordun (III.48) that a king named *Achay* (probably for Eochaid) made an alliance with the Franks. Modern scholars look to Ireland for the princes, which is sensible. Equally probable is the suggestion this might also refer to Scoti in Britain, such as Constantine. His appearance in the *Liber Vitae* of the community of St. Cuthbert shows that he was well thought of by the Northumbrian clergy, one of whose members, Alcuin, was a leading intellectual figure at the Carolingian court. A curiosity about that text is that Constantine's name is immediately preceded by Karlus, that is, Charlemagne. As demonstrated by his poem on Ninian of Whithorn, Alcuin continued his interest in the lands north of Hadrian's Wall and was collecting information about the history of Christianity in the north of Britain. Charlemagne, too, involved himself in the affairs of Northumbria

---

[18] John Hennig, "Britain's Place in the Early English Martyrologies," *Medium Aevum* 26 (1957): 17–24 (pp. 21–22).
[19] Éginhard, *Vie de Charlemagne*, ed. L. Halpern (Paris, 1967): 46.

mainly as a counterpoint to the power of Offa of Mercia. Alcuin was not the only scholar from Britain among Carolingians, for the geographer Dícuil (discussed below), the author of *Concerning the Measure of the Lands of the World*, had lived on the Isle of Iona. Information from northern Britain was finding its way to the continent, as demonstrated by Walafrid Strabo's account of a Viking raid on Iona in his *Life of Blathmac*. Farther south the court of Merfyn of Gwynedd was a gateway for those interested in traveling from across the Irish Sea region to the Carolingian realm.

Vikings and the Collapse of the Pictish Kingdoms

Shortly after Constantine had won his battle "among the Picts" a new group appears in the records of the British Isles: the Vikings. While they have the popular reputation as destroyers of churches, this is partly due to the fact that the historical records were maintained by clergy who naturally were concerned with violent attacks on religious houses. There were two famous targets for their raids north of Hadrian's Wall. In 793 the holy isle of Lindisfarne was sacked, while in 795 and again in 802 the church of Iona was attacked. The severity of the raids is suggested by an event that took place two years later, when, in 804, the Columban community on Iona received the grant of Kells for their headquarters in Ireland. Their decision to establish themselves in Ireland for the administration of their affairs on that island might have been taken before the first Viking attack on Iona. In 825 the Vikings again raided Iona, and among the monks slain was a Blathmac, who hid the shrine of Colum Cille from the raiders. His martyrdom became internationally famous and commemorated in the aforementioned poem by Walafrid Strabo.[20]

Land taking was another aspect of the Viking raids and there is evidence of settlement among the Picts by peoples from Scandinavia before the Viking raids. The evidence is supplied by the monk named Dicuil, who had been part of the church at Iona in the late eighth century and had subsequently traveled to the Carolingian court. There, during the reign of Charlemagne's son Louis the Pious he composed a geography called *Concerning the Measure of the Lands of the World* (*De Mensura Orbis Terrae*). Much of his information comes from the

---

[20] *Versus Strabi de Beati Blaithmaic Vita et Fine*, in MGH, *Poetae Latini Aevi Carolini*: ii, 297–301; and a translation in ESSH: i, 263–265.

expected classical and biblical sources, but he does add important and unique material. His account of Thule is now generally accepted to be based on reports of clergy who had landed in Iceland where, it seems, at midsummer the light was so bright that one could see to pick the lice out of one's kilt. He also mentions that men from the north were moving into the Outer Hebrides as well as the Orkney and Shetland Islands during the late eighth century.[21] Following Dicuil's internal dating, these incidents occurred around 780, showing that the Viking movement into northern Britain was taking place before the well-known attacks on the island churches of Lindisfarne and Iona. On this Dícuil is a reliable witness because the clergy were scattered throughout the northern islands, even as far as Iceland.[22] He had visited some of the island settlements himself and personally knew men who had visited others, while confirmation of this early date of settlement comes from place-name evidence.[23]

After Constantine died in 820 there is another period of obscurity, and efforts to reconcile the various sources are difficult. He was succeeded in Fortriu by Angus son of Fergus whose death in 834 is also noted in the *Annals of Ulster*; the similarity of patronymics argues that they were brothers. Simple subtraction suggests that Angus ruled for 14 years, but his reign length is given as 12 years in the earlier Y group of king-lists, while the later X lists credit him with a reign of only nine years. While several king-lists credit this Angus with the foundation of St. Andrews (see chapter 5), the greater possibility is that he has been confused with the earlier (eighth-century) Angus son of Fergus. Unlike Constantine who

---

[21] *Dicuili Liber de Mensura Orbis Terrae*, ed. J.J. Tierney (Dublin, *Scriptores Latini Hiberniae* vol. 5, 1967): 76. Archaeology provides some clues as to the merger of Pictish and Scandinavian societies; see Anna Ritchie, "Pict and Norseman in Northern Scotland," *Scottish Archaeological Forum* 6 (1974): 23–36.

[22] The Norse called them *papa*; see Ari Þorgilsson, *Íslendingabók*, ed. Anne Holtsmark, *Nordisk Filologi*, series A, vol. 5: 16.

[23] Dicuil, *Dicuili Liber de Mensura Orbis Terrae*, ed. J.J. Tierney: 72 (see p. 114 for analysis). For discussion of his geographical context see: Patrick Gautier Dalché, *Géographie et culture: La représentation de l'espace du VIe au XIIe siècle* (Aldershot, 1997): 121–165; and Werner Bermann, "Dicuils *De mensura orbis terrae*," in *Science in Western and Eastern Civilization in Carolingian Times*, ed. Paul Leo Butzer and Dietrich Lohrmann (Basel, 1993): 525–537. For place-name evidence see Nicolaisen, *Scottish Place-Names*: 85–89 for discussion and distribution charts.

appears in several separate incidents, and setting aside St. Andrews, Angus appears only in connection with the legends of a battle with an Anglo-Saxon prince named Aethelstan, who attempted an invasion of Northern Britain. Only one event is recorded during his reign, if it even happened. An Alpin called *rex Scottorum* and apparently intended to be the same man who is the father of Kenneth I, is mentioned in a thirteenth-century record now known as the *Chronicle of Huntingdon*, one of the records sent to the English king Edward I in 1290 in response to his order for materials touching on the relationship(s) between the Scots and English monarchs, which states he was slain on July 22, 834 while fighting the Picts.[24] Returning to Angus, after his death the king-lists continue with a Drest son of Constantine sharing a reign jointly with a Talorgan son of Wthoil; probably a conflation of two provincial kingships.

Drest and Talorgan are followed by Angus' son Eóganán, who is credited with a reign of three years. By this time the Vikings had been active round the British Isles for more than half a century at least (following the chronological guidance of Dicuil's geography). Appearances might be deceptive, but in comparison with the attacks on Ireland or the Anglo-Saxon kingdoms the Picts were suffering no more than their neighbors. Although it is not safe to argue from the silence of the records for the ninth century, there is little evidence of the Vikings giving any particular attention to the Picts or their neighbors in Dál Riata and there is the possibility that not all contacts were hostile. Evidence from the Shetland and Orkney Islands could be interpreted as coexistence, at least for a period of time.[25] The *Chronicle of Huntingdon* claims that the overthrow of the Picts was hastened by Viking attacks, but fails to mention any specific battle.[26] Claims of similar, unnamed, battles would be repeated in later medieval and renaissance writings. Eóganán is connected, however, with the only fight between the Picts and the Vikings that is actually recorded in the contemporary or near-contemporary records. According to the *Annals of Ulster*, in 839 "a battle was won

---

[24] *Cronica Canonicorum Beate Marie Huntingdonensis*, in Sir Francis Palgrave (ed.), *Documents and Records Illustrating the History of Scotland* ..., (London, 1837): 98–104; for a discussion of the sources used in the *Huntingdon Chronicle*, see Edward J. Cowan, "The Scottish Chronicle in the Poppleton Manuscript," *Innes Review* 32 (1981): 3–21 (pp. 13–16).

[25] On this question see Jesse Backlund, "War or Peace? The Relations between the Picts and the Norse in the Orkneys," *Northern Studies* 36 (2001): 33–47.

[26] Palgrave, *Documents and Records*: 99.

Table 7.1 The last Pictish kings.

King	Length of reign (in years)
Fergus son of Bargot	3
Brude son of Ferant	1 (or 1 month)
Kenneth son of Ferant	1
Brude son of Fodel	2
Drust son of Ferant	3

over the men of Fortriu by the Heathens, in which Eóganán son of Angus, Bran son of Angus, Áed son of Boanta, and an unnumbered others died" (*Bellum re Gennitib for firu Fortrenn, in quo ceciderunt Euganan mac Oengusa et Bran mac Oengussa, et Aed mac Boanta, et alii pene innumerabiles ceciderunt*). Complementary information comes from the narrative known as *The War of the Irish against the Vikings* (*Cocad Gáedel re Gallaib*), of which the oldest text is preserved in the *Book of Leinster*. A fleet of 65 Viking ships was active on the eastern Irish coast where they attacked Leinster and Brega (the lands to the south and north of Dublin) before sailing through the North Channel and attacking the lands of Dál Riata where Eóganán, here styled king of Dál Riata, was slain.[27] Once again the Gaelic origins of the Eóganán are clear, because only Gaels or Vikings are included in this text. *The War of the Irish against the Vikings* shows the connection of the Pictish kingdom of Fortriu with the Irish colony of Dál Riata. The collapse of the independent Pictish kingdoms might have been hastened by Viking attacks, but there is no contemporary evidence that others, such as the future Kenneth I, were in alliance with them.

The deaths of Eóganán and his brother Bran often are seen as the event that led to the career of the famous Kenneth, popularly known as the unifier of the Picts and Scots. A less tidy scenario is suggested by the king-lists. Eóganán is succeeded by two kings according to the earlier Y group of lists to which are appended another three according in the later X group (see Table 7.1). Fergus (also called Urad) and Brude are found in both the X and Y group of king-lists, while Kenneth, Brude II, and Drust are found only in the X group of lists. The reign lengths assigned to Fergus and Brude cover the period from the death of Eóganán

---

[27] R.I. Best, Osborn Bergin, M.A. O'Brien, and Anne O'Sullivan (eds.), *Book of Leinster, formerly Lebar na Núachongbála*, 6 vols. (Dublin, 1954–83): V, 1321.

to the start of Kenneth's reign. The other three kings are less easy to fit into such a neat scheme, but their appearance does make sense if one accepts the claim made by the *Huntingdon Chronicle*, followed by the fourteenth-century Scottish historian John of Fordun (*Chronica*, IV.3), that Kenneth battled the Picts for 12 of his 16 years as *rex Pictorum*.[28] There might be independent confirmation for the Ferant who was the father of Brude, Kenneth, and Drust in a document discussion in chapter 5 from the *Register of the Priory of St. Andrews*, in connection with the foundation of the church by Angus son of Fergus. *Pherath filius Bergeth* can (just) be read as a form for the name Ferant son of Bargot. A royal estate at Meigle, where the scribe Thana son of Dudabrach copied the document is suggested by the particularly important symbol stones found there.[29] Of course how much trust can be placed in one late and unreliable source is a matter requiring further study.

Union of Picts and Scots

Who was responsible for the end of the Pictish kingdoms? The answer, ever since the Middle Ages, has been one man: Kenneth son of Alpin (Old Irish *Cináed mac Ailpín*) or Kenneth I. Beginning with the mid-ninth-century record preserved in the *Scottish Chronicle* he gets the credit as the man who united the Picts with the Scots. Medieval records hail him as a pioneer, but modern scholars have been less fulsome. Doubt has been expressed about his achievement, his ancestry, and his legacy.[30] As we have seen, he and his family were certainly not the first of the *Scoti* to rule among the Picts. Even before the victory of Constantine son of Fergus around 790 the Irish presence was becoming more remarked in the records, as kings with Irish names and even a kingdom called New Ireland appeared. What was different about Kenneth's reign?

[28] Palgrave, *Documents*: 99.
[29] Printed by John Pinkerton, *An Enquiry into the History of Scotland Preceding the Reign of Malcolm III*: i, 461. On the question of power centers see: Megan Gondek, "Investing in Sculpture: Power in Early-historic Scotland," *Medieval Archaeology* 50 (2006): 105–142; and S. Driscoll, "The Archaeological Context of Assembly in Early Medieval Scotland – Scone and its *comparanda*," in A. Pantos and S. Semple (eds.), *Assembly Places and Practices in Medieval Europe* (Dublin, 2004): 73–94.
[30] D. Broun, "The Origin of Scottish Identity in its European Context," in B. Crawford (ed.), *Scotland in Dark Age Europe* (St. Andrews, 1994): 21–31.

A casual first glance at the Irish annals does not suggest much change at all. They award the title of *rex Pictorum* to Kenneth, his brother Domnall, and sons Constantine and Áed. This means that they ruled the Pictish kingdoms. Beginning with Kenneth's reign there was kept a contemporary chronicle in his kingdom; it has been called various names, but here it is the *Scottish Chronicle*.[31] The form of the chronicle imitates the structure of late antique works, such as Prosper of Aquitaine's chronicle, in which the consular years (in this case regnal years) provide the frame. The *Scottish Chronicle* originally might have been embedded in a copy of Prosper of Aquitaine's chronicle; a text called simply *Prosper* is included in the twelfth-century catalogue of library of the church dedicated to St. Serf in Loch Leven.[32] For more than a century, from the reign of Kenneth to that of his descendant and namesake Kenneth II, this chronicle gives the view from northern Britain.

The *Scottish Chronicle* is essential for understanding the outline of the collapse of the remaining Pictish kingdoms and culture. Combining the information from the Irish and Scottish chronicles, Kenneth began to reign in Dál Riata about 840 and in Pictavia about 842. He became king of Dál Riata after the battle of 839 in which Eóganán son of Angus was slain, six years after his father's death in 834.[33] How Kenneth achieved his triumph is the subject of a legend that circulated for centuries among the Irish concerning a fatal banquet that he gave for the Pictish nobles at Scone.[34] A list of the titles of *Learned Tales*, which were stories suitable for recitation at a feast by a *fili* "poet," in the *Book of Leinster* is one with the title *Braflung Scoine*, which is usually translated as "the treachery of Scone," but it can also mean "the pitfall of Scone." The same tale is mentioned in the eleventh century verse history the *Prophecy of Berchán*, where there is an allusion to the destruction of the Picts in the verses for the reign of Kenneth son of Alpín: "The fools in the east [the Picts] are deceived by him, [the Scots] dig the earth, mighty

---

[31] Hudson, "Scottish Chronicle": 129–161.

[32] ESC: 210.

[33] James Ussher, who may have been using a cognate source, also notes that Kenneth ruled two years in Dál Riata alone; see *Britannicarum Ecclesiarum Antiquitates*, ch. 15 in C.R. Elrington and J.H. Todd (eds.), *The Whole Works of the Most Rev. James Ussher, D.D.*, 17 vols. (Dublin, 1847–64): vi, 147.

[34] Benjamin Hudson, "Conquest of the Picts," *Scotia* 15 (1991): 13–25 (at pp. 18–19).

the art; a deadly pit, death by wounding, in the midst of Scone of bright shields" (st. 121).

An outline of the story is given by Gerald of Wales in his *Book of Instructions for Princes* (*Liber de Principis Instructione*), a work begun in the late twelfth century and finished after the death of King John of England.[35] The story claims that the Picts were invited to a feast where the benches had been loosened so that a peg could be drawn from them and the seat would collapse. The Pictish nobles were in the midst of eating when the Scots withdrew the pegs and, in the ensuing confusion, killed them. Study of the legend of treachery at Scone suggests that the tale received the form in which it is found in Berchán and Gerald of Wales in the eleventh century, but was a revision of an earlier story.[36] The version found in the *Instructions* may have come directly from Berchán, since Gerald knew a version of another prophecy attributed to Berchán and he could have fashioned his story during his Irish sojourn.

How can we make sense of the various scraps of what might or might not be information? One scenario is that Kenneth first established himself in Fortriu and used it as his main center of power as he extended his lordship eastwards. Taking control of new territory meant taking control of the estates of the previous rulers. One of these was a fortress at Forteviot, on the banks of the river Earn where the *Scottish Chronicle* places his death. Another seems to have been at Scone, which appears to have been an inaugural site attached to a royal estate, the scene of the destruction of the Pictish nobles according to the *Prophecy of Berchán*. In the Irish chronicles and synchronisms of the eleventh century, Scone's association with the Scottish monarchs was equivalent to the association between Tara and the Irish high-kings, and the site's importance might have begun with the Scots.[37]

Kenneth's conquest of the Picts became a complicated affair in later histories with confused accounts of what may or may not be unique information about his campaigns.[38] There are no records of mid-ninth century battles involving the Scots or Picts in the contemporary Irish records, with the exception of the battle of 839 when Eóganán was

---

[35] Gerald of Wales, *Liber de Principis Instructione* in *Geraldi Cambrensis Opera*, ed. J. Dimock and G.F. Warner, 8 vols. (London, 1861–91): viii, 97–98.
[36] See Proinsias Mac Cana, *The Learned Tales of Medieval Ireland* (Dublin, 1980): 142–145.
[37] A. Boyle, "Edinburgh Synchronisms of Irish Kings," *Celtica* 9 (1971): 169–179 (at p. 177).
[38] See Hudson, "Conquest of the Picts": 20–22.

slain fighting the Vikings. That there was more than an isolated raid in the early ninth century is suggested by comparison with the Viking activity in the lands of the Picts beginning with the reign of Kenneth I according to the *Scottish Chronicle*, where the attacks are extensive. There were Vikings raids as far as Dunkeld and Clunie in Perthshire, possibly the same Viking attack placed in the twelfth year of Kenneth's reign in the *Huntingdon Chronicle*, around 854. Kenneth's son Constantine was killed during a battle with the Vikings in 876.

The problem seems to be one of the source materials' interests. Later medieval writers, who had materials that have not survived, claimed that Viking raids assisted the Scots in the conquest of the Picts. According to John of Fordun (*Chronica*, IV.3), Kenneth took advantage of Scandinavian raids on the Picts to further his own interests, a notion that may reflect Fordun's reading of the *Huntingdon Chronicle* or a document with similar information. The suggestion has been offered that the success of Kenneth son of Alpín was due, at least in part, to alliance with another dynasty from Ireland, one with a distinct Scandinavian aspect. The seventeenth-century compilation known as the *Annals of the Kingdom of Ireland by the Four Masters* claims, among the events of 836: "Gofraid, the son of Fergus, ruler of Oriel [*toiseach Oirghiall*], went to Scotland to strengthen Dál Riata, at the request of Kenneth son of Alpín." Gofraid's obit is found in the same chronicle for the year 853, where he is then styled *toisech Innsi Gall* ("ruler of the Hebrides") and he also appears in a Clan Ranald genealogy now preserved in several manuscript versions.[39] On the basis of that information, it has been proposed that a Hiberno-Scandinavian was the leader of troops from the northern Irish kingdom of Airgialla and that he led them into Scotland at that time. Unfortunately, such a theory fails to find any support in the medieval records, and one searches the contemporary records in vain for any mention of Gofraid son of Fergus, who does not appear in the genealogies of the Airgialla nor in any of the contemporary, or near-contemporary, chronicles. Doubt about that version of history seems to have been present among their historians. A seventeenth-century reworking of their family origins found in the volume known as the *Black Book of Clanranald* knows nothing of Gofraid's adventure in Ireland. Instead credit for the family's

---

[39] W.D.H. Sellar, "The Origins and Ancestry of Somerled," *Scottish Historical Review* 45 (1966): 123–142 (p. 128).

establishment in Scotland is given to a Gilla Brigte, the father of the famous Somerled, who led his followers from Fermanagh to Ardgour and Movern in the late eleventh/early twelfth century.[40]

At this point it is necessary to consider the ancestry of Kenneth. Medieval records are united in their insistence that he was a Scot and that the supremacy of the *Scoti* throughout northern Britain had nothing to do with his lineage, but everything to do with military success. The topic needs to be revisited because of speculation that Kenneth was actually connected with the Picts and that his medieval fame as the "champion of the Scots" who took control in the east is an example of historical revisionism. The easiest way to study the problem is to place Kenneth in the context of his Irish background, the evidence for which comes from amalgamating several records of differing ages. As has been noted, the *Scottish Chronicle* entries begin after his movement into the lands of the Picts. There is an independent date for the death of his father Alpín son of Echdach on July 22, 834, but it comes from only one record, a thirteenth-century copy of chronicle extracts sent by the community of St. Mary's, Huntingdon, to the English king Edward I; to go back even farther, his grandfather Eochaid son of Áed is known only from genealogies. These genealogies survive in different contexts. One is attached to the tract *History of the Men of Britain (Senchus Fer nAlban)* in a tenth-century version, and another is in a twelfth-century collection of Irish genealogies.[41] The pedigree reads (moving backwards) Kenneth son of Alpin son of Eochaid son of Áed Find son of Eochaid, which might seem suspect and repetitious. Comparison with other royal dynasties shows, however, that they used a limited number of personal names. The objections to the deficiencies in Kenneth's ancestry can be overridden by comparison with the royal line among Cenél nEógain, one of the dominant kindreds in the Uí Néill confederation for the same period. The sequence of names here is Áed son of Niall son of Áed son of Niall, and only four generations cover the same time as the five generations for Kenneth's family. There is no doubt about the truth of that sequence since all the men are mentioned in the annals as well as the genealogies.

---

[40] The legend is printed in Alexander Macbain and Rev. John Kennedy (eds.), *Reliquiae Celticae: Texts, Papers and Studies Left by the Late Rev. Alexander Cameron, LL.D.*, 2 vols. (Inverness, 1894): ii, 152–154. For a more extensive discussion of this problem see KCS: 41–42.

[41] Michael O'Brien, *Corpus Genealogiarum Hiberniae* (Dublin, 1962): 328–329.

So there is no immediate reason to discard the genealogy found for Kenneth among the princely dynasties of Dál Riata.

Demonstrating his descent from the kings of Dál Riata on his father's side still leaves the question of a Pictish connection with Kenneth's mother. She is completely unrecorded and no contemporary or near-contemporary source makes any mention of a Pictish ancestry for Kenneth. At this point one must violate a rule of historical writing: do not base an argument on the silence of the sources. This is especially pertinent for an era when the records are few, laconic, and maintained in a manner that cannot now be established. The reason for disregarding this rightly important rule is simple: if Kenneth had any Pictish ancestry it would have been convenient for his, and later, apologists to have mentioned the fact. The Picts were Christian, and any attack on fellow believers was frowned upon by the Church. But justification in the form of hereditary right, even a slight or irrelevant one, would provide the necessary vindication for such a course of action. This claim is never advanced in the contemporary or near-contemporary records. Only by the late Middle Ages, during the Anglo-Scottish wars, is there the suggestion of a connection of Kenneth with the Picts, and it is offered tentatively.[42] The best that the contemporary record preserved in the *Scottish Chronicle* can do to make the actions of Kenneth palatable to a Christian audience is to claim that the Picts were not behaving like Christians and the Scots were divine instruments bringing down the proud. When the lists of kings were composed in the late eleventh century, the Scots princes are simply grafted onto the catalogue of Pictish lords with little or no comment.

Did the Church play a role in the general pacification of the Picts, as did other successful intruders, such as the Carolingians for their conquests among the Saxons? Constantine son of Fergus has the credit for founding an ecclesiastical community at Dunkeld in one group of king-lists, which would place it in the first quarter of the ninth century. There has been a suggestion that Kenneth and his family worked in tandem with the churches connected with Iona through dedication to St. Columba.[43] The *Scottish Chronicle* claims that Kenneth had the relics of

---

[42] For the development of the legend of Scottish claim to lordship over the Picts by ancestry, see Hudson, "Conquest of the Picts": 20–21.

[43] John Bannerman, "The Scottish Takeover of Pictland and the Relics of Columba," *Innes Review* 48 (1997): 27–44.

Columba moved to a church generally thought to be Dunkeld.[44] If any church was being used in the interests of the now-dominant Scots the evidence points to St. Andrews. One late legend claims that Kenneth transferred the bishopric of the Picts from Abernethy to St. Andrews.[45] This may have been reworked with St. Andrews' interests in mind, for the foundation legend of Abernethy claims a royal patron in the Pictish king Nechtan son of Erp, whose grant to St. Brigit was due to her spiritual comfort while he was an exile.[46] There was also a bishop at St. Andrews and the *Scottish Chronicle* notes that about 906 Bishop Cellach joined Kenneth's grandson Constantine at the royal monastery (*civitas*) of Scone where they pledged to guard the laws and disciplines of the faith, and that the rights of the churches and gospels should be kept in conformity with the Scots; the chronicle goes on to claim from that day the hill has had the name of the Hill of Belief.[47] Application of that ordinance might be seen at Dunkeld. There is evidence of an episcopal administration for the churches and the first entry concerning Dunkeld in the *Annals of Ulster* is the obit in 865 for Tuathal son of Artgusso, who is called chief bishop of Fortriu and abbot of Dunkeld. The offices he held indicate episcopal administration of the churches in Fortriu at least. When Tuathal's successor Flaithbertach son of Muichertaich died in 873, he is styled *princeps*, the usual Irish designation for an abbot with the extended meaning of bishop. Yet, by the tenth and eleventh century there are references only to abbots of Dunkeld.

A reading of the *Scottish Chronicle* shows a deliberate policy by Kenneth to realign his new conquest politically and reshape it culturally. The chronicle gives a list of those kingdoms Kenneth attacked and one of his favorite targets was Northumbria, one of the Picts' allies. He invaded *Saxonia* (referring to Northumbria) six times, burning Dunbar and ravaging "Marlos." Dunbar was a royal *villa* of the Northumbrian royal dynasty of Bernicia located on the coast south of the Haddington

---

[44] For observations on the location see G. Donaldsson, "Scottish Bishops' Sees before the Reign of David I," PSAS 87 (1952–53): 106–117 (at p. 109); and D.W. Rollason, "Lists of Saints' Resting Places," *Anglo-Saxon England* 7 (1978): 61–93.
[45] Alexander Penrose Forbes (ed.), *Kalendar of Scottish Saints* (Edinburgh, 1872): 267.
[46] KES: 248; the brief foundation legend is inserted in a list of the Pictish kings.
[47] For brief considerations of the presence of a monastery at Scone, see D.E. Easson, *Medieval Religious Houses: Scotland* (London, 1962): 83, 192.

Tyne while Marlos is a scribal corruption of *Malros*, now known as Old Melrose, one of the main centers of the community of St. Cuthbert. The direction of Kenneth's raid can be surmised since Old Melrose is close by the Roman road that extended northwards from Hadrian's Wall.[48] Kenneth however, had competitors in the Britons of Strathclyde who moved eastwards to burn Dunblane.

The Aftermath

The title King of the Picts continued to be used for the half-century after the death of Kenneth I. His sons and brother are referred to as "kings of the Picts" (*reges Pictorum*) while their domain is known as "the land of the Picts" (*terra Pictorum*) or "kingdom of the Cruithne" (*Cruithentúaith*). A benefit for those keeping the records was that Kenneth fitted within the series of the Pictish kings. The compiler of the late eleventh-century king-list designated B, composed for Malcolm Canmore, attached the dynasties of both Constantine son of Fergus and Kenneth to the list of kings of the Picts.[49] The title of *rex Pictorum* in the Irish records demonstrates how an acceptable way of referring to a king was by the name of the people over whom he reigned. As the years passed, the artificiality of the title become more pronounced, and by the death of Kenneth's grandson Donald the Madman in the year 900 the kings were identified by the geographical term *Alba*, formerly a designation for Britain as a whole, which had now acquired the more limited definition of the region of the Scots in Britain.[50]

A more significant indication that Kenneth's reign was different from that of Constantine son of Fergus is the deliberate effort to change the administration of his new lands. The *Scottish Chronicle* notes that Kenneth's brother and successor Domnall proclaimed the rights and laws of Áed Find son of Echdach, his great-grandfather: "in his time the rights and laws of the kingdom, of Áed son of Echdach, were made by the Gaels with their king at Forteviot." Domnall's legislation suggests that he was seizing the opportunity provided by the conquest to

---

[48] I.A. Richmond, "Ancient Rome and Northern England," *Antiquity* 14 (1940): 292–300 (at p. 293).

[49] Benjamin Hudson, "Historical Literature of Early Scotland," *Studies in Scottish Literature* 26 (1991): 141–155 (at pp. 147–148).

[50] O'Rahilly, *Early Irish History and Mythology*: 385–387.

regularize the laws in both Dál Riata and the Pictish kingdoms. This would prove to be a long-running concern for the Scots princes who throughout the Middle Ages had to respond to the enlargement of their lands. Recognition of the separate identities of his subjects explains the specific reference to the Gaels, and an echo of this comes from the twelfth-century charters of the Scottish kings with their references to their French, English, and Scottish subjects. Although Latin *leges* is also found as a translation of Old Irish *cáin*, an ecclesiastical proclamation that was often issued in conjunction with a saint, the reference to a monarch rather than a saint, however, implies that *leges* should be translated simply as "laws." Donald's introduction of Gaelic laws and customs was within the Irish tradition, for among the prerogatives of a king was a statement of rights.[51] There might be an historical memory of that legislation, for a fourteenth-century legal text called the MacAlpine Laws was attributed to Kenneth I by John of Fordun (*Chronica*, IV.8), but the "MacAlpine" could equally have been his brother Donald.

A glimpse of the ethnography of northern Britain appears in an entry in the *Annals of Ulster* concerning a Viking expedition made by two men named Olaf and Ivar during the years 870–71. The primary target seems to have been the kingdom of Strathclyde. King Arthgal retreated to the fortress at Ail Cluathe (on Dumbarton Rock), usually a guarantee of safety. This time, however, the refuge became a prison. The summer of 870 from June to August was one of great drought and the continental chronicles mention the oppressive summer heat.[52] Arthgal's garrison held out for four months on Dumbarton Rock, but finally was forced to yield, not because of flaws in the fortress or disloyalty among his subjects, but due to the unheard of drying-up of the fort's well.[53] The defeat of Strathclyde was famous; a literary version of the siege was composed and included in the list of historical sagas in the *Book of Leinster*.[54] The siege was the only recorded incident of what must have been a series of campaigns against not just the men of Strathclyde, but also the Picts and

---

[51] See Máirín Ó Daly, "A Poem on the Airgialla," *Ériu* 16 (1952): 179–188 (pp. 181 ff.), after M. Gerriets, "The King's Judges in Early Ireland," *Celtica* 20 (1988): 29–52 (p. 41).
[52] D.J. Schove, *Chronology of Eclipses and Comets*, AD 1–1000 (Woodbridge, 1984): 325.
[53] Joan Radnor, *Fragmentary Annals of Ireland* (Dublin, 1976): 142.
[54] Best et al., *Book of Leinster*: iv, 836.

Anglo-Saxons. The *Annals of Ulster* describe the triumphant return of Olaf to Dublin in 871 leading 200 ships filled with captive Angles, Britons, and Picts. Slightly later there is another reference to the Picts as a people. In 875 the Viking force known as the Great Army, which had ravaged Mercia and Northumbria, separated into autonomous bands. One of these moved north under the leadership of Hálfdan who established a base along the river Tyne and, according to the *Anglo-Saxon Chronicle*, led raids against the English, Picts, and Strathclyde. Possible references to the raids of Hálfdan are in the *Scottish Chronicle*, which notes a Viking army that was victorious at Dollar and the harrying of territory as far as Atholl.

Summary

The history of the last years of the Pictish kingdoms and the beginning of the Scots kingdom has been carefully sifted over the centuries. One of the problems has been the few bits of information and what to do with them, so story has stepped in to supply the details. This has led to efforts to tidy and fumigate accounts of the ninth century as are clear from reading late medieval narratives such as those of John of Fordun and Andrew of Wyntoun. Their accounts need to be considered carefully because it is clear that they used materials that are now lost, but at the same time it is also clear that they are deliberately choosing the information that fits with their positive presentation of the history of Scotland. Nonetheless, stray names or events emerge that remind us to use the surviving materials with care. What does become apparent is that the eventual triumph of Kenneth I and his dynasty did not occur in isolation, but was part of a process that had been happening for decades. Since the seventh century there had been efforts on the part of the princes of the Picts, of Dál Riata and of the Angles of Northumbria to impose their lordship over their neighbors. This is completely in keeping with the general drift of European political history, and all three groups had, at various times, had some success in their endeavors. After the ninth century the Scoti of Dál Riata were successful in making the final union. This conquest was not made in one battle or by one man and its beginnings should be dated to the eighth, rather than ninth, century. There were two conquests, one round the Moray Firth and the other north of the Firth of Forth. For the former, the conquest seems to have begun in the first half of the eighth century and moved north following the Great Glen. The southern movement was later, in the last decade of the eighth century; there is no doubt that it was accomplished through conflict. The conquest of Fortriu by a branch of the Dál Riatan dynasty of Cenél nGabráin reinforced the Gaelic element that was already present in the lands north of the Antonine Wall. The royal dynasties of Dál Riata were successful in their longstanding ambition to annex the lands to their east by the end of the eighth century, but they kept control of the ancestral homeland. When Constantine took the kingship of Fortriu, apparently he and his family removed themselves to the lands in the east. They remained the overlords of Dál Riata, which is why Eóganán fought there against the Vikings, using his subjects from Fortriu. The information about Kenneth I makes clear the military nature of his conquest. His campaigns against the Picts had become elaborate genocides in the late medieval writings of John of Fordun and his followers. Despite his later fame as the conqueror of the Picts, there is little reliable information about Kenneth's career prior to his establishment in the eastern kingdoms. Even the exact chronology of his campaigns and even the year or years of his conquest(s) of the Pictish kingdoms is uncertain. There was no single moment for the transition from the Pictish to Scottish eras and what made it remarkable was its unremarkability.

Discarding the murderous fantasies of later writers, it is clear that the Scottish conquest of the Picts was a process that extended over a long period of time and may have provoked so little notice because it was so unremarkable. This was an era of small-scale warfare separated by periods of consolidation, and non-violent change could be as effective as combat, as the legislation of the Scots princes Donald and his kinsman Constantine show. The theory that Kenneth I had a genealogical right to his conquest is one that is not made by his contemporaries or near-contemporaries. Not until the fourteenth-century history of John of Fordun, writing in the final phase of the Anglo-Scots war, does heritage as an explanation appear, and even he was uncertain about its accuracy.[55] Even on such a crucial matter any argument has to be advanced tentatively because there is a lack of evidence for the maternal heritage of Constantine son of Angus or his family, or Kenneth son of Alpín or his family.

Trying to make sense of the legends and historical explanations involves more speculation than analysis of facts. What may or may not be accurate reflections of the past do suggest that memories of a long

---

[55] See Hudson, "Conquest of the Picts": 20–21.

struggle by the Scots to rule over the Picts were preserved. As we have seen, there were Scots settled in what became known as Pictland by the early eighth century at least, when there is the first appearance of the kingdom of Atholl, "New Ireland." The genealogical connection of the eighth-century Angus son of Fergus with the Éoganachta of Cashel, and its identification of his kingdom as Circenn, shows that the Gaelic presence was significant. The conquest of Fortriu by Constantine late in the eighth century was simply another intrusion into the eastern kingdom. The final collapse of the Pictish kingdoms south of the Highlands occurred during the reign of Kenneth, who deserves, at least in part, credit for the union of the Picts and Scots.

8

Literature and Remembrance

The topic of literature is associated with enquiries about the Picts in a negative way. Henry of Huntingdon's oft-quoted remark on the disappearance of the Pictish language neatly defines the problem; if nothing of their speech survived then any vernacular literature (if there was any) must also have disappeared. So there is an excuse for the popular belief that no literature composed by "Picts" survives, with the exception of those who believe in the antiquity of the king-lists, which presumably were composed in Latin. Even before the end of the independent Pictish kingdoms most of what we think we know about the Picts depends on how they fit into someone else's story. Interest in the Picts did not begin after the triumph of the Scots led by Kenneth I, but can be seen even earlier. As the centuries changed so, too, did the image of the Pict, from widely traveled mercenary to stereotypical villain to noble savage. In the process, the literary character reflects the shifting concerns of writers and the obsessions of the day.

Literature

Together with the image of the Picts as savages is that of the Picts as illiterates. This is an easy myth to dispel. We know Picts had books because these, or their satchels, can be seen on the symbol stones. Those objects are held by or draped over churchmen who, as the learned class throughout Europe, would be expected to have them. A cleric on a stone from Meigle (no. 14) is holding a book; while a figure on the St. Vigeans

The Picts, First Edition. Benjamin Hudson.
© 2014 John Wiley & Sons, Ltd. Published 2014 by John Wiley & Sons, Ltd.

stone no. 7 has a book satchel. We can assume that they are Bibles or service books, which were essential after the conversion to Christianity. The debatable point has been whether the Picts produced their own texts in the form of histories, liturgical works, or literature. This matter has been has been examined from time to time and an eminent scholar has asked "where are the writings of early Scotland"?[1] Several texts have been put forward as products of writing centers or *scriptoria* in northern Britain in support of the proposition that the churches north of the Clyde and Forth were one of the avenues along which information about northern British affairs eventually traveled to the *scriptoria* where the Irish annals were composed. Bede's claim (V.21) that the Pictish King Nechtan ordered a letter concerning the correct calculation for Easter, received from Abbot Ceolfrid of Wearmouth/Jarrow, be copied and circulated throughout his kingdom must mean that there was at least one writing center or *scriptorium* among the Picts.[2] There has been the suggestion that a brief chronicle from a Pictish *scriptorium* is embedded in the historical materials maintained by the community of St. Cuthbert.[3] A frequent and vague refrain in medieval texts is "as chronicles/histories say," which not only shows the medieval respect for antiquity but also offers the possibility that later works preserve information from works composed prior to the tenth century. John of Fordun, in the first book of the *Chronica Gentis Scotorum* (concerned with the origins of the Picts and Scots), has ten references to unnamed chronicles.[4] His fifteenth-century editor Walter Bower gives an exact calculation for the foundation of the church of Abernethy by King Garnard as 226 years, nine months and six days before the church at Dunkeld; his precision suggests that he consulted a written source, possibly an annotated ecclesiastical calendar.[5] Oral traditions

---

[1] See, for example, Kathleen Hughes, "Where are the Writings of Early Scotland?," in D. Dumville (ed.), *Celtic Britain in the Early Middle Ages*, Studies in Scottish and Welsh Sources (Woodbridge, 1980); K. Forsyth, "Literacy in Pictland," in H. Pryce (ed.), *Literacy in Medieval Celtic Societies* (Cambridge, 1998): 39–61.
[2] Bede, *Historia Ecclesiastica*, ed. Charles Plummer, 2 vols. (Oxford, 1896): i, 345.
[3] Katherine Forsyth and John Koch, "Evidence of a Lost Pictish Source in the *Historia regum Anglorum* of Symeon of Durham," in Simon Taylor (ed.), *Kings, Clerics and Chronicles in Scotland, 500–1297* (Dublin, 2000): 19–34.
[4] Benjamin Hudson, "Tracing Medieval Scotland's Lost History," in S. Arbuthnot and K. Hollo (eds.), *Fil súil nglais* (Ceann Drochaid, 2007): 63–72 (at pp. 63–64).
[5] Walter Bower, *Scotichronicon*, ed. John MacQueen and Winifred MacQueen, vol. 2 (Aberdeen, 1989): 302 and 458.

should not be ignored, and less precise, but still intriguing, is the aside offered by John of Fordun that the legend in which a ninth-century Pictish king named Angus defeated and killed an English invader named Aethelstan was preserved both in writing and in the mouths of the people to his own day.[6] The fifteenth-century poem *Fhuaras mo rogha theach mhór* (*I have found of houses my supreme choice*) by Fionnlagh Ruadh praises a house where ancient songs are heard. This begs the question of what sources survive from a contemporary northern British milieu and which are the products of learned interpretation, speculation, or composition?

The poems connected with the north British kingdoms of Gododdin and Rheged give insight into the literature of the region. Not unexpectedly, much of this is in verse and just how much can be identified and accepted as early medieval remains a controversial matter. What seems to be the earliest historical work is the Old Welsh poem *Y Gododdin*, composed about 600. Such poems generally are accepted to have an early date of composition, but they are found in manuscripts of much later date and some details may have been added or deleted in the intervening centuries. Therefore these texts must be used carefully, but some general outlines of society appear with features also found among their neighbors. Literature and information depended on contacts among aristocratic warriors, a mobile class. There is the poem's reference to a mercenary named Llifiau son of Cian. He fought for the men of Gododdin in their defeat against the Angles, but came from outside the kingdom for his home is located "beyond Bannog," which has been interpreted as referring to the hills from Stirling to Dumbarton.[7] (He is called "the foreign [i.e., non-Gododdin] horseman." This immediately calls to mind the images of the horses that are so prominent on several of the Pictish carved stones.) Two possible fellow mercenaries are mentioned later in the verses. One is a warrior named Bubon "from beyond the sea of Iuddew" who fought more ferociously than a lion. The sea of Iuddew is believed to be the Firth of Forth, which could place him north of Manaw Gododdin.[8] Another possibility is Gwid son of Peithan who was as unflinching as a rock. The similarity of his name with the Wid found in

---

[6] William Forbes Skene (ed.), *Johannis de Fordun, Chronica Gentis Scotorum* Historians of Scotland 1 and 2 (Edinburgh, 1871–72, with Latin text in vol. 1 and English translation by Felix J.H. Skene in vol. 2): i, 155–156.
[7] Kenneth Jackson, *The Gododdin* (Edinburgh, 1969): 6 and 103.
[8] Jackson, *Gododdin*: 108, and 69–75.

the so-called Pictish king-lists as the father of three princes who died in 635, 641, and 653 respectively has led to the suggestion that he is the same man.[9] If the identifications of "Bannog" and "the sea of Iuddew" are correct – and Llifiau, Bubon, and Wid were not hostages who decided to fight for their captors or fosterlings placed at a suitably famous court to be reared – then the poem *Gododdin* shows interaction among the peoples of northern Britain. It suggests more sophistication among the Picts than is usually allowed them. The society described in the *Gododdin* is dominated by a warrior aristocracy in which public displays of status are made through feasting, the quality of possessions such as weapons or horses, and the respect of one's contemporaries, occasionally described in terms of comparison with particular animals for bravery or endurance. The vocabulary can be compared with Irish or Anglo-Saxon poetry where descriptions of physical ability as well as bravado were standard parts of the poets' repertoire. Public acknowledgment of an outstanding deed was tied to the culture of the feast, which allowed the demonstration of wealth while inclusion in the event was a visible honor. The literature also shows an élite that is connected with the high-status individuals of other kingdoms through artificial ties such as hostageship or fosterage or through biological bond. Sometimes the less heroic aspects of life appear and the *Gododdin* remarks that a warrior named Gwenabwy son of Gwenn was so attentive to the needs of battle that his land was unplowed so that it was more like waste land, an unexpected reference to the lord as a farmer.[10]

Irish and Anglo-Saxon poets visited the courts of the Picts and boasted of their journeys. Visits to the courts of northern Britain were mentioned in the verses of poets who wished to show their familiarity with different peoples and the wide range of their travels. The seventh-century Old English poem *Widsith*, for example, includes the *Peohtas* among the poet's catalogue of peoples, alongside the "sliding Finns," an early reference to skiing.[11] An Irish poet's verses on the ales of sovereignty attached to the tract on status *Críth Gablach* has already been mentioned and even though its horizon is more limited – Ireland and the northern part of Britain – the intent was to reveal the sophistication of the poet.

[9] Jackson, *Gododdin*: 130–131.
[10] Jackson, *Gododdin*: 127.
[11] *Widsth*, in G.K. Krapp and E. Dobbie (eds.), *The Exeter Book* (New York, 1936): 149–153 (at l. 79): "Mid Scottum ic waes ond mid Peohtum ond mid Scridefinnum."

Remembrance

After the ninth century the Picts became part of the historical and literary memory of European literature, but into the tenth century they continued to be part of history. The historian Widikund of Corvey (*c.* 925–*c.* 973) emphasized their alliance with the Anglo-Saxons in his history of the Saxons.[12] Slightly later the Picts make their last appearance in an historical context courtesy of the Anglo-Saxon chronicler Aethelweard (died *c.* 998) who composed a Latin version of the *Anglo-Saxon Chronicle* for his relative Abbess Matilda of Essen.[13] He claimed that the "Scots and Picts bowed their necks" in defeat at the battle of Brunnanburh in 937. A similar reference to the Picts comes from the versified Welsh pseudo-prophecy known as *The Prophecy of Britain* (*Armes Prydein*), composed around 930.[14] The poem tells of the Welsh revolt against the oppression of a "great tyrant," usually assumed to be the Anglo-Saxon King Aethelstan (r. 924–39) and is a call to arms, which was answered in the battle of Brunnanburh (937). Among those invited to join the Welsh are the "Irish of Ireland, Anglesey, and Pictland" (*Gwydyl Iwerdon Mon ac Phrydyn*).[15]

Within two generations the Picts had become an historical curiosity and the study of them became what has been described in another context as "the cult of the antique by the masters of the land."[16] Among the materials in which they appeared was hagiography. The *vita* of the Welsh St. Cadog, which survives in a twelfth-century version, has the saint meet a character called Caw of Pictland (*Kaw Prydyn*).[17] The episode begins when Cadog visits the church of St. Andrews and, returning home, stops at a fort on the southern slopes of a mountain called *Bannog*, now remembered in the name Bannockburn at Stirling.[18] Under divine instruction, he tarried there for seven years. While digging the

---

[12] Widukindus, *Res gestae saxonicae sive annalium libri tres*, in MGH, SS 3: 419.
[13] Aethelweard, *Chronicon*, ed. and trans. Alistair Campbell (London, 1961). He was a distant relation of King Alfred the Great and an ealdorman somewhere in southwest England.
[14] Sir Ifor Williams (ed.), *Armes Prydein, The Prophecy of Britain from the Book of Taliesin*, trans. R. Bromwich (Dublin, 1972): xx.
[15] Williams, *Armes Prydein*: 2.
[16] F.X. Martin, *No Hero in the House: Diarmaid Mac Murchada and the Coming of the Normans to Ireland*, O Donnell Lecture xix, (Dublin, 1978).
[17] Vita Sancti Cadoci, in A.W. Wade-Evans (ed.), *Vitae Sanctorum Britanniae et Genealogiae* (Cardiff, 1944): 82–84.
[18] Jackson, *Gododdin*: 78–79, after CPS: 195–196.

foundation for the monastic building, he uncovered a huge bone and threatened a fast against God until the identity of the person was made known to him. His prayers were heard too well. The next morning a giant named Caw appeared and revealed that the bone had been his. Shocked, but unflinching, the saint asked for his story. Caw was a warlord who lived on the other side of the mountain and had been raiding in the south when he was slain and buried. The saint tells Caw that he will be permitted to be resurrected briefly in order to convert to Christianity and do penance for his transgressions. The giant gladly accepted the offer and helped the saint to build the monastery. As a reward for this feat, the kings of the Scots (*sic*) gave the saint 27 homesteads (*villae*). In what might or might not be a connection, the early Welsh genealogies know a Caw who is the ancestor of several prominent individuals, including a Gildas.[19] Whether the two men are thought to have been the same or whether the similar names led to the occasional conflation is uncertain. And finally there is another possible example, this time for a raider named Baia, whom Rhigyfarch, in his late eleventh-century life of St. David, says is Irish, but in the version of the *vita* of St. Teilo of Llandâv written in the twelfth century by Geoffrey, the brother of Bishop Urban of Llandâv (d.1133) he becomes a Pict.[20]

Some of the literary materials are connected with a place rather than a specific individual, and they are found in a catalogue of materials that today is known as the *Learned Tales of Ireland* (*Do nemthigud filed i scélib ₇ i comgnimaib*), of which the earliest two lists are in the twelfth-century encyclopedia called the *Book of Leinster*.[21] These are stories that the professional storyteller or *seanachie* was expected to know and to recite for entertainment at a feast or gathering. Competition among these performers was fierce and poetry frequently contains lines in which the author/entertainer praises his artistry while denouncing his rivals. While many of the tales are familiar, other stories are now no more than titles. Some tales seem to have a connection with northern Britain, although the supporting evidence can be slight. An example is the tale-title *Destruction of Nechtan's House* (*Togail Tige Nectain*), and other than the fact that

[19] See, for an example, the tract called *Lineage of the Saints* (*Bonedd y Saint*) in P.C. Bartrum, *Early Welsh Genealogical Tracts* (Cardiff, 1966): 63, 59.
[20] G.H. Doble, *Lives of the Welsh Saints*, ed. D. Simon Evans (Cardiff, 1971): 173.
[21] R.I. Best, Osborn Bergin, M.A. O'Brien, and Anne O'Sullivan (eds.), *Book of Leinster, formerly Lebar na Núachongbála*, 6 vols. (Dublin, 1954–83): iv, 835–837 (ff. 189b–190b).

several kings among the Picts are named Nechtan, there is no other reason for a connection with northern Britain. More certainly situated north of the river Tay is the tale *The Battle of Drum Dólech among the Cruithne* (*Cath Dromma Dólech dara díta Cruthnig*); Drum Dólech is now Drumdollo in Aberdeenshire. Another tale where the action is in Aberdeenshire is *The Destruction of Bennachie* (*Argain Benne Cé*); Bennachie is a hill in the eastern Grampian range. Slightly to the south is *The Destruction of the Plain of Cé [by] Gala son of Febal* [*Argain Maige Cé Gala mac Febail*]. A synopsis of sorts survives for the aforementioned *Pit-fall of Scone* (*Braflang Scóine*), which is found only in the later list of tales, and the story's absence from the earlier list has suggested that it came into Ireland around 1100. Among the verses for Kenneth MacAlpin is the passage "The fools [i.e., the Picts] in the east are deceived by him, they [i.e., the Scots] dig the earth, mighty the occupation; a deadly pit – death by wounding – on the floor of noble-shielded Scone." A similar and more detailed story is told by the curmudgeonly polymath Gerald de Barri, better known as Gerald of Wales, who briefly describes the destruction of the Pictish aristocracy by the Scots during a banquet in his *Instruction for Princes*. Gerald probably learned the tale while residing in Ireland during his time as tutor to the future King John of England. The story begins with the Scots inviting the Picts to a feast under a guarantee of safety. Their real motive, however, was ambush. Prior to the meal, the Scots removed pins from the benches so that the seat could be made to crumple. When the Pictish nobles found themselves trapped in the collapsed furniture, the Scots attacked and slaughtered them. Gerald claimed his story was an illustration of how a lesser people could overcome better ones, although to be fair, the Scots were merely one of the numerous peoples he did not like. Nonetheless, the story remained in circulation for generations and it is repeated by the monk of Chester named Ranulph Higden (*c*.1280–1364) in his *Polychronicon* (I.58).[22]

A text survives for the final selection from the *Learned Tales* in the *Book of Leinster* with the title *Coming of the Cruithne from Thracia to Ireland and their Coming from Ireland to Britain* (*Tochomlod Cruithnech a Tracia co Herind ⁊ a thochomlod ó Herind co Albain*). The title shows that this is the same work as a long poem called (with some variations)

---

[22] Ranulph Higden, *Polychronicon Ranulphi Higden, Monachi Cestrensis: Together with the English Translations of John of Trevisa and of an Unknown Writer in the 15th Century*, ed. C. Babington and J.R. Lumby, 9 vols., Rolls Series no. 41 (London, 1865–86): 1, 154–156.

What brought the Picts to Marvellous Britain (*Cruithnig cid dos-forglam i niat Alban amra*).[23] Two late medieval Irish encyclopedias called the *Book of Lecan* and the *Book of Ballymote* have the story embedded in their versions of *Lebor Bretnach* (*Book of the Britons*), a mid-eleventh-century Irish translation/adaptation of the *History of the Britons* attributed to Nennius. The basic story that emerges from either version claims that six brothers – Solen, Ulpa, Nechtan, Drostan, Angus, and Letenn – sailed from Thrace after the king had sullied their sister. They had nine ships containing over 300 people and they sailed looking for a new home. During a temporary stay in the land of the Franks they built a city called Pictabis, an adaptation of Pictavia, better known today as the city of Poitiers. Forced to flee once more, their sister died on the second day of the voyage toward the British Isles. They landed in Ireland in Wexford Harbor (*Inber Sláine*) and joined with the residents, themselves from Britain, in the battle of Ard Lemnacht. One of their druids used a magical cauldron of milk to heal any of their warriors who were wounded. Shortly thereafter Solen, Nechtan, Drostan, and Angus died. After a couple of generations, the Irish became concerned that the prowess of the Cruithne in combat might encourage them to seize the kingship of Tara. So they were given 300 nobly born women as wives and, led by Cathluan and Cruithne son of Cing, they sailed to Britain, where they took all the territory from Cat (Caithness) to Forcu, probably standing for Fortriu (another version claims that they landed somewhere past Islay). An interesting conclusion to the poem is in the version preserved in the manuscript TCD MS 1295 where the poem abruptly gives the number of Scottish kings (50) from Fergus, famed as the first of the kings of Dál Riata to have his capital in Britain, to the mighty "son of Bretach" (*co mac mbrigach mBhrethach*).[24] This otherwise unknown individual might be responsible for the earliest extant manifestation of the literary Pict and is better known from drama than from history: Shakespeare's great anti-hero Macbeth.

Even a cursory reading of the poem *What Brought the Picts to Marvellous Britain* reveals its debt to the story in *Senchus Mar*. Equally obvious was the nature of the poem, an example of the learned historical revisionism of the Irish literary class during the High Middle Ages. The

---

[23] The various versions with translations are in J.M.P. Calise, *Pictish Sourcebook: Documents of Medieval Legend and Dark-Age History* (Westport, 2002): 56–79.
[24] Benjamin Hudson, "Historical Literature of Early Scotland," *Studies in Scottish Literature* 26 (1991): 141–155; Calise, *Pictish Sourcebook*: 78.

language, syntax, and content point to a date of composition in the mid-eleventh century. Resorting to speculation momentarily, if an eleventh-century date is accepted and the identification of the "son of Bretach" as a play on the name Macbeth (Middle Irish *Mac Bethad*) then this represents an important point in the development of the legend of the Picts. Macbeth was the first known Scots prince to make a pilgrimage to Rome and was, for his time, a cosmopolite. By stressing that the immediate rulers of the lands then controlled by the Scots were themselves immigrants, the triumph of the dynasties from Dál Riata would be just another example of one group of immigrants displacing another. Eight years after Macbeth's death that line of argument was dangerous.

The middle of the eleventh century was a watershed in the remembrance of the Picts. If the poem *What Brought the Picts to Marvellous Britain* was harmless antiquarianism, Macbeth's successor Malcolm Canmore had a different need for the past. The successful conquest of England by Duke William of Normandy in 1066 had brought a new foe to Britain. William's moves into Scotland had to be countered both militarily and diplomatically; the former needed the assistance of historical remembrance. To present the Scots as simply another successful invader would have given the Normans the justification to attempt the same thing. So it was necessary to show the Scots as the heirs of the Picts. Sometime before Malcolm's death in a battle fought near the river Aln in 1093 a king-list was assembled tracing the line of kings from the early princes of the Picts to Malcolm. This list (now known as king-list B) survives in a later copy, but its time of composition is indicated by the statement that Malcolm was still alive.[25] In order to imply that there had been a single kingdom, names of all the rulers of Pictish kingdoms were included. The source for this was probably the Irish annals, as the existing ones have almost all the names. The jumble of names made it appear that no king's son succeeded him directly. The merger came at Kenneth MacAlpin and from that point on it was a complete capitulation to the demands of Malcolm's clan. Only three kings are included who were not part of that group; the ninth-century Giric, Macbeth, and his stepson Lulach. All three men were unavoidable; the first because he was too well-known and the last two because they were too recent.

Slightly later, while Henry of Huntingdon was launching the legend of the vanishing Picts, a new individual appears. This was the fantasy

---

[25] The list is preserved in Oxford, Bodleian MS Laud 610: f. 87r; the best edition is KES: 261-2-63, and it is discussed in Hudson, "Early Scots Literature": 148.

Pict, who became a staple character in the stories inspired by Henry's contemporary Geoffrey of Monmouth. In the year 1136, a teacher at Oxford named Geoffrey of Monmouth claimed to have translated into Latin an old book written in Welsh that had been given to him by his friend Walter the Archdeacon. Geoffrey called his work the *History of the Kings of Britain* (*Historia Regum Britanniae*), and it became one of the most influential works of its day.[26] A fictional account of the kings of Britain from a mythical figure called Brutus up to the settlement of the Anglo-Saxons began the popularity of legends about King Arthur and his court. For the following four centuries the Matter of Britain would be one of the great literary genres of medieval Europe with many tales developing from Geoffrey's work, such as *Sir Gawain and the Green Knight*. Despite the skeptical denunciations of Geoffrey's younger contemporaries Gerald of Wales and William of Newburgh, who stated plainly that he had invented his story, what is today classed as literature during the Middle Ages was considered history. Excerpts from the *History* crop up in various texts and the short geographical piece known as *The Description of Scotland* (*De Situ Albanie*) begins with an historical prologue taken from the *History of the Kings of Britain*.

In Geoffrey's hands the Picts are the savage villains of British history. Even though they are the occasional allies of the Britons, they are the antithesis of civilized Britain. The Picts are introduced in a passage copied from the opening of the Venerable Bede's *Ecclesiastical History*, as one of the five races of peoples inhabiting Britain. There follows a slightly different version of their origin legend in which Geoffrey has the Picts led from Scythia to Albany by a King Sodric. Sodric attacks the British ruler Marius, but is defeated; afterwards commemorated by a monument raised in Westmorland (IV.17). The conquered Picts are forced to settle in Caithness, but the British refuse to give them wives, so they are sent wives from the Irish. There are echoes of Nennius, with his claim that the Picts came into Britain via the Orkney Islands, combined with Bede's story, apparently from Irish sources, of the Picts being sent wives from Ireland.

The theme of confrontation with the Britons, interspersed with occasional alliances, continues throughout the *History of the Kings of Britain*. Although Geoffrey abruptly declares that he will end the account

---

[26] The edition followed here is Geoffrey of Monmouth, *The History of the Kings of Britain: An Edition and Translation of De gestis Britonum (Historia regum Britanniae)*, ed. Michael D. Reeve, trans. Neil Wright (Woodbridge, 2007).

of the Picts after giving an account of the marriage arrangements, he almost immediately returns to the theme of hostility between the Picts and the British. This time it is a British leader, Sulgenius or Fulgenius, who goes to Scythia to recruit Pictish warriors to fight the Roman emperor Severus, obviously Septimus Severus, who dies in Britain (V.2). When the same warriors are employed by Sulgenius' nephew Bassianus, they turn against him and fight for the Briton Carausius, who rewards them with the lands they originally held in *Albany*. The weaving of fact and fantasy continues later in the story when the Picts ally with the Huns during the reign of the historical late fourth-century emperor Magnus Maximus. When Magnus leads troops to the continent, the Picts attack, but are defeated and driven to Ireland. They soon reappear with their Irish allies together with, in an early appearance, the Danes and Norwegians. This coalition is defeated by a legionary force and a wall is constructed to keep the Picts out of the southern part of Britain (VI.3). This is somewhat the same story as found in Gildas, although his wall is rebuilt rather than made anew.

An interesting episode involving the Picts features another villain of Arthurian literature, the tyrant Vortigern. The Picts reappear throughout the narrative as combatants in many wars, although in one incident the Picts are brought into Britain by Vortigern for the court of Constans (VI.7). The justification is that they will act as spies on their own people and pass on news of weapons or attacks; this might be an echo of the *arcani* mentioned by Ammianus in the middle of the fourth century. In reality Vortigern planned to use the Picts and make them execute Constans, which he accomplishes by rewarding them lavishly and encouraging their excessive drinking. When his gullible followers murder the doomed king, Vortigern promptly executes them, so that no suspicion can fall on him.

Those occasional appearances of the Picts are overshadowed by the extended narrative of their battle with the great Arthur himself. The Scots and Picts besiege Arthur's nephew Hoel in the city of Alclud (modern Dumbarton Rock, northwest of Glasgow) (IX.5). Arthur leads his army to raise the siege. The attackers are defeated and flee north, described as a wild and barbarous region, where they take refuge in Loch Lomond. Arthur gathers boats for a siege, but the Picts and Scots are unexpectedly relieved by a fleet led by the king of Ireland called Gilmaurius (Gaelic *Gille Maire*, "Servant of [the Virgin] Mary"). Arthur defeats the Irish and forces them to sail home, then begins the extermination of the Scots and Picts. The slaughter is stopped when the bishops and clergy of Moray confront the king with their most precious holy relics and petition him for an end to the bloodshed. Arthur pardons the survivors and returns home. In a ceremony at York, he gives the kingdom of the Scots to Auguselus, the rule of Moray to his brother Urian, and the dukedom of Lothian to Loth. The horror of Geoffrey's Moray Massacre is relieved by a digression on the miraculous nature of Loch Lomond where it is claimed that the lake has 60 islands with 60 streams feeding it and 60 crags with 60 eagles' nests (IX.6). Like Duncan's horses in Shakespeare's drama, the eagles were prophets. Geoffrey claims that they screamed in concert before any momentous event. When Hoel remarks on the curiosity of the lake, Arthur tells him that a nearby pool was 400 ft (121 m) square with four different types of fish dwelling in each of the four corners. Those observations on local curiosities belong to the genre of "wonder" stories in which supernatural aspects are credited to geographical features. Geoffrey borrowed the Loch Lomond episode from the ninth-century *History of the Britons* by Nennius where the lake is Loch Leven, in Fife, with a single river and eagles' nests on every rock.[27] There is no mention of the birds screaming. Geoffrey merely relocated the action closer to Dumbarton, probably because he mistranslated the original. The pool with the clannish fish might also owe something of its origin to Nennius, who claims that Lough Lein in Ireland is surrounded by four circles made of four different metals: tin, lead, iron, and copper. This episode may have been inspired by the recitation of battle sites given for Arthur in Nennius' *History of the Britons*, where his seventh battle is fought in *silva Celidonis* ("in the Caledonian woods"), which the Welsh call *Cat Coit Celidon*.[28]

The basis for Geoffrey's disdain for the Picts traces back to the sixth-century Gildas' *Ruin of Britain* which mentions invasions of the Britons by combined forces of Pictish and Scottish raiders.[29] An additional reason for the particular episodes may be that Geoffrey was using the Picts as arcetypical "wild men." The Wild Man genre was a precursor of the noble savage, except that wild men were not noble but bestial: animals in human form. By the end of the Middle Ages they were a standard feature of literary life and became more famous as a theatrical motif in

---

[27] Nennius, *The British History and Annals*, ed. John Morris (London, 1980): 81.
[28] Nennius, *British History*: 76.
[29] Gildas, *Ruin of Britain and other works*, ed. Michael Winterbottom (Chichester, 1978): 21 and 23–24.

the Tudor era. The unwillingness of the British to send wives to the Picts is heightened later by the presentation of the land of the Picts as a complete wilderness, with the customary fey animals.

Geoffrey's interpretation of Bede and Gildas on the Picts would be followed by later writers in England, primarily those who were reworking the Arthurian legend. Two generations later, with the reworking of the Arthurian legend in Lagmon's *Brut*, the leader of the Picts was named Rodric (*sic*) apparently a mistranscription of Geoffrey's Sodric, and the former is found in Robert Mannyng's *Chronicle*, composed about 1338 during the Anglo-Scottish Wars.[30] Despite the criticisms by his contemporaries, Geoffrey's *History of the Kings of Britain* was considered to be an historical work throughout the Middle Ages and into the Renaissance. Early in the sixteenth century, Hector Boece used it as one of his primary sources of information for his *History of the Scots*, and expanded upon the original. At the conclusion of Arthur's reign his final battle was fought against the Picts, led by their king named Mordred, and Arthur is slain by them. Boece does not identify where he found this information nor does he make use of it further in his narrative. Nevertheless, the death of Arthur is removed from the realms of fantasy and placed firmly in the story of north Britain.

Whether Geoffrey of Monmouth's *History of the Kings of Britain* returned the Pict to the popular imagination or was merely one aspect of a trend, the Picts begin to reappear in historical materials connected with northern English writers. Now, however, they are located in southwest Scotland, in the area encompassed by Galloway and Dumfriesshire. During the English civil war of 1136–53 the momentous battle of the Standard was fought in 1138 between King David of Scotland, championing the cause of his niece the Empress Matilda, and the supporters of King Stephen. Richard of Hexham, the historian of the church, claims that King David's forces included Picts of Galloway, notable for their savagery and nudity; he adds the aside that they are commonly called Galwegians.[31] Richard was a canon of Hexham, a target of David's invasion, and he became prior in 1141. His contemporary Reginald of Coldingham similarly places the Picts in southwest Scotland in his tract on the miracles of St. Cuthbert, and he gives some interesting

---

[30] Robert Mannyng of Brunne, *The Chronicle*, ed. Idelle Sullens (Binghampton, NY, 1996).
[31] Richard of Hexham, *De Gestis regis Stephani in Chronicles, Stephen, Henry II and Richard I*, Rolls Series 82 (London, 1884–90): iii, 152–153.

information.[32] He claims that the church of St. Cuthbert at what is now Kirkcudbright was in the land of the Picts. Then he tells a story about some *scollofthes* at the church who violated the solemnity of Cuthbert's peace with a bull-baiting that went badly for the miscreants. (Reginald claims that the word *scollofthes* was Pictish, but it is actually Middle Irish meaning a scholar at the church school.)

Throughout the Middle Ages the Picts continued to make occasional appearances in other contexts. For example, in a late fourteenth-century manuscript, among the miracles of the Virgin Mary, Rollo, the Viking founder of Normandy, is claimed to be a Pict: "Out of the Picts' land there came a knight that Rollo was his name" ("Out of peihtes lond þer came A kniht þat Rollo was his name").[33] Somewhat differently, there is the magical or fantastic Pict who lives a life different from other people. The late twelfth-century *History of Norway* (*Historia Norvegiae*) has a passage about the Picts, who are magical pygmies.[34] They remain above ground during the night, but disappear into a subterranean hole during the day. In light of Pictish habitations at places such as Jarlshof, with its sunken wheelhouse, this obvious confusion about the reason for disappearing can be blamed on a half-understood report, probably a popular memory of the original inhabitants. Possibly this type of story is responsible for the belief that the Picts were small in stature and by the fifteenth century the name becomes synonymous with *pygmy* in the word-list called the *Catholicon Anglicum* (*c*.1475) with "A Pict or pygmy: *pigmeus*" (*A peght or pigmei: pigmeus*).[35] The episodes connected with the Picts became more fabulous, and the tract called *The Name of the Kings of the Scots* (*Nomina Regum Scotorum*) claims that hostilities between the Picts and Scots began when the Picts stole a hound.[36]

---

[32] J. Raine (ed.), *Reginald monachi Dunelmensis Libellus de admirandis Beati Cuthberti Virtutibus quae novellis patratae sunt temporibus*, Surtees Soc. 1 (1835): 178–179. Reginald was the prior of Durham and well regarded as an historian by his contemporaries; he wrote his *vita* of Godric of Finchale at the request of Ailred of Rievaulx.

[33] C. Horstmann (ed.), *The Minor Poems of the Vernon MS*, part 1, Early English Text Society 98 (1892; repr. 1987): 139.

[34] *Historia Norvegia*, in Gustav Storm (ed.), *Monumenta Historia Norvegiae* (Kristiania, 1880): 67–124 (at p. 88ff).

[35] S.J.H. Herrtage and H.B. Wheatley (eds.), *Catholicon Anglicum: An English–Latin Wordbook*, Early English Text Society 75 (Oxford, 1881): f. 93b.

[36] In D. Embree, E.D. Kennedy, and K. Daly, *Short Scottish Prose Chronicles* (Woodbridge, 2012): 164.

As shown above, from the twelfth century the Picts became a minor character in literature. They continued to appear in versions or adaptations of Geoffrey of Monmouth's work, but in a subsidiary role. All the same they continued to be mentioned in historical works, although not in as much detail as one would expect. Beginning in the fourteenth century in Scottish historiography the Picts became stereotyped as villains and the opponents of the Scots. The *Chronicle of the Scottish Nation* by John of Fordun, the reworking in the hands of Walter Bower in the fifteenth century, and the late fourteenth-/early fifteenth-century rhyming chronicle of Andrew of Wyntoun all struggle to deal with the Picts. On the one hand they cannot ignore them, although their main topic was the history of the Scots. What is clear from the narratives is how little information they had. Some of their sources are still extant and the two on which they are most dependent are Bede's history and Geoffrey of Monmouth's *History of the Kings of Britain*. Other information seems to come from the lives of saints and local topographical lore. It is also clear that they did not have the information found in the Irish annals. For example in John of Fordun's *Chronicle of the Scottish Nation*, when the Picts appear they control northern Britain. Their violent encounters with the earliest Scots immigrants are noted, and then they virtually disappear until the section dealing with the Scottish conquest of the ninth century. Much the same formula is followed in Andrew of Wyntoun's *Verse Chronicle* and in Walter Bower's edition of Fordun's work.

Sometime in the late fourteenth century, a priest in Aberdeen named John of Fordun began to write a history of the Scottish people from the earliest times to his own day. He took the surviving scraps of information on early Scottish history and fashioned them into a narrative that today is known as the *Chronicle of the Scottish Nation*. Fordun finished his narrative only to the middle of the twelfth century and the death of King David I in 1153, but his notes for the remainder of the history were appended to the finished work. That continuation had to wait until the next century when the entire narrative was re-edited, and new material added, by Walter Bower. The *Chronicle of the Scottish Nation* has information about the Picts scattered through the first three books, with a brief appearance in the fourth book with the circumstances surrounding the triumph of Kenneth son of Alpin. The first book is a collection of bits of information or what is thought to be information based largely on Bede and Geoffrey (with whom the author was not always in agreement), supplemented by Batholomaeus'

De Proprietatibus Rerum, Ranulph of Chester's *Polychronicon*, and at least one king-list from the later group designated X. Fordun gives different theories on the origins of the Picts, some of which differ radically from earlier ones. Almost immediately, in the fourth chapter of the first book, he notes that some authorities claim that the original home of the Picts was in the Baltic. But his classical education shines as he, from his reading of Julius Caesar, then places the home of the Picts in Poitiers (found, as we have seen, in medieval texts as Pictavia) in the 24th chapter of the same book, a theme to which he returns in the 29th chapter. This is grafted onto the classical story of the Picts coming to the British Isles by having them sail from Aquitaine to Ireland and then on to Britain. Over the course of several chapters Fordun then gives a brief recitation of the other, different origin legends about the Picts, ending with the revered Bede. What he cannot do, however, is allow the Picts to precede the Scots as settlers in Britain, so he claims that the wives the Picts received from the Scots were accompanied by kinsmen, who settled in Britain at the same time (ch.31). The first book concludes with the pagan Picts persecuting the Scots, until the rise of the first Scots prince among them, Fergus son of Ferechad. In the same book begins the competition between the Scots and the Picts, which Fordun describes as a feud. At the 35th chapter is information which he found in a damaged king-list, for he states that Cruithne the son of Clemens was a judge, which is a garbled rendering of "Cruchine f. Kyan clemens judex accepti monarthan in regno Pictorum" found among the X group of king-lists. The Picts return in the second and third books in connection with the missions of various saints Regulus, Palladius, Servanus, Kentigern, Ternan, Ninian, Brendan, Columban, and Drostan. There is the occasional detour into politics, as at the end of the third book where the stage is set for the final overthrow of the Picts. That is accomplished at the beginning of the fourth book and the final collapse of the Picts begins with their killing of Alpin, the father of Kenneth I. The triumph of Kenneth is presented in terms of stories, such as his appearance to the Scots nobles as an angel to encourage them, and with reference to battles which are never named or supplied with details. When, a century later, Walter Bower recopied and expanded on Fordun's narrative, he did little more than supply the occasional detail for some of the episodes.

A different approach to the history of the Picts is in the slightly later verse chronicle of Andrew of Wyntoun that also has somewhat different information.[37] He was a canon regular of St. Andrews and became prior of St. Serf's of Loch Leven (a dependency of St. Andrews) in the last decade of the fourteenth century. When a local nobleman named Sir John of Wemyss asked him to write a history of Scotland from the earliest times to his own day, Andrew obliged. The resulting work was *The Original Chronicle of Scotland;* the title merely means that the work begins with the earliest ("original") history of Scotland. This chronicle is of interest to historians not least because the surviving manuscripts show that Andrew revised his work at least once, if not twice. He was interested in how the kingdom of Scotland evolved, and to that end his work is less an encomium for the Scots and more analytical than earlier works. He attempts to place his events in chronological order by cross-references to popes and kings of the Scots. What were his sources are obscure because he alludes to unnamed chronicles, and even though their identity is not obvious it is clear that some of them are king lists. Unlike John of Fordun, however, Andrew of Wyntoun is only slightly in debt to either Bede or Geoffrey of Monmouth. Also different is the more equal representation of ecclesiastical and secular affairs. Andrew is more interested in secular participation in the foundation of churches such as Rosemarkie by Nectan Derly[ng] or Dunkeld by Constantine son of Fergus, and the patronage of St. Andrews by the ninth-century Angus son of Fergus. The Picts appear in book V and are annihilated by the eighth chapter of book VI. Like his predecessor, Andrew of Wyntoun used king-lists for his information, which he quotes at different places in the fifth book. The first list of the kings of the Picts begins with Columba's occasional host Brude.

By the end of the Middle Ages the Picts were becoming a political as well as historical concern. The writer of the late fifteenth-century *La Vraie Cronicque D'Escoce* implies that the Picts were the original inhabitants of Britain, until they were expelled by the Britons.[38] The author of the chronicle is uncertain about this, however, and devotes a substantial section of his work to an effort to find a reasonable solution. What makes

[37] The textual variations of this chronicle are at least two and possibly three. The first and third versions were edited by F.J. Amours, as *The Original Chronicle of Andrew of Wyntoun*, 6 vols., Scottish Texts Society, Old Series 50, 53, 54, 56, 57, and 63 (Edinburgh, 1903–14), and the second by David Laing, as *The Orygynale Cronykil of Scotland by Androw of Wyntoun*, 3 vols., Historians of Scotland 2, 3, and 9 (Edinburgh, 1872–79).

[38] *La Vraie Chronicque D'Escoce* in Embree et al., *Short Scottish Prose Chronicles*: 81.

this tract important is not just that it reflects learned opinion, but that it appears to have been composed for French diplomats to study prior to meeting their English counterparts at the St. Omer negotiations of 1464.

Picts and Controversy

An expansion of the literary embellishments on the Picts by Fordun and Wynton was made by Leland's contemporary Hector Boece. Hector Boece (*c*.1465–*c*.1536) was born in the city of Dundee, the port town for ships sailing the Firth of Tay and he studied at the University of Paris. Upon his return to Scotland, he became the first principal of what is now the University of Aberdeen. There he wrote *Scottorum Historiae a prima gentis origine cum aliarum et rerum et gentium illustratione non vulgari*, which is better known by the short English title *History of the Scots*.[39] While modern scholars are inclined to dismiss Boece as a fantasist, he was a trained scholar who had access to materials no longer extant. His history of the bishops of Mortlach and Aberdeen is, for its day, a commendable effort to gather the materials for an obscure diocese. Nonetheless, Boece's Scottish history is a mixture of historical items, legend, and speculation. In contrast, another contemporary John Major or Mair (1467–1550) attempted to place the early history on a rational basis. Major was a theologian and sometime historian who had been educated at the universities of Cambridge and Paris. In his *History of Greater Britain as well as England as Scotland* (*Historia majoris Britanniae tam Angliae quam Scotiae*) he tried to tie events in early British history to events of his own day and the Picts emerged from the straitjacket of conventional villains.[40]

While Major's work languished in scholarly obscurity, Boece's history entered the popular mainstream when its translation by John Bellenden, made for the Scots king James V, became the basis for Raphael Holinshed's *Chronicles of England, Scotland, and Ireland* (better known today as *Holinshed's Chronicles*), one of the sources used by many other writers including William Shakespeare. Others were at work and a contemporary of Shakespeare wrote a work that became as popular among scholars as Boece's work was, at several removes, among the general public.

[39] Hector Boece, *Scottorum Historiae a prima gentis origine cum aliarum et rerum et gentium illustratione non vulgari* (Paris, 1527).
[40] John Major, *Historia majoris Britanniae tam Angliae quam Scotiae* (Paris, 1521).

Late in the sixteenth century William Camden (1551–1623) published the influential *Britannia*. Camden was a Londoner who attended the University of Oxford and eventually became the Clarenceux King of Arms. The first edition of *Britannia* was published in 1586 and combined history with topography in an antiquarian overview of the British Isles as a single historical entity. The work was reprinted several times with the final (and expanded) edition in Latin appearing in 1607, which was followed by Philemon Holland's English translation of 1610. A small section (pp. 30–34 in the first edition) is devoted specifically to the Picts, which was followed by the material for Scotland (only 16 pages). Camden was placing this history within a unified British framework and he was also trying to discard the fictitious element by moving northern British history into a British Isles context. Among the works he consulted were classical authors, inscriptions (some no longer extant), and (then) unpublished documents such as the famous fourteenth-century Poppleton manuscript (so called by modern scholars because one of the compilers was a Robert of Poppleton), which was owned by William Cecil, Lord Burleigh, to whom Camden dedicated the first four editions of his book. This manuscript is a miscellany of texts and includes information on the Picts including a king-list, extracts from Isidore of Seville, a brief chronicle of Scottish affairs now known as the *Scottish Chronicle*, and a geographical tract called *De Situ Albanie*. For the earlier editions Camden used the *Scottish Chronicle* while the edition of 1607 has additional material from the political geography *De Situ Albanie*.[41]

The light of history, in the modern sense of the word, shone on the Picts in their own right in the eighteenth century with the research of Father Thomas Innes (1662–1744). He was a native of Drumgask in Aberdeenshire who became the principal of the Scots College in Paris. His contemporary fame rested on his *Critical Essay on the Ancient Inhabitants of the Northern Parts of Britain* (1729).[42] This work had two goals: firstly, to show that the origins of Christianity in Scotland were

---

[41] Benjamin Hudson, "The Scottish Chronicle," SHR 77 (1998): 129–161 (at p. 131).

[42] Thomas Innes, *A Critical Essay on the Ancient Inhabitants of the Northern Parts of Britain or Scotland. Containing an Account of the Romans, of the Britains betwixt the Walls, of the Caledonians or Picts, and particularly of the Scots. With an Appendix of ancient manuscript pieces*, 2 vols. (London, 1729); this was reprinted as vol. 8 of the Historians of Scotland series (Edinburgh, 1879), together with a biographical memoir by George Grub; all citations are to this edition.

part of the Roman mission; and, secondly, to prove the legitimacy of the Stuart succession via the early Pictish kings. In the process he worked through the material for the history of the early period, reserving particular opprobrium for the historian Hector Boece. A lack of scholarly generosity could present problems. Even though he devotes several chapters to the destruction of Boece's theories, Innes was forced to use his speculation that the grandmother of Kenneth MacAlpin was a Pict to make his Stuart–Pict connection.[43] An important part of his book was the appendices which contained transcriptions from the manuscript sources. These were the fruits of his efforts to seek out materials, and a search for information led Innes back to Britain, where he resided in Edinburgh during the period 1724–26. The most important document was, however, in Paris, whither the fourteenth-century Poppleton manuscript had been sold in the dispersal of Cecil's library; it was purchased by Louis XIV's minister Jean Baptiste Colbert. Innes' access to the document was due to his friendship with Colbert's librarian Étienne Baluze. The *Critical Essay* was to have been the first part of Innes' program and he planned to use those materials for the writing of a political history. The narrative was written, but it was still in manuscript at the time of his death and was not published until the mid-nineteenth century with the title *Civil and Ecclesiastical History of Scotland*, as a part of the series of Spalding Club publications.[44]

If Innes was the champion of a rational approach to Pictish history, the role of madcap was taken a generation later by John Pinkerton (1758–1826), a native of Edinburgh. The contrast between the two men is striking; the celibate and poor Innes never lost a friend while the (at least) thrice-married, man-on-the-make Pinkerton rarely kept one. Like Innes, Pinkerton wrote his history to support a particular thesis; unlike Innes, his theory was wrong. The unexpected facet of this story is that Pinkerton was a competent scholar, and his *Enquiry* is an illustration of how a good researcher can go badly wrong. His main claim to scholarly fame, for example, was *Pinkerton's Modern Atlas* (London, 1808–15), a crucial milestone in the development of modern cartography, not least because of its abandonment of elaborate and fantastic imagery in favor of greater attention to detail in the map. In his *Enquiry into the History of Scotland Preceding the Reign of Malcolm III* Pinkerton wished to

---

[43] Innes, *Critical Essay*: 93.
[44] Thomas Innes, *Civil and Ecclesiastical History of Scotland, 80 to 818*, ed. George Grub, Spalding Club (Aberdeen, 1853).

remove any significant "Celtic" element in Scottish history and argued that the Picts had no connection with the Irish, Welsh or Highlanders of Scotland, but were Goths.[45] Towards that end he argued that the many place names or their elements thought to be Celtic were actually Germanic. Needless to say those theories were controversial even in his day and contemporaries hurled themselves forward to be the champions of the Gael. Despite its flawed argument, Pinkerton's *Enquiry* is still useful mainly because of his copying of, and reliance, on primary source materials. Several pages, for example, are given to correction of Innes' errors in his transcription of Scottish items from the Poppleton Manuscript which, along with the rest of Colbert's library, had subsequently passed into the collection of King Louis XV; Pinkerton acknowledged the assistance of the librarian M. Van Praets.

Pinkerton's critics were numerous, and the flames of their censure were fanned by the virulence of his attacks on the work of others. John Buchanan, a clergyman from Comrie, states openly in the preface to his *A Defense of the Scots Highlanders in General* that his book is devoted to rebutting Pinkerton's arguments.[46] Others, with less wisdom than enthusiasm, went even further. James Grant, an advocate from Corrymony, delivered his opinion that the ancient Britons were actually Gaels (i.e., ancestors of the Highlanders) and were themselves descended from the Gauls, in *Thoughts on the Origin and Descent of the Gael* (1814).[47] He continued his ethnic genealogy with the astute observation that the name Pict had replaced "Caledonian." Sir William Betham, the Ulster King of Arms, went beyond the speculations of his fellow enthusiasts by mixing ethnography with literature and declaring that King Arthur was a Pict.[48]

[45] John Pinkerton, *An Enquiry into the History of Scotland preceding the Reign of Malcolm III or the year 1056, Including the Authentic History of that Period*, 2 vols. (London, 1789).

[46] John Lanne Buchanan, *A Defence of the Scots Highlanders, in General; and Some Learned Characters in Particular: with a new and satisfactory account of the Picts, Scots, Fingal, Ossian, and His Poems: As also, of the Macs, Clans, and Bodotria. And several other Particulars respecting the High Antiquities of Scotland* (London, 1794).

[47] James Grant, *Thoughts on the Origin and Descent of the Gael: With an Account of the Picts, Caledonians, and Scots; and Observations Relative to the Authenticity of the Poems of Ossian* (Edinburgh, 1814).

[48] Sir William Betham, *The Gael and Cymbri; or an Inquiry into the Origin and History of the Irish Scoti, Britons, and Gauls, and of the Caledonians, Picts, Welsh, Cornish, and Bretons* (Dublin, 1834).

All those earlier speculations on the Picts were swept aside by the work of the towering figure of nineteenth-century Scottish historiography William Forbes Skene. He was a practicing attorney whose historical research was reserved for his leisure hours. Even though they have been supplanted by more modern works, Skene's *Chronicle of the Picts, Chronicles of the Scots, and Other Memorials of Early Scottish History* and his three volumes *Celtic Scotland* became the standard interpretations of medieval Scots history for decades and they can still be selectively read with profit today.[49] Skene assembled the relevant materials necessary for a study of the early period in his *Chronicles*, following in the tradition of Innes and Pinkerton. Unlike them, however, he benefited from two fortunate developments. The first was an interest in the history of Scotland sparked by Walter Scott's historical novels. History clubs, patronized by the great and the good (i.e., lairds and ministers) published local records such as chartularies, histories, and memoirs. The editing might be unsatisfactory by today's standards, but the service to scholarship was immense if for no other reason than it brought forth otherwise little known or unknown texts. For the first time the riches of family archives, church records, or local depositories were presented to the public. The second opportune movement was scholarly interest in Irish language materials. The labors of Irish scholars such as the brothers-in-law Eugene O'Curry and John O'Donovan in the transcription, translation, and commentary on medieval Irish texts with references to northern Britain opened a new dimension to Pictish studies. This extended beyond the Irish annals, with their mixture of early entries in Irish and Latin, to include verse, genealogies, and hagiography.

Skene's work in source collection was continued in the twentieth century by the husband-and-wife team of Alan Orr Anderson and Majorie Ogilvie Anderson. The former compiled two major collections of source materials, his (1922) *Scottish Annals from English Chroniclers* (1908) and the two-volume *Early Sources of Scottish History* (ESSH).[50] While the earlier compendium is limited to English writers, the latter includes Continental, Irish, Scandinavian, Scottish, and Welsh materials complemented with copious notes on chronology, place names, and alternative

---

[49] William Forbes Skene, *Chronicles of the Picts, Chronicles of the Scots, and Other Early Memorials of Scottish History* (Edinburgh, 1867); and *Celtic Scotland: An History of Ancient Alba*, 3 vols. (Edinburgh, 1876–80).

[50] Alan Orr Anderson, *Scottish Annals from English Chroniclers* AD 500 to 1286 (London, 1908), and ESSH.

materials. Mrs. Anderson collected and collated the king-list materials in her *Kings and Kingship in Early Scotland* (KES) and divided the lists into two groups, one compiled in the middle twelfth century (the Y group) and the other compiled early in the thirteenth century (the X group). Historical revisionism is evident in Archibald Scott's *Pictish Nation: Its People and Its Church* (1918) that was written during the First World War and after the Irish Easter Rebellion of 1916. Scott makes no secret of his thesis that: "much of the credit for the conversion of the Picts belongs to Ninian." W.C. Dickenson's *History of Scotland* corrected some of Skene's speculations, but the work was too brief (the first volume covered earliest times to 1603) to do more than make general observations. Not a history text as such, the *Problem of the Picts*, edited by F.W. Wainwright, was devoted to the Picts. The editor's introductory essay is a useful statement of what was known in the mid-twentieth century. A decade later appeared Isabel Henderson's *The Picts*. The volume approached the topic from the aspect of the physical remains. After this we enter the "historical present" with a new generation of scholars.

While historians grappled with the written sources, physical remains were also receiving attention. Antiquarians and visitors to Scotland remarked on the monuments they encountered. One of these was Alexander Gordon (?1692 –?1755) who conducted a survey of sorts in his *Itinerarium Septentrionale*.[51] Slightly later the Welsh antiquary Thomas Pennant (1726–98) made drawings of ancient monuments during his tour of Scotland, such as the symbol stones at Meigle, which were published in his *A Tour in Scotland and Voyage to the Hebrides*.[52] At almost the end of the eighteenth century there appeared the survey known as *The First (Old) Statistical Account of Scotland* with regular mention of the symbol stones although without any images.[53] A series of questions was sent to the ministers of the established Church of Scotland in order to gauge the state of the country and provide an indication of well-being in the kingdom. One of the sections was about geography and

---

[51] Alexander Gordon, *Itinerarium Septentrionale; or, a Journey thro' most of the Counties of Scotland, and those in the North of England. . . . Part 1. Containing an Account of all the Monuments of Roman Antiquity. . . . Part 2. An Account of the Danish Invasions on Scotland . . . With sixty-six copperplates* (London, 1726).
[52] Thomas Pennant, *A Tour in Scotland and Voyage to the Hebrides MDCCLXXII*, 2 vols. (London, 1776).
[53] John Sinclair of Ulbster (ed.), *Statistical Account of Scotland*, 21 vols. (Edinburgh, 1791–99).

topography, which included the antiquities of the land. Not surprisingly the quality of the replies varied, but many include the symbol stones and visible remains of buildings and fortifications, although an attribution to the Picts was often more a guess than the result of any study. Not until Patrick Chalmers' *Ancient Sculptured Monuments of the County of Angus* in the mid-nineteenth century was there a scholarly study of the symbol stones complete with illustrations.[54] Eight years later appeared the first catalogue of rock carvings found throughout Scotland with John Stuart's *Sculptured Stones of Scotland*.[55] He brought out the second volume because so many additional stones had been found or brought to his attention, and Stuart expanded his enquiry by a comparison with similar items from elsewhere in the British Isles. Publication of the symbols stones led to as much interest in the ornamentation and scrollwork found on them as in the figures or symbols. Gilbert French argued in the mid-nineteenth century that the ornamentation was a derivative of ancient British basketwork and even suggested Druidic sacrifice was represented on some stones.[56] Almost two decades later another pioneer in the study of these stones published a paper on certain themes found on Scottish and Irish stones and evidence of continued paganism in Christian art.[57] Joseph Anderson, the author of the paper, expanded on his views in his Rhind Lectures of 1879 and 1880, which were later published as *Scotland in Early Christian Times*.[58] He is as well, or even better, known for his collaboration with J. Romilly Allen on the monumental *Early Christian Monuments of Scotland*, published by the Society of Antiquaries of Scotland in 1903. Anderson, as Keeper of the National

[54] Patrick Chalmers, *Ancient Sculptured Monuments of the County of Angus Including those at Meigle in Perthshire and One at Fordoun in the Mearns*, Bannatyne Club no. 88 (Edinburgh, 1848).

[55] John Stuart, *Sculptured Stones of Scotland*, 2 vols., Spalding Club (Aberdeen, 1856; Edinburgh, 1867).

[56] Gilbert French, *An Attempt to explain the Origin and Meaning of the Early Interlaced Ornamentation Found on the Ancient Sculptured Stones of Scotland, Ireland, and the Isle of Man* (Manchester, 1858): 15.

[57] Joseph Anderson, "Notes on the Survival of Pagan Customs in Christian Burial: With Notices of Certain Conventional Representations of 'Daniel in the Den of Lions', and 'Jonah and Whale', Engraved on Objects Found in Early Christian Graves, and on the Sculptured Stones of Scotland, and Crosses of Ireland," PSAS 11 (1866): 363–427.

[58] Joseph Anderson, *Scotland in Early Christian Times*, the Rhind Lectures for 1879 and 1880, 2 vols. (Edinburgh, 1881).

Museum of Scotland, is not surprising as author, but Allen was a civil engineer who was in charge of the construction of the Leith docks. The first volume is a catalogue of designs and figures, with a special interest in scroll- and knot-work, while the second volume is a descriptive list of the stones. While the scope of the work was comprehensive, the distribution was not and only 500 copies were made of it.[59] Up to the mid-twentieth century, the publication and scholarly study of the monumental stones and other artifacts led to some new, and some old, directions in the studies of the Picts. Dissenting views began to appear, especially as the study of art had shown affinities with remains found elsewhere in the British Isles, particularly with Ireland.

By the end of the nineteenth century there had appeared a new question about the Picts: was their language a member of the so-called Celtic group or was it completely different? The ferocity of the debate was in inverse proportion to the evidence, as only the occasional word can be identified as "Pictish." While Sir John Rhŷs, the first professor of Celtic at the University of Oxford, argued that the language of the Picts was not only not Celtic, but also non-Indo-European (non-Ayrian, using the terminology of the day), T.D. MacDonald's *Celtic Dialects* (1903) argues that the language was Celtic. He was supported after a fashion, a year later, by E.W.B. Nicolson's *Keltic Researches* (1904) which argued the Picts spoke a dialect of Goidelic, (i.e., primitive Gaelic).

Summary

Perhaps not surprisingly, interest in the Picts changed and evolved over the centuries; from their place as characters in historical and pseudo-historical materials to a cliché in histories that were interested more in their rivals the Scots. The initial interest in the Picts came from those attempting to make sense of the ethnography of Britain's inhabitants. Since the Picts were not mentioned by the earliest Roman authorities – Julius Caesar and Tacitus – then, so the reasoning went, they must have been immigrants such as the Scots or even the Romans. The search for their supposed origins led to the creation of a fabulous and eventually convoluted legend. From the stark announcement in *Senchus Már* to the complex story of *What brought the Picts to Marvellous Britain* the evolution of the tale is evident. The ferocity of the Picts impressed not only

[59] Happily the two volumes have been reissued as ECMS.

the Romans, and the Irish considered them to be fierce warriors as is clear from their description in *The Destruction of Dá Derga's Hostel*.

After the ninth-century triumph of the Scots, the Picts began to take a position among the many legendary peoples of Britain. For Geoffrey of Monmouth they were the savages of the island, little more than animals with human-like characteristics. They are vicious and deceitful, with little sense of propriety much less nobility. The shadow cast by Geoffrey was long and later historians all had to engage with his work. His contemporaries could claim that the *History of the Kings of Britain* was a fantasy, but a substantial proportion of the literate population was prepared to accept his narrative as factual. This made a difficulty for the Scots of the later Middle Ages who wanted to write a history of their kingdom. They could not ignore the Picts, but they could not praise them either or it would make the triumph of the Scots difficult to defend if presented as aggression. With the church attempting to limit warfare through diplomacy and concepts such as, in the early Middle Ages, The Law of Innocents, attributed to Adomnan of Iona or, by the later Middle Ages, the Peace of God movement, precisely how history was presented became all important. Furthermore, later historians had a bewildering variety of materials to use, many of which remain controversial. Precisely what and how many records survived remains controversial even though it is clear that written and oral materials were available from among the Irish, Scandinavians, and English, and there might have been survivals from the Picts.

Conclusion

Students of early medieval history face many different challenges, and almost all of them are present when discussing northern Britain. Dangerous as this area was – and the Romans devoted precious resources to building two walls in an attempt to exert some control – for much of the time covered in this volume we know little about this region. The obscurity is due in part to (the usual complaint of the historian) too few contemporary documents and too much scope for differing interpretations. Added to this have been efforts by earlier writers, beginning in the early Middle Ages, to make sense of events and leaving behind them what might be helpful information or secondhand speculation. Even the meager bits of information found in the extant sources usually provoke more questions than they answer. This extends beyond the customary written records to the art. Is the eagle found on the symbol stones an example of the local wildlife or is it a Christian symbol for the evangelist or is it a reference to lineage? Having given the traditional warning – that almost everything we think we know about the period is open to different interpretations – the fascination of the time and place are obvious.

The name Pict is a generic term coined by the Romans in the late third century after re-establishing control in Britain; it was a collective designation for anyone living north of Hadrian's Wall. The wall was the northernmost frontier of the Empire and, so far as the Romans were concerned, beyond it was mere barbarism. Hadrian's Wall was used by the Romans as more than an instrument of policy; it divided a Britain that was directly connected with the Mediterranean world from a Britain that remained connected with an earlier northern European world. The meaning of Latin *pictus* (whence "Pict") is "picture" and it refers to

The Picts, First Edition. Benjamin Hudson.
© 2014 John Wiley & Sons, Ltd. Published 2014 by John Wiley & Sons, Ltd.

the body decoration practiced by the northern Britons. Whether this was painting, as Julius Caesar mentioned for the Britons in the south in the last century BC, or actual tattooing (i.e., piercing of the epidermis) is not clear. The practice had disappeared in the British lands under imperial administration due to Roman horror of bodily disfigurement, which they used as a punishment. Herodian mentions the elaborate skin pictures on the ambassadors from beyond Hadrian's Wall who met the emperor Severus early in the third century. When the new men who dominated the imperial officer corps afterwards were searching for a descriptive name for the people in northern Britain, "picture people" was used. The Picture People did not call themselves that, nor did their neighbors. They were the "Britons," which is why a substitute for Pict in Irish is *Cruithne* and in Welsh is *Prydyn* or *Prydein* (both Irish and Welsh words translating as "Briton"). Despite the introduction of a convenient term, older names such as Caledonian and Meaetae continued to circulate for centuries after the appearance of the collective name; Caledonian into the fifth century, while Meaetae is found in the seventh-century *vita* of Columba. The language spoken by the Picts was a Brythonic dialect similar to the ancestor of modern Welsh or Cornish. Name elements such as *cair* (fort) or *carden* (thicket) are found throughout northern Britain. One problem is that these names survive in modern place names or in medieval records set down centuries after the Picts had come under the rule of the Scots. Many of the names have disappeared either through disuse or because they were supplanted by Gaelic names brought in by immigrants/invaders.

Modern scholars can be excused much because they merely follow earlier writers who were thought to know what they were describing. With the realization that the Romans intended the name Pict to refer to everyone north of Hadrian's Wall, we can dispense with many of the artificial divisions that have unnecessarily limited study. This means that the history of the kingdoms between the two Roman constructions of the Hadrian and Antonine Walls – Gododdin, Strathclyde, and the shadowy realm of Rheged – are as much part of the story of the Picts as are the people living to their north. These were the famous Men of the North of Welsh legend. But even if one wants to divide Britain at the Antonine Wall (by the third century no more than a large ditch and bank that might have been used as an occasional campsite), then both Gododdin and Strathclyde must still be included among the Picts. The picture has been made unnecessarily difficult by Bede who makes a contradictory statement when he claims that the river/firth of Clyde was the boundary between the Picts to the north and the Britons of Strathclyde to the south, apparently unaware that the capital of Strathclyde at Dumbarton was on the north bank of the Clyde. This means that one of the myths about the Picts – that there are no literary remains from them – must be set aside, There were, and these included the verses attributed to Taliesin and Anierin, and the long eulogy known as *Y Gododdin*. These verses show a society of aristocrats who used visible signs of wealth, such as horses, to mark their status. This aristocratically dominated kingdom had as its cultural center the hall (Latin *aula*) with its mixture of fine dining, professional entertainment, and public recognition. Pictorial representations of this class are carved onto the Pictish symbol stones with mounted warriors on the stone in the churchyard at Aberlemno, or the lady whose groom is leading her horse. The poems from the southern Picts also reveal that the Roman authorities were justified in their concern about the ability of the Picts to form temporary confederations. Following the information in *Gododdin*, the combined force that descended on the Angles at Catterick came from northern Wales, southern Scotland and possibly even farther afield.

Modern problems sometimes have older parallels and the collective name Pict became an historical problem for later commentators. Unaware of the nature of the name, it was assumed by writers beginning with Gildas that it meant a particular people. Thus began several centuries of learned speculation, with Bede repeating an Irish legend of maritime Picts from the south while a century later Nennius brought his Picts in from the north. Irish writers with their predilection for the fantastic produced ever more elaborate accounts of the Picts culminating in the eleventh-century poem *How Came the Picts to Marvellous Britain* which might have been commissioned by the famous Macbeth. The broad application of the name Pict for anyone beyond Hadrian's Wall should not lull us into the familiar error of "one Pict fits all" or to suppose that there was a homogenous culture from the river Tyne as far north as the Shetland Islands. There were variations in architecture, diet, and material culture dictated by available resources and circumstances. This is especially true for architecture, which had to adapt to the nature of local building supplies. The result is an imbalance in the archaeological record, with more traces of building in regions where stone was used and fewer in afforested areas which could provide timber. There is an additional problem of population movement. During the historical period there were at least three major settlements by peoples different in language and culture from the Picts. One group of immigrants came from Ireland, from the region of what is now County Antrim, and they established the kingdom of Dál Riata in what are now Argyllshire and the Hebrides. The second group came from Scandinavia and were in the Shetland and Orkney Islands by at least the end of the eighth century, when the Irish geographer Dicuíl included them in his *Book about the Measure of the Lands of the World*. The third group were the Anglo-Saxons, whose expansions and retreats are chronicled in part by the Venerable Bede. He is the primary source of information about the Picts for most writers, both medieval and modern.

The outline of political society which is visible in the 200 years from the beginning of the seventh to the end of the eighth century, shows that (like their neighbors) the peoples north of Hadrian's Wall were divided into separate kingdoms which occasionally cooperated and more often fought one with another. A powerful kingdom was Strathclyde, which dominated its neighbors and inserted its own dynasts into the kingdom of Fortriu. The only way that Strathclyde could be defeated in the mid-eighth century was by an alliance of the Anglo-Saxons with the Picts. When the Strathclyde dynast Brude son of Bile (then king of Fortriu) defeated the Northumbrians within the kingdom of Circenn, he might have been defending one of his satellites. A generation later a king from Circenn held the north in his hands and, in a nice reversal of fortunes, forced terms on Strathclyde. Pressures – population and military – on the Picts were constant from the fifth century until the final supremacy of the Scots under the leadership of the famous Kenneth son of Alpin. The circumstances need not always have been violent. The establishment of an Irish colony in Mag Circenn, which produced the famous Angus son of Fergus, and even the Dál Riata colony, could have been under the supervision of the Picts themselves either to reward their allies or to imitate the Romans in the tactic of "use a barbarian to fight a barbarian." The movement of Scandinavians by at least the eighth century added another element. One of the many questions about this period is what were the limits of their settlement and at what times were these occurring? The question is pertinent because the admittedly much later sources claim that there were battles between the Picts and Scandinavians on the east coast. Added to this are the interesting parallels between some of the art on the symbol stones and stones found as far east as in Götland. There is also the interpretation of the ogam inscriptions as pidgin Norse, which deserves further investigation.

Pictish society had many elements in common with other peoples throughout Europe. The population depended on agriculture as its main source of revenue. Seafood appears not to have been as significant as it later became; it was for immediate consumption and there is little evidence of the processing that would lead to the important trade in fish of the later Middle Ages. The domination of agriculture leads to the question of *pit* which is often touted as an authentically Pictish word. Unfortunately there is nothing to link it specifically with the Picts and where it is used in a compound name, the other element is usually Gaelic. Other possibilities have been overlooked such as that the name might be Old Norse *beit* (land), which would come into Middle Irish as *pit* following the analogy of Old Norse *buanar* (beans) into Middle Irish *ponar*. Or *pit* might be a form of Welsh *peth* (part). Leaving the outer for the inner man, the conversion of the Picts to Christianity was momentous. First, their new faith forbade bodily scarring (Leviticus 19:28) which explains why there is no mention of tattooing in connection with Gododdin or Strathclyde; they were Christian by the time the verses concerning them were written. The conversion of the peoples between the Antonine and Hadrian Walls was carried out by Ninian, the famous saint of Whithorn. Far more is known about the missions from the church on the island of Iona, established by Columba (Irish *Colum Cille*, or "dove of the church"). Using the hagiography written by his successor in the headship Adomnán, the picture is made of the saint and members of his community moving constantly among the Picts of the north to proselytize. Adomnán's *vita* gives glimpses of the life among the pre-Christian Picts with their sacred wells, fierce water monsters, and rival priests. Christian theology among the Picts must be extrapolated through conjectures made on the basis of their magnificent stone crosses with elaborate decorations. Later materials such as the *Breviary of Aberdeen* give notice of men who might have labored among the Picts as missionaries, but early materials have little to say about individuals beyond Ninian and Columba. Christianity among the Picts was as changeable as elsewhere and occasionally followed politics. When Nechtan of Atholl made his alliance with the Northumbrians, he expelled the community of Iona from his kingdom, to replace the *Scoti* with the Anglo-Saxons as his new allies.

When turning to political affairs among the Picts, we rely on the occasional notices in the written records. The most fulsome collections come from the peoples who were competing with the Picts, such as the Irish records in the *Annals of Ulster* and the so-called *Annals of Tigernach*. The Irish materials are supplemented from the south by isolated notices which are preserved in Anglo-Saxon materials such as the *Anglo-Saxon*

Chronicle or in the twelfth-century chronicle attributed to Symeon of Durham, but most prominent is the information supplied by the Venerable Bede, both in his *Ecclesiastical History* and his other writings such as the *Life of St. Cuthbert*. When the Scots needed to enlist Pictish history for their own uses in the eleventh century, they used earlier works to compile catalogues such as the so-called Pictish king-lists, which can be used by the modern historian, but with care. Just prior to the era of written records there was a significant Irish settlement made in northern Britain, which later records tried to explain in terms of the dynasty that would later provide the kings of Scots. This movement was occurring along the western coast of Britain. However the Irish came to be among the Picts, by the sixth century they were raiding Pictish territory during the reign of the Dál Riata king Áedan son of Gabran. This obscure period is popularly known as the Heroic Age with competition between native and newcomer. From the south came the rising power of the Angles and the destruction of the men of Gododdin in the general defeat of the men of Britain at the battle of Catterick, about 600, which was the beginning of the end for them. By 641 their fortress at Edinburgh had been destroyed. Slightly later the kingdom of Rheged, along the Solway Firth, was destroyed and by a century later the Angles had pushed on as far as the Plain of Kyle, the area round modern Ayr. The conquest of Rheged brought into Anglian control the famous church of St. Ninian at Whithorn. The expansionary ambitions of the Irish and Angles clashed at the battle of Degsastan, whose location is unknown, but possibly somewhere in Dumfriesshire. The success of the Angles cleared the way for their westward push. Their limitations were also revealed, and their northernmost expansion was to be the limit of their colonization.

North of the Clyde–Forth line the political situation is no more obvious by the late seventh century as the generic term King of Picts occasionally is supplanted by more specific designations. Also clear is that the political situation changed often, and quickly. Around 685 the victor of the Battle of Dun Nechtan is styled King of Fortriu, one of the provincial kingdoms; later this would be followed by the appearance of the name Atholl. Visible by the beginning of the eighth century is competition for power among the princes of three kingdoms: Fortriu, Atholl, and Circenn. The victor was the great Angus son of Fergus for whom the Irish annals use the word *crudelissima* (most cruel). A contemporary note in the eighth-century Irish genealogies claim him as Irish, a circumstance that is expanded in the twelfth-century synthetic history known as the *Book of Invasions of Ireland* (*Lebor Gabála Érenn*). While Angus was not able to conquer Dál Riata, his raids were becoming so frequent by 740 that the account in the *Annals of Ulster* uses the term *percussio* (hammering). Still he was the power in the north, and when the Northumbrian king Eadberht invaded Strathclyde in 756, the addition of Angus' troops led to victory.

So one of the many questions is whether or not the description "first of the Scots to rule among the Picts" should be awarded to Angus son of Fergus. The death of Angus was followed by a resurgence in the power of Dál Riata. By the last decade of the eighth century a descendant of Áedan son of Gabran named Constantine son of Fergus had conquered the kingdom of Fortriu and established there a branch of the Irish. He continued the kingdom's policy of alliance with Northumbria and was remembered, together with his successors, respectively his brother and nephew, Angus and Eóganán, in the *Liber Vitae* of the community of St. Cuthbert, then still at Lindisfarne. By the time his kinsman Kenneth son of Alpin began to move eastwards about 842, the Irish presence among the Picts was of long duration. Undoubtedly there were hostilities, but no major battles or huge shifts, because the process had already begun. What marked a difference between the dynasties of Constantine and Kenneth was the latter's insistence on cultural change. When Kenneth's brother Domnall ordered the observance of Irish law, and his grandson Constantine ordered the churches to follow Irish practice, they were merely concluding a process that had been going on for some time. Curiously there is no obvious alliance between these kings and any particular church. The only time a king legislates in connection with a member of the clergy is when Constantine son of Áed makes his proclamation concerning ecclesiastical governance in connection with Bishop Cellach of St. Andrews.

The amalgamation of the Pictish kingdoms south of the Grampians by the dynasty of Kenneth I was not the end of their memory. Stories and literature concerning them continued to flourish. By the eleventh century, the Scottish supremacy was almost two centuries old. Materials about the Picts got a new lease on life. While Henry of Huntingdon could claim that the Picts were the vanishing folk of Britain, his contemporary Geoffrey of Monmouth used the Picts as his wild-men in the *History of the Kings of Britain*. Their savagery contrasted with the restrained behavior of their opponents, especially when Arthur led a retaliatory invasion of their lands. The literary elaborations continued throughout the centuries; the Picts became vanishing pygmies in medieval Norwegian literature and the blue-skinned freedom fighters of the modern era.

Select Bibliography

Ab Ithel, J., ed., *Annales Cambriae* (London 1860).
Adomnán, *Life of Columba*, ed. A.O. Anderson and M.O. Anderson (Oxford 1991).
___ *The Life of Columba, Founder of Hy, Written by Adamnan*, ed. William Reeves (Dublin 1857).
Aethicus Ister, *The Cosmography of Aethicus Ister*, ed. Michael Herren (Turnhold 2011).
Alcock L., and E.A. Alcock, "Reconnaissance Excavations on Early Historic Fortifications and Other Royal Sites in Scotland 1974–84, 4: Excavations at Alt Clut, Clyde Rock, Strathclyde, 1974–75," PSAS 120 (1990): 95–150.
Alcock, L., E.A. Alcock, and S. Driscoll, "Reconnaissance Excavations on Early Historic Fortifications and Other Royal Sites in Scotland 1974–84, 3: Excavations at Dundurn, St. Fillians, Perthshire," PSAS 119 (1989): 189–220.
Allen, J. Romilly, *Celtic Art in Pagan and Christian Times* (London 1904).
Allen, J. Romilly, and Joseph Anderson, *The Early Christian Monuments of Scotland*, intro. Isabel Henderson, 2 vols. (Balgavies 1993).
Ammianus Marcellus, *Rerum Gestarum Libri*, ed. John C. Rolfe, 3 vols. (Cambridge, MA, 1935–39).
Anderson, Alan Orr, *Early Sources of Scottish History* AD 500 to 1286, 2 vols. (Edinburgh 1922), re-edited with corrections by Marjorie O. Anderson (Stamford 1990).
___ *Scottish Annals from English Chroniclers* AD 500 to 1286 (London 1908).
Anderson, Joseph, "Notes on the Survival of Pagan Customs in Christian Burial: With Notices of Certain Conventional Representations of 'Daniel in the Den of Lions', and 'Jonah and Whale,' Engraved on Objects Found in Early Christian Graves, and on the Sculptured Stones of Scotland, and Crosses of Ireland," PSAS 11 (1876): 363–427.

The Picts, First Edition. Benjamin Hudson.
© 2014 John Wiley & Sons, Ltd. Published 2014 by John Wiley & Sons, Ltd.

___ *Scotland in Early Christian Times*, Rhind Lectures for 1879 and 1880, 2 vols. (Edinburgh 1881).
Anderson, Marjorie O., "The Celtic Church in Kinrimund," in David Roberts, ed., *The Medieval Church of St Andrews* (Glasgow 1976), pp. 1–10.
___ *Kings and Kingship in Early Scotland* (Edinburgh 1973).
___ "St. Andrews before Alexander I," in G.W.S. Barrow, ed., *The Scottish Tradition, Essays in Honour of Ronald Gordon Cant* (Edinburgh 1974), pp. 1–13.
Andrew of Wyntoun, *The Original Chronicle of Andrew of Wyntoun*, ed. F.J. Amours, 6 vols., Scottish Texts Society, Old Series 50, 53, 54, 56, 57, and 63 (Edinburgh 1903–14).
___ *The Orygynale Cronykil of Scotland by Androw of Wyntoun*, ed. David Laing, 3 vols., Historians of Scotland vols. 2, 3, and 9 (Edinburgh 1872–79).
Ari Þorgilsson, *Íslendingabók*, ed. Anne Holtsmark, *Nordisk Filologi*, series A, vol. 5 (Oslo 1967).
Ausonius, *Decimi Magni Ausonii Opera*, ed. R.P.H. Green (Oxford 1999).
Backlund, Jesse, "War or Peace? The Relations between the Picts and the Norse in the Orkneys," *Northern Studies* 36 (2001): 33–47.
Bannerman, John, "The Scottish Takeover of Pictland and the Relics of Columba," *Innes Review* 48 (1997): 27–44.
___ *Studies in the History of Dalriada* (Edinburgh 1974).
Barrett, J.H., A.M. Locker, and C.M. Roberts, "'Dark Age Economics' Revisited: The English Fish Bone Evidence 600–1600," *Antiquity* 78 (2004): 618–636.
Barrow, G.W.S., "The Childhood of Scottish Christianity: A Note on Some Place-Name Evidence," *Scottish Studies* 27 (1983): 1–15.
___ ed., *Regesta Regum Scottorum*, vol. I (Edinburgh 1960).
Bartrum, P.C., *Early Welsh Genealogical Tracts* (Cardiff 1966).
Bede, *Historia Ecclesiastica*, in *Venerabilis Baedae Opera Historica*, ed. Charles Plummer, 2 vols. (Oxford 1896).
Bergin, Osborn, R. I. Best, Kuno Meyer, and J. G. O'Keeffe, eds., *Anecdota from Irish Manuscript*, 4 vols. (Halle 1907–12).
Bermann, Werner, "Dicuils *De mensura orbis terrae*," in Paul Leo Butzer and Dietrich Lohrmann, eds., *Science in Western and Eastern Civilization in Carolingian Times* (Basel 1993), pp. 525–537.
Best, R.I., and Osborn Bergin, eds., *Lebor Na Huidre, Book of the Dun Cow* (Dublin 1929).
Best, R.I. Osborn Bergin, M.A. O'Brien, and Anne O'Sullivan, eds., *Book of Leinster, formerly Lebar na Núachongbála*, 6 vols. (Dublin 1954–83).
Betham, William, *The Gael and Cymbri; Or an Inquiry into the Origin and History of the Irish Scoti, Britons, and Gauls, and of the Caledonians, Picts, Welsh, Cornish, and Bretons* (Dublin 1834).
Bieler, Ludwig, *The Patrician Texts in the Book of Armagh* (Dublin 1979).

Binchy, D.A., *Corpus iuris hibernici: ad fidem codicum manuscriptorum*, 6 vols. (Dublin 1978).
___ "Patrick and his Biographers, Ancient and Modern," *Studia Hibernica* 2 (1962): 7–173.
___ "Pseudo-historical Prologue to the *Senchas Már*," *Studia Celtica* 10–11 (1975–76): 15–28.
___ ed., *Scéla Cano meic Gartnáin* (Dublin 1975; first pub. 1963).
Blathmac, *Versus Strabi de Beati Blaithmaic Vita et Fine*, in MGH, *Poetae Latini Aevi Carolini*, ii, 297–301.
Bollandus, J. et al. *Acta sanctorum* ... (Brussels 1642–).
Bonner, Gerald, "The Pelagian Controversy in Britain and Ireland," *Peritia* 16 (2002): 144–155.
Borsje, Jacqueline, "The Monster in the River Ness in *Vita Sancti Columbae*: A Study of a Miracle," *Peritia* 8 (1994): 27–34.
Bourke, Cormac, "The Hand-Bells of the Early Scottish Church," *Proceedings of the Society of Antiquaries of Scotland* 113 (1983): 464–468.
Bowen, E.G., *Britain and the Western Seaways* (London 1972).
___ "Cult of St. Brigit," *Studia Celtica* 8/9 (1973/74): 33–47.
Boyle, A., "The Edinburgh Synchronisms of Irish Kings," *Celtica* 9 (1971): 169–179.
___ "Notes on Scottish Saints," *Innes Review* 32 (1981): 59–82.
Boynton, Susan, "Prayer as Liturgical Performance in Eleventh- and Twelfth-Century Monastic Psalters," *Speculum* 82 (2007): 896–931.
Breeze, Andrew, "St. Cuthbert, Bede, and the Niduari of Pictland," *Northern History* 40 (2003): 365–368.
___ "Pictish Chains and Welsh Forgeries," *PSAS* 121 (1998): 481–484.
British Geological Survey, *Minerals in Britain: Gold* (London 1999).
Broun, D., "The Origin of Scottish Identity in its European Context," in B. Crawford, ed., *Scotland in Dark Age Europe* (St. Andrews 1994), pp. 21–31.
Brown, Peter, *The World of Late Antiquity* (London 1971).
Buchanan, John Lanne, *A Defence of the Scots Highlanders, in General; And Some Learned Characters in Particular: With a new and satisfactory account of the Picts, Scots, Fingal, Ossian, and histor Poems: As also, of the Macs, Clans, and Bodotria. And several other Particulars respecting the High Antiquities of Scotland* (London 1794).
Bugge, Alexander, *Vesterlandenes Inflydelse paa Nordboernes og saerlig Normandenes ydre Kultur, Lovesaet og Samfundsforhold i Vikingetiden*, Videnskabs-Selskabets Skrifter 2, Historisk-Filosofisk Klass, 1904, 1 (Christiana 1905).
Burl, Aubrey, *A Guide to the Stone Circles of Britain, Ireland and Brittany* (New Haven, CT, 2005).
Calise, J.M.P., "Genealogies and History: A Reassessment of Cenél nGabráin," in B. Hudson, ed., *Familia and Household in the Medieval Atlantic World* (Tempe, AR, 2011), pp. 19–50.
___ *Pictish Sourcebook. Documents of Medieval Legend and Dark-Age History* (Westport 2002).

Campbell, Ewan, "The Archaeological Evidence for Contacts: Imports, Trade and Economy in Celtic Britain AD 400–800' in K.R. Dark, ed., *External Contacts and the Economy of Late Roman and Post-Roman Britain* (Woodbridge 1996), pp. 83–96.
___ "Trade in the Dark-Age West," in Barbara Crawford, ed., *Scotland in Dark Age Britain* (St. Andrews 1996), pp. 79–91.
Campbell, James, *The Anglo-Saxons* (London 1991).
___ "Bede's Words for Places," *Essays in Anglo-Saxon History* (London 1986), pp. 99–120.
Carver, Martin, *Portmahomack, Monastery of the Picts* (Edinburgh 2008).
Cessford, Craig, "The multiple crescent and V-rod – an Anomalous Symbol Grouping," *Pictish Arts Society Journal* 11 (1997): 31–32.
Chadwick, H.M., *Early Scotland* (Cambridge 1949).
Chadwick, Norah, *Celtic Britain* (Newcastle, CA, repr. 1989).
Chalmers, Patrick, *Ancient Sculptured Monuments of the County of Angus Including Those at Meigle in Perthshire and One at Fordoun in the Mearns*, Bannatyne Club 88 (Edinburgh 1848).
Charles-Edwards, T.M.O., *Early Irish and Welsh Kinship* (Oxford 1993).
___ "The Ui Neill 695–743: the Rise and Fall of Dynasties," *Peritia* 16 (2002): 396–418.
Clanchy, T.O., "Philosopher-King: Nechtan mac Der-Ilei," *Scottish Historical Review* 83 (2004): 135–149.
___ "The Real St. Ninian," *Innes Review* 52 (2001): 1–26.
___ "Saints' Cults and National Identities in the Early Middle Ages," in Alan Thacker and Richard Sharpe, eds., *Local Saints and Local Churches in the Early Medieval West* (Oxford 2002), pp. 397–421.
Clancy, Thomas Owen., and Gilbert Márkus, *Iona, the Earliest Poetry of a Celtic Monastery* (Edinburgh 1995).
Clarke, David, Alice Blackwell, and Martin Goldberg, *Early Medieval Scotland: Individuals, Communities and Ideas* (Edinburgh 2012).
Claudian, *Clavdii Clavdiani Carmina*, ed. John Barrie Hall (Leipzig 1985).
Close-Brooks, Joanna, "Excavations at Clatchard Craig, Fife," *PSAS* 116 (1986): 117–184.
Colgrave, Bertram, *Two Lives of Saint Cuthbert* (Cambridge 1940).
Constance of Lyon, *Vie de Saint Germain d'Auxerre* ed. René Borius, Sources Chrétiennes 112 (Paris 1965).
Constantinus of Lyon, "Life of Germanus of Auxerre," trans. F.R. Hoare, in T.F.X. Noble and T. Head, eds., *Soldiers of Christ* (University Park, PA, 1994): 75–106.
Cowan, Edward, "Myth and Identity in Early Medieval Scotland," *Scottish Historical Review* 63 (1984): 111–135.
___ "The Scottish Chronicle in the Poppleton Manuscript," *Innes Review* 32 (1981): 3–21.
Cox, Richard, *The Language of the Ogam Inscriptions of Scotland* (Aberdeen 1999).

___ "Modern Scottish Gaelic Reflexes of two Pictish words; *pett and *lannerc," *Nomina* (1998): 47–58.
Cramp, Rosemary, gen. ed., *Corpus of Anglo-Saxon Stone Sculpture in England* (Oxford 1984–).
Crudden, S.E., "Excavations at Birsay, Orkney," in A. Small, ed., *The Fourth Viking Conference* (Edinburgh 1965), pp. 22–31.
Cummins, W.A., *The Picts and their Symbols* (Stroud 1999).
Cunliffe, Sir Barry, *The Ancient Celts* (London 1997).
Dalché, Patrick Gautier, *Géographie et culture: La représentation de l'espace du VIe au XIIe siècle* (Aldershot, 1997).
Dickinson, William Croft, *Scotland from the Earliest Times to 1603* (London 1961).
Dicuil, *Dicuili Liber de Mensura Orbis Terrae*, ed. J.J. Tierney, *Scriptores Latini Hiberniae*, vol. 5 (Dublin 1967).
Dio, *Roman Histories*, ed. Earnest Cary (New York 1927).
Dobbs, Margaret E., "History of the Descendants of Ir (part 1)," *Zeitschrift für celtische philologie* 13 (1921): 308–359.
___ "History of the Descendants of Ir (part 2)," *Zeitschrift für celtische philologie* 14 (1923): 43–144.
Doble, G.H., *Lives of the Welsh Saints*, ed. D. Simon Evans (Cardiff 1971).
Donaldsson, Gordon, "Scottish Bishops' Sees before the Reign of David I," PSAS 87 (1952–53): 106–117.
Drinkwater, John, *The Alamanni and Rome 213–496 (Caracalla to Clovis)* (Oxford 2007).
Driscoll, S., "The Archaeological Context of Assembly in Early Medieval Scotland — Scone and its *Comparanda*," in A. Pantos and S. Semple (eds.), *Assembly Places and Practices in Medieval Europe* (Dublin 2004): 73–94.
Duncan, A.A.M. "Bede, Iona and the Picts," in R.H.C. Davis and J. M. Wallace-Hadrill, eds., *The Writing of History in the Middle Ages: Essays Presented to Richard William Southern* (Oxford 1981), pp. 1–42.
___ *Scotland: The Making of the Kingdom*, Edinburgh History of Scotland 1 (Edinburgh 1978).
Duval, Paul-Marie, "Teutates, Esus, Taranis," *Études Celtiques* 8 (1958/59): 41–58.
Dillon, Myles, "The Story of the Finding of Cashel," *Ériu* 16 (1952): 61–73.
Earle, John, and Charles Plummer, *Two of the Saxon Chronicles, Parallel*, 2 vols. (Oxford 1892–99).
Easson, D.E., *Medieval Religious Houses: Scotland* (London 1962).
Eddius Stephanus, *The Life of Bishop Wilfrid*, ed. Bertram Colgrave (Cambridge, repr. 1985).
Edwards, Kevin J., and Ian B.M. Ralston, eds., *Scotland after the Ice Age* (Edinburgh 2003).
Einhard, *Vie de Charlemagne*, ed. L. Halpern (Paris 1967).

Elphinstone, William, ed., *Breviary of Aberdeen* (Edinburgh 1507).
Embree, D., E.D. Kennedy, and K. Daly, *Short Scottish Prose Chronicles* (Woodbridge 2012).
Eoin Mac Neill, *Phases of Irish History* (Dublin 1919).
Espérandieu, E. (Lantier-), *Recueil General des Bas-Reliefs, Statues et Bustes de la Gaule Romaine*, 10 vols. (Paris 1910).
Etchingham, Colman, and Catharine Swift, "English and Pictish Terms for a Brooch in an 8th-Century Irish Law-Text," *Medieval Archaeology* 48 (2004): 31–49.
Evans, Nicholas, "Royal Succession and Kingship among the Picts," *Innes Review* 59 (2008): 1–48.
Feachem, R.W., "Hill-forts of Northern Britain," in A.L.F. Rivet, ed., *The Iron Age in Northern Britain* (Edinburgh 1966), pp. 59–88.
Finsen, Vilhjálmur, *Grágás, Islaendernes lovbog i fristatens tid*, 2 vols. (Kjøbenhavn 1852–70).
Fojut, N., *Guide to Prehistoric and Viking Shetland* (Lerwick 1993).
Forbes, Alexander Penrose, ed., *Kalendar of Scottish Saints* (Edinburgh 1872).
___ *Lives of S. Ninian and S. Kentigern*, Historians of Scotland 5 (Edinburgh 1874).
Forsyth, Katherine, *Language in Pictland: The Case Against Non-Indo European Pictish* (Utrecht 1997).
___ "The Latinus Stone: Whithorn's Earliest Christian Monument," in J. Murray, ed., *St Ninian and the Earliest Christianity in Scotland: Papers from the Conference Held by the Friends of the Whithorn Trust in Whithorn on September 15th, 2007*, BAR British series 483 (Oxford 2009), pp. 19–41.
___ "The Ogham-Inscribe Spindle Whorl from Buckquoy: Evidence for the Irish language in Pre-Viking Orkney?' *PSAS* 125 (1995): 677–696.
___ "Some Thoughts on Pictish Symbols as a Formal Writing System," in David Henry, ed., *The Worm, the Germ, and the Thorn: Pictish and Related Studies Presented to Isabel Henderson* (Balgavies 1997), pp. 85–98.
___ ed., *Studies on the Book of Deer* (Dublin 2008).
Forsyth, Katherine, and John Koch, "Evidence of a Lost Pictish Source in the *Historia regum Anglorum* of Symeon of Durham," in Simon Taylor, ed., *Kings, Clerics and Chronicles in Scotland, 500–1297* (Dublin 2000): 19–34.
Foster, Sally M., ed., *The St Andrews Sarcophagus: A Pictish Masterpiece and its International Connections* (Dublin 1998).
___ "The Strength of Belief; The Impact of Christianity on Early Historic Scotland," in Guy de Boe and Frans Verhaeghe, eds., *Religion and Belief in Medieval Europe* (Zellik 1997), pp. 229–240.
Fraser, James E., "Adomnán, Cumméne Ailbe and the Picts," *Peritia* 17–18 (2004): 183–198.
___ *From Caledonia to Pictland: Scotland to 795* (Edinburgh 2009).

Fraser, John, "The Question of the Picts," *Scottish Gaelic Studies* 2 (1927): 172–201.
French, Gilbert, *An Attempt to Explain the Origin and Meaning of the Early Interlaced Ornamentation Found on the Ancient Sculptured Stones of Scotland, Ireland, and the Isle of Man* (Manchester 1858).
Garner, F.H., *The Cattle of Britain* (London 1944).
Garrett, Brett, *Celtic Knots with and beyond J. Romilly Allen* (Zürich 2009).
Geoffrey of Monmouth, *The History of the Kings of Britain: An Edition and Translation of De gestis Britonum (Historia regum Britanniae)*, ed. Michael D. Reeve, trans. Neil Wright (Woodbridge 2007).
Gerald of Wales, *Liber de Principis Instructione* in *Geraldi Cambrensis Opera*, ed. J. Dimock and G. F. Warner, 8 vols., Rolls Series 21 (London 1861–91).
Gildas, *The Ruin of Britain and Other Works*, ed. Michael Winterbottom (Chichester 1978).
Gondek, Megan, "Investing in Sculpture: Power in Early-historic Scotland," *Medieval Archaeology* 50 (2006): 105–142.
Gordon, Alexander, *Itinerarium Septentrionale; Or, a Journey thro' Most of the Counties of Scotland, and Those in the North of England. ... Part 1. Containing an Account of all the Monuments of Roman Antiquity. ... Part 2. An Account of the Danish Invasions on Scotland ... With Sixty-Six Copperplates* (London 1726).
Gordon, C.A., "The Pictish Animals Observed," *PSAS* 98 (1967): 215–224.
Grant, James, *Thoughts on the Origin and Descent of the Gael: With an Account of the Picts, Caledonians, and Scots; and Observations Relative to the Authenticity of the Poems of Ossian* (Edinburgh 1814).
Grigg, Julianna, "Pascal Dating in Pictland: Abbot Ceolfrid's Letter to King Nechtan," *Journal of the Australian Early Medieval Association* 2 (2006): 85–101.
Gwynn, E., *Metrical Dindshenchas*, 5 parts (Dublin 1903–35).
Haddan, Arthur, and William Stubbs, *Councils and Ecclesiastical Documents relating to Great Britain and Ireland*, 3 vols. (Oxford 1869–78).
Hamilton, J.R.C., *Excavations at Clickhimin, Shetland* (London 1968).
Hancock, W.N., A.G. Richey, and R. Atkinson, eds., *Ancient Laws of Ireland*, 6 vols. (Dublin 1865–1901).
Hariot, Thomas, *A Briefe and True Report of the New Found Land of Virginia. The 1590 Theodor de Bry Latin Edition* (Charlottesville 2007).
Helskog, Knut, "Landscapes in Rock-Art: Rock-Carving and Ritual in the Old European North," in Christopher Chippindale and George Nash, eds., *The Figured Landscapes of Rock-Art* (Cambridge 2004), pp. 265–288.
Henderson, George, "The Representations of the Apostles in Insular Art with Special Reference to the New Apostles Frieze at Tarbat, Ross-shire," in Alastair Minnis and Jane Roberts, eds., *Text, Image, Interpretation: Studies*

in *Anglo-Saxon Literature and its Insular Context in Honour of Éamonn Ó Carragáin* (Turnhout 2007), pp. 437–494.

Henderson, George, and Isabel Henderson, *The Art of the Picts: Sculpture and Metalwork in Early Medieval Scotland* (London 2004).

Henderson, Isabel, "Monasteries and Sculpture in the Insular Pre-Viking Ages: The Pictish Evidence," in Benjamin Thompson, ed., *Monasteries and Society in Medieval Britain: Proceedings of the 1994 Harlaxton Symposium* (Stamford 1999), pp. 75–96.

___ *The Picts* (London 1967).

Hennig, John, "Britain's Place in the Early English Martyrologies," *Medium Aevum* 26 (1957): 17–24.

Henry, P.L., *Saoithiúlacht na Sean-Ghaeilge* (Dublin 1978).

Herbert, Máire, and Pádraig O Riain, eds., *Betha Adamnáin*, Irish Texts Society 54 (London 1988).

Heritage, S.J.H., and H.B. Wheatley, eds., *Catholicon Anglicum: An English-Latin Wordbook*, Early English Text Society 75 (Oxford 1881).

Herodian, *History of the Empire from the Time of Marcus Aurelius*, ed. C.R. Whittaker (Cambridge, MA, 1969).

Higgitt, John, "The Pictish Latin Inscription at Tarbat in Ross-shire," *PSAS* 112 (1982): 300–321.

Hogan, James, "The Irish Law of Kingship, with Special Reference to Ailech and Cenél Eoghain," *Proceedings of the Royal Irish Academy* 40 C (1932): 186–254.

Hood, A.B.E., ed., *St. Patrick, His Writings and Muirchu's Life* (Chichester 1978).

Horstmann, C., ed., *Minor Poems of the Vernon MS*, part 1, Early English Text Society 98 (Oxford 1892; repr. 1987).

Hübner, Ernst Willibald Emil, *Inscriptiones Britanniae latinae: Consilio et auctoritate Academiae litterarum regiae borussicae* (Berlin 1959).

Hughes, Kathleen, *Celtic Britain in the Early Middle Ages, Studies in Scottish and Welsh Sources*, ed. D. Dumville (Woodbridge 1980).

Hughson, Irene, "Pictish Horse Carvings," *Glasgow Archaeological Journal* 17 (1991–92): 53–62.

Hull, Vernon, "Conall Corc and the Corco Luigde," *Publications of the Modern Language Association* 62 (1947): 887–909.

Innes, Thomas, *A Critical Essay on the Ancient Inhabitants of the Northern Parts of Britain or Scotland. Containing an Account of the Romans, of the Britains betwixt the Walls, of the Caledonians or Picts, and particularly of the Scots. With an Appendix of Ancient Manuscript Pieces*, 2 vols. (London 1729; repr. with a biographical memoir by George Grub, Historians of Scotland 8, Edinburgh 1879).

___ *Civil and Ecclesiastical History of Scotland, 80 to 818*, ed. George Grub, Spalding Club (Aberdeen 1853).

Isidore of Seville, *Etymologiarvm Sive Originvm*, ed. W.M. Lindsay, 2 vols. (Oxford 1911).
Jackson, Anthony, *Symbol Stones of Scotland* (Stromness 1984).
Jackson, Kenneth, *Gaelic Notes in the Book of Deer* (Cambridge 1972).
___ *The Gododdin* (Edinburgh 1969).
___ "The Language of the Picts," in F.T. Wainwright, ed., *The Problem of the Picts* (Edinburgh 1955).
Jones, Michael, "The Historicity of the Alleluia Victory," in J. France and K. deVries, eds., *Warfare in the Dark Ages* (Aldershot 2008).
Kelly, Fergus, *Early Irish Law* (Dublin 1988).
Kermack, Stuart, "An Attempt on the Meaning of the Pictish Symbols – Part 1," *Pictish Arts Society Journal* 11 (1997): 9–18.
Kirby, D. P., "... per universas Pictorum provincias," in Gerald Bonner, ed., *Famulus Christi: Essays in Commemoration of the Thirteenth Centenary of the Birth of the Venerable Bede* (London 1976), 286–324.
Knott, Eleanor, ed., *Togail Bruidne Dá Derga*, Medieval and Modern Irish Series 8 (Dublin, repr. 1975)
Koch, John T., *The Celtic Heroic Age* (Andover 1997).
Krapp, G.K., and E. Dobbie, eds. *Exeter Book* (New York 1936).
Lacey, Brian, "Fahan, Tory, Cenél nEógain and the Picts," *Peritia* 20 (2008): 331–345.
Laing, Lloyd, *The Archaeology of Celtic Britain and Ireland* (Cambridge 2006).
___ "The Chronology and Context of Pictish Relief Sculpture," *Medieval Archaeology* 44 (2000): 81–114.
___ "The Hoard of Pictish Silver from Norrie's Law, Fife," *Studia Celtica* 28 (1994): 11–38.
Laing, Lloyd, and Jennifer Laing, "Archaeological Notes on Some Scottish Early Christian Sculptures," *PSAS* 114 (1984): 277–287.
___ *The Picts and the Scots* (Stroud 1993).
Lanting, J.N., "Dates for the Origin and Diffusion of the European Log Boat," *Palaeohistoria* 39/40 (1997/98): 627–650.
Lawrie, Sir Archibald, *Early Scottish Charters prior to 1153* (Glasgow 1905).
Lehman, Ruth, *Fled Dúin na nGéd, Lochlann* 4 (1969): 131–159.
Lethbridge, T.C., *Herdsmen and Hermits, Celtic Seafarers in the Northern Seas* (Cambridge 1950).
Levison, Wilhelm, "An Eighth-Century Poem on St. Ninian," *Antiquity* xiv (1940): 280–291.
Lindqvist, Sune, *Gotlands Bildsteine*, 2 vols. (Stockholm 1941–42).
Lowe, H., "Findan von Rheinau: Eine Irische Peregrinatio im 9. Jahrhundert," *Deutsches Archiv für Erforschung des mittelalters* 42 (1986): 25–85.
Mac Cana, P., *The Learned Tales of Medieval Ireland* (Dublin 1980).
Mac Eóin, Géaroid, "On the Irish Legend of the Origins of the Picts," *Studia Hibernica* 4 (1964): 138–154.

Mac Airt, S. and G. Mac Niocaill, eds., *Annals of Ulster to 1131* (Dublin 1984).
Macalister, R.A.S., *Corpus Inscriptionum Insularum Celticarum*, 2 vols. (Dublin 1945–49; vol. 1 repr. 1996, with a preface by Damian McManus).
___ *Lebor Gabála Érenn*, vol. 5, Irish Text Society 44 (London 1956).
Macbain Alexander, and Rev. John Kennedy, eds., *Reliquiae Celticae: Texts, Papers and Studies Left by the Late Rev. Alexander Cameron, LL.D.*, 2 vols. (Inverness 1894).
Maclean, Douglas, "Knapdale Dedications to a Leinster Saint: Sculpture, Hagiography and Oral Tradition," *Scottish Studies* 27 (1983): 49–65.
___ "Snake-Bosses and Redemption at Iona and in Pictland," in R.M. Spearman and John Higgitt, eds., *The Age of Migrating Ideas: Early Medieval Art in Northern Britain and Ireland* (Stroud 1993), pp. 244–253.
MacNeill, Eoin, *Phases of Irish History* (Dublin 1919).
Mac Niocaill, G., *Ireland before the Vikings* (Dublin 1972).
MacQueen, John, *St. Nynia* (Edinburgh 1961).
Macquarrie, Alan, The Career of Saint Kentigern of Glasgow: *Vitae, Lectiones* and Glimpses of Fact, *Innes Review* 37 (1984): 3–24.
___ *Legends of Scottish Saints. Readings, Hymns and Prayers for the Commemoration of Scottish Saints in the Aberdeen Breviary* (Dublin 2012).
___ "*Vita Sancti Servani*: The Life of St. Serf," *Innes Review* 44 (1993): 122–152.
Martin, F.X., *No Hero in the House: Diarmaid Mac Murchada and the Coming of the Normans to Ireland*, O Donnell Lecture 19 (Dublin 1978).
Mathisen, Ralph W., "Catalogues of Barbarians in Late Antiquity," in Ralph W. Mathisen and Danuta Shanzer, eds., *Romans, Barbarians, and the Transformation of the Roman World* (Burlington, VT, 2011), pp. 17–32.
McCarthy, Daniel M., "The Chronological Apparatus of the Annals of Ulster AS 431–1131," *Peritia* 8 (1994): 46–79.
___ "The Chronological Apparatus of the Annals of Ulster AD 82–1019," *Peritia* 16 (2002): 256–283.
McGrail, Sean, *Ancient Boats in North-West Europe: The Archaeology of Water Transport to AD 1500* (London 1998).
Mckerral, Andrew, "The Lesser Land and administrative Divisions in Celtic Scotland," PSAS 85 (1950–51): 52–64.
McNeill, Peter G.B., and Hector L.MacQueen, eds., *Atlas of Scottish History* (Edinburgh 1996).
Megaw, Ruth, and Vincent Megaw, *Celtic Art* (London 1990).
Menzies, Gordon, ed., *Who Are the Scots?* (London 1971).
Meyer, Kuno, *Voyage of Bran son of Febal*, 2 vols. (London 1895).
Migne, J.-P., ed., *Patrologiae Cursus Completus, sive bibliotheca universalis ... omnium S.S. Patrum, Doctorum, Scriptorumque ecclesiasticorum qui ab aevo apostolico ad Innocentii III tempora floruerunt. Series latina*, 221 vols. (Paris 1844–91).

Miller, Molly, "Matriliny by Treaty; The Pictish Foundation Legend," in D. Whitelock, R. Mckitterick, and D. Dumville, eds, *Ireland in Early Medieval Europe* (Cambridge 1982): 133-161.
Moisl, H., "The Bernician Royal Dynasty and the Irish in the Seventh Century," *Peritia* 2 (1983): 103-126.
Muir, Richard, *Shell Guide to Reading the Celtic Landscape* (London 1985).
Mulchrone, K., *Bethu Phatraic* (Dublin 1939).
Mullins, Juliet, "Trouble at the White House: Anglo-Irish Relations and the Cult of St. Martin," *Proceedings of the British Academy* 157 (2009): 113-127.
Nennius, *The British History and Annals*, ed. John Morris (London 1980).
Nicolaisen, W.F.H., *Scottish Place-Names* (London 1975).
Ní Dhonnchadha, Máirín, "The Guarantor List of *Cáin Adomnáin*, 697," *Peritia* 1 (1982): 178-215.
Nixon, C.E.V., and Barbara Saylor Rodgers, eds., *In Praise of the Later Roman Emperors: The Panegyrici Latini* (Berkeley 1994).
Ó Baoill, Colm, and Nancy McGuire, eds., *Rannsachadh na Gàidhlig 2000* (Aberdeen 2002).
O'Brien, Michael, *Corpus Genealogiarum Hiberniae* (Dublin 1962).
Ó Corráin, Donnchadh, "Creating the Past: The Early Irish Genealogical Tradition," *Peritia* 12 (1998): 177-208.
Ó Cróinín, Dáibhí, "Who was Palladius 'First Bishop of the Irish'?" *Peritia* 12 (2000): 205-237.
Ó Cuív, Brian, "Some Irish Items relating to the MacDonnells of Antrim," *Celtica* 16 (1984): 139-156.
Ó Daly, Máirín, "A Poem on the Airgialla," *Ériu* 16 (1952): 179-188.
O'Donovan, John, ed., *Annals of the Kingdom of Ireland by the Four Masters, from the Earliest Period to 1616*, 7 vols. (Dublin 1851).
Ó Murchadha, Diarmuid, "Nationality Names in the Irish Annals," *Nomina* 16 (1991/92): 49-70.
O'Rahilly, Cecile, ed., *The Stowe Version of Táin Bó Cuailnge* (Dublin 1973).
O'Rahilly, T.F., *Early Irish History and Mythology* (Dublin 1946).
___ *The Two Patricks: A Lecture on the History of Christianity in Fifth-Century Ireland* (Dublin 1942).
Origen, *Homilies on Luke, Fragments on Luke*, trans. Joseph Lienhard SJ (Washington, DC, 1996).
Palgrave, Sir Francis, ed., *Documents and Records Illustrating the History of Scotland ...* (London 1837).
Pennant, Thomas, *A Tour in Scotland and Voyage to the Hebrides MDCCLXXII*, 2 vols. (London 1776).
Pharr, Clyde, ed., *Theodosian Code and Novels and the Sirmondian Constitutions* (New York 1952).
Piggott, Stuart, "Three Metalwork Hoards in Southern Scotland," *PSAS* 82 (1952/53): 68-123.

Piggott, Stuart and R.J.C. Atkinson, "The Torrs Chamfrein," *Archaeologia* 94 (1955): 197–235.
Pinkerton, John, *An Enquiry into the History of Scotland Preceding the Reign of Malcolm III or the Year 1056, Including the Authentic History of that Period*, 2 vols. (London 1789).
Plummer, Charles, ed., *Bethada Náem nÉrenn*, 2 vols. (Oxford 1922).
___ ed., *Vitae Sanctorum Hiberniae*, 2 vols. (Oxford 1910).
Procopius, *History of the Wars*, ed. and trans. H.B. Dewing, 7 vols. (Cambridge, MA, 1914–40).
Purser, John, *Scotland's Music* (Edinburgh 1992).
Radnor, Joan, *Fragmentary Annals of Ireland* (Dublin 1976).
Rance, Philip, "Attacotti, Déisi and Magnus Maximus: The Case for Irish Federates in Later Roman Britain," *Britannia* 32 (2001): 243–270.
Ranulf Higden, *Polychronicon Ranulphi Higden, Monachi Cestrensis: Together with the English Translations of John of Trevisa and of an Unknown Writer in the 15th Century*, ed. C. Babington and J.R. Lumby, 9 vols., Rolls Series 41 (London 1865–86).
Reginald of Durham, *Libellus de admirandis Beati Cuthberti, Virtutibus quae novellis patratae sunt temporibus*, ed. J. Raine, Surtees Society 1 (London 1835).
Richard of Hexham, *De Gestis regis Stephani*, in *Chronicles, Stephen, Henry II and Richard I*, Rolls Series 82 (London 1884–90).
Richmond, I.A., "Ancient Rome and Northern England," *Antiquity* 14 (1940): 292–300.
___ ed., *Roman and Native in North Britain* (London 1958).
Riese, A., ed. *Geographia latini minores* (Hildesheim, repr. 1964).
Ritchie, Anna, "Clothing among the Picts," *Costume* 39 (2005): 28–42.
___ "Pict and Norseman in Northern Scotland," *Scottish Archaeological Forum* 6 (1974): 23–36.
Robert Mannyng of Brunne, *The Chronicle*, ed. Idelle Sullens (Binghampton, NY, 1996).
Rollason, David W. "Lists of Saints' Resting Places," *Anglo-Saxon England* 7 (1978): 61–93.
___ and Lynda Rollason, eds., *Durham Liber vitae: London, British Library, MS Cotton Domitian A.VII: Edition and digital facsimile with introduction, codicological, prosopographical and linguistic commentary, and indexes including the Biographical Register of Durham Cathedral Priory (1083–1539) by A. J. Piper*, 3 vols. (London 2007).
Ross, Anne, *Pagan Celtic Britain* (London 1974).
Salway, Peter, *Roman Britain* (Oxford 1981).
Samson, Ross, "The Reinterpretation of the Pictish Symbols," *Journal of the British. Archaeological Association* 145 (1992): 29–65.
Schove, D. J., *Chronology of Eclipses and Comets, AD 1–1000* (Woodbridge 1984).

Sellar, W.D.H., "The Origins and Ancestry of Somerled," *Scottish Historical Review* 45 (1966): 123–142.
___ "Sueno's Stone and its Interpreters," in W.D.H. Sellar, ed., *Moray: Province and People* (Edinburgh 1993): 97–116.
Sinclair of Ulbster, John, ed. *Statistical Account of Scotland*, 21 vols. (Edinburgh 1791–99).
Sidonius, *Sidoine Apollinaire*, ed. André Loyen, 3 vols. (Paris 2003).
Skene, William Forbes, *Celtic Scotland: An History of Ancient Alba*, 3 vols. (Edinburgh 1876–80).
___ *Chronicles of the Picts, Chronicles of the Scots, and Other Early Memorials of Scottish History* (Edinburgh 1867).
___ (ed.), *Johannis de Fordun, Chronica Gentis Scotorum*, Historians of Scotland vols. 1 and 2 (Edinburgh 1871–72), with Latin text in vol. 1 and English trans. by Felix J.H. Skene in vol. 2.
Small, A., "Excavations at Underhoull, Unst, Shetland," *PSAS* 98 (1966): 225–248.
Small, Alan, Charles Thomas, David M. Wilson, et al., *St. Ninian's Isle and Its Treasure*, 2 vols. (Oxford 1973).
Smiles, Sam, "John White and British Antiquity: Savage Origins in the Context of Tudor Historiography," in Kim Sloan, ed., *European Visions: American Voices*, British Museum Research Publication 172 (London 2009), pp. 106–112.
Smith, Ian, "The Origins and Development of Christianity in North England and Southern Pictland," in John Blair and Carol Pyrah, eds., *Church Archaeology: Research Directions for the Future* (York 1996), pp. 19–37.
Snyder, Christopher, *The Britons* (Oxford 2003).
Stamp, L.D., *Man and the Land*, New Naturalist Series (London 1955).
Stenton, Frank, *Anglo-Saxon England*, ed. Mary Stenton (Oxford, 3rd edn, 1971).
Stevenson, R.B.K., "The Inchyra Stone and Other Unpublished Early Christian Monuments," *PSAS* 92 (1958/59): 33–55.
Stokes, Whitley, ed. "The Fragmentary Annals of Tigernach," *Revue Celtique* 16 (1895): 374–419; 17 (1896): 6–33, 119–263, 337–420; 18 (1897): 9–59, 150–197, 267–303, 374–391.
___ (ed.), *Martyrology of Oengus the Culdee: Félire Óengusso Céli Dé, Kalendar of Oengus* (Dublin, repr. 1984).
___ "Rennes Dindshenchas," *Revue Celtique* 15 (1894): 272–484.
___ (ed.), *Three Irish Glossaries* (London 1862).
___ *The Tripartite Life of Patrick*, 2 vols., Rolls Series 89 (London 1888).
Stokes, Whitley, and J. Strachan, *Thesaurus Palaeohibernicus*, 2 vols. (Dublin, repr. 1975).
Strecker, Karl, "Zu den Quellen für das Leben des hl. Ninian," *Neues Archiv der Gesellschaft für ältere deutsche Geshichstunde* xliii (1920–22): 1–26.

Stuart, John, *Sculptured Stones of Scotland*, 2 vols., Spalding Club (Aberdeen 1856; Edinburgh 1867).
Sweet, Henry, ed., *Liber Vitae*, in *The Oldest English Texts*, Early English Text Society 83 (Oxford 1885).
Symeon of Durham, *Historia Regum* in *Symeonis Monachi Opera Omnia*, ed. Thomas Arnold, 2 vols. (London 1883–85).
Talbot, C.H., *Anglo-Saxon Missionaries in Germany* (New York 1954).
Tertullian, *Adversus Iudaeos*, in *Opera*, ed. Eligius Dekkers, 2 vols., *Corpus Christianorum Series Latinae* 1 and II (Turnhout, 1953–54), ii, 1337–1398.
Thomas, Charles, "Animal Art of the Scottish Iron Age and its Origins," *Archaeological Journal* 118 (1963): 14–16.
___ *The Early Christian Archaeology of North Britain* (Oxford 1971).
___ "The "Monster" Episode in Adomnan's Life of St. Columba," *Cryptozoology* 7 (1988): 38–45.
Thompson, A. Hamilton, ed., *Liber Vitae Ecclesiae Dunelmensis. A Collotype Facsimile of the Original Manuscript, with Introductory Essay and Notes*, Surtees Society 136 (London 1923).
Thompson, E.A., *St. Germanus* (Woodbridge 1984).
Thomson, W.P.L., "St. Findan and the Pictish-Norse Transition," in R.J. Berry and H. Firth, eds., *The People of Orkney* (Kirkwall 1986), pp. 279–283.
Thurneysen, Rudolf, *Die irische Helden- und Königsage* (Halle 1921).
___ "Synchronismen der irischen Könige," *Zeitschrift für celtische Phiologie* 19 (1933): 81–99.
Ussher, James, *Britannicarum Ecclesiarum Antiquitates*, in C.R. Elrington and J.H. Todd, eds., *The Whole Works of the Most Rev. James Ussher, D.D.*, 17 vols. (Dublin 1847–64).
Van de Noort, Robert, *North Sea Archaeologies: A Maritime Biography, 10,000 BC–AD 1500* (Oxford 2011).
Vegetius, P. *Flavii Vegeti Renati, Epitoma Rei Militaris*, ed. Alf Önnerfors (Leipzig 1995).
Wade-Evans, A.W., ed., *Vitae Sanctorum Britanniae et Genealogiae* (Cardiff 1944).
___ *Welsh Medieval Law* (Oxford 1909).
Wainwright, F.T., "Nechtansmere," *Antiquity* 22 (1948): 82–97.
___ ed., *The Problem of the Picts* (Edinburgh 1955).
___ "Souterrains in Scotland," *Antiquity* 27 (1952): 219–232.
___ *The Souterrains of Southern Pictland* (London 1963).
Wallace-Hadrill, J.M., *Bede's Ecclesiastical History of the English People* (Oxford 1988).
Watson, W.J., *The History of the Celtic Place-Names of Scotland* (Edinburgh 1926).
Weinmann, Cornelia, *Der Hausbau in Skandinavien vom Neolithikum bis zum Mittelalter* (Berlin 1994).

Whittington, G. and J.A. Soulsby, "A Preliminary Report on an Investigation into Pit Place-names," *Scottish Geographical Magazine* 84 (1968): 117–125.
Williams, Sir Ifor, *Armes Prydein*, trans. R. Bromwich (Dublin 1972).
___ *Canu Aneirin* (Cardiff 1938).
___ *Poems of Taliesin* (Dublin 1975).
Wilson, C. Anne, *Food and Drink in Britain* (Harmondsworth 1976).
Woolf, Alex, "AU 729.2 and the Last Years of Nechtan mac Der-Ilei," *Scottish Historical Review* 85 (2006): 131–137.
___ "Dun Nechtain, Fortriu and the Geography of the Picts," *Scottish Historical Review* 85 (2006): 182–201.
___ *From Pictland to Alba: Scotland 789–1070* (Edinburgh 2007).
Wormald, Patrick, "The Emergence of the *Regnum Scottorum*: A Carolingian Hegemony?" in B. Crawford, ed., *Scotland in Dark Age Britain* (St. Andrews 1996): 131–147.
Wright, T., ed., *Alexandri Neckham de Naturis Rerum with Neckham's poem De Laudibus Divinae Sapientiae naturis*, Rolls Series 34 (London 1863).
Youngs, Susan, "Anglo-Saxon, Irish and British Relations: Hanging Bowls Reconsidered," *Proceedings of the British Academy* 157 (2009): 205–230.
Zosimus, *New History*, ed. and trans. Ronald I. Ridley (Sydney 1982).

Index

Abercorn, 10, 45, 61, 65, 74, 80, 150
Aberdeen Breviary, 113, 114, 152, 237
Aberlemno, 76, 77, 78, 108, 109, 118, 121, 164, 166, 167, 168, 169, 171, 172, 173, 174, 175, 235
Abernethy, 148, 153, 154, 171, 201, 208
Adomnán of Iona, 5, 9, 10, 41, 42, 48, 50, 60, 61, 62, 71, 73, 82, 94, 95, 97, 98, 100, 102, 105, 109, 115, 116, 127, 128, 129, 130, 134, 137, 139, 140, 144, 145, 146, 148, 149, 150, 152, 155, 158, 159, 161, 237
Adventu Saxonum, 58
Áed, 183, 185, 196, 199, 202
Áedan, bishop of Lindisfarne, 11
Áedan son of Gabran, 61, 62, 63, 70, 73, 85, 184, 238, 239
Aethelstan, English king, 48, 156, 193, 209, 211
Aethelweard, 6, 211
AEthicus Ister, 48, 124, 130
Ailred of Rievaulx, 43, 142, 143, 220
Ainfcellach, 89, 189
Alba, 189, 202, 228
Alcuin, 142, 188, 190, 191
alder, 70, 127
ale, 103, 104
Alemani, 15, 24, 37

Alhred, 92, 185
Allectus, 21, 22
Alleluia Victory, 35, 36
Alpin, son of Eochaid, father of Kenneth I, 193, 199, 222
Alpin son of Ferent, 13, 82, 86, 87
Alpin son of Nechtan, 80
altar, 140, 149, 186
Altus Prositor, 146
Ammianus Marcellinus, 3, 8, 24, 25, 26, 27, 28, 30, 38, 56, 57, 58, 217
Amra Coluim Chille, see Columba's Breastplate
Anderson, Alan O., 8, 228, 229
Anderson, M.O., 228
Andrew of Wyntoun, 12, 204, 221, 222, 223
Aneirin, 9, 64, 101
Angles, 3, 4, 16, 58, 63, 65, 71, 80, 92, 93, 150, 153, 183, 188, 204, 209, 235, 238
Anglo-Saxon Chronicle, 10, 42, 80, 123, 211
Angus (region), 48, 85, 112, 166, 181, 230
Angus son of Fergus (died 761), 3, 13, 68, 81–93, 97, 110, 156, 157, 183, 184, 187, 188, 195, 206, 236, 238, 239

The Picts, First Edition. Benjamin Hudson.
© 2014 John Wiley & Sons, Ltd. Published 2014 by John Wiley & Sons, Ltd.

Angus son of Fergus (died 834), 192, 193, 223
Angus son of Nechtan, 70
Annals of Tigernach, 11, 12, 42, 70, 75, 86, 88, 92, 237
Annals of Ulster, 11, 12, 47, 60, 73, 75, 80, 83, 85, 87, 89, 90, 91, 92, 110, 129, 145, 146, 155, 158, 183, 185, 186, 192, 193, 201, 203, 204, 237, 239
Antonine Itinerary, 31
Antonine Wall, 16, 17, 18, 31, 40, 42, 45, 49, 62, 76, 205, 234
Applecross, 148
Aquitaine, 6, 144, 196, 222
arcani, 27, 28, 217
Argyllshire, 30, 45, 59, 103, 136, 236
Arian heresy, 8
Artbranán, 148
Arthur, 6, 32, 59, 113, 216, 217, 218, 219, 227, 239
Arthurian legend, 217, 219
Atholl, 13, 48, 83, 84, 89, 90, 94, 204
Atlantic, 4, 5, 6, 7, 17, 20, 24, 37, 60, 99, 112, 125, 126, 136, 180
Attacotti, 26, 27, 28, 31
Augustine of Hippo, 34
Ausonius, 24, 26, 122, 130, 131
Avon, river in Linlithgow, 42, 80

Báetan son of Cairill, 60
Baia, 212
Baltic, 138, 178, 222
Bamburgh, 65, 77, 79
barbarian 15, 23, 24, 25, 26, 27, 28, 31, 33, 37, 38, 56, 62, 63, 65, 76, 128, 140
Barbarian Conspiracy, 5, 25, 27, 28, 56, 58
Barbarian Nations that sprang up under the [Romans], 15
barley, 20, 111, 114, 115
Barra, 121

Battle of Brunnanburh, 6
Battle of Drum Dólech, 213
Beccan, 148, 149
Bede, 2, 5, 9, 10, 11, 44, 45, 46, 49, 51, 53, 54, 55, 58, 62, 69, 74–80, 84, 85, 91, 92, 93, 104–108, 131, 134, 141–146, 149, 150, 151, 152, 155, 159, 182, 185, 208, 216, 219, 221, 222, 223, 234, 235, 236, 238
Ecclesiastical History, 2, 5, 9, 10, 55, 75, 84, 104, 131, 134, 142, 145, 150, 216, 226, 238
Bennachie, 48, 213
Beornhaeth, 74, 75
Berht, 75
Bertfrid, 42
Bible, 124, 138, 167, 208
Bicoet, 87
Black Isle, 115
Blathmac, 191
boar, 103, 113, 118, 121, 122, 152, 176
boat, 95, 115, 129, 131, 137, 178, 217
  Pict boat, 30, 128
  skin boat, 125–126
  wooden boat, 125, 126–128
Boece, Hector, 219, 224, 226
bog butter, 119
Boniface, Anglo-Saxon missionary, 106, 150, 151, 154
Book of Cuanu, 73
Book of Deer, 51, 116, 155, 164, 171
Book of the Dun Cow (Lebor na Huidre), 66, 144, 145
Book of Invasions (Leabor Gabála), 54, 68, 238
Book of Leinster, 101, 203, 212
Book of Life (Liber Vitae), 92, 188
Bower, Walter, 208, 221, 222
Bran son of Angus, 194
Brandsbutt Stone, 165, 167, 171, 175
Brega, 75, 194
Briton, 24, 34, 43, 142, 217, 234

Britons, 2, 16, 18, 19, 21, 22–25, 35, 36, 39, 41–46, 53, 54, 56, 58, 64, 68, 76, 86, 128, 130, 140, 144, 151, 202, 204, 216, 218, 223, 227, 234, 235
broch, 111
Broichan, 93, 95, 96, 97, 101, 102, 138, 139, 159
brooches, 180
Brude, king of Fortriu (died 753), 92
Brude son of Angus (died 736), 88, 89, 110
Brude son of Bile, king of Fortriu (died 693), 11, 69, 71, 75, 79, 80, 236
Brude son of Deirili (died 706), 81, 82, 148, 154
Brude son of Dergard, 154
Brude son of Ferant, 194
Brude son of Fid (died 641), 70
Brude son of Fodel, 194
Brude son of Maelcon (died 584), 11, 12, 48, 60–63, 73, 91, 93, 95, 96, 97, 98, 100, 102, 129, 138, 139, 145, 146, 158, 159
Bubbon, 66
bull, carved on stone, 176
bull-baiting, 43, 220
Burghead, 99, 100, 119, 176
Burghley, 47

Cadog, 211
Caereni, 16, 137
Caesar, Julius, 6, 7, 18, 21, 22, 23, 24, 25, 41, 52, 55, 96, 99, 138, 222, 231, 234
cáin, 117, 203
Cainnech, 97, 149
Caithness, region, 16, 48, 137, 159, 214, 216, *see also* Cat
Caledonian forest, 20, 41, 48, 218
Caledonian shore, 130, 131
Caledonians, 15, 16, 18, 22, 24, 37, 41, 54, 56, 75, 96, 130, 227

Camden, William, 46, 225
Caracalla, 18, 24
Carausius', 21
Carnonacae, 16
Carron, river in Linlithgow, 42, 80
Cat, kingdom, 47, 48, 184, 214, 218, *see also* Caithness
Cathusach, 44
Catraeth (? in Yorkshire), 65
Catroe, 90, 184
cattle, 54, 111, 113, 117, 118, 119, 120, 121, 124, 126, 138, 190
Cattle Raid of Cooley, 117, 179
cauldron, 67, 136, 139, 214
Caw, 211, 212
Ce, kingdom, 47, 48
cellular houses, 112
Cenél Conaill, 89, 90, 145
Cenél Loairn, 84, 88, 89, 90, 183, 184
Cenél nAngusa, 69
Cenél nEógain, 90, 199
Cenél nGabráin, 74, 82, 88, 90, 184, 205
centaurs, 171, 176
Ceolfrid, 62, 84, 149, 152, 208
Cernunnos, 136, 152, 175
chains, silver, *see* silver chains
chickens, 121
Chronicle of Huntingdon, 193, 195, 198
Cinadhon (Kenneth, Cinaed) son of Wredech, (died 774), 92, 184–185
Cindaeladh, 12
Cindrigmonath, *see* St. Andrews
Cinedon son of Lugthren, 70
Circenn, kingdom, 13, 47, 48, 53, 63, 68, 79, 80, 81, 85, 86, 87, 91, 104, 206, 236, 238
Clatchard Craig, fortress, 100
Claudius Claudianus (Claudian), 8, 24, 28, 29, 33, 35, 41, 45
Clava cairns, 135
claymore, 69
Clonmacnoise, church, 68

clothing, 1, 30, 120, 128
Clunie, 198
Clyde, 14, 17, 26, 32, 36, 37, 45, 62, 63, 99, 105, 123, 128, 179, 208, 234, 235, 238
Coire Breccáin, 129, 130
Colmán, 130
Columba of Iona, 10, 11, 32, 41, 42, 60, 62, 63, 64, 66, 70, 73, 82, 93, 94, 95, 97, 98, 100–103, 109, 115, 128, 129, 130, 137–140, 142, 145–148, 150, 153, 155, 158, 159, 160, 161, 184, 200, 201, 223, 234, 237
Columba's Breastplate (Amra Choluim Chille), 32, 103, 147
Comgall of Bangor, 126, 149
Coming of the Cruithne from Thracia, 213
Conaire, 67
Conall, 49, 67, 68, 69, 86, 98, 146, 186, 187
Conall son of Tadc, 186
Conception of Mongan, 63
Congal, 73
Cononish, 123
Constans, 8, 26, 217
Constantine, biographer of St. Germanus, 34, 35,
Constantine son of Áed, king, 82,
Constantine son of Fergus, king of Fortriu (died 820), 157, 186–192, 195, 196, 198, 200, 201, 202, 205, 206, 223, 239
Constantine son of Kenneth I, king, 113, 117
Constantine the Great, emperor, 26
Constantius the Pale (*Chlorus*), emperor 21–26, 37, 38, 55
copper, 20, 124, 218
coracle, 30, 125, 126, 129, 143
coral, 130
Cormac, 49, 98, 129

Cornavii, 16, 137
Coroticus, 36, 42, 141
Cossans symbol stone, 126, 127, 178
Crenoes, 16
Críth Gablach, 210
Cruithne/Cruithen/Cruithnech, 13, 43, 44, 47, 49, 53, 54, 55, 63, 66, 67, 68, 70, 82, 86, 104, 136, 187, 202, 214, 234
Cruithnechán, 68
Cumuseach, 70
Cunedda, 31, 58
Curitan, 148
Curnach, 67
Cuthbert of Lindisfarne, bishop, 10, 43, 65, 75, 77, 79, 150, 219,
   Community of St. Cuthbert, 92, 188, 190, 202, 208, 220, 239
   Life (Vita) of St. Cuthbert, 10, 79, 150, 238
cymbal, 101

Dagda, 190
dairy, 117, 119
Dál nAraide, 44, 63
Dál Riata, 4, 12, 25, 44, 45, 52, 59, 60, 62, 63, 66, 69, 71–74, 84, 85, 87–90, 93, 94, 109, 110, 131, 146, 148, 149, 156, 165, 182, 183, 184, 187, 189, 193, 194, 196, 198, 200, 203, 204, 205, 214, 215, 236, 238, 239
Damnonii, 17
Decantae, 16
deer, animal, 118, 122, 176
Deer, church, 51, 61, 146, 154, 155, 159, 164
Degsastan, battle of, 63, 70, 73, 238
Deirili, 81, 83, 84, 87
Delcros, 115
Description of Scotland, 216
Destruction of Bennachie, 213
Destruction of Da Derga's Hostel, 66, 69

Destruction of Nechtan's House, 212
Destruction of the Plain of Cé, 213
Dícuil, 191, 192
Dio (Dion Cassius), 18, 19, 22, 41, 56, 62, 75, 76, 121
divination, 138
Domnall Brecc (Freckled), king of Dál Riata, 66, 73, 239
Domnall son of Alpin, king of Scots, 196, 202, 239
Donnán of Eigg, 48, 118, 131, 159, 160
Doon Hill, 101
Dorsum Britanniae, see Druim Alban
double disc symbols, 162
Drest son of Constantine, 193
Drest son of Wroid, 185
Drostan son of Donald, king (died 678), 71, 83, 84
Drostan, saint, 147, 222
Drostan, disciple of Columba (possibly same man as St. Drostan), 155, 159
druid, 54, 138
Druim Alban (Ridge of Britain), 17, 84, 87, 98, 149, 153, 184
Druim Dearg, 87
Drostan/Drust, king (died 729) 82, 87
Drust (form of Drost and Drostan), 13, 83
Drust son of Talorgan, 88
Drust son of Ferant, king, 194
Dub Longes, 67
Dubtholargg (Dubtolarg son of Angus), king (died 782), 92, 185
Dumbarton Rock (Ail Cluaide of Strathclyde), 36, 45, 46, 61, 66, 91, 99, 203, 209, 217, 218, 235
Dumfriesshire, 17, 42, 63, 165, 219, 238
Dumyat, fortress, 99
Dun Edin, *see* Edinburgh
Dun Nechtan (Nechtan's Mere), 3, 11, 69, 74, 75, 79, 80, 97, 167

Dunachton, 78, 79
Dunadd, 61, 72, 89, 103, 113
Dunbaitte, siege of, 72
Dunbar, 201
Dunchad, 73
Dundurn, 61, 72, 99, 115, 118, 120, 121, 123, 124
Dungal, 89, 110
Dunkeld, church of, 47, 61, 157, 158, 189, 198, 200, 201, 208, 223
  fortress of King's Seat, 99
  Litany of, 188, 189
Dunnichen, 77, 78, 80
Dunnottar, fortress, 72, 100
Dunolly, fortress, 73
Dupplin Cross, 101
Durham, 43, 176, 188, 220, 238
Dyce, symbol stones at St. Fergus, 165, 166, 171, 172

eagle,
  artistic representation, 140, 173, 174, 175, 176, 233
  prophetic animal, 137, 218
Eanfrith, son of Aethelfrith, 69
Early Christian Monuments of Scotland, 164–165, 230
Earn, river, 86, 187, 197
Ecgfrith, king of Northumbria, 11, 12, 69, 74, 75, 76, 79, 80, 97, 152
Edinburgh (Dun Etain/Edin), 9, 64, 65, 74, 86, 226, 238
Eigg, island, 48, 118, 131, 148, 159, 160
Eithne, princess, 185
Elidon Hill North, 101
Elpin son of Wroid, king (died *circa* 780), 185
Eochaid *Buide* son of Áedan, 73,
Eochaid Oversea, 25, 52, 59
Eochaid son of Echdach, 90, 183, 184, 190, 199
Eóganán son of Angus (died 839), 188, 193, 194, 196, 197, 205, 239

exactores, 82, 87, 97, 123
Expulsion of the Déisi, 25, 189

farm, 57, 111, 113, 117
Fergus son of Bargot, ninth-century king, 194
Fergus son of Eochaid of Dál Riata (died 781) 183, 185
Fergus son of Erc of Dál Riata, 59, 60, 214
Fergus son of Ferechad, legendary king, 222
Fergussan son of Maelcon (died 703), 80, 81, 85, 88, 92
Ferith, 70
Ferot, 87
Fid (?Gwid son of Peithan), 66, 70, 71
Fidach, kingdom, 47, 48
Fife (Fib), kingdom and region, 32, 47, 48, 80, 92, 100, 112, 116, 117, 123, 126, 150, 180, 181, 218
Findan, 48, 49, 122
Findchán, 115
Finding of Cashel, 67
Finguine son of Drostan, 87
Finnguine son of Deileroth, 80
fish, 19, 20, 118, 131, 171, 175, 218, 237
Fled Dúin na nGéd, 103
Fordun, church of, 145
Forteviot, 197, 202
Forth, river and firth, 10, 14, 16, 17, 20, 37, 45, 46, 58, 62, 64, 66, 71, 74, 75, 76, 80, 85, 87, 92, 93, 105, 115, 116, 123, 136, 147, 150, 162, 165, 179, 185, 204, 208, 209, 238
fortress, 18, 30, 36, 40, 61, 64, 65, 77, 79, 86, 89, 91, 99–101, 139, 149, 159, 197, 203, 238
Fortress of Belief/Hill of Belief, at Scone, 82, 87
Fortriu, kingdom, 13, 47, 48, 53, 62, 71, 75, 78, 79, 81, 82, 84, 90, 92, 94, 158, 184, 187, 192, 194, 197, 201, 205, 206, 214, 236, 238, 239
fosterage, 96, 97, 210
foster-father, 93, 95, 138, 159
Fragmentary Annals of Ireland, 11, 114, 203

Galloway, 17, 20, 35, 37, 42, 43, 91, 99, 143, 159, 163, 165, 219
Gartnan (Gartnat) son of Domelch, king (died 601), 70,
Gartnat son of Accidan (died 649), 83
Gaul, 6, 8, 14, 21, 23, 24, 26, 28, 31, 32, 34, 37, 129, 130, 131, 139
Geoffrey of Monmouth, 6, 59, 137, 138, 216, 219, 221, 223, 239
geometric figures, 162
Gerald, 35, 197, 213, 216
Germanus, 32, 34, 35, 36, 57, 58, 153, 186
Gildas, 2, 9, 29, 30, 34, 35, 36, 42, 45, 53, 54, 55, 58, 59, 64, 86, 106, 125, 126, 128, 129, 144, 186, 212, 217, 218, 219, 235
Giric son of Dungaile, 99, 189, 215
glass, 101
Glen Clova, 123
Glen Morison, 73
goats, 111
Gododdin, kingdom and poem, 9, 37, 42, 43, 46, 47, 58, 64, 65, 66, 70, 71, 89, 92, 94, 100, 101, 105, 107, 108, 141, 147, 150, 160, 174, 175, 176, 209, 210, 211, 234, 235, 237, 238
Gofraid son of Fergus, 198
gold, 6, 20, 23, 82, 87, 123, 124, 179, 190
Gotland, 4, 178
Grampians, highland range, 38, 46, 73, 78, 79, 87, 127, 185, 213, 239
Great Glen, 61, 90, 111, 122, 127, 146, 152, 184, 205

Gregory II, pope, 106, 150, 151
Gregory III, pope, 151
Gundestrup Cauldron, 136, 175, 178
Gureit, king of Strathclyde (died 658), 71
Gwid (Fid), 66, 71, 209

Hadrian's Wall, 2, 3, 8, 9, 17, 18, 19, 20–24, 26, 28, 31, 32, 34, 37, 39, 41–43, 45, 50, 52, 53, 56, 59, 64, 65, 93, 94, 123, 130, 140–144, 146, 150, 151, 160, 163, 165, 182, 190, 191, 202, 233–236
Halfdan, 42
hanging bowl, 180
Hariot, Thomas, *A Briefe and True Report of the New Found Land of*, 1
harp, 101, 102
Hebrides, 17, 25, 45, 59, 92, 110, 111, 119, 120, 121, 122, 130, 146, 192, 198, 229, 236
Helmsdale, 123
Henry of Huntingdon, 5, 6, 50, 207, 215
Herodian (Herodianus), 18, 19, 22, 23, 37, 56, 75, 76, 234
Higden, Ranulph (Ranulf of Chester), 43, 213, 222
High Rochester, 18, 40
History of the Britons, 9, 54, 58, 137, 144, 214, 218
 see also Nennius
History of the Descendants of Ir, 44, 53
History of Norway, 220
Holinshed, Raphael, 224
Honorius, emperor, 8, 24, 28, 32, 33, 35, 129, 144
horned god/hero, 67, 136, 137, 152, 175
horse, 121, 137, 235
How Culwuch Won Olwen, 113
hunting, 118, 121, 162, 167, 171, 181

Iceland, 148, 192
Innes, Thomas, 144–148, 158, 193, 200, 225–228
Ioain of Eigg, 148
Iogenan, 160
Iona, church of, 10, 11, 41, 60, 61, 69, 73, 82, 83, 84, 93, 94, 95, 105, 127, 136, 139, 142, 145, 146, 147, 149, 152, 153, 156, 159, 161, 175, 191, 192, 200, 232, 237
Ireland, 3, 13, 25, 29, 30, 33, 36, 44, 49, 52, 53, 54, 55, 59, 60, 66, 67, 68, 72, 74, 75, 77, 80, 82, 85, 89, 90, 93, 94, 97, 103, 104, 111, 112, 119, 122, 126, 129, 130, 131, 136, 140, 143, 144, 145, 148, 149, 153, 154, 160, 161, 165, 175, 180, 185, 189, 190, 191, 193, 198, 210, 211, 213, 214, 216, 217, 218, 222, 231, 235
Irish, 2, 4, 5, 8, 9, 10, 11, 12, 13, 17, 21, 24, 25, 27, 30, 32, 36, 38, 42, 43, 44, 47–56, 59, 60, 61, 62, 63, 66, 67, 68, 69, 71, 73, 74, 75, 79, 80, 81, 85, 86, 90, 92, 93, 94, 96, 97, 101–108, 113, 114, 117, 122, 123, 124, 126, 128, 130, 136, 138, 142–146, 148, 150, 151, 153, 155, 156, 158, 159, 160, 179–182, 187, 189, 190, 191, 194–199, 201, 202, 203, 208, 210, 211, 212, 214, 215, 216, 217, 220, 221, 227, 228, 229, 230, 232, 234–239
Irish Sea, 17, 30, 44, 60, 75, 93, 122, 143, 191
Irish World Chronicle, 11
iron, 18, 20, 22, 38, 124, 165, 179, 218
Isidore of Seville, 38, 39, 124, 225
Isle of Man, 44, 60, 62, 179, 230
Ivar, 203

Jarlshof, 111, 112, 220
Jerome, church father, 27, 31
jewelry, 2, 64, 130, 131, 162
Jocelin of Furness, 147
John of Fordun, 12, 147, 153, 156, 190, 195, 198, 203, 204, 205, 208, 209, 221–224
Jonathan's Cave, 126

Kells, 191
Kenneth (Cináed) I son of Alpin (MacAlpin), 52, 84, 85, 97, 156, 158, 183, 187, 193–207, 213, 215, 221, 222, 226, 236, 239
Kenneth (Cináed) son of Deirili, king (died 713), 81, 82,
Kenneth son of Ferant, 194
Kenneth son of Wredech, *see* Cinadhon
Kentigern, 142, 143, 147, 148, 160, 170, 222
king-lists, 12, 63, 70, 71, 81, 105, 148, 153, 154, 158, 184, 185, 189, 192, 193, 194, 207, 210, 222, 223, 238
kingship, 14, 67
  abdication, 189
  inauguration/kingmaking, 102, 103
  succession to, 4, 54, 55, 96, 104, 105, 106, 107, 114, 151, 226
Kintyre, 59, 90, 137, 186, 187, 190
Kirkbuddo, fortress, 100, 149
Kirkcudbright, 43, 139, 220

Lagmon's *Brut*, 219
language, Pictish, 5, 13, 16, 40, 43, 49–52, 56, 67, 207, 231, 234, 235
Law of Innocents (Cáin Adomnáin), 10, 82, 148, 232
Laws of Hywel Dda, 107
Lay of the son of Dwywai, 101
Learned Tales of Ireland, 196, 197, 212, 213

Lebor Gabála, *see Book of Invasions*
Leinster, 44, 54, 101, 103, 122, 160, 189, 194, 196, 203, 212, 213
Leland, John, 2, 3, 224
Lemnacht, 54, 136, 214
Lia Fail, 103
Life of Columba, 5, 9, 10, 42, 48, 50, 60, 61, 62, 72, 73, 95, 98, 100, 102, 105, 109, 115, 116, 127, 128, 129, 130, 134, 137, 139, 140, 145, 146, 148, 152, 153
Lindisfarne, 10, 79, 92, 136, 150, 176, 188, 191, 192, 239
literature, 5, 6, 12, 19, 23, 29, 36, 42, 49, 55, 66, 68, 95, 112, 117, 123, 138, 143, 155, 175, 176, 207–211, 216, 217, 221, 227, 239
Livy, 41
Llifiau, 66, 209, 210
Llŷn, 44
Loanhead of Daviot, 135
Loch Abac (?Loch Awe), 129
Loch Lomond, 137, 217, 218
Loch/river Ness, 73, 127, 137, 150
Locharbriggs, 126
Lochene, 70
lord of the animals, 137
Lothian, 17, 42, 43, 64, 101, 218
Lugi, 16

Macbeth, 214, 215, 235
Machar, missionary,114, 115, 147, 152
Maeatae, 18, 19, 37, 41, 62, 75, 96
Máel Duin, bishop of St. Andrews, 156
Máel Ruba of Applecross, 148
Magnus, 27, 29, 33, 217
magus (wise man, magician), 93, 95, 101, 102, 138, 139
Maiden Stane, 176
Malcolm II son of Kenneth II, king, 164
Malcolm III son of Duncan (Canmore), king, 123, 202, 215
Manannán mac Lír, 63

Manau, 42, 46, 47, 62, 63, 64, 80
manufacturing, 122, 132
Mar, 48, 53, 55, 106, 214
martyrdom, 48, 118, 131, 159, 189, 191
Martyrology of Óengus, 48
matrilineal succession/matriliny, 14, 104, 105, 107, 108
Mearns, 48, 145, 230
meat, 113, 117
Meigle, 123, 152, 166, 195, 207, 229, 230
mercenaries, 58, 66, 67, 69, 86, 93, 209
Midmar, 135
Mo Chuda, Irish saint, 190
Moncrieff Hill, 86, 87
Moray, 16, 20, 48, 90, 99, 111, 114, 115, 116, 158, 163, 176, 178, 184, 204, 218
Mote of Mark (Trusty's Hill, Galloway), 99, 123
Mounth, *see* Grampians
Muckros, 156

Naiton, 152, 154
Nechtan (Naiton), bishop, 141, 154
Nechtan, Irish blacksmith, 123
Nechtan, saint, 113, 115
Nechtan, saint of Devon and Cornwall, 154
Nechtan of Deer, 155
Nechtan son of Chelturan, 157
Nechtan son of Deirili, king (died 732), 81, 82, 84, 87, 97, 105
Nechtan son of Drostan, 83, 84
Nechtan son of Drostan (Naiton), king, 11, 62, 98, 149, 152, 153, 185, 208
Nechtan son of Erp, *see* Nechtan son of Uerb
Nechtan son of Gwyddno (?Wid or Fid), 71,
Nechtan son of Uerb (?Erp), 70, 148, 153, 154, 171, 201
Nechtan, unidentified king, 100, 131, 149

Nechtan, warrior of Thrace, 214
Neckham, Alexander, 43
Nennius, 9, 54, 55, 58, 59, 137, 144, 214, 216, 218, 235
Niall of the Nine Hostages, 36
Nicolaus (?), bishop, 141
Nigg, 101
Ninian, 45, 135, 141–144, 147, 160, 170, 180, 185, 190, 222, 229, 237, 238
Norrie's Law, 32
North Channel, 44, 59, 91, 194
North Sea, 4, 17, 47, 51, 92, 100, 122, 124, 125, 126, 136
Northumberland, 18, 176
Northumbria, 11, 12, 43, 44, 45, 63, 69, 71, 74, 76, 80, 91, 92, 106, 142, 183, 185, 188, 190, 201, 204, 239
Northumbrians, 3, 11, 77, 80, 91, 92, 94, 150, 152, 187, 236, 237
Novantae, 17

oak, 128
oats, 20, 114, 115
O'Curry, Eugene, 228
O'Donovan, John, 228
ogam, 14, 49, 50, 67, 166, 236
Olaf, 203, 204
Old Melrose, 202
Origen, 141
Orkney Islands, 17, 33, 48, 49, 51, 54, 55, 61, 98, 112, 115, 118, 122, 124, 129, 130, 148, 149, 158, 192, 193, 216, 236
Osbald, 188
Oswy, 12, 69, 150
Otadini, 17
oysters, 130, 131

Palladius, 144, 145, 147, 222
Patrick, saint, 30, 32, 36, 42, 59, 60, 74, 141, 144, 188, 192, 230

pearls, 130, 131
Pehthelm, 43
Pehtwine, 43
Pelagian heresy, 34
Pelagius, 34
Perth, 86, 136
Pes-rut (red cloak), 31
Phantom's Frenzy, 103
Pict boat, *see* boats
Pictish water-beast, symbol, 171, 175
Pictones, 6, 7, 14, 23, 37, 55
pigs, 111, 117, 118, 121
Pinkerton, 50, 157, 195, 226, 227, 228
Pit, name element, 51, 116, 117, 125, 155, 197, 213, 237
Pitcarmick house, 112
Pit-fall of Scone, 196, 213
plowing, 114
Poppleton manuscript, Paris Bibliothèque Nationale ms Latin 2146, 46, 148, 153, 193, 225, 226, 227
Portmahomack, 124, 158, 163
Procopius, 20, 39, 138
prophecy, 69, 103, 136, 138, 146, 187, 197
Prophecy of Berchán, 97, 113, 187, 190, 196, 197
Prophecy of Britain, 211
Prosper of Aquitaine, 144, 196
Prydyn, 43, 44, 64, 211, 234
Prythein, 43
Ptolemy of Alexandria, 16, 19, 31, 137

Rannoch Moor, 82
Rathmore, 44
Ravenna Cosmography, 31, 103
Reginald of Coldingham, also known as Reginald of Durham, 43, 219, 220
Register of St. Andrews, 123, 154, 156, 195
Rheged, 37, 44, 94, 105, 143, 160, 209, 234, 238

Rhynie, 20, 123
Rhynie Man, 114
Richard of Hexham, 219
rock, 84, 120, 155, 163, 165, 166, 209, 218, 230
Rome, 6, 7, 21, 23, 24, 26, 27, 29, 32, 33, 34, 35, 38, 52, 57, 142, 149, 150, 202, 215
Rosemarkie, 148, 223
Ross, 16, 88, 90, 136, 137, 152, 153, 173, 174, 175
Rum, 148
rye, 114

sailing, 77, 129
salmon, 20, 118, 131, 162, 175
sanctuary, 89, 110, 185, 188
Saxons, 5, 28, 33, 58, 63, 104, 128, 200
Scalloway, 115
Scone, 61, 82, 87, 102, 195, 196, 197, 201, 213
Scots, 6, 25, 26, 28, 29, 30, 33–36, 42, 45, 52, 53, 55, 58, 63, 66, 69, 73, 82, 85, 90, 94, 97, 98, 99, 103, 114, 125, 129, 144, 153, 155, 165, 183, 184, 194, 195, 196, 197, 198, 199, 200, 201, 202, 203, 204, 205, 206, 208, 213, 215, 217, 218, 220, 221, 222, 223, 231, 232, 234, 236, 238, 239
  see also Dál Riata
Scottish Chronicle, 82, 158, 182, 195, 196, 197, 198, 199, 200, 201, 202, 204, 225
Scriptorium, 208
Scythia, 53, 54, 55, 104, 106, 216, 217
sea, 7, 17, 20, 30, 46, 63, 77, 79, 86, 87, 111, 116, 128, 129, 130, 131, 133, 143, 209
seaweed, 20, 130
Selbach, 89, 110, 189
Selgovae, 17

Senchus Fer nAlban, 44, 53, 55, 59, 66, 69, 106, 199, 214, 231
Septimus Severus, emperor, 18, 19, 22, 56, 76, 121, 217, 234
Servanus (Serf), saint, 147, 222
Shakespeare, William, 214, 218, 224
sheep, 111, 117, 118, 120, 131, 159, 190
shellfish, 20
Shetland Islands, 17, 48, 110, 111, 112, 120, 121, 124, 131, 149, 163, 192, 193, 235, 236
ships, 7, 19, 28, 30, 32, 49, 88, 122, 124, 178, 194, 204, 214, 224
  see also boats
Sidonius Apollinaris (C. Sollius Sidonius Apollinaris), 24, 41
silver, 32, 82, 87, 179, 180, 190
silver chains, 162, 179, 181
Skara Brae, 111
Skene, William Forbes, 228, 229
Skye, Isle of, 50, 73, 74, 120, 128, 148
slave/slavery, 5, 23, 30, 36, 82, 95, 96, 107, 138, 139, 190
Smertae, 16
smith, 123, 179
soil type, 111, 116, 133
Solway firth, 29, 43, 63, 93, 238
souterrain, 112
Speckled Book, 145
spoon, 180
St. Andrews, 61, 154, 155, 156, 157, 189, 192, 193, 195, 201, 211, 223, 239
St. Andrews sarcophagus, 170
St. Buite, 100, 149
St. Martin of Tours, 142
Statistical Account of Scotland, 164, 229
Stenton, Sir Frank, 46
Stilicho, 9, 29, 33
Strathclyde, kingdom, 3, 36, 37, 41, 42, 43, 47, 63, 66, 71, 84, 85, 91, 94, 99, 107, 141, 143, 160, 202, 203, 204, 234, 235, 236, 237, 239

Strathearn, 72, 87, 123
Strathfillan, 82
succession, *see* kingship
Sueno's Stone, 167, 177, 178
Sutherland, 16, 123, 124, 137
Symbol stones, 4, 5, 14, 123, 146, 164, 209
  Class 1 symbol stones, 165, 167, 175
  Class 2 symbol stones, 166, 168, 170, 178
  Class 3 symbol stones, 168, 169
Symeon of Durham, 10, 48, 91, 92, 185, 188, 208
Synod of St. Albans, 153

Tacitus, 16, 23, 35, 41, 52, 54, 55, 96, 112, 130, 138, 179, 231
Taexali, 16
Tale of Cano, 73, 104, 148
Talorcan (died 617), 70
Talorgan son of Ainfrith (died 657), king, 69, 73
Talorgan son of Angus, 185
Talorgan son of Congusso of Dál Riata, 88
Talorgan son of Drostan (died 739), king, 13, 83, 84, 89
Talorgan son of Fergus (died 750), 88, 90, 91
Talorgan son of Wthoil, 193
Tara, 103, 197, 214
Tarain, 66, 80, 109, 139, 140
Tarbat, 51, 153, 158, 163, 174
tattoo/-ing, 14, 18, 23, 38, 39, 234, 237
taxes, 98
Tay, river and firth, 20, 32, 76, 86, 102, 103, 147, 163, 213, 224
Ternan, saint, 114, 145, 147, 222
Tertullian (Q. Septimus Florens Tertullianus), church father, 140
Theodosius, 28, 29, 32, 33, 128
Thrace, 53, 55, 106, 214
threshing floor, 116

Thule, Isle of, 22, 33, 192
Tiree, Isle of, 149
Torannán, saint, 145
trade and trade routes, 122, 131
Traprain Law, 64, 100, 170
treasury, 102
Trebaut, 67
Tripartite Life of Patrick, 60
triple pipe, 101
Troup Head, 88
Trumwine, bishop, 45, 65, 74, 80, 150
Tuathal son of Artgusso, abbot of Dunkeld and bishop of Fortriu, 47, 156, 158, 201
Tuathalan (died 743), abbot of Cindrigmonath, 155
Tweed, river, 43, 141
Tyndrum, 82, 87, 88, 123
Tyne, river, 4, 42, 202, 204, 235

Uí Néill, 59, 90, 145, 156, 199
Ulstermen, 44, 59, 60
Ultan, 44

Vacomagi, 16
Vegetius (P. Flavius Vegetius Renatus), 30, 128
Veneti, 7
Venicones, 16
Viking/-s, 2, 4, 30, 42, 44, 48, 49, 51, 75, 110, 111, 122, 125, 149, 158, 168, 177, 180, 183, 191–194, 198, 203, 204, 205, 220

Vita of St. Cuthbert, 10
Vortigern, 58, 217
Votadini, 64, 100
V–rod, symbol, 166, 167, 169, 171

Wainwright, F.T., 16, 46, 50, 83, 112, 165, 229
Wales, 25, 30, 44, 52, 59, 65, 68, 92, 114, 119, 235
War of the Irish against the Vikings, 194
wetlands, 20, 76, 78
What brought the Picts to Marvellous Britain, 138, 214, 231
wheat, 20, 98, 114, 115
wheel house, 111
Whitby, 80, 149
White, John, 1–3
Whithorn, 42, 45, 123, 142, 143, 144, 160, 190, 237, 238
Wick, 149
wicker structure, 136, 138
Widikund of Corvey, 211
Widsith, 210
Wild Man, 218
Wilfred, 74
woad, 18, 23
wool, 120

York, 21, 26, 106, 142, 151, 218

Zosimus, 26
Z-rod, 43, 162, 166, 180